THE
BIG
RED
BOOK

OF MODERN CHINESE LITERATURE

ALSO BY YUNTE HUANG

Charlie Chan: The Untold Story of the Honorable Detective and His Rendezvous with American History

Transpacific Imaginations: History, Literature, Counterpoetics

CRIBS (poetry)

Transpacific Displacement: Ethnography, Translation, and Intertextual Travel in Twentieth-Century American Literature

Shi: A Radical Reading of Chinese Poetry

THE BIG RED BOOK

OF MODERN CHINESE LITERATURE

WRITINGS FROM THE MAINLAND IN THE
LONG TWENTIETH CENTURY

EDITED BY YUNTE HUANG

W. W. NORTON & COMPANY

Independent Publishers Since 1923

New York | London

Dedicated to my father
who taught me
the power and perils of Chinese literature

For information about special discounts for bulk purchases, please contact
W. W. Norton Special Sales at specialsales@wwnorton.com or 800-233-4830

Manufacturing by Quad Graphics Fairfield
Book design by Chris Welch Design
Production manager: Julia Druskin

Library of Congress Cataloging-in-Publication Data
Names: Huang, Yunte, editor.
Title: The big red book of modern Chinese literature : writings from the
mainland in the long twentieth century / edited by Yunte Huang.
Description: First edition. | New York : W. W. Norton & Company, 2016. |
Includes bibliographical references.
Identifiers: LCCN 2015037505 | ISBN 9780393239485 (hardcover)
Subjects: LCSH: Chinese literature—20th century.
Classification: LCC PL2513 .B54 2016 | DDC 895.108/005—dc23 LC record available at
http://lccn.loc.gov/2015037505

W. W. Norton & Company, Inc.
500 Fifth Avenue, New York, N.Y. 10110
www.wwnorton.com

W. W. Norton & Company Ltd.
Castle House, 75/76 Wells Street, London W1T 3QT

1 2 3 4 5 6 7 8 9 10

Contents

PART TWO: 1949 – 1976

PART THREE: 1976 – Present

Acknowledgments

As befits a project grappling with a nation's collective memory, this book would not exist without the collective efforts of many people who have helped me in various ways and whose names I cannot possibly all list here.

I owe an enormous debt to my editor at Norton, Alane Salierno Mason, who first approached me with the idea of doing this book and since then has expertly and patiently guided me through the long, at times tortuous, process of putting together an anthology with an ironic, yet deadly serious, title. I also want to thank Glenn Mott, who has always done more than his share as an agent and a friend in making my dreams possible. As a gifted poet and translator, Glenn has contributed invaluable work to this volume.

Since this book relies on translation, I want to express my profound admiration for the trailblazing work by Julia Lin, Yang Hsien-yi and Gladys Yang, Sidney Shapiro, Howard Goldblatt, Mabel Lee, Eva Hung, Jeffrey Kinkley, David Pollard, and others who have made modern Chinese literature what it is today in the English-language translation. These pioneers are followed by other equally talented and devoted translators, including Gregory Lee, Timothy Wong, Jeffrey Yang, Tani Barlow, Michael Duke, Bonnie McDougall, Mary Fung, Madeleine Zelin, Andrew Jones, Aaron Crippen, Dan Murphy, Lucas Klein, Andrea Lingenfeller, and Fiona Sze-Lorrain. It is my fortune to be able to include the works by many of these translators but my deep regret having to leave out some selections due to the complexity of copyright clearance.

It especially pains me to drop two of my favorite works, *Love in a*

Fallen City by Eileen Chang and *Fortress Besieged* by Qian Zhongshu. Despite my repeated attempts and desperate pleas, the literary executors who control the rights for these works declined to oblige. I also encountered insurmountable roadblocks erected by the arcane system of subsidiary rights in China, demands for unreasonable fees by some English-language publishers, and the incompatibility between American and Chinese practices of copyright protection.

Difficulties notwithstanding, I have enjoyed the support, assistance, and encouragement from the following friends, fellow travelers, and editors at various journals and publishing companies: Jianhua Chen, Yiye Huang, Bei Dao, Xi Chuan, Zishan Chen, Dongfeng Wang, Yu Xinqiao, Theodore Huters and Stephanie Wong at *Renditions*, Peter London at HarperCollins, Sam Moore at Penguin, Kelsey Ford at New Directions, Angelina Wong at Chinese University of Hong Kong Press, Elizabeth Clementson at W. W. Norton, Michael Duckworth at University of Hawaii Press, Ryan Mita at Beacon Press, Greta Lindquist at University of California Press, Liz Hamilton at Northwestern University Press, Norah Perkins at Curtis Brown Group Ltd., Peter Froehlich at Indiana University Press, Kit Yee Wong at Anvil Press Poetry, and Michael Purwin at Columbia University Press. I especially want to thank my college friend and now an editor at People's Literature Publishing House in China, Helen Liu, who gave me a key to the mystery of the Chinese publishing world. I am also grateful to Tan Lin, who generously granted me the permissions to reprint some of his late mother's pioneering work.

Last but not least, I want to thank my father, who allowed me to pursue a career in literature, an opportunity which was denied to him when he was a young man in Mao's China. I initially agreed to take on this book project because I wanted to pay tribute to him and millions of other struggling Chinese souls who, despite the perils, have never stopped dreaming.

Introduction

This book is a search for the soul of modern China.

As such, it is less an anthology, or à la carte sampling, than a story that, carrying the historical weight of a nation in its most tumultuous century, seeks a coherence lying on the page and beyond.

Twentieth century China saw two apocalyptic events that defined its character and destiny. In 1912, the overthrow of Qing Dynasty shattered the shackles of two thousand years of monarchical rule and ushered in a modern nation. In 1949, the founding of the People's Republic took the country on a long march toward a utopian, Communist future that never materialized, a perilous path some may say it is still treading on today, at least in name if not in reality. Around these two watershed events were other, often bloody, episodes: the Boxer Rebellion, the Republican era's reign of terror, the Japanese invasion, a civil war, the Cultural Revolution, the Tiananmen Square massacre. Any soul that has plumbed the depths of these horrors must be at pains to find a voice to speak the unspeakable.

Beginning with Lu Xun's *Call to Arms*, Chinese writers have tried, often at the cost of their lives, to come to terms with a world gone awry, a culture in crisis, and a nation on the brink of annihilation. The Opium Wars and clash with Western imperial powers and repeated defeats and internal rebellions since the nineteenth century plunged many Chinese into doubt about the viability of their once-proud civilization. Lu Xun likened the Middle Kingdom to a sepulchral "iron house" in which sound sleepers will never wake up. Wen Yiduo, gunned down by secret agents of the Kuomintang in 1946, compared China to "a ditch of hopelessly dead water," where "no clear breeze can raise half a ripple" on its sordid surface.

Yet, the Republican era (1911–49) was also a time of radical transformations in literature. The end of monarchy gave the Chinese literati an opportunity to absorb influences from the West and imagine a brave new world. The May Fourth Movement, a student-led protest that began in Peking in May 1919, calling for democracy and science, had a lasting impact on the Chinese mind. Transitioning from *wenyan* (the archaic, classical form of Chinese) to *baihua* (the vernacular of common speech), Chinese literature was reborn. Novels by Lu Xun, Mao Dun, Ba Jin, Ding Ling, and Shen Congwen, poetry by Dai Wangshu, Xu Zhimo, Wen Yiduo, and Li Jinfa, and essays by Zhou Zuoren, Lin Yutang, and Zhu Ziqing, all combined to create a kaleidoscopic vista of the Chinese literary imagination. The sense of newness ran so deep, and occasionally wild, that some even proposed a face-lift for the ideographic ancient language, replacing it with an alphabetic system as the medium for writing.

This golden age of modern Chinese literature came to an abrupt end when communism took over the country in 1949. Mao Zedong, the Great Helmsman and a poet, exerted an ironclad control over literary expression, dictating that literature serve politics. Works produced in this period of totalitarian rule, up to Mao's death in 1976, may rightly be regarded as propaganda, or at best formulaic potboilers that rarely deviate from party lines. Read through the prisms of the West, which regards individual free expression as the golden rule for artistic production, revolutionary literature may indeed lack aesthetic value. While this is hardly the place to dispute the validity of aesthetic principles, it is worth noting, however, that the belief in literature as an expression of a free individual is as ideologically suspect as the revolutionary *mot justes* in *Mao's Little Red Book*. Communism may have done much damage to literature, but at least it takes art seriously, so seriously that it wants to control all forms of artistic expression, weeding out the "one hundred flowers" that dare to blossom.

Selections from the so-called revolutionary literature in this book, therefore, must be read with an open mind. The works by Ai Qing, Zhao Shuli, Wang Meng, and others, are not relics from a bygone period, but a record of creative souls struggling, negotiating, and coping with a national dream gone bad. They remind me of my father's red notebook. When I was growing up in the waning days of Mao's China, my father once showed me a notebook he had kept since he was young. It had a red plastic cover, making it look like *Mao's Little Red Book*. Inside he had pasted many clippings, all poems and essays he had published under various pseudonyms in newspapers and magazines. His grandfather (my great-grandfather) was a landlord, from an "exploitive and parasitic class," a factor which doomed my father's future. Going to college, a privilege reserved only for working-class children, was a dream beyond his reach, and he became instead a "barefoot doctor," carrying a medicine kit, roaming the countryside to cure sick peasants. A literary aficionado, he did not stop writing, a secret he had long kept from everyone, including his family. I found the notebook by accident one day when I, a curious kid, was rummaging through his things. Shocked a little, he got me to promise never to tell anyone, and then he let me read a few short poems. From what I can remember, those tofu-sized poems were mostly about the virtues of the proletarian revolution, joys of agricultural harvesting, and other topics common to Communist literature. Despite the formulaic quality of the writing, even my prepubescent eye could see that my father's love for literature and desire for creativity were as real as the heartbeats pulsing under his bare skin.

The end of the Cultural Revolution in 1976 and the ensuing economic reform led to an era of unprecedented openness. After decades of writing under the threat of the Communist Sword of Damocles, Chinese writers finally enjoyed some freedom of expression. Censorship persisted, but it was no match for the sudden burst of creativity, as if a dam had cracked open. The generation born under the red flag and coming of age during the Cultural Revolution led the way. From Bei Dao's bold proclamation, "I do not believe," to Gu Cheng's ironic lines, "the black night gave me black eyes / still I use them to seek the light," the Misty School of poetry broke the ice that had long frozen literary imagination. Novels by Mo Yan, Yu Hua, Su Tong, Wang Anyi, Can Xue, and others explored topics such as sex, love, and bestiality, which had long been taboos. Literature no longer had to function only in the service of politics. The Chinese soul, long tortured and deeply scarred, finally seemed to be able to roam freely. As the peripatetic narrator in Gao Xingjian's Nobel-Prize-winning novel *Soul Mountain* puts it, "I would rather drift here and there without leaving traces."

Freedom, however, was short-lived. The rumbling tanks and roaring gunfire at Tiananmen Square in the wee hours of June 4, 1989, pulled the curtain on a decade of cultural fever and spiritual euphoria. In those dark days after the massacre, Beijing broiled in the stifling heat of a deadly summer. The ancient capital city appeared to be plagued by something unknown, as if a mysterious disease, lying dormant for thousands of years, suddenly came alive and turned viral, attacking the city mercilessly. Spilled innocent blood might have been washed off the streets, but the stink of death lingered on in the air.

I was still a college sophomore. Hai Zi, a young poet and fellow student at Peking University, had just committed suicide earlier that year. He had done so by lying on the railroad tracks near the crown jewel of our national pride, the Great Wall, as if naked flesh could stop the train of what Lu Xun's madman once called "four thousand years of cannibalistic history." We held a candlelight vigil for Hai Zi one night, accompanied by poetry readings and watched by an unknown number of undercover cops. After the event, I took a walk by the campus lake. A pale moon hung in the night sky. Reflected in the inky water, the moon looked like a period artificially placed there, failing to anchor a sentence that had no meaning. Someone was singing and playing guitar on the other side of the lake. The words of the popular song "The Orphan of Asia" by Luo Dayou drifted waywardly, like broken radio signals, in the muggy night air: "The orphan of Asia is crying in the wind / Red mud on his yellow face . . ." At that moment, only a few months before the event of Tiananmen Square, I already felt all hope had indeed been lost, the soul of China sinking like the paper-thin moon to the muddy bottom of the lake.

And yet, two decades later, China rises again, as a world superpower flexing its economic, military, and political prowess everywhere. In his monumental search for the zeitgeist of modern China, Jonathan Spence writes, "The swings of its political life, the switches in its cultural moods, the lurches in its economy . . . all combine to keep us in a state of bewilderment as to China's real nature." Looking back at the undulations of the Chinese experience in the twentieth century, remembering the red plastic cover of my father's secret notebook, and thinking about that ominous pale moon I once saw in one dark night in Chinese history, I often wonder: How did the Chinese soul endure these tortures and horrors? How did China rise from that lifeless mirage flickering at the bottom of dead water?

That is the story this book tells.

PART ONE

1911–1949

CHRONOLOGY

1912	Abdication of Emperor Puyi, end of Qing monarchy
1919	May Fourth Movement
1921	Founding of the Chinese Communist Party
1927	Chiang Kai-shek consolidates power, reign of "White Terror"
1931	Japan occupies Manchuria
1934–35	The Long March led by Mao Zedong
1937–45	Sino-Japanese War
1945	Japan surrenders, beginning of the civil war
1949	Founding of the People's Republic of China

Introduction to the Republican Era

For millennia China had regarded itself as the center of the universe, a vast land of unimaginable wealth and a most advanced civilization. Beginning in the nineteenth century, however, when British gunboats arrived in the China seas, the self-labeled "Middle Kingdom" experienced a rude awakening. The ensuing clash with the West led to a dramatic shift in the Chinese mind, a change of self-consciousness aptly described by Joseph R. Levenson as "the contraction of China from a world to a nation in the world." Not just any nation, but one that was defeated and humiliated time and again by the Western powers that were carving up the country like a juicy melon through unfair treaties involving territorial concessions. Internal strife—regional and nation-wide rebellions—also added to the pressure on the Manchu regime teetering on the verge of collapsing. Barely able to maintain its imperial façade, the Middle Kingdom had by the late nineteenth century acquired a new epithet, the "Sick Man of East Asia."

Modern Chinese literature was born in this crucible of national crisis. In 1912, Qing Dynasty was toppled, ending monarchism in China. In 1919, the May Fourth Movement began with students marching through the streets of Peking, demanding change. The zeitgeist of this transitional period may best be captured by Lu Xun's *Call to Arms* (1923), with its dark metaphor for China ("an iron house") and the madman's desperate plea ("Save the children"). Lu Xun's call was echoed, among others, by Guo Moruo's *Goddesses* (1921), in which the poet imagines the rebirth of China like a phoenix out of the ashes. Interestingly, as leaders of the New Culture Movement, both Lu and Guo began as students of medicine and then realized that it was more important to save the soul than the body of the "Sick Man of East Asia." This perceived centrality of literature to the life of a nation speaks to a dilemma that was faced, though often unacknowledged, by modern Chinese writers: in their bold attempts to dismantle traditional literature and culture, they unwittingly inherited the Confucian belief in the ties between writing and governance, the assumption that literature is essential to morality, social life, and politics. Shelley's statement that "poets are the unacknowledged legislators of the world" did not fall on deaf ears when translated for China, where for centuries the ability to write well was considered the prerequisite for, if not simply equivalent to, the ability to govern or legislate. Twentieth century Chinese writers would pay dearly, and occasionally get paid handsomely, for this belief in the power of literature. But we are ahead of our story.

Lu and Guo were also representative in another respect: they both studied abroad, in Japan. The repeated defeats suffered by China at the hands of foreign powers—in two Opium Wars with Britain, the 1894 war with Japan, the siege of Peking by the Eight-Nation Alliance (including the United States) in the wake of the Boxer Rebellion in 1900, to name just a few—made the Chinese realize that traditional Chinese culture had become a roadblock to progress and that they needed to learn from the powerful nations that had just bullied them. The experience of study abroad, predominantly in Europe, the United States, and Japan, produced a generation of writers who transformed modern Chinese literature: Hu Shih, Liu Bannong, Wen Yiduo, Xu Dishan, Ba Jin, Yu Dafu, Xu Zhimo, Bing Xin, Dai Wangshu, Li Jinfa, Zhou Zuoren, Lin Yutang, Qian Zhongshu, and so on. While direct exposure to foreign cultures helped to train the pioneers of modern Chinese writing, translations from Western literature also created a hotbed for new ideas and literary experiments. The unbridled wildness of Guo Moruo's work claimed lineage from Shelley, Goethe, and Whitman. It was under the influence of British Romanticism that Xu Zhimo wrote the most beautiful lyrical poems penned since Chinese poetry had broken free from classical verse. Hu Shih's famous proposal for replacing classical

Chinese with vernacular Chinese as the literary language had much to do with his devotion to American pragmatism, a school of philosophy that taught him to question absolute authority, including the tyranny of the Chinese classics. Ba Jin's indictment against feudal patriarchy in his novels was inspired by the anarchist and utopian ideas he had picked up while living in the Latin Quarter in Paris as well as from translated texts. The list can go on.

The disaster of the First World War might have made some Chinese intellectuals question the virtues of Western civilizations, but the success of the Russian revolution brought more radical ideas to China. Especially after the founding of the Chinese Communist Party in 1921, literature and politics seemed to have become conjoined. While in the first quarter of the century Chinese writers had enjoyed a degree of freedom in the absence of a strong political regime, Chiang Kai-shek's consolidation of power in 1927 and his subsequent purge and persecution of communist sympathizers ushered in a period called the "Reign of White Terror." The temporary setback to radical politics led to an outburst of both soul-searching and socially engaged writings, including Ding Ling's *Miss Sophia's Diary* (1928), Mao Dun's *Rainbow* (1930), and Ba Jin's *Family* (1931).

In 1931 Japan occupied Manchuria, alarming all Chinese that their country might be doomed. The rising tide of patriotism brought renewed energy to Chinese literature. Xiao Hong wrote her first novel, *The Field of Life and Death* (1935), after she had been displaced from her native Manchuria, followed by a semi-autobiographical piece, *Tales of Hulan River*, about a birthplace she would never see again. Shen Congwen published *Border Town* in 1934, a novel about western Hunan, a frontier area of pristine natural beauty and a simple way of life threatened by war and other human deviltries. In his 1936 novel *Rickshaw*, Lao She created a memorable character of a rickshaw puller whose life takes an unexpected turn after he is kidnapped by the army.

The full-blown Sino-Japanese War in 1937 further galvanized Chinese writers, many of whom participated directly in the resistance movement. The Communists, after a brutal Long March, had by this time gained a foothold in the Yan'an area in northern China. In 1942, Mao Zedong delivered a famous speech on art and literature, proclaiming that "literature must serve politics." The full effect of Mao's speech would not be felt until 1949, when the Communists defeated Chiang Kai-shek's Nationalists after a civil war (1945–49) in the wake of the Japanese surrender and gained control of the country.

Yet we should not forget writers who self-consciously turned away from overt ideological agendas and dwelled instead on topics of everyday life, pop culture, leisure, and so on. The rise in the 1920s of the School of Mandarin Duck and Butterfly, a genre of fiction featuring romantic love, scandals, and mysteries, as exemplified by He Haiming's "For the Love of Her Feet" (1923), testifies to the vitality of popular literature. Lin Yutang's gently humorous prose in *My Country and My People* (1935) made him the foremost interpreter of Chinese culture to the English-speaking world in the 1930s. He once stated that he would prefer to write about his toothbrush than about current national issues. Like Lin, Zhou Zuoren wrote about reading in the lavatory and other seemingly trivial matters. The kind of satirical verve and comic spirit so masterfully cultivated by Chinese literati for centuries found perhaps its best expression in Qian Zhongshu's *Fortress Besieged* (1947), a novel of disarming wit and utter delight, a gem of fiction that would unfortunately be buried in the annals of literary history as twentieth century China entered the Revolutionary Era under Communist rule.*

---

* Due to difficulty in clearing permission from the Qian Zhongshu estate, we are unfortunately unable to include an excerpt from *Fortress Besieged*. For the same reason we are unable to include *Love in a Fallen City* by Eileen Chang.

LU XUN
(1881–1936)

Born Zhou Shuren in Zhejiang, Lu Xun, the foremost writer of modern China, started out with an ambition to be a doctor in order to cure the diseases of his people. While studying medicine in Japan (1904-1906), he realized that it would be far more important to save souls than bodies, as he recounts in his autobiographical "Preface to Call to Arms," which follows. He turned to literature and adopted the pen name "Lu Xun," as in "revolution." In 1918 he published "A Madman's Diary," one of the earliest stories written in vernacular Chinese and a scathing critique of the hypocrisy and inhumanity of the feudalist, Confucian tradition. A daunting and fearless fighter wielding his pen as a weapon, he wrote, in addition to many stories, more than six hundred polemical and occasional essays. When he died of tuberculosis in 1936, mourners covered his body with a silk banner that read "Soul of the Nation."

Preface to *Call to Arms*

When I was young I, too, had many dreams. Most of them came to be forgotten, but I see nothing in this to regret. For although recalling the past may make you happy, it may sometimes also make you lonely, and there is no point in clinging in spirit to lonely bygone days. However, my trouble is that I cannot forget completely, and these stories have resulted from what I have been unable to erase from my memory.

For more than four years I used to go, almost daily, to a pawnbroker's and to a medicine shop. I cannot remember how old I was then; but the counter in the medicine shop was the same height as I, and that in the pawnbroker's twice my height. I used to hand clothes and trinkets up to the counter twice my height, take the money proffered with contempt, then go to the counter the same height as I to buy medicine for my father who had long been ill. On my return home I had other things to keep me busy, for since the physician who made out the prescriptions was very well-known, he used unusual drugs: aloe root dug up in winter, sugarcane that had been three years exposed to frost, twin crickets, and *ardisia* . . . all of which were difficult to procure. But my father's illness went from bad to worse until he died.

I believe those who sink from prosperity to poverty will probably come, in the process, to understand what the world is really like. I wanted to go to the K—— school in N——,* perhaps because I was in search of a change of scene and faces. There was nothing for my mother to do but to raise eight dollars for my traveling expenses, and say I might do as I pleased. That she cried was only natural, for at that time the proper thing was to study the classics and take the official examinations. Anyone who studied "foreign subjects" was looked down upon as a fellow good for nothing, who, out of desperation, was forced to sell his soul to foreign devils. Besides, she was sorry to part with me. But in spite of that, I went to N—— and entered the K—— school; and it was there that I heard for the first time the names of such subjects as natural science, arithmetic, geography, history, drawing, and physical training. They had no physiology course, but we saw wood block editions of such works as *A New Course on the Human Body* and *Essays on Chemistry and Hygiene*. Recalling the talk and prescriptions of physicians

* The Kiangnan Naval Academy in Nanjing.

I had known and comparing them with what I now knew, I came to the conclusion those physicians must be either unwitting or deliberate charlatans; and I began to sympathize with the invalids and families who suffered at their hands. From translated histories I also learned that the Japanese Reformation had originated, to a great extent, with the introduction of Western medical science to Japan.

These inklings took me to a provincial medical college in Japan. I dreamed a beautiful dream that on my return to China I would cure patients like my father, who had been wrongly treated, while if war broke out I would serve as an army doctor, at the same time strengthening my countrymen's faith in reformation.

I do not know what advanced methods are now used to teach microbiology, but at that time lantern slides were used to show the microbes; and if the lecture ended early, the instructor might show slides of natural scenery or news to fill up the time. This was during the Russo-Japanese War, so there were many war films, and I had to join in the clapping and cheering in the lecture hall along with the other students. It was a long time since I had seen any compatriots, but one day I saw a film showing some Chinese, one of whom was bound, while many others stood around him. They were all strong fellows but appeared completely apathetic. According to the commentary, the one with his hands bound was a spy working for the Russians, who was to have his head cut off by the Japanese military as a warning to others, while the Chinese beside him had come to enjoy the spectacle.

Before the term was over I had left for Tokyo, because after this film I felt that medical science was not so important after all. The people of a weak and backward country, however strong and healthy they may be, can only serve to be made examples of, or to witness such futile spectacles; and it doesn't really matter how many of them die of illness. The most important thing, therefore, was to change their spirit, and since at that time I felt that literature was the best means to this end, I determined to promote a literary movement. There were many

Chinese students in Tokyo studying law, political science, physics, and chemistry, even police work and engineering, but not one studying literature or art. However, even in this uncongenial atmosphere I was fortunate enough to find some kindred spirits. We gathered the few others we needed, and after discussion our first step, of course, was to publish a magazine, the title of which denoted that this was a new birth. As we were then rather classically inclined, we called it *Xin Sheng* (*New Life*).

When the time for publication drew near, some of our contributors dropped out, and then our funds were withdrawn, until finally there were only three of us left, and we were penniless. Since we had started our magazine at an unlucky hour, there was naturally no one to whom we could complain when we failed; but later even we three were destined to part, and our discussions of a dream future had to cease. So ended this abortive *New Life*.

Only later did I feel the futility of it all; at that time I did not really understand anything. Later I felt if a man's proposals met with approval, it should encourage him; if they met with opposition, it should make him fight back; but the real tragedy for him was to lift up his voice among the living and meet with no response, neither approval nor opposition, just as if he were left helpless in a boundless desert. So I began to feel lonely.

And this feeling of loneliness grew day by day, coiling about my soul like a huge poisonous snake. Yet in spite of my unaccountable sadness, I felt no indignation; for this experience had made me reflect and see that I was definitely not the heroic type who could rally multitudes at his call.

However, my loneliness had to be dispelled, for it was causing me agony. So I used various means to dull my senses, both by conforming to the spirit of the time and turning to the past. Later I experienced or witnessed even greater loneliness and sadness, which I do not like to recall, preferring that it should perish with me. Still my attempt to deaden my senses was not unsuccessful—I had lost the enthusiasm and fervor of my youth.

||||||||||||||||

IN S——* HOSTEL there were three rooms where it was said a woman had lived who hanged herself on the locust tree in the courtyard. Although the tree had grown so tall that its branches could no longer be reached, the rooms remained deserted. For some years I stayed here, copying ancient inscriptions. I had few visitors, there were no political problems or issues in those inscriptions, and my only desire was that my life should slip quietly away like this. On summer nights, when there were too many mosquitoes, I would sit under the locust tree, waving my fan and looking at the specks of sky through the thick leaves, while the caterpillars which came out in the evening would fall, icy-cold, onto my neck.

The only visitor to come for an occasional talk was my old friend Chin Hsin-yi. He would put his big portfolio down on the broken table, take off his long gown, and sit facing me, looking as if his heart was still beating fast after braving the dogs.

"What is the use of copying these?" he demanded inquisitively one night, after looking through the inscriptions I had copied.

"No use at all."

"Then why copy them?"

"For no particular reason."

"I think you might write something. . . ."

I understood. They were editing the magazine *New Youth*,† but hitherto there seemed to have been no reaction, favorable or otherwise, and I guessed they must be feeling lonely. However, I said:

"Imagine an iron house without windows, absolutely indestructible, with many people fast asleep inside who will soon die of suffocation. But you know since they will die in their sleep, they will not feel the pain of death. Now if you cry aloud to wake a few of the lighter sleepers,

* Shaoxing.
† The most influential magazine in the cultural revolution of that time.

making those unfortunate few suffer the agony of irrevocable death, do you think you are doing them a good turn?"

"But if a few awake, you can't say there is no hope of destroying the iron house."

True, in spite of my own conviction, I could not blot out hope, for hope lies in the future. I could not use my own evidence to refute his assertion that it might exist. So I agreed to write, and the result was my first story, A Madman's Diary. From that time onwards, I could not stop writing, and would write some sort of short story from time to time at the request of friends, until I had more than a dozen of them.

As for myself, I no longer feel any great urge to express myself; yet, perhaps because I have not entirely forgotten the grief of my past loneliness, I sometimes call out, to encourage those fighters who are galloping on in loneliness, so that they do not lose heart. Whether my cry is brave or sad, repellent or ridiculous, I do not care. However, since it is a call to arms, I must naturally obey my general's orders. This is why I often resort to innuendoes, as when I made a wreath appear from nowhere at the son's grave in "Medicine," while in "Tomorrow" I did not say that Fourth Shan's Wife had no dreams of her little boy. For our chiefs then were against pessimism. And I, for my part, did not want to infect with the loneliness I had found so bitter those young people who were still dreaming pleasant dreams, just as I had done when young.

It is clear, then, that my short stories fall far short of being works of art; hence I count myself fortunate that they are still known as stories, and are even being compiled in one book. Although such good fortune makes me uneasy, I am nevertheless pleased to think they have readers in the world of men, for the time being at least.

Since these short stories of mine are being reprinted in one collection, owing to the reasons given above, I have chosen the title Na Han (Call to Arms).

December 3, 1922, Peking

A Madman's Diary

Two brothers, whose names I need not mention here, were both good friends of mine in high school; but after a separation of many years we gradually lost touch. Some time ago I happened to hear that one of them was seriously ill, and since I was going back to my old home I broke my journey to call on them. I saw only one, however, who told me that the invalid was his younger brother.

"I appreciate your coming such a long way to see us," he said, "but my brother recovered some time ago and has gone elsewhere to take up an official post." Then, laughing, he produced two volumes of his brother's diary, saying that from these the nature of his past illness could be seen, and that there was no harm in showing them to an old friend. I took the diary away, read it through, and found that he had suffered from a form of persecution complex. The writing was most confused and incoherent, and he had made many wild statements; moreover he had omitted to give any dates, so that only by the color of the ink and the differences in the writing could one tell that it was not written at one time. Certain sections, however, were not altogether disconnected, and I have copied out a part to serve as a subject for medical research. I have not altered a single illogicality in the diary and have changed only the names, even though the people referred to are all country folk, unknown to the world and of no consequence. As for the title, it was chosen by the diarist himself after his recovery, and I did not change it.

1

Tonight the moon is very bright.

I have not seen it for over thirty years, so today when I saw it I felt in unusually high spirits. I begin to realize that during the past thirty-odd years I have been in the dark; but now I must be extremely careful. Otherwise why should that dog at the Chao house have looked at me twice?

I have reason for my fear.

2

Tonight there is no moon at all, I know that this bodes ill. This morning when I went out cautiously, Mr. Chao had a strange look in his eyes, as if he were afraid of me, as if he wanted to murder me. There were seven or eight others, who discussed me in a whisper. And they were afraid of my seeing them. All the people I passed were like that. The fiercest among them grinned at me; whereupon I shivered from head to foot, knowing that their preparations were complete.

I was not afraid, however, but continued on my way. A group of children in front were also discussing me, and the look in their eyes was just like that in Mr. Chao's, while their faces too were ghastly pale. I wondered what grudge these children could have against me to make them behave like this. I could not help calling out: "Tell me!" But then they ran away.

I wonder what grudge Mr. Chao can have against me, what grudge the people on the road can have against me. I can think of nothing except that twenty years ago I trod on Mr. Ku Chiu's* account sheets for many years past, and Mr. Ku was very displeased. Although Mr. Chao does not know him, he must have heard talk of this and decided to avenge him, so he is conspiring against me with the people on the road. But then what of the children? At that time they were not yet born, so why should they eye me so strangely today, as if they were afraid of me, as if they wanted to murder me? This really frightens me, it is so bewildering and upsetting.

I know. They must have learned this from their parents!

3

I can't sleep at night. Everything requires careful consideration if one is to understand it.

* Ku Chiu means "Ancient Times." Lu Xun had in mind the long history of feudal oppression in China.

Those people, some of whom have been pilloried by the magistrate, slapped on the face by the local gentry, had their wives taken away by bailiffs, or their parents driven to suicide by creditors, never looked as frightened and as fierce then as they did yesterday.

The most extraordinary thing was that woman on the street yesterday who spanked her son and said, "Little devil! I'd like to bite several mouthfuls out of you to work off my feelings!" Yet all the time she looked at me. I gave a start, unable to control myself; then all those green-faced, long-toothed people began to laugh derisively. Old Chen hurried forward and dragged me home.

He dragged me home. The folk at home all pretended not to know me; they had the same look in their eyes as all the others. When I went into the study, they locked the door outside as if cooping up a chicken or a duck. This incident left me even more bewildered.

A few days ago a tenant of ours from Wolf Cub Village came to report the failure of the crops, and told my elder brother that a notorious character in their village had been beaten to death; then some people had taken out his heart and liver, fried them in oil, and eaten them, as a means of increasing their courage. When I interrupted, the tenant and my brother both stared at me. Only today have I realized that they had exactly the same look in their eyes as those people outside.

Just to think of it sets me shivering from the crown of my head to the soles of my feet.

They eat human beings, so they may eat me.

I see that woman's "bite several mouthfuls out of you," the laughter of those green-faced, long-toothed people, and the tenant's story the other day are obviously secret signs. I realize all the poison in their speech, all the daggers in their laughter. Their teeth are white and glistening: they are all man-eaters.

It seems to me, although I am not a bad man, ever since I trod on Mr. Ku's accounts it has been touch-and-go. They seem to have secrets which I cannot guess, and once they are angry they will call anyone a bad character. I remember when my elder brother taught me to write compositions, no matter how good a man was, if I produced arguments to the contrary he would mark that passage to show his approval; while if I excused evildoers, he would say: "Good for you, that shows original-ity." How can I possibly guess their secret thoughts—especially when they are ready to eat people?

Everything requires careful consideration if one is to understand it. In ancient times, as I recollect, people often ate human beings, but I am rather hazy about it. I tried to look this up, but my history has no chronology, and scrawled all over each page are the words: "Virtue and Morality." Since I could not sleep anyway, I read intently half the night, until I began to see words between the lines, the whole book being filled with the two words—"Eat people."

All these words written in the book, all the words spoken by our tenant, gaze at me strangely with an enigmatic smile.

I too am a man, and they want to eat me!

4

In the morning I sat quietly for some time. Old Chen brought lunch in: one bowl of vegetables, one bowl of steamed fish. The eyes of the fish were white and hard, and its mouth was open just like those people who want to eat human beings. After a few mouthfuls I could not tell whether the slippery morsels were fish or human flesh, so I brought it all up.

I said, "Old Chen, tell my brother that I feel quite suffocated, and want to have a stroll in the garden." Old Chen said nothing but went out, and presently he came back and opened the gate.

I did not move, but watched to see how they would treat me, feeling certain that they would not let me go. Sure enough! My elder brother came slowly out, leading an old man. There was a murderous gleam in his eyes, and fearing that I would see it he lowered his head, stealing glances at me from the side of his spectacles.

"You seem to be very well today," said my brother.

"Yes," said I.

"I have invited Mr. Ho here today," said my brother, "to examine you."

"All right," said I. Actually I knew quite well that this old man was the executioner in disguise! He simply used the pretext of feeling my pulse to see how fat I was; for by so doing he would receive a share of my flesh. Still I was not afraid. Although I do not eat men, my courage is greater than theirs. I held out my two fists, to see what he would do. The old man sat down, closed his eyes, fumbled for some time, and remained still for some time; then he opened his shifty eyes and said, "Don't let your imagination run away with you. Rest quietly for a few days, and you will be all right."

Don't let your imagination run away with you! Rest quietly for a few days! When I have grown fat, naturally they will have more to eat; but what good will it do me, or how can it be "all right"? All these people wanting to eat human flesh and at the same time stealthily trying to keep up appearances, not daring to act promptly, really made me nearly die of laughter. I could not help roaring with laughter, I was so amused. I knew that in this laughter were courage and integrity. Both the old man and my brother turned pale, awed by my courage and integrity.

But just because I am brave they are the more eager to eat me, in order to acquire some of my courage. The old man went out of the gate, but before he had gone far he said to my brother in a low voice, "To be eaten at once!" And my brother nodded. So you are in it too! This stupendous discovery, although it came as a shock, is yet no more than I had expected: the accomplice in eating me is my elder brother!

The eater of human flesh is my elder brother!

I am the younger brother of an eater of human flesh!

I myself will be eaten by others, but nonetheless I am the younger brother of an eater of human flesh!

5

These few days I have been thinking again: suppose that old man were not an executioner in disguise, but a real doctor; he would be nonetheless an eater of human flesh. In that book on herbs, written by his pre-decessor Li Shih-chen,* it is clearly stated that men's flesh can be boiled and eaten; so can he still say that he does not eat men?

As for my elder brother, I have also good reason to suspect him. When he was teaching me, he said with his own lips, "People exchange their sons to eat." And once in discussing a bad man, he said that not only did he deserve to be killed, he should "have his flesh eaten and his hide slept on."† I was still young then, and my heart beat faster for some time, he was not at all surprised by the story that our tenant from Wolf Cub Village told us the other day about eating a man's heart and liver, but kept nodding his head. He is evidently just as cruel as before. Since it is possible to "exchange sons to eat," then anything can be exchanged, anyone can be eaten. In the past I simply listened to his explanations, and let it go at that; now I know that when he explained it to me, not only was there human fat at the corner of his lips, but his whole heart was set on eating men.

6

Pitch-dark. I don't know whether it is day or night. The Chao family dog has started barking again.

The fierceness of a lion, the timidity of a rabbit, the craftiness of a fox. . . .

7

I know their way; they are not willing to kill anyone outright, nor do they dare, for fear of the consequences. Instead they have banded together and set traps everywhere, to force me to kill myself. The

---

*   A famous pharmacologist (1518–93), author of *Ben-cao-gang-mu*, the *Materia Medica*.

†   These are quotations from the old classic *Zuo Zhuan*.

behavior of the men and women in the street a few days ago, and my elder brother's attitude these last few days, make it quite obvious. What they like best is for a man to take off his belt, and hang himself from a beam; for then they can enjoy their heart's desire without being blamed for murder. Naturally that sets them roaring with delighted laughter. On the other hand, if a man is frightened or worried to death, although that makes him rather thin, they still nod in approval.

They only eat dead flesh! I remember reading somewhere of a hideous beast, with an ugly look in its eye, called "hyena," which often eats dead flesh. Even the largest bones it grinds into fragments and swallows: the mere thought of this is enough to terrify one. Hyenas are related to wolves, and wolves belong to the canine species. The other day the dog in the Chao house looked at me several times; obviously it is in the plot too and has become their accomplice. The old man's eyes were cast down, but that did not deceive me!

The most deplorable is my elder brother. He is also a man, so why is he not afraid, why is he plotting with others to eat me? Is it that when one is used to it he no longer thinks it a crime? Or is it that he has hardened his heart to do something he knows is wrong?

In cursing man-eaters, I shall start with my brother, and in dissuading man-eaters, I shall start with him too.

8

Actually, such arguments should have convinced them long ago. . . .

Suddenly someone came in. He was only about twenty years old and I did not see his features very clearly. His face was wreathed in smiles, but when he nodded to me his smile did not seem genuine. I asked him: "Is it right to eat human beings?"

Still smiling, he replied, "When there is no famine how can one eat human beings?"

I realized at once, he was one of them; but still I summoned up courage to repeat my question:

"Is it right?"

"What makes you ask such a thing? You really are . . . fond of a joke. . . . It is very fine today."

"It is fine, and the moon is very bright. But I want to ask you: Is it right?"

He looked disconcerted, and muttered: "No. . . ."

"No? Then why do they still do it?"

"What are you talking about?"

"What am I talking about? They are eating men now in Wolf Cub Village, and you can see it written all over the books, in fresh red ink."

His expression changed, and he grew ghastly pale. "It may be so," he said, staring at me. "It has always been like that. . . ."

"Is it right because it has always been like that?"

"I refuse to discuss these things with you. Anyway, you shouldn't talk about it. Whoever talks about it is in the wrong!"

I leaped up and opened my eyes wide, but the man had vanished. I was soaked with perspiration. He was much younger than my elder brother, but even so he was in it. He must have been taught by his parents. And I am afraid he has already taught his son: that is why even the children look at me so fiercely.

9

Wanting to eat men, at the same time afraid of being eaten themselves, they all look at each other with the deepest suspicion. . . .

How comfortable life would be for them if they could rid themselves of such obsessions and go to work, walk, eat, and sleep at ease. They have only this one step to take. Yet fathers and sons, husbands and wives, brothers, friends, teachers and students, sworn enemies and even strangers, have all joined in this conspiracy, discouraging and preventing each other from taking this step.

10

Early this morning I went to look for my elder brother. He was standing outside the hall door looking at the sky, when I walked up behind him, stood between him and the door, and with exceptional poise and politeness said to him:

"Brother, I have something to say to you."

"Well, what is it?" he asked, quickly turning toward me and nodding.

"It is very little, but I find it difficult to say. Brother, probably all primitive people ate a little human flesh to begin with. Later, because their outlook changed, some of them stopped, and because they tried to be good they changed into men, changed into real men. But some are still eating—just like reptiles. Some have changed into fish, birds, monkeys, and finally men; but some do not try to be good and remain reptiles still. When those who eat men compare themselves with those who do not, how ashamed they must be. Probably much more ashamed than the reptiles are before monkeys.

"In ancient times Yi Ya boiled his son for Chieh and Chou to eat; that is the old story.* But actually since the creation of heaven and earth by Pan Ku men have been eating each other, from the time of Yi Ya's son to the time of Hsu Hsi-lin,† and from the time of Hsu Hsi-lin down to the man caught in Wolf Cub Village. Last year they executed a criminal in the city, and a consumptive soaked a piece of bread in his blood and sucked it.

"They want to eat me, and of course you can do nothing about it single-handed; but why should you join them? As man-eaters they are capable of anything. If they eat me, they can eat you as well; members of

* According to ancient records, Yi Ya cooked his son and presented him to Duke Huan of Qi, who reigned from 685 to 643 B.C. Chieh and Chou were tyrants of an earlier age. The madman has made a mistake here.
† A revolutionary at the end of the Qing dynasty (1644–1911), Hsu Hsi-lin was executed in 1907 for assassinating a Qing official. His heart and liver were eaten.

the same group can still eat each other. But if you will just change your ways immediately, then everyone will have peace. Although this has been going on since time immemorial, today we could make a special effort to be good, and say this is not to be done! I'm sure you can say so, brother. The other day when the tenant wanted the rent reduced, you said it couldn't be done."

At first he only smiled cynically, then a murderous gleam came into his eyes, and when I spoke of their secret his face turned pale. Outside the gate stood a group of people, including Mr. Chao and his dog, all craning their necks to peer in. I could not see all their faces, for they seemed to be masked in cloths; some of them looked pale and ghastly still, concealing their laughter. I knew they were one band, all eaters of human flesh. But I also knew that they did not all think alike by any means. Some of them thought that since it had always been so, men should be eaten. Some of them knew that they should not eat men, but still wanted to; and they were afraid people might discover their secret; thus when they heard me they became angry, but they still smiled their cynical, tight-lipped smile.

Suddenly my brother looked furious, and shouted in a loud voice:

"Get out of here, all of you! What is the point of looking at a madman?"

Then I realized part of their cunning. They would never be willing to change their stand, and their plans were all laid; they had stigmatized me as a madman. In the future when I was eaten, not only would there be no trouble, but people would probably be grateful to them. When our tenant spoke of the villagers eating a bad character, it was exactly the same device. This is their old trick.

Old Chen came in too, in a great temper, but they could not stop my mouth, I had to speak to those people:

"You should change, change from the bottom of your hearts!" I said. "You must know that in the future there will be no place for man-eaters in the world.

"If you don't change, you may all be eaten by each other. Although so many are born, they will be wiped out by the real men, just like wolves killed by hunters. Just like reptiles!"

Old Chen drove everybody away. My brother had disappeared. Old Chen advised me to go back to my room. The room was pitch-dark. The beams and rafters shook above my head. After shaking for some time they grew larger. They piled on top of me.

The weight was so great, I could not move. They meant that I should die. I knew that the weight was false, so I struggled out, covered in perspiration. But I had to say:

"You should change at once, change from the bottom of your hearts! You must know that in the future there will be no place for man-eaters in the world."

11

The sun does not shine, the door is not opened, every day two meals.

I took up my chopsticks, then thought of my elder brother; I know now how my little sister died: it was all through him. My sister was only five at the time. I can still remember how lovable and pathetic she looked. Mother cried and cried, but he begged her not to cry, probably because he had eaten her himself, and so her crying made him feel ashamed. If he had any sense of shame. . . .

My sister was eaten by my brother, but I don't know whether Mother realized it or not.

I think Mother must have known, but when she cried she did not say so outright, probably because she thought it proper too. I remember when I was four or five years old, sitting in the cool of the hall, my brother told me that if a man's parents were ill, he should cut off a piece of his flesh and boil it for them if he wanted to be considered a good son; and Mother did not contradict him. If one piece could be eaten, obviously so could the whole. And yet just to think of the mourning then still makes my heart bleed; that is the extraordinary thing about it!

12

I can't bear to think of it.

I have only just realized that I have been living all these years in a place where for four thousand years they have been eating human flesh. My brother had just taken over the charge of the house when our sister died, and he may well have used her flesh in our rice and dishes, making us eat it unwittingly.

It is possible that I ate several pieces of my sister's flesh unwittingly, and now it is my turn. . . .

How can a man like myself, after four thousand years of man-eating history—even though I knew nothing about it at first—ever hope to face real men?

13

Perhaps there are still children who have not eaten men? Save the children.

April 1918
(Translated by Yang Hsien-yi and Gladys Yang)

HU SHIH
(1891–1962)

A leader of the New Culture Movement, Hu Shih was born in Shanghai in 1891. In 1910 he went to America to study agriculture at Cornell University, but soon switched his major to philosophy and literature. After graduation, he pursued a doctoral degree in philosophy at Columbia University and became a lifelong follower of John Dewey's Pragmatism. In 1917 Hu published "A Modest Proposal for the Reform of Literature," in which he proposes to replace classical Chinese with vernacular Chinese as a literary language, thereby breaking the tyranny of the classics. His book Experimental Verses, published in 1920, was the first volume of poetry written in vernacular Chinese. A key figure in twentieth century literature and scholarship, Hu also served as China's ambassador to the United States (1938-42), Chancellor of Peking University (1946-48), and president of the Academia Sinica in Taiwan, where he died of a heart attack in 1962.

The Butterflies

Two yellow butterflies
In pair fly to the skies;
I don't know why
One suddenly returns

Leaving the other one
Lonely and pitiful.
It too has no heart to fly into the skies,
For heaven is too lonely a place.

—*1916*

Dream and Poetry

All is commonplace experience,
All is commonplace impression.
By chance they rush into a dream
They are transformed into many new patterns.

All is commonplace sentiment,
All is commonplace word,
By chance they meet a poet
They are transformed into many new poems.

Only after being drunk does one know the wine is strong,
Only after having loved does one know the depth of love.
You can never write my poems,
I can never dream your dreams.

—*1920*

One Smile

Over ten years ago
Someone gave me a smile.
At the time—I did not know why—
I only felt that he smiled well.

I don't know what happened to that man,
But his smile remained;
Not only could I not forget him,
But the longer the smile lasted, the more lovable it became.

I have written many love poems on it,
I have made many different settings for it;
Some felt sad reading the verse,
Others felt gay reading the verse.

Gay or sad,
It is only a smile.
I have never found that man who smiled,
But I am grateful for his lovely smile.

—1920
(Translated by Julia C. Lin)

To the Tune of Shengzhazi

Wishing to have no love at all
And avoid the bitterness of loveless love
But after weighing my options
Willing to have lovesick thoughts of love

—1919
(Translated by Glenn D. Mott)

GUO MORUO
(1892–1978)

A pioneer in new verse, Guo Moruo was a major figure in twentieth century China. Son of a small-town landlord in Sichuan, Guo went to study medicine in Japan in 1914. There he fell in love with a Japanese nurse named Sato Tomiko and revoked his earlier arranged marriage. He lived with Sato for twenty years and had five children with her. Influenced by Western romantic poets such as Shelley, Goethe, and Whitman, Guo in 1921 published a collection of poems, Goddesses. Exploding with intense emotions and espousing individualism and pantheism, his work fully grasped the zeitgeist of the May Fourth Movement. Versatile, energetic, rebellious, Guo was influential in both state politics and scholarly pursuits, holding important official positions and claiming expertise in history, archeology, and other disciplines.

The Streets of Heaven

The streetlights in the distance have brightened
Like countless bright stars sparkling.
The bright stars in heaven have appeared
Like countless luminous streetlights.

Surely in that misty sky
There are lovely streets.
The items displayed there
Must be treasures unfound on this earth.

Look, that shallow Milky Way
Surely cannot be too wide.
The cowherd and weaving maid across the river
Surely can ride their buffaloes to meet each other.

I think just at this moment, they
Surely must be strolling along those streets of heaven.
If you do not believe me, look at the blooming comet.
It must be the lantern they carry on their walk.

—1921

The Sky Dog

Ya, I am a sky dog!
I have swallowed the moon,
I have swallowed the sun.
I have swallowed all the planets,
I have swallowed the entire universe.
I am I!

I am the light of the moon,
I am the light of the sun.
I am the light of all the planets,
I am the light of *X-ray*,
I am the total *energy* of the entire universe.*

---

* Both "X-ray" and "energy" were English in the original poem.

I am flying,
I am screaming,
I am burning,
I am burning like a fierce fire!
I am screaming like the mighty ocean!
I am running like electricity!
I am running,
I am running,
I tear my skin,
I eat my flesh,
I chew my heart,
I am running on my nerves,
I am running on my spines,
I am running in my brain.

I am I!
The I of I is about to explode!

—1920

The Nirvana of the Feng and Huang: Prelude

On the threshold of the new year, there in the sky
The Feng and Huang fly back and forth.*
Singing mournful tunes as they fly away,
Bearing twigs of fragrant wood as they return,
Return to Tan-hsüeh Mountain.

* Both Feng and Huang in Chinese mean "phoenix," with Feng being the male bird and Huang the female.

To the right of the mountain is the withered Wu-t'ung tree,
To the left of the mountain is the dried-up spring.
Before the mountain is the wide expanse of the sea,
Behind the mountain is the vast dreary plain,
And over the mountain a frozen sky of bitter winds.

The sky is now darkened,
The fragrant wood is now piled high,
The Feng is now wearied from flying,
The Huang is now wearied from flying,
Their hour of death is nearing.

The Feng pecks at the fragrant wood,
Sparks of fire upward dart;
The Huang fans the fire sparks,
Strands of smoke rise upward.

Again pecks the Feng,
Again pecks the Huang,
On the mountain the scented smoke swirls,
On the mountain the firelight fills the sky.

The night has deepened,
The fragrant wood is lighted,
The Feng is wearied from pecking,
The Huang is wearied from fanning,
Their hour of death is nearing!

Ah, ah,
Sad, sad are Feng and Huang!
Feng starts his dance, now slow, now high!
Huang starts her songs, now sad, now exalted!
Again Feng dances,

Again Huang sings,
A flock of birds has now flown over
Beyond the sky to attend the burial.

—1920

(Translated by Julia C. Lin)

LIU BANNONG
(1891–1934)

A native of Jiangsu, Liu Bannong was a child prodigy who turned against the old education system. A high school dropout but a reputable writer, he was offered in 1917 a professorship at Peking University, where he edited the New Culture Movement's flagship journal New Youth. In 1920 he went to study in England, followed by four years at the University of Paris, where he pursued a doctoral degree in linguistics. One of the earliest practitioners of new verse, Liu turned his attention to folk songs and often wrote about the working class. His most famous poem, "How Can I Not Miss Her" (1920), was later set to music by Yuen Ren Chao and became a hit in the 1930s. It was also in this poem that Liu coined the first modern Chinese feminine pronoun 她 (she, or her). In 1925, Liu returned to China and resumed teaching at Peking University. He died at the age of forty-three from an insect bite during linguistic fieldwork in Mongolia.

How Can I Not Miss Her

Light clouds drift in the sky
Gentle breezes blow on earth
Alas!
Gentle breezes brushing my hair
How can I not miss her?

The moonlight loves the ocean
The ocean loves the moonlight
Alas!
On this night of sweet silver
How can I not miss her?

Fallen flowers float on water
Fish swim slowly under there
Alas!
My swallow, what did you whisper?
How can I not miss her?

A withered tree sways in the chilly wind
A prairie fire burns the dusk
Alas!
In the west twilights linger
How can I not miss her?

Paper Thin

Inside the house a stove fire burns.
"Open the windows and buy fruit,"
　　　the master commanded.
Saying, "The weather is not cold,
But you will roast me with such a fire."
Outside the house lies a beggar
Teeth clenched against the north wind
Crying, "Die, Damn you!"
Pity that between indoors and out
Is a partition thin as paper.

(Translated by Yunte Huang)

XU DISHAN
(1893–1941)

Born in Taiwan, Xu Dishan was an active participant in the May Fourth Movement when he was a student at Yenching University (later Peking University). Along with Mao Dun, Ye Shengtao, and others, he founded the Literary Research Society in 1921 and edited the influential journal Short Story Monthly. He studied philosophy and religion at Columbia University in 1923 and then at Oxford University in 1924. A highly regarded writer, scholar, and translator, Xu died of a heart attack at the age of forty-eight while teaching in Hong Kong. Xu was known for his plain-styled essays, like "The Peanut" and "I Think," in which the author meditates on philosophical, religious, and ethical themes.

The Peanut

Behind our house there used to be half an acre of empty field. Mom said, "It's a pity to let it lie fallow. Since you all enjoy peanuts so much, let's turn it into a peanut patch." We siblings and the house girls all loved the idea. So we bought the seeds, dug the soil, and watered the field. A few months later, we had a harvest!

Mom said, "We should celebrate our harvest tonight and invite your dad to taste our new peanuts, okay?" We all agreed. Mother went on to make half a dozen peanut dishes. She also told us to hold our celebration at the thatched pavilion in the garden.

The weather wasn't great that night, but Dad came—how amazing! Dad asked, "Do you all like peanuts?"

"Yes!" we replied eagerly.

"Who can name the virtues of the peanut?"

"Peanuts smell good," answered elder sister.

"Peanuts give us cooking oil," said elder brother.

"Everyone, rich or poor, can buy them cheaply and everyone enjoys eating them," said I. "That is the virtue of the peanut."

Dad said, "There're indeed many uses for the peanut, but one of them is the most precious. The tiny bean is not like an apple, peach, or pomegranate, which hangs its fruit on the branches, in bright red or fresh green, drawing attention from admirers. Instead, it buries the fruit underneath the soil, to be dug out only when ripe. If you happen to see a peanut plant curling up above the ground, you can't tell right away whether it bears any fruit, until you see the whole of it."

"That's true," we all said. Mom also nodded her head, as Dad continued, "So you should all be like a peanut, being a useful thing, but not a mighty one that looks conspicuously pretty."

I asked, "Does it mean I should try to be a useful person, not one dignified by might?"

"That is indeed my hope for you," said Dad.

We chatted till late at night. All the peanut dishes were gone, but Dad's words left an indelible impression on my heart.

I Think

What am I thinking?

In my heart there used to be a road leading to the Garden of Paradise, once treaded by a woman. But now she's gone, and the road is so deserted and overgrown with weeds, wildflowers, thorny brush, and twisted vines that I can hardly see it.

I have long been thinking about that road, which exists not for her alone. Since she's gone, why can't I take strolls there by myself?

The weeds and wildflowers are lovely and fragrant; how can I bear to get rid of them? The thorny underbrush and entangled vines are so overflowing and extensive; without any tool in hand, how do I dare touch them? I've thought about wandering alone on that road, but haven't set off.

Days pass, and I begin to forget where the road leads. I can only walk to the edge of the road and sit there quietly by a little pond gazing listlessly, contemplating that grass-covered and vine-locked path.

As a gust of wind blows petals into the water, pond koi rush to the surface to nibble, mistaking flowers for some delicacy. My thoughts also float on water, nibbled and then spat out by the fish like bubbling foams, drifting back into the air.

The fish are still swimming happily. I am not willing to blaze the trail myself, nor would I abandon my thoughts. Alas!

I fix my gaze on the koi bobbing up and down, while my recollections also wander up and down.

Ah, woman! You've now turned into the koi in my "pond of memory." Sometimes you float to the surface, showing yourself to me; sometimes you sink, making me wonder where you are, beneath which fallen leaf, between what rocks and sands.

But where that road leads I have long forgotten. I can only sit by the water every day, waiting for you to emerge from the bottom of the pond.

(Translated by Yunte Huang)

BING XIN
(1900–1999)

Born in Fujian, Bing Xin, real name Xie Wanying, was brought up in Shandong, where her father was the head of a naval college. In 1918 she attended the Peking Union College for Women (later amalgamated with Yenching University) and became active in student protest and literary reform. Influenced by Rabindranath Tagore's Stray Birds, she published A Maze of Stars (1921) and Spring Water (1922), both collections of "mini poems," which are influenced by classical Chinese jueju and Japanese haiku, and reminiscent of Greek epigrams. She studied at Wellesley College from 1923 to 1926 and graduated with a master's degree in English literature. In her ensuing long career spanning the entire twentieth century, she remained an influential poet, novelist, essayist, translator, and writer of children's literature.

A Maze of Stars (selections)

19

My heart—
A lonely vessel
cuts through the ebb and swell of time.

34

That which creates the new shoreline
is not the rolling wave
but the tiny grains of sand beneath it.

44

Nature,
allow me just one question,
one serious question:
"Haven't I mistaken you?"

49

Fragmented lines,
a little spray on the sea of learning.
Yet the lights in them gleam and sparkle:
a maze of stars set into the heavens of the heart.

73

Worthless words,
thrown on the fire,
transformed into worthless light.

74

The child
is a great poet,
with an imperfect tongue,
lisping perfect verse.

81

Deep night—
I am tired, let me
lay down my pen
and share a brief quiet moment with you.

97

Is it true?
The heart is just a music box,
always churning out the same old song.
                    (Translated by John Cayley)

Spring Water (selections)

14

Nature called aloud and said—
"Take your pen,
Dip it into my ocean;
Humanity's heart is too dry and parched."

17

The setting sun shines on the withered grass of the red wall.
Go down quickly, O sun!
You cause many young people to age early.

37

Space!
Tear away your net of stars.
Let me see the face of your light.

79

I wish before I leave this world
That I might softly, softly say to it—
"O world—   ·
I thoroughly understand you."

100

When the burden on the shoulder of the young
Suddenly lightens,
The brave heart—
Because of this very relief, becomes lonely and sad.

102

My questions,
My heart
Never answers in the midst of light.
But my dreams
In darkness, give me their solution.

144

The poet writes in vain,
One little heart—
Could it bring comfort
To wanderers suffering bitterly in the rain?

(Translated by Grace Boynton)

LI JINFA
(1900–1976)

Although little is known of the life of the elusive "poet eccentric" of the 1920s, Li Jinfa was credited with introducing French Symbolism to China. Born Li Shuliang in Guangdong, he adopted the pen name "Jinfa" (literally meaning "golden hair") because of a recurring dream in which he was flying in the sky, led by a blond goddess. In 1919 he went to study sculpture and painting in France, where he became enamored with the poetic symbolism of Charles Baudelaire and Paul Verlaine. He wrote his best symbolist poems in the early 1920s, incorporating French words in his lines, which irritated many contemporary and later critics. Upon returning to China in 1925, he taught art history and was once appointed China's ambassador to Iraq. After the founding of the People's Republic in 1949, Li left China and lived a reclusive life on a chicken farm in New Jersey. He died in Long Island in 1976.

The Abandoned Woman

Long hair hangs disheveled before my eyes,
Severing all hostile stares of contempt,
And the quick flow of fresh blood, the deep sleep of dried bones.
The dark night and mosquitoes arrive slowly together,
Over the corner of this low wall,

To scream behind my clean white ears
Like the crazed winds raging in the wilderness,
Frightening the wandering shepherds.

With a blade of grass, I come and go with the spirit of
        God in the empty valley.
My sorrow can be deeply imprinted only in the brains of
        roaming bees.
Or with the waterfalls, let it be dashed down the hanging cliffs,
To be then drifted away with the red leaves.

The hidden grief burdens her every move.
No fire of setting sun can melt the ennui of time
Into ashes, and fly away through the chimney
To color the wings of the roaming crows,
And with them perch on the rocks of a roaring sea
To listen quietly to the boatman's song.

The frail old skirt mournfully sighs
As she wanders among the graves.
 Never will there be hot tears
To drop on the lawn
To adorn the world.

The Expression of Time

1

Wind and rain in the ocean,
Wild deer dead in my heart.
Look, autumn dream has spread its wings and departed,
Leaving behind only this wilted soul.

2

I seek abandoned desires,
I mourn discolored lips.
Ah, in the gloom of dark grass,
The moon gathers our deep silence.

3

In love's ancient palace,
Our nuptials have fallen ill.
Take a discarded candle,
Dusk has shrouded the fields.

4

What do I need at this moment?
As if in fear of being scorched to death by the sun!
Go, the garden gate is unfastened;
The roaming bees have come in winged sandals.

5

I await the waking of dream,
I await my wakefulness to sleep.
But with your tears in my eyes,
I have no strength to see the past.

6

Leaning against snow, you long for spring;
Amid the faded grass, I listen to the cicadas' cries.
Our lives are withered, too wasted,
Like a rice field after a stampede.

7

I sing rhymeless folk songs
With my heart keeping the beat.
Entrust your sorrows in my bosom
Where they will be cured.

8

The sleeping lotus in the shade
Cannot understand the glory of sun and moon.
Row your boat to the wide pond,
And let it learn a bit of love in the world of men.

9

Our memories
Are searching for a way home from the wilderness.

(Translated by Julia C. Lin)

YU DAFU

(1896–1945)

Born into an impoverished genteel family in Zhejiang, Yu Dafu went to study in Japan in 1913. As a student of economics at Tokyo Imperial University, he lived a bohemian life, and in 1921 he published Sinking, *the first collection of short stories written in vernacular in modern China. Lyrical, decadent, and honest, his stories often portray the psychodramas of young intellectuals caught in the crossfire of the new and old in a changing world and extend, in the words of C. T. Hsia, "the psychological and moral frontiers of modern Chinese fiction." A founding member of the Creation Society in 1921 and the Chinese League of Left-Wing Writers in 1930, Yu struggled against radical politics and ideology. At the outbreak of the Sino-Japanese War, he joined the national alliance of resistance and became an editor in Singapore. When the city fell, he fled to Indonesia and lived under a pseudonym. In 1945, he was tracked down and killed by Japanese military police in Sumatra.*

Malady of Spring Nights

1

For half a year I lived in Shanghai with no job, and because I was unemployed, it was necessary to change my lodgings three times. At first I lived in a birdcage apartment on Bubbling Well Road, a prison cell without guards that never saw sunlight. Except for a few tailors who looked like ferocious gangsters, the inmates of this place were mostly pitiable unknown men of letters. Hence my epithet for the place: Yellow Grub Street. After a month in Grub Street, the rent suddenly went up, forcing me to pack up a few tattered books and move to a small hotel I knew near the racecourse. At the hotel I suffered all sorts of ill treatment and had to move again. I looked around on Dent Road to the north of the Garden Bridge, a slum opposite Rixinli Lane. I found a small room there and relocated.

The houses on Dent Road stood no higher than about twenty feet. My chamber on the upper floor was so small and low that if I stretched out to yawn, my arms would poke through the dusty gray roof. Coming through the front door from an alley, you first entered the landlord's room. Edging your way around piles of rags, mounds of old tins, bottles, and rusty detritus, you would come to a rickety ladder with missing rungs leaning against the wall. Climbing the ladder to a dark hole of two square feet, you would arrive at the second floor. This dim little space, no bigger than a cat's face, was partitioned by the landlord into two tiny rooms. The inner room was occupied by a woman who worked at the N Cigarette Company. As she had to come and go through my cubby at the top of the ladder to get to hers at the back, my monthly rent was a few coppers cheaper than hers.

The landlord, a man in his fifties with a bent back, looked older than his age. His sallow face had a dark oily sheen. His eyes were of different size perched above high cheekbones. The wrinkles on his forehead and face were filled with a fine coal dust, which, despite his efforts every morning, could not be washed out. He got up at eight or nine every day. After a fit of coughing, he went out with a pair of bamboo baskets dangling on a shoulder pole. He returned around three or four most afternoons, still carrying two empty baskets. Occasionally he came back with the baskets full, loaded with the same kinds of rags, rusty junk, bottles, and so on that already littered his chambers. On these nights, he would get some wine and sit by the edge of the bed drinking by himself, cursing freely in an incomprehensible dialect.

My first encounter with my housemate on the other side of the partition was on the afternoon I moved in. At about five o'clock, when the fleeting light of a spring day drew close to dusk, I lit a candle and began to arrange the few books I had brought with me from the hotel. I divided them into two stacks, one big and one small. Then I placed two large picture frames on top of the larger stack. I had sold all my furniture, so this setup of books and picture frames would have to serve as a desk during the day and a bed at night. Done with the task, I sat down on the smaller stack for a smoke, facing my newfangled desk. With my back turned against the trapdoor, I pulled slowly on the cigarette and stared at the candle. Just then I heard a movement from the ladder. Turning around, I could see nothing but my own enlarged shadow, but my ears plainly told me that someone was coming up. I stared into the darkness for a moment, and then a pale oval face and the slender torso of a female figure came into view. Seeing her face, I knew instantly that she must be my housemate on the other side of the partition. Earlier when I had come looking for a place, the landlord had told me that besides him, there was only a female worker living in this house. Liking the cheap rent and the fact that there was no actual housewife or kids around, I took the place without any hesitation.

I waited until she came up the ladder, stood up, and bowed to her politely. "Excuse me," I said, "I just moved in today. I hope you will not mind."

She made no reply, but her big dark eyes looked at me solemnly. She then unlocked her room and went in. Ours was just a brief encounter, but for some unknown reason I felt a kind of pity for the waif. Her high-bridged nose, pale oval face, and slight wispy figure, all appealed to my sympathy. But as someone struggling to make ends meet myself, I had no time to care for someone who at least had a job. A moment later, I returned to my previous state, sitting still on the small stack of books, staring at the candle.

A week had passed since I moved into the slum. Every day my neighbor went to work at seven in the morning and returned after six that evening. She would always find me sitting on top of my books, staring at the candle flame or oil lamp. Perhaps my long idling stirred her curiosity; one day when she returned from work, came upstairs, and saw me standing there, letting her pass like the first day, she suddenly stopped and looked directly at me. "What are you reading every day?" she stammered in a halting voice. She spoke a pure lilting Suzhou dialect, producing an effect on me beyond description, so I will only transcribe her words in plain Chinese.

Her question made me blush. Even though I was sitting there day in and day out peering into several foreign books I had opened, my mind was in such a state of confusion that I wasn't able to read a single line. Sometimes I let my imagination conjure up strange patterns and plugged them into the space between the lines. Other times I only flipped through pages looking at the illustrations and invented fantasies inspired by the images. Due to my insomnia and malnutrition, this trancelike state was not difficult to induce. I saw it as a form of sickness. Also, my heavy padded gown—my only worldly possession—was so threadbare that I could not go out in it for walks. As there was no natural light in the room, I had to light a lamp or candle day and night, causing my overall health to decline still further, my eyesight weakened, leg muscles atrophied. In such a sorry state, how could I not feel exposed by her question? So I replied vaguely, "I wasn't really reading. It's just that it doesn't look good sitting around idly all day. That's why I put books in front of me."

She gave me another searching glance, seemingly confused by what I had said, and then disappeared into her partition.

It would be untrue to say that in those days I had completely abandoned the idea of employment or had not done anything at all. There were times when my mind hadn't been so cloudy, and I'd translated a few poems from English and French, as well as short stories from German that were each about four thousand words in length. I sneaked out quietly at night, after everyone had gone to sleep, to mail these translations to some new publishers. Since my hope for finding employment in other fields was all but dashed, this line of work, relying on my dried-up brains, remained the only possibility for me. If the editors happened to like my work and publish those pieces, it wouldn't be hard to get paid a few dollars in royalty. Since my relocation to Dent Road, by the time she first spoke to me, I had submitted three or four such pieces of translation.

2

Living in the muddled foreign concessions in Shanghai, one hardly noticed the change of seasons or passage of time. After my move to the slum on Dent Road, I felt that my ragged cotton gown was getting heavier and warmer day by day. I thought, "Perhaps spring will be over soon?"

Even so, without two nickels to rub together, I couldn't afford to go anywhere, and could only stay in my dark cubby, sitting by the light, day and night. One day, sometime around late afternoon, when I was sitting there as usual, my housemate suddenly came upstairs with two paper bags. When I stood up to let her pass, she put down one bag on my desk and said, "Here's some grape jam bread for you. You can have it tomorrow. I also bought some bananas. Would you like to come eat them in my room?"

While I helped her with the bag, she unlocked the door to her room and invited me in. We had shared the loft for two weeks, which seemed to have bolstered her trust in me as an honest and respectable man. All trace of suspicion on her face during our first meeting was gone. After we went in, I saw that it was not yet dark outside. There was in her room a south-facing window, through which reflected sunlight could enter and shine on this small space containing a bed made of two planks, a black lacquer side table, a wooden chest, and a round stool. The bed wasn't equipped with a mosquito net, but with two clean blue-cloth quilts. On the side table there was a small foreign tin box, perhaps for her toiletries, that was spotted with grease. Picking up the few half-worn cotton gowns and work pants from the stool and putting them on the bed, she invited me to sit down. I felt a bit uneasy because of her hospitable gestures, so I said, "We are housemates; there's no need to be so polite."

"I'm not being polite. It's just that every day I come home, you always stand up to let me pass. I feel much obliged."

With those words, she opened the bag of bananas and handed them to me. She also took one for herself, sitting on the bed, peeling and eating.

"Why do you stay at home every day? Why not go out and get a job?"

"My plan was to get a job, but I couldn't find anything. I tried."

"Do you have any friends?"

"Yes, but given my circumstance, no one's disposed to see me anymore."

"Did you go to school?"

"I studied at a foreign school for a few years."

"Where are you from? Why don't you go home?"

Her questions made me suddenly aware of my own situation, of how I'd become, since the previous year, so dejected day by day that I had totally forgotten things such as, "Who am I?" "What is my current situation?" or even "Am I happy or sad?" At her questioning, I began to recall all the difficulties endured over the past six months. I became speechless, sitting there looking at her. My silence must have made her think that I was also a vagabond; an expression of sadness mixed with loneliness spread across her face, followed by a gentle sigh. "Ah, are you just like me?"

After another sigh, she lapsed into silence, her eyes moist and red. I tried to divert her with a question. "What do you do at the factory?"

"I pack cigarettes."

"How many hours do you have to work each day?"

"From seven in the morning to six in the afternoon, a one-hour break at noon, that's ten hours of work a day. They cut your pay if you work less than that."

"How much is the pay?"

"Nine dollars a month, that's three dollars for ten days, or three cents an hour."

"How much do the meals cost?"

"Four dollars a month."

"So, if you work for ten hours a day without an absence, your income would be five dollars a month. Is that enough for rent and clothes?"

"Hardly! Besides, that manager is . . . well . . . I . . . I hate that factory. Do you smoke?"

"Yes."

"You'd better not smoke. And if you must, don't smoke our brand. I really hate it."

I noticed her teeth were clenching, and decided to drop the topic. When I finished my banana, darkness had crept into the room. I stood up, thanked her, and left for my cubby. Usually, because she was exhausted by work, she would go to sleep immediately after coming home. But that night, she seemed to have stayed up till midnight. After that evening, she would always talk to me when she got home and I learned about her past.

Her name was Ermei Chen, born in Dongxiang, Suzhou, but she was raised in the countryside near Shanghai. Her father, before passing away the previous fall, had also worked at the cigarette factory. They had shared the same tiny room and gone to work together every day, but now she was left alone. The month after her father's death, she would cry all the way to work in the morning and cry again on the way back in the evening. Seventeen years old, she had no siblings or close relatives. The cost for her father's burial was covered by the fifteen dollars he had entrusted to the landlord downstairs before dying, who indeed took sole charge of the matter.

"He is a good man, our landlord," she said. "He never takes advantage of me; otherwise, I wouldn't have been able to go to work every day just like when my father was still alive. But that factory foreman, Mr. Li, is an evil man. Knowing my father is dead, he's been harassing me."

I now knew the outline of her childhood and life with her father, but what about her mother? Was she alive or dead? Ermei never mentioned her.

3

The weather seemed to be changing. Over the last several days my small stuffy room filled with putrid air like in a steam oven, making me dizzy. In this climate, as spring turns to summer, I usually develop a seasonal case of nerves, weakening my disposition—it drove me half mad. I began to take walks at night, when there was little traffic on the street. It did me good to stroll down an empty road alone, gazing up at the stars in the narrow strip of deep navy sky, and let my mind wander off into fantasy. On such intoxicating spring nights, I could do nothing but walk around aimlessly, and wouldn't go home until dawn. Exhausted, I would go to bed immediately and sleep till noon. Sometimes I didn't even get up until around the time Ermei returned from work. With sufficient sleep, my health slowly improved. Ordinarily my stomach could handle no more than half a pound of bread, but since my regimen of nightly exercises, my appetite had increased to almost double, a disaster for my purse but good news for my brain, which could now focus, being better nourished. After my strolls and before bed, I even wrote a few short stories in the style of Edgar Allan Poe. Reading them over, I found they weren't bad. I revised them a few times, made copies, and then mailed them off. Feeling a slim hope, I also remembered that there had been no news at all about those translations I had submitted earlier. Pretty soon, I forgot about these stories, too.

As for Ermei, I now only saw her occasionally when she returned in the afternoon, since I was usually still asleep when she left her room for work in the morning. But I sensed, for some unknown reason, her attitude toward me had reverted back to the suspicion she harbored when we first met. Sometimes she would give me a searching glance, her dark, clear eyes seeming reproachful and full of admonition.

It had been over twenty days since my move to this slum. One afternoon, when I was reading by candlelight a novel I had bought from a used bookstore, Ermei hurried upstairs and said to me, "There's a mailman downstairs. He wants you to bring your seal and sign for a letter."

With these words, her look of suspicion became more pronounced, as if suggesting, "Aha, now we know what you are up to." Annoyed by her attitude, I replied sharply, "What letter? I'm not expecting a letter. It can't be mine."

My reply had somehow made her feel triumphant, and a smile instantly appeared on her face. "Go take a look yourself," she said coldly. "Only you know your own affairs."

At that moment I heard the impatient mailman call from downstairs, "A registered letter!"

When I got the letter and opened it, my heart skipped a beat. It turned out one of my translations of a German story had been accepted by a magazine. The letter contained a five-dollar money order. I was about to go broke, and now these five bucks would not only cover my next month's rent due soon, but also pay for food in the next few days. No one could guess how critical these five dollars were to me at this moment.

The next afternoon, I went to the post office and cashed the money order. It didn't take long after walking in the bright sunlit street before I was soon perspiring heavily. Noticing the look of other people on the street, and then looking down at myself, I couldn't help but feel shame. Beads of sweat ran down my head and neck. All those late nights when I wandered through the streets, with a spring chill lingering in deserted lanes, there had been no sun to contend with before dawn broke in the east. On those nights I had not felt that my ragged padded gown was out of season. But now, on a warm afternoon under the spring sun, I still wore the same shabby gown, strolling down the streets, unaware that my fellow creatures had all adapted to the change of seasons. How could I not feel ashamed of myself? For a moment I became oblivious to the fact that my rent would be due soon and my wallet was almost empty; I started walking toward the clothing stores on Zha Road. Not having been out and about in broad daylight for a while, I momentarily felt I had entered paradise as I watched cars and rickshaws carrying well-dressed young men and women to and fro on the streets, roadside silk shops and jewelry stores displaying luxurious items, and I listened to the beehive-like cacophony of human voices, footfalls, and bell rings.

Oblivious to my own existence, and wanting to join in the songs and dance of my fellow citizens, I inadvertently started humming an old Peking Opera tune. But this illusory nirvana was shattered by the sudden ringing of a bell as I tried to cross the street and turn into Zha Road. I looked up and saw that a trolley bus was charging toward me and the fat driver, leaning halfway out of the window, glared at me and cursed loudly:

"You pigheaded imbecile! Are you blind? You deserve to be run over like a yellow dog!"

I yielded, feeling foolish, as the northbound trolley bus rumbled past in a cloud of dust. Out of nowhere, a fit of laughter overtook me. I didn't stop laughing until I noticed passersby were giving me dirty looks. Blushing, I entered Zha Road.

At the clothier's, I asked about prices for lined gowns and haggled to the best of my ability. The clerks, as if coached by the same master, all looked down their noses, mocking me. "You must be kidding! Don't bother us if you can't afford to buy anything."

Finally I arrived at a small shop on the Fifth Avenue. At this point I realized there was no way I could get a lined gown, so I settled on a plain cotton gown and immediately changed into it. Carrying the old padded robe in my arms, I walked toward home in silence, while contemplating an idea.

"The money won't be enough for anything now. Why not just go on a spree and be done with it?" I thought to myself. I remembered the day when Ermei brought me bread and bananas. Without a second thought, I stepped into the confectioner's and bought a dollar's worth of chocolates, banana candies, and cakes. Standing at the counter and waiting for the clerk to wrap them up, I suddenly remembered that I hadn't had a bath in a month. Why not go and have one?

By the time I had the bath and got to Dent Road with my two packages, my padded robe in one hand and a bag of goodies in the other, it was already quite late, with shops along the street lit up, traffic scarce, and a cold evening wind from the Bund sending me into shivers. Arriving back at my room, I lit a candle and looked at the door of Ermei's room to find she hadn't returned yet. Even though I was starving, I wasn't willing to open the bag of goodies. I wanted to wait for Ermei to come home and share them with her. I started reading, while swallowing hard from hunger. After a long wait, Ermei still had not come home. At some point, I was overcome by fatigue and fell asleep on a pile of books.

4

The sound of Ermei's footsteps on the ladder woke me. I saw that the candle had burned down two inches. I asked her what time it was, and she said, "The ten-o'clock siren's just sounded."

"Why did you come home so late today?"

"The factory has received more orders, so they want us to work night shifts. More pay, but too tiring."

"Can't you refuse the overtime hours?"

"They are short of workers. We have no choice."

With this, tears ran down her face. I thought she was crying from exhaustion, and felt pity for her, but I was also a little amused to see that she was still a child at heart. Opening the bag of candies, I invited her to try some, saying, "It takes time to get used to night shifts; that's why you feel so tired. But when you get used to it, it'll be nothing."

She sat quietly by my makeshift desk, ate a few chocolates, and glanced at me as if she wanted to say something but couldn't. So I urged her, "Do you want to tell me something?"

After another pause, she stammered a question:

"I . . . I . . . wanted to ask you this. Recently you went out every night. Were you mixed up with bad men?"

I was taken aback by this idea, her suspicion of me mixing with thieves and gangsters all these nights. When I stayed silent, she was convinced that she must be right about me and had found me out. "Why must you eat such fine food and wear such fine clothes?" She tried to persuade me, speaking gently but pleading. "Do you know what you are doing is risky? What if you get caught? How would you face other people then? We'd let bygones be bygones, but from now on I beg you to stop. . . ."

My eyes widened, my jaw dropped, I stared at her, speechless, for her ideas were so absurd that I didn't know how to respond. Pausing for a second, she resumed:

"Take your smoking, for instance, if you quit, you can at least save a few coppers a day. I advised you long ago not to smoke, especially not the brand made by my hated factory, but you won't listen."

Again her eyes welled up with tears. I supposed she was crying out of resentment for her factory, but my heart wouldn't allow myself that idea; instead, I convinced myself that her tears were shed for my sake. I mused on this for a moment, waiting for her to calm down, and then told her everything: how the registered letter had come about yesterday, how I had cashed the money order and gone on a shopping spree today, and my insomnia and the necessity of going out for long walks every night to calm my nerves. Listening to my explanations, she began to believe in me. When I was done, she noticeably blushed, lowering her head to avoid my eyes, and said shyly, "Oh, I was wrong, I was wrong. Please don't mind what I said, I didn't mean any harm. Your behavior was so strange, that's why my thoughts went to crazy ideas. As long as you work hard, it will all be fine. The thing you just mentioned, what is it called again? One piece can sell for five dollars. If you can do one a day, how wonderful will that be?"

Touched by her naïveté, I suddenly had an unthinkable urge, a desire to reach out and snatch her into my arms. But my senses checked me, saying, "Commit no sin! Don't you know the shape you're in? Do you really want to poison this pure girl? Devil, devil, you have no right to love anyone now!"

When I had the sudden notion to embrace her, I shut my eyes for a few seconds. When reason won out, I opened my eyes again, and felt my surroundings brighter than before. With a gentle smile, I said to her, "It's getting late, you should go to bed. Haven't you got work to do in the morning? I promise you, I will quit smoking from now on."

At this, she stood up instantly, and went happily back to her room.

After she left, I lit another candle, and sat there thinking things over. "From the fruits of my labor, the first five dollars I made, I have spent three. Adding to what I originally had, a bit over a dollar, I'll have only a few dimes left after paying the rent. What shall I do?

"I could pawn my old padded robe, but I'm afraid no pawnshop will take it.

"This girl is pitiable. But my own situation is worse. She doesn't want to work and yet the job forces her to work overtime. I want to work and yet I can't find a job.

"Maybe I can try manual labor? But can my soft noodle limbs handle the weight of a rickshaw?

"I could kill myself; if I had the courage, I would have done it long ago. But since the idea still appeals to me, it means I'm not a complete coward.

"Aha, what did that trolley bus driver call me today?

"Yellow dog! That's a good name for me.

" . . . . . "

Out of my mind's unconnected and scattered thoughts, I couldn't find one good idea to dig myself out of the plight. A siren from a nearby factory sounded; it must have just announced midnight. I got up and put on my old padded robe, blew out the candle, and went out for a walk.

By now the inhabitants of the slum had all gone quietly to sleep. On Dent Road, facing me, there stood the modern blocks of Rixinli, with a few high windows lit up with colored lights. Balalaika music and snatches of melancholic songs, clear and lyrical, drifted into the chilly dead of night—probably it was a White Russian émigré making her living as a singer. Above it all, a layer of ashen clouds, heavy like decaying corpses, draped themselves over the sky. Where there was a tear in the drapery, one or two stars blinked through. But around these stars, even the dark sky appeared to harbor a gloomy and mysterious sadness.

July 15, 1923

(Translated by Yunte Huang and Glenn Mott)

HE HAIMING
(1887–1944)

Born in Hong Kong and a native of Hunan, He Haiming was an important member of the School of Mandarin Duck and Butterfly, a genre of popular fiction that features romantic love, knights-errant, scandals, and detective mysteries. Early in life He attended a teachers' college in Hubei and then a military school, where he befriended young revolutionaries aspiring to overthrow the Qing monarchy. He was jailed for his editorship of a radical magazine and was sentenced to death, but the Wuchang Uprising in July 1911, which led to the demise of Qing Dynasty, saved him from death row. After a brief sojourn in Japan, he returned to Shanghai in 1915 and made a living by writing stories that often portray courtesan love. Despite his success, the income from writing was hardly sufficient to support his life of extravagance and debauchery. He died in poverty in Nanjing during the Japanese occupation.

For the Love of Her Feet

The store selling medium-priced leather footwear was located next to a large amusement park, so that the men and women entering and exiting the park each day had to pass by the storefront. Nearly everyone inside could see the bustle. The store consisted of two and a half stories, with an interior layout as follows. The upper story was made up of offices for the manager and the various bookkeepers; it also served as a storage area for a certain amount of stock. The lower story was the shop, with the commotion of a bevy of clerks making sales. The remaining half story was the basement, which housed the only factory for the enterprise.

An apprentice named Ah Fa, who had just completed his initial training, worked in this factory. He was only seventeen but had already labored in the basement for three years.

Three whole years! For a young man, shouldn't they be as precious as gold? Wasn't it regrettable to have to spend them in an underground factory? And yet, the skill of putting together shoes by hand had undeniably been acquired there, so that the time did not seem to have been expended in vain. It's just that the fervent spirit of youth could never actually be shut up in any dungeon. The two street-level windows never stopped flashing with light, letting in sights of the outside world for him, as if to keep him enticed.

The daily routine of his life, on the other hand, was utterly monotonous. He was a very tiny person in a very tiny place, using his very tiny hands to do a very tiny job. Whenever he looked around, his tools and the workbench next to him all appeared so small. In his seemingly detached world of limited sunshine, everything was miniaturized according to scale. Still, he was able to leave this workspace in spirit, to uncover those little eyeballs that so rarely encountered direct sunlight, to peek semiconsciously out a street-level window time and time again. But would this limited line of vision possibly allow him to see everything in human society? Could it show him the kaleidoscopic world that he imagined existed outside his half-buried environment?

The reader ought to know that according to practice, basement windows of this sort were situated at sidewalk level along the thoroughfare. The line of vision of anyone looking out from them was exactly at the shoe level of passersby. Hence, the result of Ah Fa's close observation of human society outside his domain was the sight of different feet—large, small, long, short—as well as shoes of varying styles for both men and women. The sidewalk outside his window, moreover, was a place everyone entering or exiting the amusement park had to pass. So the foot traffic there was far more dense than anywhere else. Bedazzled by the colorful variety of what he saw, he gradually developed a certain expertise at what had begun as curious observation.

"All these feet," he secretly mused. "What sort of people do they belong to? Why is it that they gad about like that, so thoroughly unrestrained? Can they just be running around outside all day long? Ah, I too have a pair of feet. Why then do I have to confine myself to this little bit of space all the time, without being able to make a single spontaneous move?" His thoughts thus led from the unfettered feet of others to his own confined ones, making him feel the sharp pain of lost freedom. Then his mind began to stir once more. "Don't those feet constantly go in and out of that park next door? The people go to seek amusement day in and day out, never tiring of doing so. I've only been there once myself, during New Year's. Ah, feet! How unlucky for you to be at the end of my legs! I'm really rather sorry for you." As if to mock him, the music from the park, carried by the wind, came through the window in waves, the clear and pleasant notes making the itch in his feet all the harder to bear. He so wanted to pick them up and rush right over there. But this dungeon of a basement was watched over by a foreman as if he were a prison guard. No one could escape using just a pair of feet. So even though he had long since flown off in his imagination, he still had to pretend to focus on the work in front of him, to do it over and over. The stitch after hempen stitch he was applying to the shiny black leather of a pair of women's shoes seemed also to be sewing up the inner chambers of his heart. Who was there to know his pain, or to comfort him in his depression?

The greater his suffering and vexation, the more he liked to peek out the window, as if searching for the comfort he craved. For a long, long time, he found nothing at all. But looking out like that did add to his powers of perception. He was actually able to identify the feet of a good number of men and women who frequented the park. Among them was a pair belonging to a female, which he never tired of looking at, and which he could never erase from his mind. It is reasonable to suppose that any cobbler would naturally have a heightened ability to judge the aesthetics of feet. This particularly feminine pair was neither too large nor too small, too fat nor too thin. They were perfect in size, and the pair of black leather pumps they had on complemented them well. The flair they displayed when they walked made them especially attractive. No one other than a gorgeous young woman could possibly have feet like those, he thought. After that, in order to substantiate his hypothesis, he once actually hurried over to the window to look up when he saw the feet passing by. Indeed, she was as he imagined. Too bad she was walking past so quickly he was only able to catch her profile. Still, that one glance erased all questions regarding her appearance.

From that day on, he was no longer satisfied just looking at her footsteps. Several times he was able to escape the notice of the others and, boldly yet carefully, stole glimpses of the woman with the beautiful feet. He put together the various profile angles to form a mental portrait, which he kept locked in the inner recesses of his heart. She was lovely beyond compare. Fortunately, the girl liked to visit the park day after day. Thus, he had regular opportunities to catch sight of those feet, which drove out all of his other desires, including his interest in looking at anything else around them. Each day, his eyes waited hungrily for this particular pair of feet. Seeing them time and again, he developed an inexplicable obsession: He had to look at them constantly. On any given day when the feet came around later than usual, his heart would be at his throat in his longing for them. Whenever they suddenly arrived as he was thinking about them, a wild feeling of joy would come over him and a smile would instantly appear on his face. Sometimes, as the feet left the park to return home, he would hardly be able to bear seeing them go. He would then suppress the urge to bid them good night and promise to see them again on the morrow. When the feet would stay away for an entire day, his disappointment would know no bounds. He would go about with a heavy heart, worried that the girl could have perhaps fallen ill. In sum, each time he saw her yielded a feeling of gladness, each time he did not, a feeling of woe. His moods swung between the extremes of joy and sorrow. Caught in this emotional turmoil, he had no idea what to do. He began by falling in love with a pair of feet and ended up falling in love with the whole person. His opportunities varied by the day, however. Mostly, he saw the feet, far less often the person. Chances for seeing the feet came easily, those for seeing the person came rarely. In the abstract sense, he did indeed become enamored of those feet. But in terms of actual feelings, how could he have helped extending this love to include the one to whom the feet belonged?

After pondering the matter for an extended time, he came to realize that he had fallen hard for this girl. How wonderful it would be if he could exchange names with her, or escort her to the amusement park. And, thinking ahead another step, if they were to get married, that would be better still. He would then be able to watch over her feet all his life. At this thought, his face felt a little feverish, and he was embarrassed enough to chide himself. "Aren't you going too far?" he muttered. "She looks like a person of means, the daughter of a wealthy family, while you, with your ragged clothes, are no more than a pauper of a cobbler. How on earth could you match up with her? *Ai*. . . . What is it that has made you so poor ever since you were born?" (*The same thought sequence has turned the determined into successes, the crafty into criminals, and the cowardly into suicide victims.*) Then another thought occurred to him. "Not so. She and I are the same sort of people. Our ages are similar. So why can't we be married? I may be relatively poor right now, but who's to say I won't become rich in the future? There are many in the world who overcame a destitute childhood to end up tycoons. Everything is the result of what one does. It doesn't seem to be all that impossible for me to become wealthy. So, fine! From now on I resolve to be an earnest, hardworking young man, to advance my position so that I can marry this girl in the future and have a fulfilling family life with her. Otherwise, it's useless to go on fantasizing as I have day in and day out."

Making up his mind at that moment, he indeed strove to succeed with extraordinary determination. He showed an exceptional eagerness for learning, rushing to handle every task. He mastered all the required skills to near perfection. On his time off from his job, he regularly attended night classes to advance his academic knowledge. Through it all, he was happy to be able to see those feet outside the window every day. Looking at them each time, he would resolve once again to strive harder. It was as if they were actively encouraging him. Eventually, thanks to the strenuous effort he expended for their sake, he attained his goals.

For a businessman, time never passes so easily. For a storyteller, however, a decade can go by with a mere stroke of the pen. The Ah Fa after that time was no longer the earlier Ah Fa. From the young apprentice he had been, he became one of the successful people in the world of industry. At first, the manager in the store noticed his excellent work and sent him to another town to be foreman at a branch. Then, when the manager's position opened up there, he was promoted to fill it. Business boomed during the next several years, allowing him to save some money. He then quickly became a stockholder in the enterprise. Toward the end of the period, the business was greatly expanded and was reorganized into a limited corporation issuing stock. In this way, he became an important founding member of the firm. At the elections to fill the firm's various posts during its establishment, he was voted by the stockholders into the position of vice president in charge of managing the main store. In this way he returned to his original location.

What we must settle at this point is whether, through all this, he had forgotten the person whose feet he had been so infatuated with as a youth. Even as he was being transferred out of the main store, he could not help having lingering regrets about the move: he would miss those feet. But business came first (*those words constituting a fundamental principle for his major accomplishments*), and he could not very well have remained in the basement just for those feet outside the window. To go out and take care of proper business, moreover, was clearly one very good way to eventually possess those feet. So he had determinedly gone on his way, not daring to tarry. There was more and more work at his post each day, and he was getting older and older each year. Eventually, as we might expect, the infatuation he first felt as a lad gradually faded. There were times, however, when the memories did come sneaking back, memories he had some trouble brushing off. But other than laughing at himself, there was nothing he could do about them. How ludicrous, to lavish such fantasies on nothing more than a pair of feet!

Now that he had returned and was successful, he lived with several shareholders in a large hotel. Venturing out in daylight, he felt a flutter in his heart when he saw the feet of so many women. That first night, he could not get to sleep, as various thoughts came back to him. The image of those feet from the past, long embedded in his brain, seemed to reappear with stark clarity before his eyes, like a movie film placed in the light of a projector. All he had to do was shut his eyelids and they would be there. Evidently, the first love of one's youth cannot ever be forgotten. In pondering the past, his thoughts went as follows: "Why are those feet still in my head? Why do I still love them? Could I still be as naive as I was as a young man? Since I'm not able to free myself from them, I ought to exhaust all means, to plunge myself into the mass of humanity in order to seek them out. And yet, realistically speaking, that would be an impossible task. Too bad I was such a dope then, wallowing in my own infatuation without bothering to find out her background or address. If I were to look for her now, where would I begin?"

Then one evening, having finished his work, he rested alone in his hotel room, stretched out comfortably on a sofa. The image of the feet was again welling up in his mind. It happened that he had left his door open. Since the sofa was directly opposite it, his line of vision was unconsciously directed outside the room. Even though a swinging door was still in the way, he could see out the unobstructed area beneath it. The feet of various hotel guests went past from the corridor outside, reminding him of what he saw out the basement window years before. Yes, uncanny coincidences do indeed happen. For, in a flash, he again caught sight of *those* feet.

Having looked at them so many times, he had long known by instinct their exact width and length, how they were pointed at the toes and rounded at the heels, as well as the way they moved either in a hurry or at a leisurely pace. Should you ask him to explain this knowledge in detail, he wouldn't of course be able to do so. But encountering them again suddenly was like rereading an old book: Instantly he was certain of what he saw. One thing about them had not changed, moreover: even now, those feet had on shiny black shoes. For a former cobbler, the ability to determine the size and style of leather footwear was of course unerring. In addition, there was one other feature that made the feet easily identifiable. The bone at the second joint of each big toe jutted out at a sharp angle. Here was a truly remarkable encounter, and he wasn't about to let this rarest of opportunities pass. So he rushed out after her.

It was all right. She had not gone far, only to the table at the corner of the corridor. What's more, she was standing right there, turning her head to ask a bellhop where room 107 was, and learning that it was upstairs to the west. As she nodded her thanks, her face became distinctly visible from a distance. Surely she had to be the one. Her attire was even more gaudy than before, even though it had been ten years and she was now a woman of twenty-five or twenty-six. Could she still be single? Why wasn't she wearing a skirt? Why was she dressed like the teenager she'd not been in years? Looking again, he saw a girl by her side, someone much younger but made up with so much powder and rouge that she appeared to be a prostitute. What were they doing together? Who were they looking for in the hotel?

Befuddled for the moment, he called the bellhop over after the two went off, and asked who they were. "They're both call girls," the young man replied with a smirk. "The younger one is Hibiscus Blossom; the other is Old Number Five. She tells people she's the older sister. But she's really the well-known courtesan Spring Hibiscus Number Five." How had she come to this? He wanted badly to find out everything from her. So he went back to his room and filled out an order for the bellhop to bring her there.

In short order she arrived, Hibiscus Blossom in tow. He invited her to sit down, then greeted her by announcing, "We haven't seen each other for a very long time."

She searched her memory for a time without coming up with anything. "We've met before . . . somewhere," she responded vaguely.

"It's something that happened quite some time ago," he said with a smile. "It was I, though, who was acquainted with you, not at all the other way around. As to what I recognize in you, I'm afraid it's just those feet of yours—not you as a total person."

She thought this exceedingly strange. "How is it that you recognize my feet?" she immediately asked. "Perhaps you're playing with me. . . ."

"It's all true," he said. "You'll understand after I explain."

He then recounted all that had happened years ago, as if he were telling her a story. At the end, he let out a sigh. "I had no idea I would see you here today, not to mention finding you in such straits," he said. "Just talking about everything grieves me deeply. (*We shed tears on reading these words.*) Now that I've told you all about me, can you tell me about yourself?"

She and Hibiscus Blossom were both dumbfounded at the story, and she, especially, was deeply moved. "How in the world," she thought, "could there be such a single-minded fool? He fell in love with my feet, then extended that love to all of me. At least he appears to care a lot for me. So why not bare my soul to him?"

Thereupon she laid out in detail for him all that had happened to her over the past ten years. Her father, it turned out, died when she was little, leaving her to grow up with only her mother. Until she was fifteen or so, she had attended school. But she had always been fond of going to the amusement park, even at the cost of neglecting her studies. Then she was charmed by a slick young man, to whom she lost her virginity. Her mother became so upset she took ill and died. Thereafter, she descended into the world of prostitution. After becoming a veteran in the trade, she began to get into the business side of it as well. At present she was an assistant in the organization. In retrospect she could see that everything was the consequence of her early attraction to the amusement park. (*Those who are similarly addicted today ought to take note of this.*) And yet, had she not gone there so often during those years, she would never have left her footprints so deeply in his mind. The whole thing was a kind of karma, something ordained by fate.

Hearing all this, he could only let out sigh after sigh. Then he took on a very serious air. "Our meeting today is the result of your feet acting as our go-between," he said to her. "From what you tell me now, your decade of misfortune also came about because of your fun-loving feet. For my part, though, what success I enjoy today has been given to me by those same feet of yours. If not for them, I would not have accomplished what I have. So I should give great thanks to them in appreciation for the good they have provided me for ten years, for motivating me to get better and better. After all, your feet are nothing but an appendage of your whole self, and I can't think of any appropriate gift to offer them. To get them a few pairs of shoes, for example, would hardly be suffi-cient. So I have no choice but to go from feet to person, to express my heartfelt gratitude. What are you in need of right now? Please tell me without hesitation. As long as it lies within my powers, I am willing to provide you whatever you ask for."

Old Number Five pondered for a while. "I would never guess that these feet of mine would lead to any good; they have only taken me to dissipation and ruin," she frankly admitted. "Now, after meeting a car-ing person such as yourself, I'm overwhelmingly ashamed of what I've done. To think someone would strive so hard for the love of my feet. Even though I have my own heartaches, I could never seek to profit from you the way I've always sought to profit from my ordinary cus-tomers. For the sake of what you have felt for my feet, I beg you to allow all of me to become your dependent. Since you have loved them so, you won't be able to bear seeing them wander about in the world forever, without ever having a place to call home. So please take me in. You can make me your concubine or maidservant. . . ." (*These were not words of gratitude, but words of love.*) Tears were running all over her face by the time she concluded. (*How could she not shed them?*) She looked up at him, waiting for a reply.

He could not help being moved by this unexpected request, which he quickly agreed to grant. "These last few years, I have been so occupied with my work I have not even taken a wife," he told her. "In my heart, I have of course wished for a day like this. You may have betrayed your own feet, but they have not betrayed me. They have made me a success in my profession, and you will be marrying me only because of them. So, in the end, your feet are a boon to you. From now on, may you keep them under control for my sake, so that I can be close to them each and every day. Then may I redouble my efforts and renew my resolve to strive for even greater success in my work. Your feet have now taken you through the gate of good fortune to a peaceful and happy existence. You have no reason to grieve anymore."

As they were thus agreeing to marry, Miss Hibiscus Blossom prudently slipped away to return alone to the brothel. "Fifth Sister is going to get married," she proclaimed to everyone there. "I heard the groom is Zhao Fa, the vice president and manager of China Leather Goods." Another decade after that, another news item was spread around. "Zhao Fa has become a tycoon. In consultation with his wife, he has bought out the large amusement park, turning it into a department store for Chinese products. Footwear produced by the China Leather Goods Company is on display in the basement. Most remarkably, Manager Zhao's office has been located there all along. He said that a person should never forget where he comes from." (*He achieved his current success only because he was always mindful. All of you who work for a living should take Zhao Fa as a model.*)

1923

(*Translated by Timothy C. Wong*)

ZHU ZIQING
(1898–1948)

A virtuoso belle-lettrist, Zhu Ziqing was also a pioneer of the new verse and a renowned scholar of classical Chinese literature. Born in Jiangsu, he entered Peking University in 1916 and upon graduation taught at high schools in many cities. In 1921 he joined the Literary Research Society, and the next year started Poetry Monthly, *the first poetry journal founded after the May Fourth Movement. In 1925 he was offered a professorship at Tsinghua University, whose beautiful campus would become the locale for his universally admired essay "The Moonlit Lotus Pond." The year 1928 saw the publication of his first collection of essays,* A Silhouette. *A patriot and peace activist, he opposed Chiang Kai-shek, who started the civil war in 1946. He died of hunger in 1948 because he refused to accept food aid from Chiang's backer, the United States.*

The Moonlit Lotus Pond

These past few days I have been exceedingly restless. This evening, as I sat in my courtyard enjoying the cool night air, I suddenly thought of the lotus pond along which I was used to taking daily walks, and I imagined that it must look quite different under the light of this full moon. Slowly the moon climbed in the sky, and beyond the wall the laughter of children playing on the road could no longer be heard. My wife was inside patting Run'er* as she hummed a faint lullaby. I gently threw a wrap over my shoulders and walked out, closing the gate behind me.

Bordering the pond is a meandering little cinder path. It is a secluded path; during the day few people use it, and at night it is even lonelier. There are great numbers of trees growing on all sides of the lotus pond, lush and fertile. On one side of the path there are some willow trees and several varieties of trees whose names I do not know. On moonless nights this path is dark and forbidden, giving one an eerie feeling. But this evening it was quite nice, even though the rays of the moon were pale. Finding myself alone on the path, I folded my hands behind me and strolled along. The stretch of land and sky that spread out before me seemed to belong to me, and I could transcend my own existence and enter another world. I love noise, but I also love quiet; I love crowds, but I also love seclusion. On a night like tonight, all alone under this vast expanse of moonlight, I can think whatever I wish, or think of nothing if I wish. I feel myself to be a truly free man. The things I must do and the words I must say during the daytime I need not concern myself with now: this is an exquisite secluded spot, a place where I can enjoy the limitless fragrance of the lotuses and the light of the moon.

On the surface of the winding and twisting lotus pond floated an immense field of leaves. The leaves lay high in the water, rising up like the skirts of a dancing girl. Amid the layers of leaves white blossoms adorned the vista, some beguilingly open and others bashfully holding their petals in. Just like a string of bright pearls or stars in a blue sky, or like lovely maidens just emerging from their bath. A gentle breeze floated by, bringing with it waves of a crisp fragrance like strains of a vague melody sent over from distant towering buildings. When that happened the leaves and blossoms trembled briefly, as though a bolt of lightning had streaked across the lotus pond. The leaves themselves were

---

* The name of one of the author's children.

densely crowded together, pushing back and forth, and they seemed to be a cresting wave of solid green. Beneath the leaves restrained currents of water flowed, imprisoned beneath them, the color forever hidden, while the stirrings of the leaves were even more pronounced.

The moon's rays were like flowing waters, gently depositing their moisture on the layer of leaves and blossoms. A light green mist floated just above the lotus pond. The leaves and blossoms looked as though they had been bathed in milk, or like a blurred dream swathed in airy gauze. Although the moon was full, a light covering of clouds in the sky prevented it from shining brightly; yet I had the pleasant feeling that I had come to a fine spot. For just as one cannot do without deep slumber, still a light sleep has its own delights. The moon's rays filtered down through the trees, and dark, uneven shadows of varying shades were cast by the dense foliage on the high ground, perilously dark and spooky. The bewitching shadows cast by the sparse, twisted willow trees seemed to be painted on the lotus leaves. The moonlight on the pond was spread unevenly, but the rays and the shadows were a concert of harmony, like a celebrated tune played on a violin.

On all sides of the lotus pond, far and near, on high ground and low, there are trees, most of them willows. These trees completely envelop the whole of the lotus pond; only by the side of the path are there gaps, here and there showing through, seemingly left there just so the moon can shine in. The colors of the trees are uniformly dark. At first glance they resemble a bank of fog and mist, but the slender, graceful forms of the willows can still be distinguished in that fog and mist. Above the treetops a row of mountains can be seen ever so indistinctly, just the hint of their shapes, while one or two faint glimmers of roadside lamps seep through the openings of the branches, appearing like the weary eyes of a tired man. Now the spot was at its noisiest, if you count the chirping of cicadas in the trees and the croaking of frogs in the water. But the noise was theirs alone; I added nothing to it.

All of a sudden I was reminded of lotus gathering. The gathering of lotuses is an old custom south of the Yangtze, whose origins probably date from very early on but that flourished during the Six Dynasties period.* This we know from the poems and ballads of the time. The lotus gatherers were young maidens who drifted in small boats and sang their songs of love. It goes without saying that there were great numbers of lotus gatherers as well as those who came to watch them, for that was a festive and a romantic occasion. "The Lotus Gatherers" by Emperor Yuan of the Liang dynasty† tells it well:

> Princely lads and alluring maidens
> Adrift in a boat, their hearts in accord;
> The boat's prow describes a slow turn
> As they exchange wine cups;
> The oars become intertwined,
> And the boat moves across the floating duckweed;
> The maidens with their slender waists simply bound
> Cast glances behind them.
> Summer begins where the spring leaves off;
> The leaves are tender, the flowers in bloom.
> Protecting their dresses from the dampness, smiles adorning their
>   faces,
> They gather up their skirts, taking care not to capsize the boat.

This paints for us a picture of the pleasant excursions of those days. They must have been truly memorable events; it is a pity that we can no longer enjoy such pastimes.

I then recalled the lines from "Tune of the West Isle":

> Gathering lotuses at Nantang in the fall,
> The lotus blossoms rise above our heads.
> Bending over to pluck the lotus seeds,
> Lotus seeds as transparent as the water.

---

*   A.D. 317–588.

†   A.D. 552–555.

If tonight there were lotus gatherers, the lotus blossoms here too would "rise above their heads." But it is not enough to have before me only these rippling shadows. All of this stirred up in me a sense of longing for the South. With these thoughts in my mind I suddenly raised my head and found that my steps had carried me to my own gate; I softly pushed it open and entered. I was greeted by complete silence; my wife had long since fallen fast asleep.

1927

(Translated by Howard Goldblatt)

XU ZHIMO
(1897–1931)

Born into a wealthy banker family in Zhejiang, Xu Zhimo was a roman-
tic poet who lived a romantic life and died a romantic death. Influenced
by his father, Xu first pursued a career in banking, with an ambition to
be a "Chinese Hamilton" (after Alexander Hamilton). In 1918 he attended
Clark University and then Columbia University. In 1921 he studied polit-
ical science at Cambridge, where he encountered British Romanticism
and began writing poetry. Returning to China in 1923, Xu taught at
Peking University till a love scandal forced him to resign in 1925. Like
Wen Yiduo and other Crescent Moon Society poets—a label derived
from their journal Crescent Monthly, *founded in 1928—Xu was inter-*
ested in metrics, trying to develop a suitable form for the new verse. His
exceptional gift for blending classical diction with the colloquial, as evi-
denced by "Second Farewell to Cambridge," made him the best-known
poet in modern China. On November 19, 1931, Xu flew from Nanjing to
Beijing to see a woman he had fallen for. The plane crashed, and he
died at the age of thirty-four.

Second Farewell to Cambridge

Quietly I am leaving,
　　Just as quietly I came;
Quietly I wave goodbye
　　To clouds blazing the western sky.

The golden willow by the river
    Is a bride at sunset;
In sparkling waves a radiant reflection
    Ripples through my heart.

Waterlilies in soft mud,
    Lush, beckoning from deep;
In the gentle waves of River Cam
    I'd rather be a waterweed!

The pool under the elm's shade
    Not a spring, but a heavenly rainbow
Scattered among floating algae
    Settling into a rainbow-colored dream.

Looking for a dream? Get a long pole,
    Row toward the greenest of grass,
Carry a boatload of starlight,
    And sing aloud in starlight's splendor.

But I cannot sing aloud,
    Silence is the tune of departure;
Even summer insects stay mute for me,
    Mute is tonight's Cambridge.

Silently I am leaving,
    Just as silently I came;
I straighten my sleeves,
    And carry not a patch of cloud.

—*1928*

By Chance

I am a patch of cloud in the sky
Casting by chance a shadow on your heart
       Don't be surprised
       Still less overjoyed
A trace vanishes in the blink of an eye

On the sea of dark night we met
You have your destination, I have mine
       It's fine if you remember
       But best if you forget
The sparks set off by this encounter.

—1926
(Translated by Yunte Huang)

WEN YIDUO

(1899–1946)

Steeped in Chinese literary classics, Wen Yiduo was exposed to Western-style education early in life. He spent eight years at Tsinghua College (later Tsinghua University), which prepared him for study abroad. In 1922 he attended the Art Institute of Chicago, and in 1923 he published his first collection of poetry, The Red Candle. *A formalist and experimenter, he focused attention on the visual and auditory, emphasizing what he called the "three beauties of poetry": the beauties of music, painting, and architecture. In 1928 he published* The Dead Water, *in which he exposed grim and sordid Chinese reality with fresh images, evoking complex emotions. A diehard patriot and fiercely outspoken critic of the Nationalist government, he was assassinated after a rousing speech in Kunming, Yunnan in July, 1946.*

The Dead Water

This is a ditch of hopelessly dead water.
No clear breeze can raise half a ripple on it.
Why not throw in some rusty metal scraps,
Or even some of your leftover food and soup?

Perhaps the copper will turn its green patina into jade,
And on the tin can rust will bloom into peach blossoms;
Then let grease weave a layer of silk brocade,
And germs brew out colored clouds.

Let the dead water ferment into a ditch of green wine,
Filled with the floating pearllike white foam,
The laughter of small pearls turning into large pearls
Only to be pierced when gnats come to steal the wine.

Thus, a ditch of hopelessly dead water
May yet claim some small measure of splendor.
And if the frogs cannot bear the loneliness,
Let the dead water burst into song.

This is a ditch of hopelessly dead water,
A place where beauty can never live.
Might as well let vice cultivate it,
And see what kind of world it can create.

Perhaps (A Dirge)

Perhaps you are indeed too wearied from too much weeping.
Perhaps, perhaps you wish to fall asleep now.
Then ask the night owl not to cough,
The frogs not to croak and bats not to fly.

Let no sunshine pierce your eyelids,
Let no clear winds touch your brows,
And whoever he may be, let him not startle you.
With an umbrella of pine I shall guard your sleep.

Perhaps you hear earthworms turning the soil,
The grass roots sucking water.
Perhaps the music you hear now
Is lovelier than men's cursing voices.

Close tight your eyes then,
I shall let you sleep, let you sleep.
I'll gently cover you with yellow earth
And ask the ashes of paper money to rise slowly.

Confession

I do not deceive you when I say I am no poet,
Even though I love the integrity of the white rocks,
The green pines and the vast sea, the sunset on the crow's back,
The twilight woven with the wings of bats.
You know that I love heroes and tall mountains.
I love, too, the national flag outspread in the breeze,
The chrysanthemums colored from soft yellow to antique bronze.
But remember that my food is a pot of bitter tea!
And there is another "I." Will you be afraid to know it?
The flylike thought crawling in the garbage can!

(Translated by Julia C. Lin)

DING LING
(1904–1986)

The life of Ding Ling is a powerful testament to the uneasy relationship between feminism and revolution in modern China. Born Jiang Bing-zhi into a genteel family in Hunan, Ding Ling lost her father when she was only four and was brought up by her independent mother. Always a free spirit, she went to Peking in 1924 and lived with an editor who would later become a revolutionary martyr. In 1928, the publication of Miss Sophia's Diary, an anarcho-feminist novella about a tubercular young woman's emotional life and erotic passion, brought her into prominence. In 1932 she joined the Communist Party and became a pioneer of revolutionary literature, but still with a penchant for independent thinking, a character trait that often got her in deep water. Her novel about land reform, The Sun Shines over the Sanggan River (1948), won the Stalin Prize in Literature. After the founding of the People's Republic of China, she enjoyed appointments in key positions and continued to publish widely, until 1955 when she became a target of political purge and suffered over twenty years of exile, persecution, and imprisonment. She was rehabilitated in 1979 and allowed to write and publish again.

Miss Sophia's Diary (excerpt)

December 24

The wind's up again today. The blowing woke me before day broke. Then the boy came in to start the stove. I know I'll never get back to sleep again. I also know that my head will start whirling if I don't get up. Too many strange thoughts run through my mind when I lie wrapped in the covers. The doctor's instructions are to sleep and eat a lot and not to read or think. Exactly what I find most impossible. I can never get to sleep until two or three o'clock in the morning and I'm awake again before dawn. On a windy day like today, it's impossible to keep from brooding over every little thing. I can't go outside when the wind's this strong. What else can I do but brood, cooped up in this room with nothing to read? I can't just sit vacantly by myself and wait for time to pass, can I? I endure it one day at a time, longing for winter to be over fast. When it gets warmer, my cough is bound to clear up a little. Then if I wanted to go south or back to school, I could. Oh, God, this winter is endless!

As the sunlight hit the paper window, I was boiling my milk for the third time. I did it four times yesterday. I'm never really sure that it suits my taste, no matter how often I do it, but it's the only thing that releases frustration on a windy day. Actually, though it gets me through an hour or so, I usually end up even more irritable than I was before. So all last week I didn't play with it. Then out of desperation, I did, relying on it, as though I was already old, just to pass time. I read the newspaper as soon as it comes. I start, systematically, with the headlines, the national news, the important foreign reports, local gossip, and then . . . when I've finished the items on education, party propaganda, economics, and the stock market, I go back to the same announcements I read so thoroughly yesterday . . . and the day before . . . the ones recruiting new students, the notices of lawsuits over division of family property. I even read stuff like ads for "606" and "Mongolian Lark" venereal tonics, cosmetics, announcements of the latest shows at the Kaiming Theater, and the Zhenguang Movie Theater listing. When I've finished everything I toss the paper away, reluctantly. Every once in a while, of course, I find a new advertisement. But what I can never get free of are the fifth- and sixth-year anniversary sales at the fabric shops, and the obituaries— with apologies to those not contacted personally.

NOTHING TO DO after the paper except sit alone by the stove and work myself into a rage. What infuriates me is the daily routine. I get a nervous headache every day as I sit listening to the other inmates yell at the attendants. Such loud, braying, coarse, monotonous voices, "Attendant, bring hot water!" or "Washbasin, attendant!" You can imagine how ugly it sounds. And there is always somebody downstairs shouting into the telephone. Yet when the noise does let up, the silence scares me to death. Particularly inside the four whitewashed walls that stare blankly back at me no matter where I sit. If I try to escape by lying on the bed, I'm crushed by the ceiling, just as oppressively white. I can't really find a single thing here that *doesn't* disgust me: the pockmarked attendant, for example, and the food that always tastes like a filthy rag, the impossibly grimy window frame, and that mirror over the washbasin. Glancing from one side you've got a face a foot long; tilt your head slightly to the side and suddenly it gets so flat you startle yourself. . . . It all infuriates me. Maybe I'm the only one affected. Still I'd really like a few fresh complaints and dissatisfactions. Novelty, for better or worse, always seems just out of reach.

Weidi came over after lunch. The familiar hurried sound of his leather shoes carried all the way from the other end of the corridor and comforted me, as though I'd suddenly been released from a suffocating room. But I couldn't show it. So when he came in, I simply glanced silently at him. Weidi thought I was peeved again. He clasped my hands tightly and cried, "Sister, Elder Sister!" over and over. I smiled. Of course. Why? Oh, I know. I know what's behind those shy glowing eyes.

I understand what it is that he'd rather keep from others. You've been in love with me for such a long time, Weidi. Has he captured me? That is not my responsibility. I act as women are supposed to act. Actually, I've been quite aboveboard with him. There isn't another woman alive who would have resisted toying with him, as I have. Besides, I'm genuinely sorry for him. There have been times when I couldn't stand it any longer, when I wanted so badly to say, "Look, Weidi, can't you find some better way of going about this? You're making me sick." I'd like Weidi a whole lot better if he'd wise up, but he persists with these stupid abandoned displays of affection.

Weidi was satisfied when I smiled. Rushing around to the other end of the bed, he tore off his overcoat and leather hat. If he'd turned his head and glanced at me just then, he'd have been saddened by my eyes. Why doesn't he understand me better?

I've always wanted a man who would really understand me. If he doesn't understand me and my needs, then what good are love and empathy? Father, my sisters, and all my friends end up blindly indulging me, although I never have figured out what it is in me that they love. Is it my arrogance, my temper? Or do they just pity me because I have TB? At times they infuriate me because of it, and then all their blind love and soothing words have the opposite effect. Those are the times that I wish I had someone who really understood. Even if he reviled me, I'd be proud and happy.

I think about them when they forget me. Or I get mad at them. But then when somebody finally does come, I end up harassing him without really meaning to. It's an impossible situation. Lately I've been trying to discipline myself not to say whatever jumps into my mind, so I don't accidentally hurt people's secret feelings when I'm really only joking. My resulting state of mind as I sat with Weidi can easily be imagined. If Weidi had stood up to go, I'd have hated him because of my depression and fear of loneliness. Weidi has known this for a long time, so he didn't leave me until ten o'clock. But I deceive no one, certainly not myself. The fact that Weidi waited around so long gave him no special advantage. In fact, I ended up pitying him because he's so easy to exploit and because he has such a gift for doing the wrong thing in love.

December 28

I invited Yufang and Yunlin out to the movies today. Yufang asked Jianru along, which made me so furious I almost burst into tears. Instead I started laughing. Oh, Jianru, Jianru, how you've crushed my self-respect. She looks and acts so much like a girlfriend I had when I was younger, that without being aware of what I was doing, I started chasing her. Initially she encouraged my intimacies. But I met with intolerable treatment from her in the end. Whenever I think about it, I hate myself for what I did in the past, for my regrettably unscrupulous behavior. One week I wrote her at least eight long letters, maybe more, and she didn't pay the slightest bit of attention to me. Whatever possessed Yufang to invite Jianru when she knows I don't want to dredge up my past all over again? It's as though she wanted to make me mad on purpose. I was furious.

Though there was no reason for Yufang and Yunlin to notice any change in my laugh, Jianru must have sensed something. But she can fake it—play stupid—so she went along as though there was nothing between us. I wanted to curse; the words were on the tip of my tongue, when I thought of the resolution I'd set myself. Also I felt that if I were that vehement she'd get even more stuck on herself. So I just kept my feelings to myself and went out with them.

We got to the Zhenguang Theater early and met some girls from our province at the door. Those girls and their practiced smiles make me sick. I ignored them. Then I got inexplicably angry at all the people waiting to see the movie. So I capitalized on the situation, and as Yufang talked heatedly with the girls, I slipped away from my guests and came home.

I am the only person who can excuse what I did. They all criticize me, but they don't know the feelings I endure when I am with other people. People say I am eccentric, but no one notices how often I'm willing to toady for affection and approval. No one will ever encourage me to say things that contradict my first impulses. They endure my eccentricities constantly, which gives me even more cause to reflect on my behavior, and that ends up alienating me even further from them.

It is very late and the entire residence is quiet. I've been lying here on the bed a long time. I have thought through a lot of things. Why am I still so upset?

December 29

Yufang phoned me early this morning. She's a good person and wouldn't lie, so I suppose Jianru really is sick. Yufang told me that Jianru is sick because of me and wants me to come over so she can explain herself. Yufang and Jianru couldn't be more mistaken. Sophia is not a person who likes listening to explanations. I see no need for explanations of any kind. If friends get along that's great; when you have a falling-out and give someone a hard time, that's fair enough too. I think I am big enough not to require more revenge. Jianru got sick because of me. I think that's great. I'd never refuse the lovely news that somebody had gotten sick over me. Anyway, Jianru's illness eases some of the self-loathing I've been feeling.

I really don't know what to make of myself. Sometimes I can feel a kind of boundless unfathomable misery at the sight of a white cloud being blown and scattered by the wind. Yet faced with a young man of, what, about twenty-five?—Weidi is actually four years older than I—I find myself laughing with the satisfaction of a savage as his tears fall on my folded hands. Weidi came over from Dongcheng with a gift of stationery and envelopes. Because he was happy and laughing, I teased him mercilessly until he burst into tears. That cheered me up, so I said, "Please, please! Spare the tears. Don't imagine I'm so feminine and weak that I can't resist a tear. If you want to cry, go home and do it. You're bothering me." He didn't leave. He didn't make any excuses, either, or get sullen, of course. . . . He just curled up in the corner of the chair, as tears from God knows where streamed openly, soundlessly, down his face. While this pleased me, I was still a little ashamed of myself. So I patted his head in a sisterly way and told him to go wash his face. He smiled through his tears.

When this honest, open man was here, I used all the cruelty of my nature to make him suffer. Yet once he'd left, there was nothing I wanted more than to snatch him back and plead with him: "I know I was wrong. Don't love a woman so undeserving of your affection as I am."

January 1

I don't know how people who like to party spent their New Year's. I just added an egg to my milk. I had the egg left over from the twenty that Weidi brought me yesterday. I've boiled seven eggs in a tea broth; the remaining thirteen are probably enough to last me for the next two weeks. If Weidi had come while I was eating lunch, I'd have had a chance to get a couple of canned things. I really hoped he'd come. In anticipation, I went out to the Danpai Building and bought four boxes of candy, two cartons of *dianxin*, and a basket of fruit to feed him when he got here. I was that certain he'd be the only one to come today. But lunch came and went and Weidi hadn't arrived.

I sat and wrote five letters with the fine pen and stationery he'd brought me a few days ago. I'd been hoping I'd get some New Year's picture postcards in the mail, but I didn't. Even the few girlfriends I have who most enjoy this kind of thing forgot that they owed me. I shouldn't be surprised that I don't get postcards. Still, when they forget about me completely, it does make me mad. On the other hand, considering that I never paid anyone else a New Year's visit—forget it! I deserve it.

I was very annoyed when I had to eat dinner all by myself.

Toward evening Yufang and Yunlin did come over, bringing a tall young fellow with them. How fortunate they are. Yufang has Yunlin to love her and that satisfies them both. Happiness isn't just possessing a lover. It's two people, neither of whom wants anything more than each other, passing their days in peace and conversation. Some people might find such a pedestrian life unsatisfying, but then not everyone is like my Yufang.

She's terrific. Since she has her Yunlin, she wants "all lovers to be united." Last year she tried to arrange a love match for Marie. She wants things to work out for Weidi and me, too, so every time she comes over she asks about him. She, Yunlin, and the tall man ate up all the food I'd bought for Weidi.

That tall guy is stunning. For the first time, I found myself really attracted to masculine beauty. I'd never paid much attention before. I've always felt that it was normal for men to be glib, phony, cautious; that's about the extent of it. But today as I watched the tall one, I saw how a man could be cast in a different, a noble, mold. Yunlin looked so insignificant and clumsy by comparison. . . . Pity overwhelmed me. How painful Yunlin would find his own coarse appearance and rude behavior, if he could see himself. I wonder what Yufang feels when she compares the two, one tall, the other not.

How can I describe the beauty of this strange man? His stature, pale delicate features, fine lips, and soft hair are quite dazzling enough. But there is an elegance to him, difficult to describe, an elusive quality, that shook me profoundly. When I asked his name, he handed me his name card with extraordinary grace and finesse. I raised my eyes. I looked at his soft, red, moist, deeply inset lips, and let out my breath slightly. How could I admit to anyone that I gazed at those provocative lips like a small hungry child eyeing sweets? I know very well that in this society I'm forbidden to take what I need to gratify my desires and frustrations, even when it clearly wouldn't hurt anybody. I did the only thing I could. I lowered my head patiently and quietly read the name printed on the card, "Ling Jishi, Singapore. . . ."

Ling Jishi laughed and talked uninhibitedly with us as though he were with old, intimate friends; or was he flirting with me? I was so eager to avoid seduction that I didn't dare look directly at him. It made me furious when I could not bring myself to go into the lighted area in front of the table. My ragged slippers had never bothered me before, yet now I found myself ashamed of them. That made me angry at myself: How can I have been so restrained and boring? Usually I find undue attention to social form despicable. Today I found out how moronic and graceless I could seem. Mmm! He must think I'm right off the farm.

Yufang and Yunlin got the feeling that I didn't like him, I was acting so woodenly, so they kept interrupting the conversation. Before long they took him off. They meant well. I just can't find it in me to be grateful. When I saw their shadows—two short, one tall—disappearing through the downstairs courtyard, I really didn't want to return to my room, now suffused with the marks of his shoes, his sounds, the crumbs of his cake.

January 3

I've spent two full nights coughing. I've lost all faith in the medicine. Is there no relationship at all between medicine and illness? I am sick to death of the bitter medicine, but still I take it on schedule, as prescribed; if I refuse medication, how can I allow myself any hope for recovery? God arranges all sorts of pain for us before we die to make us patient and to prevent us from rushing toward death too eagerly. Me? My time is brief, so I love life with greater urgency than most. I don't fear death. I just feel that I haven't gotten any pleasure out of life. I want . . . all I want is to be happy. I spend days and nights dreaming up ways I could die without regret. I imagine myself resting on a bed in a gorgeous bedroom, my sisters nearby on a bearskin rug praying for me, and my father sighing as he gazes quietly out the window. I'll be reading long letters from those who love me, friends who will remember me with their tears. I urgently need emotional support from all these people; I long for the impossible. What do I get from them? I have been imprisoned in this residence for two full days: no one has visited me and I haven't even gotten any mail. I lie in bed and cough; I sit on the stove and cough; I go in front of the table and cough—all the time brooding over these repulsive people. . . . Actually, I did receive a letter, but that just completed my total wretchedness. It was from a tough Anhui guy who was pestering me a year ago. I ripped it up before I had even finished reading it. It made my flesh crawl, reading page after page of "love, love, love, love, love." How I despise grandstand affection from people I loathe.

But can I name what I really need?

January 4

I just don't know how things went so wrong. Why did I want to move? In all the fuss and confusion I've also deceived Yunlin. The lies came so easily I felt I almost had an instinct for it. Were Yunlin to know Sophia was capable of deceiving him, how wretched he would be. Sophia is the baby sister they love so much. Of course I'm upset now, and I regret everything. But I still can't make up my mind. Should I move? Or not?

I had to admit to myself, "You're dreaming about that tall man." And it's true: for the last few days and nights I have been enmeshed in wonderful fantasies. Why hasn't he come over on his own? He should know better than to let me languish for so long. I'd feel so much better if he'd come over and tell me that he'd been thinking of me too. If he did, I know I wouldn't have been able to control myself, and I'd have listened to him declare his love for me and then I'd let him know what I wanted. But he didn't come. I guess fairy tales don't usually come true. Should I go looking for him? A woman that uninhibited would risk having everything blow up in her face. I still want people to respect me. Since I couldn't think of a good solution, I decided to go to Yunlin's place and see what would happen. After lunch I braved the wind and set off for Dongcheng.

Yunlin is a student at Jingdu University and rents a room in a house in Qingnian Lane near the university, between the first and second colleges. Fortunately I got there before he'd left and before Yufang had arrived. Yunlin was surprised to see me out on such a windy day, but wasn't suspicious when I told him I'd been to the German Hospital and was just stopping by on my way home. He asked about my health. I led the conversation around to the other evening. Without wasting any energy, I found out that Ling Jishi lives in Dormitory No. 4 in the second college. After a while I started to sigh and talk in vivid terms about my life at Xicheng Residence Hall, how lonely and dismal it was. And then I lied again. I said I wanted to move because I want to be near Yufang. (I already know that Yufang was going to move in with him.) When I asked Yunlin if he would come help me find a room near theirs, he seemed delighted and didn't hesitate to offer his help.

While we were looking around for a room, we just happened to run into Ling Jishi. So he joined us. I was ecstatic and the ecstasy made me bold enough to look right at him several times. He didn't notice. When he asked about my health and I told him I'd completely recovered, he just smiled, skeptically.

I settled on a small, moldy room with low ceilings in the Dayuan Apartment House next door to Yunlin. Both Ling Jishi and Yunlin said it was too damp, but nothing they said could shake my determination to move in the next day. The reason I gave was that I was tired of the other place and desperately needed to be near Yufang. There was nothing Yunlin could do, so he agreed and said that he and Yufang would be over to help me tomorrow.

How can I admit to anyone that my only reason for choosing that room was because it's located between the fourth dormitory and Yunlin's place?

He didn't say good-bye to me so I went back to Yunlin's with them, mustering all my courage to keep on chatting and laughing. Meanwhile I subjected him to the most searching scrutiny. I was possessed with a desire to mark every part of his body with my lips. Has he any idea how I'm sizing him up? Later I deliberately said that I wanted to ask Ling Jishi to help me with my English. When Yunlin laughed, Ling Jishi was taken aback and gave a vague, embarrassed reply. He can't be too much of a bastard, I thought to myself, otherwise—a big tall man like that— he'd never have blushed so red in the face. My passion raged with new ferocity. But since I was concerned that the others would notice and see through me too easily, I dismissed myself and came home early.

Now that I have time for reflection, I can't imagine my impulsiveness driving me into any worse situation. Let me stay in this room with its iron stove. How can I say I'm in love with this man from Singapore? I don't know anything about him. All this stuff about his lips, his eyebrows, his eyelashes, his hands, is pure fantasy. These aren't things a person should need. I've become obsessive if that's all I can think about now. I refuse to move. I'm determined to stay here and recover my health.

I'm decided now. I'm so full of regret! I regret all the wrong things I did today, things a decent woman would never do.

January 6

Everyone said I was being terribly foolish when they heard I'd moved. And when Jin Ying from Nancheng and Jiang and Zhou from Xicheng all came over to my damp little room to see me and I started laughing and rolling around on the bed, they all said I was acting like a baby. That amused me all the more and made me consider telling them what's really on my mind. Weidi dropped by this afternoon too, miserable because I'd moved without discussing it with him first and because now I'm even farther from him. He looked straight through Yunlin when he saw him. Yunlin, who couldn't figure out why he was so angry, stared right back. Weidi's face darkened even further. I was amused. "Too bad," I said to myself, "Weidi's blaming the wrong man."

Yufang never brings up the subject of Jianru anymore. She has decided to move into Yunlin's room in two or three days. She knows I want to be near her and won't leave me alone longer than that. She and Yunlin have been even warmer than ever.

January 10

I've seen Ling Jishi every day, but I've never spoken more than a few words to him, and I'm determined it's not going to be me who mentions the English lessons first. It makes me laugh to see how he goes to Yunlin's twice a day now. I'm certain he's never been this close to him before. I haven't invited Ling Jishi over either; and although he's asked several times how things are going now that I've moved, I've pretended not to get the hint and just smile back. It's like planning a battle. Now I'm concentrating all my energy on strategy. I want something, but I'm not willing to go and take it. I must find a tactic that gets it offered to me voluntarily. I understand myself completely. I am a thoroughly female woman, and women concentrate everything on the man they've got in their sights. I want to possess him. I want unconditional surrender of his heart. I want him kneeling down in front of me, begging me to kiss him. I'm delirious. I go over and over the steps I must take to implement my scheme. I've lost my mind.

Yufang and Yunlin don't detect my excitement; they just tell me I'll be getting better soon. Actually, I don't want them to know. When they say how improved I am, I act as if I'm pleased.

January 12

Yufang already moved in, but Yunlin moved out. I can't believe the two of them; they're so afraid of her getting pregnant that they won't live together. I suppose they feel that since they can't trust themselves to make "good" decisions when they're in bed together, the best solution is to remove sexual temptation completely. According to them, necking is not too dangerous, so their list of proscriptions doesn't preclude the occasional stolen encounter. I can't help scoffing at her asceticism. Why shouldn't you embrace your lover's naked body? Why repress this part of love? How can they be so preoccupied with all the details before they've even slept together! I won't believe love is so logical and scientific.

Of course, when I tease them they never get angry. They're proud of their purity, and laugh at my childishness. I suppose I understand how they feel; it's just another one of those strange, unexplained things that happen in life.

I went to Yunlin's tonight (I guess I should call it Yufang's now) and we told ghost stories, so I didn't get back until ten o'clock. When I was a child I used to sit in my auntie's lap and listen to Uncle tell strange tales from the *Liaozhai* all the time. I loved to hear them, especially at night;

but I never let anyone know how much they frightened me, because if you said you were afraid, that was the end of the stories. The children wouldn't be allowed out of bed and Uncle would have disappeared back into the study. Later, in school, I learned some rudimentary science from the teachers, and pockmarked Mr. Zhou inspired me enough to trust the books so I outgrew my terror of ghosts. Now that I'm grown up, I always deny the existence of ghosts. But you can't halt fear by simple declaration, and the thought of ghosts still makes my hair stand on end. No one grasps fully how eager I am to change the subject when the topic comes up. That's because later, when I'm sleeping alone under the covers at night, I think about my dead auntie and uncle and it breaks my heart.

On the way back, I felt a little jumpy when I saw the dark alleyway. What would I do, I thought, if a monstrous yellow face appeared in the corner, or a pair of hairy hands reached out at me from that frozen alley? But a glance at the tall strapping man beside me—Ling Jishi—acting as my bodyguard, reassured me. So when Yufang asked me if I was frightened, I just said, "No. No, I'm not."

Yunlin left with us to go back to his new room. He went south, and we went north, so we'd only gone three or four steps when the sound of his rubber-soled shoes on the muddy boards was no longer audible. "Sophia, you must be scared," said Ling Jishi, reaching out to put his arm around my waist. I considered freeing myself, but couldn't. My head rested on his shoulder. What would I look like in the light, I thought, wrapped in the arms of a man so much taller than I am? I wriggled and slipped free of him. He let go, stood beside me, and knocked at the door.

The alley was extremely dark. But I could clearly see which way he was looking. My heart fluttered slightly as I waited for the gate to open.

"Sophia, you're frightened."

The bolt creaked open as the doorman asked who was there.

"Good ni—" I said, but before I'd finished, Ling Jishi was holding my hand tightly.

Seeing the large man standing beside me, the doorman looked surprised.

When the two of us were alone in my room, my bravado disappeared. I tried to conceal my discomfort with a little conventional chatter, but couldn't manage that either. "Sit down," was all that came out, and I went to wash my face. I can't remember how we got off the subject of the supernatural.

"Sophia, are you still interested in studying English?" he suddenly asked.

It was he who had come looking for me. He's the one who brought up the subject of English. He'd never sacrifice his time just to help me with my English, and no one as old as I, over twenty, could be deceived by such an offer. I smiled and said, "I'm too stupid. I probably wouldn't do very well. I'd just make a fool out of myself."

He didn't say anything, just picked up a photograph from the table and toyed with it. It was a picture of my older sister's daughter, who had just turned one.

By that time I'd finished washing my face and was sitting at the end of the table. He looked at me and then back at the little girl, then at me again. It's quite true. She does look a lot like me, so I asked him, "Cute, isn't she? Does she remind you of me?"

"Who is she?" There was unusual earnestness in his voice.

"Tell me, don't you think she's cute?"

He asked again who she was.

Suddenly I realized what he meant by the question, and I had an impulse to lie about it. "She's mine." I snatched the photograph and kissed it.

He believed me. I made a fool of him. My lie was a complete success. His seductiveness faded in the face of my triumph. Otherwise how—once he'd revealed such naïveté—how was I suddenly able to ignore the power of his eyes and become so indifferent to his lips? I had triumphed indeed, but it cast a chill over my heated passion. After he left, I was consumed with regret for all the obvious chances I'd let slip away. If I'd shown more interest when he pressed my hand, if I'd let him know I couldn't refuse him, he'd have gone a lot further. I'm convinced that if you dare to have sex with someone you find reasonably attractive, the pleasure must be like bones dissolving, flesh melting. Why was I so strict and tight with him? Why had I moved to this shabby room in the first place?

January 15

I certainly haven't been lonely recently. Every day I go next door to visit, and at night I sit and talk to my new friend. Yet my condition continues to deteriorate. That discourages me, naturally, since nothing I desire ever ends up helping me. Is this craving really love? It's all so completely absurd. Yet when I think about dying—and I think about it frequently—I'm filled with despair. Every time I see Dr. Kelly's expression I think to myself, it's true, say what you like: there's no hope left, is there? I laugh to mask the tears. No one knows how I cry my eyes out late at night.

Ling Jishi has been over several nights in a row, and he's telling everybody he's helping me with my English. Yunlin asked me how it was going, but what could I say? This evening I took a copy of *Poor Folk* and put it in front of Ling Jishi, who actually began to tutor me, but then I threw the book aside. "You needn't tell people you are helping me with my English anymore," I said. "I'm sick and no one believes it anyway." "Sophia," he said hastily, "shall we wait until you're feeling better? I'll do whatever you want, Sophia."

My new friend is quite captivating. Yet for some reason I can't bring myself to pay much attention to him. Every night as I watch him leave morosely, I feel intense regret. Tonight, as he put on his overcoat I said to him, "I'm sorry. Forgive me, but I'm sick." He misunderstood what I meant, took it for convention. "It doesn't matter. I'm not afraid of infection," he said. Later I thought that over. Perhaps his comment had a double meaning. I don't dare believe people are as simple as they appear on the surface.

January 16

Today I received a letter from Yunjie in Shanghai that has plunged me into a deep depression. How will I ever find the right words to comfort her? In her letter she said, "My life, my love are meaningless now." Meaning, I suppose, that she has less need than ever for my condolences or tears shed for her. I can imagine from her letter what married life has been like even though she doesn't spell it out in detail. Why does God play tricks on people in love like her? Yunjie is a very emotional and passionate person, so it's not surprising that she finds her husband's growing indifference, his badly concealed pretense at affection, unbearable. . . . I'd like her to come to Beijing, but is it possible? I doubt it.

I gave Yunjie's letter to Weidi when he came over, and he was genuinely upset because the very man making Yunjie despair is, unfortunately, his own older brother. I told Weidi about my new "philosophy of life." And, true to form, he did the only thing instinct gives him leave to do—he burst into tears. I watched impassively as his eyes turned red and he dried them with his hands. Then I taunted him with a cruel running commentary on his little crying jag. It simply didn't occur to me then that he might indeed be the exception, a genuinely sincere person. Before long I slipped off quietly by myself.

In order to avoid everyone I know, I walked alone around the frigid, lonely park until very late. I don't know how I endured the time. I was obsessed with one thought: "How meaningless everything is, how I'd rather die and have done with it."

January 17

I was just thinking, maybe I'm going crazy. It's fine with me if I lose my mind. I think, once I've got to that point, life's sorrows will never touch me again. . . . It's been six months since I stopped drinking because of my illness. Today I drank again, seriously. I can see that what I'm puking now as a consequence is blood-redder than wine. But my heart seemed commanded by something else, and I drank as though the liquor might ease me toward my death tonight. I'm so tired of being obsessed by these same endless complications.

January 18

Right now I'm still resting in my bed. But before long I'll be leaving this room, maybe forever. Can I be certain I'll ever have the pleasure of touching these things again—this pillow, my quilt? Yufang, Yunlin, Weidi, and Jinxia are all sitting protectively in a gloomy little circle around me, waiting anxiously for dawn when they can send me to the hospital. I was awakened by their sad whispers. Since I didn't feel much like talking, I lay back and thought carefully over what had happened yesterday morning. It wasn't until I smelled the stench of blood and wine in the room that I was overcome with agony and convulsive tears. I had a premonition of death as I lay in the heavy silence and watched their dark, anguished faces. Suppose I were to sleep on like this and never wake up . . . would they sit just as silently and oppressively around my cold, hard corpse? When they saw I was awake, they drew near me to ask how I felt. That's when I felt the full horror of death and separation. I grabbed at each of them and scrutinized their faces, as though to preserve the memory forever. They all wept, feeling, it seemed, that I was departing for the land of the dead. Especially Weidi; his whole face was swollen, distorted with tears. Oh! I thought, please, dear friends, cheer me up, don't make me feel worse. Then, quite unexpectedly, I started to laugh. I asked them to arrange a few things for me, so out from under my bed they dragged the big rattan box where I kept several little bundles wrapped in embroidered hankies. "Those are the ones I want with me when I go to Union Medical College," I told them. When they handed me the packages I showed them they were stuffed full of letters. I smiled again and said, "All your letters are here," which cheered them up a bit. I also had to smile when Weidi took a picture album from the drawer and pressed it on me as though he wanted me to take that along too. It contains a half dozen or so photographs exclusively of Weidi. As a special favor I let him hold my hand, kiss it, and caress his face with it; and so, just as we'd finally dispelled the sensation that there was a corpse in the room, the pale light of day broke across the horizon. They all rushed about in an anxious flurry searching for a cab. Thus my life in the hospital began.

March 4

It was twenty days ago that I got the telegram notice of Yunjie's death. Yet for me each passing day means more hope of recovery. On the first of this month, the crowd that had brought me to the hospital moved me back to the freshly cleaned and tidied residence. Fearing I might get cold, they'd even set up a little iron coal stove. I have no idea how to convey my thanks. Especially to Weidi and Yufang. Jin and Zhou also stayed two nights before they had to go. Everyone has played nursemaid, letting me lie in bed all day feeling so comfortable it's hard to believe I'm living in a residence and not at home with my family. Yufang decided she's going to stay with me a couple more days, and then, when it warms up, she'll go to the Western Hills to find me a good place to convalesce. I am so looking forward to getting out of Beijing, but here it is March and it's still so cold! Yufang insists on staying here with me. And I can't really refuse, so the cot set up for Jin and Zhou remains for her to use.

I had a change of heart about some things during my stay in the hospital. I must credit it to the overwhelming kindness and generosity of my friends. Now the universe seems full of love. I am especially grateful to Ling Jishi. It made me so proud when he visited me in the hospital. I thought that only a man as handsome as he should be allowed to come to the hospital to visit a sick girlfriend. Of course, I was also aware of how much the nurses envied me. One day that gorgeous Miss Yang asked me, "What's that tall man to you?"

"A friend." I ignored the crude implication.

"Is he from your home area?"

"No, he's an overseas Chinese from Singapore."

"Then he's a classmate, right?"

"No, he isn't."

She smiled knowingly. "He's just a friend, right?"

Of course I had no reason to blush and I could have called her on her rudeness, but I was ashamed to. She watched the way I closed my eyes indecisively, pretending to be sleepy. Finally she gave a satisfied laugh and walked off. After that she always annoyed me. To avoid further trouble, I lied whenever anyone asked about Weidi. I said he was my brother. There was a little guy who was a good friend of Zhou's whom I also lied about. I told them that he was a relative or close friend of the family from my home province.

When Yufang leaves for class and I am alone in the room, I reread all the letters I've gotten in the last month or so. It makes me feel happy and satisfied to know there are so many people who still remember me. I need to be remembered. The more the better. Father, needless to say, sent me another picture of himself, hair whiter than ever. My older sisters are all fine, but too busy taking care of their children to write more often.

I hadn't yet finished rereading my letters when Ling Jishi came by again. I wanted to get up but he restrained me. When he took my hand, I could have wept for joy.

"Did you ever think I'd make it back to this room?" I asked him. He gazed, tangibly disappointed, at the spare bed shoved up against the wall. I told him that my guests were gone but that the bed was left up for Yufang. When he heard that, he told me that he was afraid of annoying Yufang and so he wouldn't return that evening. I was ecstatic. "Aren't you afraid that I'll be annoyed?" I said.

He sat on the bed and told me in detail what had happened over the past month, how he had clashed with Yunlin over a difference of opinion: Ling Jishi felt I should have left the hospital earlier, but Yunlin had steadfastly refused to allow it. Yufang had agreed with Yunlin. Ling Jishi realized he hadn't known me very long and that therefore his opinion did not carry much weight. So he gave up. When he happened to run into Yunlin at the hospital, he would leave first.

I knew what he meant, but I pretended not to understand. "You're always talking about Yunlin," I said. "If it hadn't been for Yunlin, I wouldn't have left the hospital at all, I was so much more comfortable there." I watched him turn his head silently to one side. He didn't answer.

When he thought Yufang was about to return, he told me quietly that he'd be back tomorrow. Then he left. Shortly after that Yufang came home. Yufang didn't ask and I didn't tell her anything. She doesn't like to talk too much, since with my illness I might easily exhaust myself. That was fine with me. It gave me a chance to think my own thoughts.

March 6

After Yufang went to class, leaving me alone in the room, I started thinking about weird things that go on between men and women. It's not that I love boasting, actually, it's just that my training in this regard is far greater than all of my friends' combined. Still, recently I've felt at a spectacular loss to understand what is happening. When I sit alone with Ling Jishi, my heart leaps and I'm humiliated, frightened. But he just sits there, nonchalantly, reaching over to grasp my hand from time to time, and tells stories about his past with apparent naïveté. Although he carries on with supremely natural ease, I find that my fingers cannot rest quietly in his massive hand; they burn. Yet when he rises to go, I feel an attack of anxiety as though I am about to stumble into something really horrible. So I stare at him, and I'm not really sure whether my eyes seek pity or flash with resentment. Whatever he sees there, he ignores. But he seems to understand how I feel. "Yufang will be back soon," he says. What can I say to that? He's still afraid of Yufang! Normally I wouldn't like to have anybody know what kind of private fantasies I've been having recently; on the other hand, I do feel the need to have someone understand my feelings. I've tried to talk indirectly with Yufang about this, but she just covers me with the quilt loyally and fusses about my medication. It depresses me.

March 8

Yufang has moved out, and Weidi wants to take over her job. I knew I would be more comfortable with him here than I was when Yufang nursed me. If I wanted tea in the middle of the night, for instance, I wouldn't have to creep back under my quilt with disappointment, as I did when I heard Yufang snoring and I didn't think it would be fair to disturb her sleep. But I refused his kind offer, naturally. When he insisted, I told him bluntly, "If you are here I will be inconvenienced in a number of ways, and anyway I'm feeling better."

He kept insisting that the room next door was empty and he could live there. I was just at my wit's end when Ling Jishi came in. I didn't think they knew each other, but Ling Jishi shook Weidi's hand and told me they'd met twice before at the hospital. Weidi ignored him coldly.

"This is my little brother," I said with a laugh to Ling Jishi. "He's just a kid who doesn't know how to act in mixed company. Drop by more often and we'll have a great time together." With that Weidi really did turn into a child, pulling a long face as he rose and left. I was annoyed that somebody had been present when this took place, and I felt it would be best to change the subject. I also felt apologetic toward Ling Jishi. But he didn't seem to notice particularly. Instead he just asked, "Isn't his last name Bai? How can he be your younger brother?"

I laughed. "So you only let people surnamed Ling call you 'Little Brother' or 'Big Brother,'" I said to him, making him chuckle.

These days when young people get together, they love to explore the meaning of the word "love." Although I feel at times that I understand love, in the end I can never really explain it. I know all about what goes on between men and women. Perhaps what I already know about it makes love seem vague, makes it hard for me to believe in love between the sexes, makes it impossible to think of myself as someone pure enough, innocent enough to be loved. I am skeptical of what everyone calls "love." I'm just as skeptical of the love I've received.

I was just becoming aware of the realities of life when those who loved me made me suffer by allowing outsiders the chance to humiliate and slander me. Even my most intimate friends abandoned me. And it was precisely for fear of the threat of love that I left school. Although I mature more each day, those previous liaisons influenced me so much that I still have doubts about love and sometimes thoroughly despise the intimacy love brings. Weidi claims he loves me. Then why does he make me so miserable all the time? He came over again this evening, for instance, and as soon as he got here, he burst into tears and sobbed his eyes out. No matter what I said—"What's wrong with you? Please talk to me," or "Weidi, say something, I beg you"—he just carried on as before. Nothing quite like this had ever happened before. I exhausted myself trying to guess what catastrophe had befallen him until I couldn't think of any other possibilities. Eventually he cried himself out. Then he started in on me.

"I don't like him."

"Who's bullying you, Weidi? Who made you cry and throw this tantrum?"

"I don't like that tall guy. The one you're so close to now."

Oh! I really hadn't realized until then that he was furious over something I had done. Without thinking, I started to chuckle. This insipid jealousy, this selfish possessiveness, this is love? I couldn't help myself. I broke into laughter. And that, of course, did nothing to calm poor Weidi's raging heart. In fact, my condescending attitude increased his fury. Watching his blazing eyes, I got the feeling that what he really wanted was to rip me to shreds. "Go ahead and do it," I thought to myself. But he just put his head down, started bawling again, and, rubbing tears from his eyes, staggered out the door.

A scene like this might conceivably be considered an ardent expression of tempestuous love. Yet Weidi stages these things for me with such artless lack of forethought that he defeats himself. I'm not asking him to be false or affected in the expression of his love. It's just I feel it's futile for him to try to move me by acting like a child. Maybe I'm just hard by nature. If so, I deserve all the anxiety and heartbreak that my failure to live up to people's expectations has brought me.

As soon as Weidi left, I scrutinized my own intentions. I recalled in vivid detail someone else's tenderness, someone else's warmth, generosity, and openly passionate bearing, and I was so drunk with sweet joy that I took out a postcard, wrote a few sentences, and ordered the attendant to take it over to Dormitory No. 4.

March 9

When I see Ling Jishi sit so relaxed and casually in my room, I can't help pitying Weidi. I pray that not every woman in the world will neglect and disdain his great sincerity, as I do, thus submerging myself in a morass of guilty sorrow I cannot get free of. More than that, I hope a pure young girl comes along who will redeem Weidi's love, fill the emptiness he must feel.

(Translated by Tani E. Barlow)

MAO DUN
(1896–1981)

After Lu Xun, Mao Dun is universally regarded as the greatest writer in twentieth century China. Born in Zhejiang into a family sympathetic to social reform, Mao Dun, whose real name was Shen Yanbing, entered Peking University in 1914. A member of the Literary Research Society, he edited Short Story Monthly *and became actively involved in the insurgent Communist movement. A political setback caused by Chiang Kaishek's purge of Communists led to Mao Dun's disillusion and despair in the late 1920s and early 1930s, a period in which he produced his best work: a trilogy entitled* The Eclipse *was published in 1927, followed by* Rainbow *(1930), considered by many his finest for a psychological depth new to Chinese literature, and then the novel* The Midnight *followed in 1933. In the People's Republic era, Mao Dun was a towering figure, serving as the minister of culture from 1949 to 1965 and the chairman of China's Writers Association from 1949 to 1981.*

Rainbow (excerpt)

Chapter One

The golden rays of the rising sun pierced the light smoky mist that hung over the Yangtze River, dispersing it to reveal the blue-green of the mountain peaks on either shore. The east wind played a soft, enchanting melody. The muddy waters of the Yangtze gradually plunged through the narrow gorges, now and then producing a bevy of small whirlpools in its wake.

An indistinct growl, like the roar of a great animal, issued forth from behind the wall of mountains upstream. After a few minutes it grew into a long, proud bellow, transforming itself into a thundering echo between the cliffs on the two sides of the river. A light green steamship burst majestically through the remaining fog, sailing effortlessly downstream. In an instant, the heavy rumbling noise of its engine swelled up on the surface of the river.

It was the renowned steamship *Longmao*, which plied the Sichuan waters of the Yangtze River. On this day it had pulled up anchor at dawn in Kuifu and was rushing to make the journey to Yichang by two or three in the afternoon. Although it was only eight in the morning, the ship was already packed to the rails with third-class passengers who had come up for a breath of fresh air. The passageway outside the dining hall on the uppermost deck was not as crowded. In fact, there were only two women leaning against the green iron railing, looking out into the distance at the magnificent, clear view of the Wu Gorge.

They stood shoulder to shoulder, facing the bow of the ship. One, her body slightly turned at the waist, her left forearm leaning on the railing, looked about twenty years old. She wore a pale blue soft satin waist-length blouse, beneath which a long black skirt that billowed out in the wind accentuated the elegance of her slender and graceful body. She had short hair. Two jet-black wisps of hair brushed the cheeks of her oval face, complementing a pair of long, thin eyebrows, a straight nose, two teasingly beautiful eyes, and small, round lips. She displayed all the characteristics of a flawless Oriental beauty. If viewed from behind, she appeared to be the essence of tenderness. But her eyes revealed a vigorous and straightforward spirit. And her small mouth, which was usually tightly closed, gave proof of her resolute disposition. She was the kind of person who knew her goal and never turned back.

Her companion was a short, fat, middle-aged woman. Her face was not unattractive, but her thick lips drooped at the corners, imparting an air of gloom to her appearance. Her clothes were of high-quality material, but their style was old-fashioned. Her feet had once been bound but were now released from their confinement. Encased in black boots that were too large, their humplike deformity looked like two round balls. Next to the long, narrow natural feet of her young companion, they looked quite miserable and pathetic.

The two did not speak to each other. The grandeur of the scenery had long since cleansed their minds of all thoughts. Their hearts were empty, free of concerns, intoxicated by the vastness of the natural beauty surrounding them.

The boat's whistle shrieked once again. Far off in the distance a cliff intruded on the landscape, blocking the river and piercing the sky. The river cut through the tall peaks that lined both banks. They seemed to form two towering natural dikes, barring any possibility of continued forward passage. The sun shone like a ray of gold, sparingly clothing only the tops of the high peaks in its brilliance, leaving the mountain below a carpet of dark green. The boat continued to push unswervingly forward, its whistle blasting with ever more urgency. The cliffs that all but obstructed the river moved gradually toward the two women, higher and higher, more and more imposing, the luxurious growth of trees halfway up their sides becoming faintly visible.

"This is only the first of the twelve peaks of Wushan." The middle-aged woman, as she addressed her companion, nodded her head with an air of self-importance and such vigor that the large but loosely fastened bun anchored to the back of her skull bounced back and forth as if about to fall off.

The young woman replied with a smile, turning her head to avoid the foul odors that emanated from the large bun. Slowly she took a step forward, concentrating even more intently on the vista ahead. The precipice rushing toward her was now so close she could no longer see its tip. Clusters of jade-green cedars spread like a belt diagonally across the middle of the mountain. Below, thrust directly into the water, were reddish brown rocks dotted here and there with climbing plants. All of this, this screen of mountains, grew slowly larger, moved slowly closer.

Then, suddenly, it shuddered and gently turned around, as if to show off another aspect of its glory.

Bu . . . hong! The whistle gave a joyous cry, and the boat navigated the bend in the river. On the right the mountains that had been soaring to the heavens moved out of the way; once again the limitless waters of the Yangtze rushed between the mountain peaks.

"That's just like the Yangtze! From a distance it looks impassable. It's only when you get there that you see there's a way through. Who knows how many bends like this there are. Miss Mei, this is your first time. You must find it very interesting indeed!" the middle-aged woman called out loudly from behind. Unfortunately, the east wind was so strong that her words of experience were scattered with it. Mei, who was gazing absentmindedly at the eastward-flowing Yangtze, did not hear a thing.

The unbelievable beauty of the Wu Gorge had deeply moved her. She thought of her own past. It too had been so treacherous, so quick to change. It too had had its dead ends and rebirths. Light and darkness were interwoven into the fabric of her life. She had already courageously made it halfway through. What would the rest be like? This puzzle called the future! Mei had no fantasies. Yet neither was she pessimistic. She was simply waiting, quietly, like a boxing master who has established his position and is waiting for his opponent. Hardship was deeply branded on this young life.

Quite a few people probably envied her life. But she herself still saw her past as worthy of the word "vicissitude." During the last four years she had begun to attract people's attention as a "prominent member of the nouveaux riches." In west and south Sichuan everyone knew of Miss Mei. She was no ordinary girl. She was like a rainbow. But she had never wanted her life to be like this, nor was she happy this way. She simply charged forward with the spirit of a warrior, doing what circumstance dictated. Indeed, her special talent was "charging forward." Her only ambition was to overcome her environment, overcome her fate. During the last few years her only goal had been to rein in her strong feminine nature and her even stronger maternal instincts.

On bright spring days and sorrowful rainy nights, she would occasionally feel the ancient legacy of being female stirring in her heart. At such times she would stare into space, immersed in a flood of loneliness and remorse. It was also at times like these that she fell to lamenting her unfortunate fate and conjuring up a million regrets about the vicissitudes of her existence. Nevertheless, her hardships had already cast her life into a new mold, and the whirlwind May Fourth Movement had already blown her thinking in a new direction. She could not look back. She could only strive to suppress and eradicate the traditional in her nature and adapt to a new world, a new life. She did not pause. She did not hesitate. She felt no contradictions.

The Yangtze was now struggling with difficulty to squeeze through the Wuxia Mountains. The river seemed a symbol of her past. But she hoped her future would be as open and surging as the Yangtze would be below the Kui Pass.

Mei could not suppress a smile. She turned her head and saw the middle-aged woman squinting at her, a reminder that the woman had been jabbering at her with that air of authority that older people so often displayed. Mei did not really like this companion, with her dejected look, but neither was she willing to needlessly offend her. Besides, as long as Mei did not have to smell that rancid hair, she didn't mind listening to the woman's pretentious din.

"Mrs. Wen, the wind is strong. Aren't you scared?" Mei spoke cordially. Stepping daintily inside, she deliberately took a position upwind.

"What hardships and bitterness haven't these old bones known? How could I be scared of the wind? This spring when we demonstrated for women's suffrage, the wind was stronger than this and there was a raging rainstorm too. That didn't scare me. Without even opening my umbrella, I led the sisters to the provincial governor's office to make our demands."

Mrs. Wen spoke excitedly, the bun at the back of her head bobbing unceasingly.

Mei pursed her lips to hold back a smile, all the while feigning total admiration.

"Why didn't you participate then, Miss Mei? Oh, yes, you're the governor's private secretary, the trusted lieutenant of the boss. You're already an official. But Miss Mei, being an official isn't the same as suffrage. Suffrage is . . ."

As she reached this point, the woman paused for a moment and moved a bit closer to Mei in preparation for an extended harangue. Mei took a half step back to guard her position upwind and adroitly interrupted the other woman: "I'm only the provincial governor's family tutor. What's all this about being a private secretary? That's just a rumor started by people who want to ridicule me. And that's not all people have been saying. It's better to just laugh it off. Mrs. Wen, you lost your husband as a young woman. You of all people should know that people with loose tongues like nothing more than to insult a woman, to spread reckless gossip."

Mrs. Wen's jowls twitched, but she did not reply. Any mention of her youth always depressed her. Nevertheless, her days of "fearing rumors" had long since passed. She was now a wholehearted member of the movement for political suffrage. Yet on the day they had rushed into the provincial assembly and she had heard the guards cursing her as an "old tigress on the prowl," for some reason her ardent spirit had flagged. Subconsciously, she thought back to the past indiscretion that had cast a shadow over her future. She felt that as a woman, the only prerequisite for taking a role in society was that she be pure and above reproach. In believing that a woman should remain ever faithful to one husband and never remarry, she was of one mind with many of those who opposed the suffrage movement.

"The provincial governor advocates the new thought. On the question of relations between the sexes, he has some special views. No doubt Mrs. Wen has heard people speak of them?"

Seeing her companion's discomfort, Mei laughed and changed the direction of the conversation. But the term "relations between the sexes" was probably still very alien to the ears of this eloquent and ardent supporter of women's suffrage. She looked slightly puzzled at Mei and did not answer. Mei winked knowingly and continued, "This special viewpoint goes like this: A wife is a companion for life. A companion is a friend. The more friends the better!"

Suddenly the boat's whistle sounded again, two short spurts followed by a long, loud wail. The warning bell on top of the boat also began to clang wildly. Hiding in the hollows carved out of the hills on both banks of the river, local bandits had begun firing guns in the direction of the boat. This happened quite often. Suddenly the boat was filled with the chaotic sound of passengers' footsteps. By the time Mei grabbed Mrs. Wen and ran to the passageway in front of the dining hall, she had already heard the intermittent and then continuous sounds of gunfire coming from the left. The first-class passengers, who had already arisen, were now pushing and shoving to be first to squeeze down the narrow stairway leading to the cabins below. One of the crew gestured at Mei and her companion to go below as well. Without thinking, Mei took a step forward, but her nose was instantly assaulted by the stench of Mrs. Wen's hair. She stopped.

"I'm not going down. A boat moving with the current goes very fast. Even bandits' bullets won't be able to reach us," Mei said with a slight smile.

She did not wait for Mrs. Wen's reply but walked sprightly through the dining hall to her own cabin, lay down on the bed, picked up a book, and began to read. As it happened, her cabin was on the right-hand side of the boat. The reflection of the sun flashed across the window. Mei got up, thinking to pull down the curtains, when she saw a wooden junk on the water unfurl its sails. It moved along the edge of the cliff and in an instant was gone. She listened carefully. The gunfire had stopped. She returned to her bed, lay down, and yawned. Her nights had been filled with dreams, her sleep unsettled. Once again this morning she had arisen too early. She felt very tired. Folding her hands under her head, she lay back on the pillow and closed her eyes.

The doorknob to the cabin turned softly. Mei opened her eyes lazily and saw Mrs. Wen standing in front of the bed. She must have been jostled by the crowd, for her bun was about to come apart. It drooped limply down the back of her neck, and her temples were sticky with beads of sweat.

"How dare those gangsters even open fire on foreign ships. Aiya! But you're the bold one, Miss Mei. Bullets don't have eyes. It's not worth getting yourself killed." Mrs. Wen sank heavily onto the bed. She spoke breathlessly.

Mei smiled charmingly, sat up, walked to the window, and leaned over the dressing table. She considered advising Mrs. Wen to rearrange her bun, but in the end Mei changed her mind.

"The pity is it interrupted our conversation. Mrs. Wen, do you think what the governor said was correct?"

"Important people think differently from us common folk."

A casual observer might have thought that Mrs. Wen was just being polite, but her attitude was exceedingly earnest. Mei laughed faintly. She lifted her foot and lightly kicked the tassels on the lower part of the curtains with the pointed toes of her white leather high-heeled foreign shoes.

"But he said only that a wife is a companion for life, not that a husband and wife are companions for life."

Mrs. Wen opened her eyes wide in total incomprehension.

"He now has five of these companions for life," Mei quickly continued. "He treats them very thoughtfully and equally, but he guards them jealously. You'd almost think he used eunuchs in that famous garden of his. It's practically his Afang Palace."*

Mrs. Wen did not grasp the point of these words. But the number five conjured up rumors she had heard and aroused her interest. "I've heard that some are extremely ugly. Is it true?"

This time it was Mei who did not entirely understand. But just as she threw Mrs. Wen a startled glance, Mei realized what her companion was referring to. With a laugh, she stretched and coldly replied, "There was one who once wrote a poem containing the lines, 'I'd rather be con-

---

* The Afang Palace housed the harem of the first emperor of the Qin Dynasty (221–207 B.C.).

cubine to a hero / than be the wife of a common man.' She'd probably qualify as the world's ugliest woman."

The sun's rays outside the window abruptly fell into shadow, as if the boat had entered a tunnel of some kind. Mei craned her neck to see but noticed only an exceedingly tall cliff slowly receding, its peak hidden from view. Suddenly, suspended before her eyes were row after row of trees, both tall and short, their trunks straight and thin like those of the hemp. Mei drew back her head and looked at Mrs. Wen's dazed expression. "One of the peculiarities of the general* of the Afang Palace," Mei added, "is that almost all his companions are kind of ugly."

A profound silence crept into the room. The normally talkative Mrs. Wen seemed to have been stricken speechless. She suddenly lay back on the bed and covered her face with her hands. Her fat, clumsy body and her unnaturally small feet all reminded Mei of that woman dwelling deep within the Afang Palace who would rather not be the "wife of a common man."

Images out of the past slowly began to congeal in Mei's mind, enveloping her consciousness like a veil of smoke. As in a dream, she was once again a family tutor in that large garden. She saw the familiar layout of man-made hills, the fish pond, and the Western-style gazebo. Ah! That unforgettable gazebo. It was there that she had refused the temptation of money and jewels. It was not that she did not like luxuries but that she valued her freedom more. Above all, she did not want to become a prisoner of the Afang Palace. It was also there that she had come to know the jealousy that had been bred in women by thousands of years of dependence on men. The vision of a small round face with a pair of fierce triangular eyebrows rushed into her mind. And then the smooth, shiny barrel of a Browning revolver, staring at her like the eye of some bizarre monster.

A barely audible snort of contempt rose up from deep within Mei,

---

* Mei refers to the governor as a general because most provincial governors during this so-called warlord period of Chinese history were powerful commanders of personal armies whose political role grew out of their military power.

waking her out of her gloomy reverie. It was the same snort with which the *yuanzhu* bird in Zhuangzi's famous story replied to the owl who was cherishing his piece of rotting rat meat as if it were a precious jewel.* In fact, the last lesson Mei had taught as a family tutor was that very fable, "The Owl Gets a Rotten Rat."

A faint snoring arose from the bed. Mrs. Wen had fallen asleep. Mei glanced out the window and then walked softly out of the cabin, back to the passageway outside the dining hall. She sat down on one of the rattan chairs.

On both banks of the river, mountains so tall they had never been inhabited jutted out of the muddy waves and pierced the sky like two high walls. The steamship *Longmao* puffed asthmatically down the middle of the river. Every once in a while a junk or two appeared on either side, but they clung so closely to the cliffs that it seemed as if those aboard could stretch out a hand and pick the wisteria growing on the rocks. Below the distant towering cliffs ahead were several small wooden boats. Crowded together as if immobile in the narrow pass, they seemed to leave no space for the steamship to squeeze through. But only a few minutes later, with a triumphant blast of its whistle, the *Longmao* was hurrying past. Only then was it clear that the Yangtze was really wide enough for four steamships. The wake created by the steamship's propellers dashed against the shore, and the snail-like wooden boats clinging to the cliffs swayed like a gathering of drunken men.

Mei smiled as she looked at the wooden boats. She admired the great power of this machine and had no pity for the snail-like objects being buffeted by the violence it created. She had complete faith in the huge monstrosity that carried her and was intensely conscious that this mammoth product of modern civilization would bring her to a new

* This is a reference to the section in *Zhuangzi* entitled "The Floods of Autumn," in which the philosopher chides the prime minister of the kingdom of Liang for fearing his job is coveted by the philosopher. He likens the prime minister to an owl who has just caught a rat and fears it will be stolen by the phoenix flying overhead. Just as the phoenix eats and drinks only the purest and most delicate foods and would not want the rat, Zhuangzi would have no interest in such a job.

future. Although before her was a world unimaginably strange, it was surely more vast and more exciting than anything she had known. Of this she was firmly and unalterably convinced.

But she had no illusions. The experience of the last four or five years had taught her three lessons: never long for the past, never daydream about the future, but seize the present and use all your abilities to cope with it. Her past was just like a boat moving through the Wuxia Mountains. She often saw precipices blocking her path, convincing her that there was no way out. But if she bravely and resolutely pressed on, she would always discover that the road ahead was actually very wide. Then as she went a little farther on, the cliffs would again loom before her, and a way out would seem even more remote. If at that point she had looked back from whence she had come, she would have seen that the mountains were already hidden by clouds. To look back on the past was unbearable. The future was indistinct and full of hazards. She could only seize the present and press forward with both feet planted firmly on the ground. She was a "disciple of the present."

A hot wind passed over her. The sun's rays danced on the water like myriad specks of gold. It was almost noon. Mei leaned back in the rattan chair and felt her eyelids grow heavy. Although the scenery before her was fascinating, it now made her feel somewhat weary. The endless river pressed between the barren mountains, twisting and turning interminably as the torrents of water rushed ceaselessly forward, always promising new mysteries and yet always the same. And amidst it all, the ever-present triumphant, yet mournful, sound of the ship's whistle.

She slumped down in the chair, letting herself drowse off to escape the monotony. No thoughts of the past disturbed her peace, and no thoughts of the future came to arouse her emotions.

A waiter arrived to call her to lunch. She found out from him that it would be around three o'clock before they reached Yichang and concluded that this so-called fast steamship was no better than a slow boat after all. She wished she could cross the Kui Pass immediately. The closer they approached the Sichuan border, the more her impatience

grew. To Mei, everything about Sichuan was narrow, small, meandering, just like the river flowing before her.

After lunch, taking advantage of a reprieve from Mrs. Wen's inces-
sant chatter, Mei withdrew into the cabin to take a nap. She had long
since found this leading member of the women's suffrage movement
boring. Now Mei had begun to hate her. She hated her vulgar manners;
she hated her extreme narrow-mindedness; she hated the way she put
on airs to mask her base nature; she hated her extremely muddled ideas
on women's rights.

Half consciously, she compared herself to Mrs. Wen. Then, suddenly,
Mei thought of what would happen after they reached Shanghai. She
asked herself, "We are representatives, but as a group, what do we represent? How will we be able to accomplish our collective mission?" She
could not but laugh. She admitted to herself that she had used her attendance at the National Student League conference as a pretext to evade
the advances of that diminutive warlord. She knew if she did not escape
now, it would be difficult to avoid being forced into becoming one of
the ladies of the Afang Palace. As to whether her companion, Mrs. Wen,
also had personal motives for attending, Mei was even less inclined to
speculate.

All thought of sleep departed. From Mrs. Wen, Mei's mind wandered
to recollections of other acquaintances. Xu, a good friend from middle
school with whom she had kept in touch until two years ago, when she
was a teacher in southern Sichuan, leaped into her mind. "She's in Nanjing," Mei thought excitedly. And with this a multitude of disconnected
memories streamed into Mei's head, finally driving her from her bed.

A rumbling sound arose from the deck. From outside the window
came the sound of swarming footsteps. Mrs. Wen stuck her head in
through the window and shouted joyfully, "Don't you want to see the
Kui Pass? We're almost there!"

Mei replied with a smile. The enthusiasm of the throng outside made
her feel hot. She changed into a muslin blouse, wiped her face with a
towel, and ran nimbly out to the passageway.

Lofty cliffs still stood on both banks, but now they were not so high and had begun to slope slightly. Behind them rose row after row of mountains, each taller than the ones before. The rays of the sun had now turned them a brilliant golden color. The wind had died down to a gentle breeze, as if it too had barely awoken from its afternoon nap.

The boat seemed to be moving more slowly. The splashing of the waves became more even. The whistle emitted a constant arrogant bellow like the cries of the heralds in ancient times who ordered the people to make way for an approaching official.

Many people were lined up along the railing, staring straight ahead. Mrs. Wen was among them. Mei stood in the passageway. She clasped her hands behind her neck and gently swayed her shoulders from side to side. Her short sleeves fell back to her shoulders, revealing her snow-white arms like two triangles on either side of her head. The sight of her bare skin attracted quite a few sideward glances. Mei bit her lip and grinned as if no one else were there. Then, impulsively, she raised her eyebrows and skipped off, cutting right through the clusters of passengers to the door of the captain's cabin.

About one hundred feet from the front of the ship, two walls of stone jutted out of the water and faced each other across the river, so vertical and smooth they seemed to be sliced out of the rocks with a knife. There were no trees, no vines, no ferns, only the pitch-black rocks looming majestically over the river like a monumental doorframe without its top. Joining these two strange stones were row after row of undulating mountains. Each billowing wave of the Yangtze rushed to be first to reach the shore, crashing violently against the foot of the cliffs.

The boat's whistle once again let out a long earsplitting shriek as the *Longmao* sailed into the great stone gateway. Mei craned her neck to see. The intensity of the sun made her dizzy. She felt as though the rapidly receding stone precipice was swaying, about to topple. Instinctively, she closed her eyes. She saw a flash of red light and then all was dark.

Mei buried her face in her hands and thought to herself, "So this is the Kui Pass. This is the great pass out of Sichuan. This is the demon pass* that separates Sichuan from the rest of the world!" These thoughts left Mei momentarily distracted, until the boat's whistle once again roused her. She lifted her head and felt a blinding flash from the returning sunlight. The Yangtze opened up before her, so broad that she could not see the shore. All that was visible were distant, smoky objects like the shadows of clouds lying on the horizon. As if a great weight had been lifted from her chest, Mei smiled, raised her arms high, and took a deep breath. She paid tribute to this glorious work of nature. It was only at that moment that she fully realized the vastness and power of the Yangtze River.

She turned her head to the right. The cliffs of the Kui Pass were still faintly visible. The pass itself now seemed but a crack among the myriad peaks, and within the crack lay a mysterious darkness.

"From here on you won't be seeing any more good scenery. Once you leave Sichuan the Yangtze is really quite ordinary. The Kui Pass is a natural boundary."

From her left came the sound of Mrs. Wen's voice. Mei turned her head and saw Mrs. Wen straining to move her small feet. As she nodded and walked away, Mei pursed her lips in a smile and called gently after her, "This is also the last time we'll be following a meandering, narrow, dangerous, mazelike route. From here on we enter the broad vast world of freedom!"

Chapter Two

When Mei was eighteen years old she was enrolled as a student at the Yizhou Girls' School in Chengdu. It was in that same year, on May 4, that the students of Beijing began their historic mass movement. Their initial attack on the Zhao mansion† gave rise to the raging tide of "May

---

*   This is a pun on the word *gui,* or demon, and the name of the pass as well as an expression of Mei's hatred of her isolation in Sichuan.

†   This was the home of Cao Rulin, minister of communications in the central warlord government and one of the three pro-Japanese officials who were targets of student wrath following China's mistreatment at Versailles.

Fourth." The flames that burned through the Zhao mansion set fire to the zeal of young people throughout China.

Within a month this raging tide, this spark, had burst forth and spread all the way to Chengdu, that remote and enigmatic land on China's western frontier. Mei had gone to Shaocheng Park to witness the activity generated by a rally to boycott Japanese goods. The slogan of the rally was "patriotism." Of course, Mei knew that she should love her country, but the slogan was too general, too broad to arouse her enthusiasm. She remained only a spectator. At the time she was too caught up in her own personal dilemma, one that she could not resolve. Only three days earlier, without her consent, her father had betrothed her to her first cousin, Liu Yuchun.

When she returned home from the rally that evening, her father had himself just returned from getting drunk at the Lius'. He had apparently heard something at the Liu Dry Goods Store because instead of going straight to sleep as usual, he summoned Mei and began to rant, "So, this is our great republic! Students meddling in other people's private affairs! They plan to go to the dry goods store to inspect it for Japanese goods. If they find any they'll confiscate them, and they even intend to impose a fine. It's ridiculous. It's impossible. I can't believe the *yamen*[*] won't take any action."

Mei lowered her head and said nothing. The words "inspect the dry goods store" pierced her like a knife. The earthshaking patriotic cries at Shaocheng Park, which had seemed so remote to her this afternoon, now turned out to be directly related to her personal problem. In the future she would have to be the proprietress of a store that secretly sold Japanese goods. This prospect intensified her misery. That day, when she heard people shout, "Patriotism," she hadn't given it a second thought, for she knew she had never sold out her country. Now her complacency was gone. Suddenly she felt like a notorious traitor.

"Heh! What they say *sounds* good enough. They say they want us to buy Chinese products. Well, I'm a genuine doctor of Chinese medicine,

---

[*]   A *yamen* was the office of the head of any administrative unit.

the real article. But in recent years look how unpopular, how poor I've become!"

Her father spoke wheezingly, filling the room with the stench of alcohol. From the students, he moved on to his usual routine of cursing his son. His tongue thick from drink, he laboriously recited the past events that Mei had heard so often before. How he had sold off family property to send his son to study in America. How, later, he had sold more family property to pull the right strings to get his son a job. How his son, who was happily living far away, never even asked whether his father was dead or alive. His eyes were completely red by the time he finished his tale.

"The year before last he was employed in the office of the Shaanxi military governor, but he still wired home again and again asking for money. Last year he became a magistrate and he stopped coming to me for money. But his telegrams and express letters also stopped. Ah! This is the way a son who studies abroad and becomes an official acts. The one with real promise is that child Yuchun. He was an orphan. I took him into our home only because he was related to us. Later, when I sent him to be an apprentice at the Hong Yuan Dry Goods Store at the Yuelai market, it was only so he'd have a way to make a living. And with nothing but his bare hands he turned around and made a fortune."

Her father closed his eyes and nodded his head in satisfaction. Then, abruptly, he opened them wide and shouted, "How dare those student bastards prevent people from selling Japanese goods!" Repeating himself once more with venom, Mei's father then staggered into his own room.

Mei watched his retreating figure and heaved a great sigh. If there hadn't been a maid still standing in a dark corner of the room, Mei would have already let the tears welling in her eyes pour out. Her eyes darted in every direction, like a drowning person searching desperately for something to hang on to. There was nothing, only the flickering flames of the kerosene lamp leaping toward her, the ancient wooden furniture gaping dumbly all around her, and the chill of a household in decline that pierced her to the marrow.

Biting her lip to hold back the tears, Mei fled into her own bedroom. Here the warmer atmosphere comforted her somewhat. On a delicate pear-wood table were arranged the mementos of the blissful days of her childhood: an exquisitely dressed doll; a red-lipped, white-toothed Negro figure with a small clock in its protruding belly; two peacock feathers inserted in a tea-green triangular glass vase. These were all relics of better times, five or six years ago, before her mother had died. Mei, without a mother and without sisters, had used these toys to replace the intimacy of real flesh-and-blood relatives. Now she stared absentmindedly at these mute, though almost human, friends. Confused thoughts crossed her mind, but none took root in her consciousness. It was as though she were being assaulted by disconnected images—the dry goods store, Japanese products, Cousin Liu, marriage, the rally at Shaocheng Park—each throbbing feverishly in her head.

Impulsively, she went to her bed and took out a small inlaid ebony box. She lifted the lid. It was completely empty except for a single photograph of the face of a slightly feminine-looking young man. Mei gazed at the photo for a few minutes, then closed the box and lay down on the bed. A vision of another man flashed before her eyes. On his round face were two broad, thick eyebrows and a pair of shrewd eyes. He was not basically bad-looking. He just displayed too much of the vulgarity of the crafty businessman.

Mei buried her face in the pillow and gritted her teeth. How she hated that man! Her secret hatred of him was as great as her secret love for the other man. But it was not her secret love for the one that caused her to hate the other. She had hated him for a long time. Both were her cousins, but for some reason she had never felt as close to her father's sister's son, who had been raised in her own family, as she felt toward her other cousin on her mother's side. Although she did not want him to, the former continually pursued her. From the time Mei was barely old enough to know about sex, he, already an adult, had constantly looked for opportunities to flirt with her. She still had a scar on her arm where he had scratched her. This was something a proud girl like Mei could not tolerate. She carried in her bosom the secret of this humiliation. She secretly detested this man. Yet it had now been decided that she was to spend the rest of her life with this very person.

A feeling of having been vanquished, of having been taken prisoner, overcame her. Worse, there seemed no hope of escape. The marriage agreement had been concluded. The wedding would probably take place next year. What means could she use to resist? What means did she have to resist? Still worse, she had heard that the man she loved was also about to get married. At the latest it would probably be this winter. Last week when they had met and talked at the Wangjiang teahouse, had he not said to her, "Meimei,* circumstances demand that we part. Even if I was not engaged, would Uncle want a poor orphan like me? And even if Uncle agreed, I'm only a clerk in the army divisional headquarters. Could I make you happy? I know you're willing to suffer, but how can I bear to see the one I love sacrifice on my account? The doctor says I have tuberculosis. I probably don't have long to live. That's even more reason not to sacrifice your future."†

Two rows of tears streamed from Mei's eyes, but they were tears of happiness. She was glad she had tasted the bittersweet joy of true love. She sank once more into her memories, reliving that moment as if it were displayed before her like a motion picture. When her emotions had reached their peak, she had looked to see that there was no one around and pressed her face against her cousin's shoulder. Then slowly, half unconsciously, she moved her lips closer to his. A shiver ran through his whole body. He drew gently back and said in an unsteady voice, "Cousin, I have tuberculosis." Oh! Oh! Tuberculosis! Will it keep me from embracing this man while he is alive? Will it only let me cry at his grave?

A wild passion overtook Mei's heart. She did not blame her cousin for

* "Meimei" is a term used to address a younger sister. Here it demonstrates affection and the fact that the two are cousins.

† Traditional Chinese morality contained strong proscriptions against the remarriage of widows.

his seeming aloofness. On the contrary, she was even more grateful, felt even more respect and love for his pure and honest nature. She wanted to know only why she did not have the right to love the one she loved, why she was only worthy of being a prisoner, a piece of soft, warm flesh to be toyed with. She hated the teachers at school and the old revolutionary spinster headmistress, Miss Cui, for never having discussed problems of this kind.

These two questions went around and around in her mind, but she had no answers. Finally, her nerves, half numb with exhaustion, led her to that age-old explanation: an unfortunate fate. This simple answer wrenched her, tortured her, haunted her, gnawed at her until the chirping of the birds praising the dawn aroused her with a start. The sun shone obliquely on the eaves of the house. The clock in the belly of the Negro doll ticked steadily. All was beautiful. All was calm.

Mei rolled over and sat up. In a daze, she balanced herself on the edge of the bed. She could not believe a whole night had passed. She noticed mosquito bites all over her pale upper arm. Her neck also itched. When she walked toward the window to look in the mirror, she saw that there were faint blue circles under her eyes and that her cheeks were flushed blood-red. Putting down the mirror, she sank into a nearby chair and stared vacantly at the doll sitting atop the pear-wood table.

The big hand on the Negro doll's belly had marked the passing of a full ten minutes when Mei suddenly jumped up. She dashed off a short letter, combed her hair, changed into a pale lilac muslin skirt and blouse, and called one of the family's maids to bring her breakfast. Her lips had recovered their smile, and her eyes, which minutes before were suffering from lack of sleep, once again radiated determination.

Mei went to school as usual. As she dropped the letter into a mailbox on the way, an unconscious smile crossed her face. No formal classes were held that day. Yesterday's rally had already stirred up some of these normally sedate young ladies. Everywhere could be heard the buzzing of female voices absorbed in curious gossip. The old revolutionary, Headmistress Cui, suddenly became an object of great interest. Wherever she went, her long braid bouncing behind her,* there were always pockets of students secretly watching her every move. The reading room in particular was alive with activity. Group after group of students fought over month-old newspapers from Shanghai and Hankou to see how the students in Beijing had set fire to the minister's house and beaten up a high government official, to see how afterward they had taken to the streets to make speeches, and to see how several hundreds of them had been arrested by the police. A few of the more discerning girls went a step further and searched out five or six dusty volumes of *New Youth* magazine. The whole school shook with nervous agitation.

Mei was no exception. But unlike the others, she was not absorbed in this intense research into recent events. Rather, she used it as a means to make the time pass more quickly. In reality, she was preoccupied with the date she had made with Cousin Wei Yu for later that day. She was also afraid that she would hear people say things like "the dry goods store sells nothing but Japanese products." Whenever Mei ran into classmates who were talking about the boycott, she could not help feeling a bit jumpy, as if her own hidden sins had been discovered.

At ten past four Mei sneaked away to the Ziyun Pavilion. A tall, emaciated young man was already there waiting for her. They smiled and stood gazing silently at one another, then walked slowly to a large *wutong* tree behind the pavilion, each deep in thought, as if pondering what to say first.

"Meimei, your letter gave me quite a scare." The young man spoke softly, his gentle eyes fixed on Mei's face.

Mei replied with a tender smile, "Why weren't you able to sleep well last night? You look pale and your eyes are a bit swollen. You were crying last night, weren't you?"

The young man sighed faintly, hung his head, and allowed two imperceptible tears to drip down his cheeks.

---

* Traditionally only young unmarried girls in China wore their hair in braids. Used by a middle-aged woman like Miss Cui, this hairstyle could become a symbol of feminism and the rejection of marriage.

Mei did not reply. Her lips drew together as if to speak, but she held back. She kicked a clump of grass at the foot of the tree with her toe and began mechanically fingering the hem of her muslin blouse. She hesitated for a full half minute before she said calmly, "Cousin Yu, I don't know what was on my mind last night. But you needn't worry. It doesn't matter. Last night was nonsense, meaningless nonsense. But this morning I came to a decision. Let's work out a plan to go away."

Wei Yu raised his head in alarm and fixed his gentle gaze on Mei as if he had not understood what she meant by "go away." Nevertheless, a look of intense gratitude was revealed as his eyes slowly filled with tears. Mei smiled and added softly, "If we go away together, there might still be hope. If we split up, the future will be unendurable!"

Tears were his only reply. Two thoughts did battle in the mind of this overly sensitive young man. He could not bear to hurt her by saying no, but he felt he should not say yes. After a painful silence, he forced out these few words: "I am not worthy of such true love, Meimei."

This time it was Mei's face that turned pale. She began to have the uneasy feeling that the man she loved was a coward.

"I'm a sick man. At most I'll live another two or three years. I don't deserve to enjoy life. Even more, I shouldn't let the shadow hanging over my life blot out your chances for happiness. If you continue to think of me, then I will die with a smile on my face. Knowing that your future will be a good one, I'll be able to die content."

Although there was a slight tremor in his voice, he spoke these words with resolve. He had the aura of a martyr about to die for his principles. He shed no more tears. His cheeks were flushed with excitement.

Mei silently bowed her head. Then suddenly she spoke with total conviction: "My future most certainly will not be good."

"Huh?"

"Because I don't love him. I hate him."

"Do you hate him for the reason you mentioned last time? If he's too aggressive, it's probably because he loves you so much."

Mei could not but purse her lips and laugh. She shot a glance at Wei

Yu and said with an air of disapproval, "When did you learn how to defend other people so well?"

"I'm not defending him. I'm just telling you the truth."

"You call that the truth?"

Mei spoke sharply. She was clearly angry. If this had not been her trusted Wei Yu, she would certainly have thought Liu Yuchun had bribed him to lobby on Liu's behalf. But coming from Wei Yu's lips this sort of talk was quite unexpected. She looked at him intently, waiting for an answer.

"Meimei, I was wrong. Please forgive me. Of course I don't want someone else to love you. But at the same time I really wish there was someone who could truly love you and whom you could love in return." Wei Yu tried to dispel his feelings of guilt by defending himself.

"When did you start having such thoughts?"

"Since I found out that I had tuberculosis and knew I couldn't make you happy."

Again, tuberculosis. Mei's heart pounded. She sensed that the dark shadow of this disease would tear them apart forever. She wanted to curse this godforsaken tuberculosis, but Wei Yu had already resumed speaking.

"Last year I didn't feel this way. Meimei, at that time we were both very shy. We never talked openly about our feelings. But in our hearts we both knew. We thought about each other all the time. At that time I hated myself for being too poor. I resented Uncle for not giving his consent. But recently I've been reading some stories and magazines and my way of thinking has changed. . . ."

"Now you just speak the truth, huh?" There was considerable dismay in her voice as she interrupted him.

"No. I've just come to realize that when you love someone it doesn't mean you have to possess her. To really love someone is to put her happiness ahead of your own. . . ."

"People only say that sort of thing in novels," Mei interrupted Wei Yu a second time. Clearly she was not pleased with what he had to say. Moreover, she did not understand what he meant by "possess."

"It's not from novels. It's philosophy—Tolstoy's philosophy," Wei Yu corrected her earnestly. But noticing Mei's exhausted appearance, he lowered his head and discontinued his argument.

There was a short silence. For the first time they heard the sound of the cicadas chirping among the leaves of the *wutong* tree. The breeze rustled Mei's muslin skirt. The sun shone obliquely on the sides of the pavilion. Mei wrinkled her eyebrows slightly and stared into space. In the end it was Mei who spoke first, her eyes gliding over Wei Yu's face. "That business of yours later this year, has the date been set?"

He replied with a resigned nod of the head. But after a brief interval, he began to defend himself: "It was all my uncle's idea. I told him that right now I'm not in a position to take care of a family, but he refused to listen."

"But did you bring up your tuberculosis and the fact that you have only three or four years to live?"

"No. It wouldn't have done any good."

"Then aren't you going to hurt *her* future?"

Wei Yu looked at Mei with a puzzled expression. For a moment he could not think of an appropriate reply.

"Do you think it's all right because you don't love her? But how can you know that she doesn't love you? How can you turn around and cold-bloodedly ruin the life of someone who loves you?"

"I can't worry about everything. Even if it will destroy her, it's my uncle who is the executioner. I'm only the sword. A sword can't move by itself."

"But when someone wants to throw herself on the blade of this sword, then it is able to come alive, isn't it? Then it is able to move out of the way!"

With this mild rebuttal, Mei turned her back on Wei Yu and began walking slowly toward the pavilion. She could no longer suppress the nagging suspicion, the uncomfortable sensation that gnawed at her insides. Her cousin was too passive, too timid. He was too lazy. Wei Yu only wanted to ensure his own immediate comfort. So much so that he was unwilling to brave danger for the one he loved. He placed his own comfort above all else.

By the time she stepped up onto the stone steps in front of the pavilion she could bear it no longer and turned around. But when she did, it was only to find that Wei Yu was right behind her. His feelings of apprehension brought her to a halt. They looked at each other for several seconds before Wei Yu spoke excitedly. "I'm a weakling, a good-for-nothing weakling. Meimei, you are wrong to love me. But you know what's in my heart. I worship you. To me you are a goddess. I beg you not to be miserable because of me. I beg you to forget me. I beg you to despise me. I beg you, just let me lock my love for you away in my heart; just let me repay your kindness to me with my tears. Ah! I might as well tell you everything. I'm an evil person. Two months ago, in the middle of the night, when I was thinking of you, I found myself hugging the covers passionately, squeezing them so tight, as if they were you. Oh, I'm a beast. It's only in the daytime, when I stand before you, that I become human again, an honest gentleman. I detest myself. When I read stories, when I look at magazines, it is in the hope of deriving some comfort from their pages, in the hope of discovering in their pages a way to save myself and save you. Now I've found it! A glorious ideal has relieved me of my agony, has made up for losing you. Now if I could only see you live a long prosperous life, I would be the happiest man in the world!"

Having said this, Wei Yu opened wide his troubled eyes and stared off into space. It was as if there, beyond the treetops, amid the glow of the setting sun, was the new, glorious ideal to which he owed his salvation. As if there in the distance stood an infinitely compassionate, infinitely sympathetic sage, beckoning to him with a raised hand.

Tears the shape of pearls welled up in his eyes. Was this a natural expression of his humanity, or was it the last remnant of his desire? Wei Yu was not certain himself. He merely felt an extraordinary sense of relief, as though he had just spit out something that had been lodged in his guts a long, long time.

Mei leaned against a pillar of the pavilion engrossed in thought. She did not reply. After a while she turned around and, with a strained expression, said softly, "I know what is in your heart. It's not just fate that's brought us to this impasse, is it? Please don't worry. I understand what you're saying. But please, spare me the philosophy from now on. I also have principles. I refuse to be a prisoner. It's getting late, Cousin Yu. Good-bye!"

Mei turned and took one last look at Wei Yu, then followed the path on the right of the pavilion and walked determinedly away. Wei Yu followed slowly behind her. After about ten steps she stopped, turned around once more, and said to him, "Those stories and magazines you spoke of, I also want to read them. Would you send them to my house?"

Suddenly the evening breeze blew through Mei's muslin blouse, revealing the hem of her pale pink camisole. Like rosy clouds it dazzled Wei Yu's eyes and aroused his passions. Instinctively he rushed forward, about to press Mei to his bosom, but he instantly recovered his composure and stopped. In a daze, he nodded his head, turned toward a different path, and ran away.

Mei returned home bewildered. Her image of Wei Yu had begun to blur. She had always felt she understood Wei Yu completely. Now she was not sure. A few strange books had changed her Wei Yu. But how they had changed him, Mei did not really know. She just felt as though some kind of mysterious spirit had possessed Wei Yu, making his way of thinking different from other people's, different from her own. He had become even more cowardly, even more indifferent. It could even be said that he had become frigid and aloof. But that was not the whole story. Beneath his cowardice he had a new daring and determination; beneath that icy aloofness burned a passionate desire to sacrifice himself for the happiness of another.

There was only one thing of which Mei was still absolutely certain, and that was Wei Yu's faithfulness to her. This gave her incomparable comfort. In imitation of Wei Yu, she had come close to saying, "Even if my future knows no happiness, as long as there is someone who loves me with all his heart, my life will not have been lived in vain."

In such a mood Mei began to feel the days pass more easily. At the same time her native eagerness to explore new things encouraged her to devour the stories and magazines Wei Yu sent over. She thirsted for an immediate knowledge of the mysterious spirit that had changed Wei Yu.

As for the fervent activity of the "patriotic movement," she was still just a bystander. She could not get herself interested. Although the words "inspect the dry goods store for Japanese goods" occasionally upset her, when she thought of her decision "not to be a prisoner" she became inured, feeling that the matter of Japanese products at the dry goods store had, after all, nothing to do with her. She viewed the continued progress of this convulsive mass movement as she had before, as something totally unrelated to her own personal interests.

But the patriotic movement to boycott Japanese goods was slowly developing a new focus. The students of the city's highest educational institution, the Teachers' College, had proclaimed a new slogan: "Liberalize social relations between the sexes." Mei recalled that several of Wei Yu's magazines had mentioned this, but she had not paid it any attention. Following Wei Yu's instructions, she had read only the essays on Tolstoy. The stories were also by Tolstoy. In her excitement she had already read them twice, but they did not seem to say anything about open social relations. With a new curiosity and hope she perused them yet again.

One day on the way home from school Mei caught a glimpse of several eye-catching magazines arranged in the window of a bookseller's shop. Each and every one had the word "new" in the title. On the front covers were also prominently displayed article titles such as "The Cannibalism of Traditional Morality." She looked at them with surprise and joy and regretted that she was not carrying any money. The next day on the way to school she made a point of deliberately stopping in to buy one, but they were all sold out.

Dispirited, she went to school but was in no mood to listen to the lectures. Instead she daydreamed. She imagined that she saw a rush of powerful roaring waves rolling over all that was old and rotten. She was convinced that extraordinary and new things were spreading everywhere. Her small corner of the world was the only place they had not yet reached. And even if they did, she would never get her hands on them. Restlessly she gazed around the room. She despised her dull, lazy, torpid classmates. Then suddenly, unexpectedly, she saw a student, Xu Qijun, sitting not far from her, reading one of the magazines with the word "new" in the title.

After class Mei rushed over to Xu Qijun. Peering over her shoulder, Mei saw that this was the very magazine that had slipped through her fingers. "Ah, I never suspected you were the one who bought it," Mei called out gleefully. She turned half around and leaned on Xu Qijun's shoulder as though they were old friends. Xu turned her head, looked at Mei with dark, penetrating eyes, and said with a smile, "Are these also on sale in the city? Mine were sent to me by my brother in Beijing."

The two classmates, who had barely known each other by sight, suddenly began an intimate conversation. An indescribable but clearly sensed force drew them together. In the course of this animated discussion Mei again heard many strange new terms. Although she did not yet fully understand their meaning, each one gave her a feeling of rapture, of exhilaration. The two girls did not even hear the bell signaling the next class.

When Mei returned home that day she carried under her arm a bundle of magazines, all lent to her by Xu Qijun. Although the weight under her arm had increased, there was a greater spring in her steps. She felt that a new world had opened up before her. She had only to walk in and there would be happiness and light.

Her exploration of the new thought and the sudden acquisition of a new friend made Mei temporarily forget the anxieties evoked by her personal problems. From the crack of dawn when they went to school until the evening when it grew dark, she and Xu Qijun were inseparable. The two of them became a target of gossip at school. Some even suspected them of lesbianism. Summer vacation was near. The dates for final examinations had already been set. But Mei and Xu remained engrossed in the new books and magazines. The only time they opened their textbooks was in class, when they propped them up on their desks to fool their teachers.

Because of Wei Yu's original suggestion, Mei still concentrated on Tolstoy. But Xu seemed to be a disciple of Ibsen. Every other word out of her mouth was Ibsen. Each saw herself as the representative of her chosen writer. In reality, neither really understood the works of these two great masters. They had only a very vague idea of their meaning and even misinterpreted them in many places. But at the same time they shared a common conviction: Tolstoy and Ibsen were both new, and because they were new they were definitely good. This common faith strengthened the girls' friendship and brought their very souls together.

Examinations finally ended. On the evening of July 1, the first day of vacation, Mei's father suddenly took ill. The old man had returned home drunk at eight o'clock. At ten he started complaining of stomach pains, after which he threw up everything he had eaten. He wrote himself a prescription, which he himself prepared, but it had no effect. Mei did not sleep all night. She sat in her father's sickroom, wild and confused thoughts pouring through her agitated mind. Just before dawn her father seemed a bit calmer, but within half an hour he went into a rage over his son's lack of filial piety. Gasping, he jumped up and began ranting about dragging his son back and reporting him to the magistrate for disobedience to his father. All Mei and the maid could do was muster their strength to pull the old man back to bed. This melodrama lasted until eight o'clock the next morning, when the patient finally calmed down and Mei frantically sent for a doctor.

Later that morning, when the patient appeared to be resting easily, Mei returned to her own room to try getting a little sleep. But in her overly excited condition she could do no more than close her burning eyes and let her muddled thoughts overcome her. She pondered the fact that Xu Qijun would be returning home to Chongqing today. Mei's new friend had promised to mail her more new books, but Mei did not know when they would arrive. She also wondered whether her plans to spend the vacation reading would be upset and hoped her father would get well quickly. It also troubled her that Wei Yu had not been by all week. She turned these matters over and over in her mind. Time and again she rolled over to place her feverish cheeks on the coolest part of the mat.* Mei dimly heard the singing of birds in the trees outside her window. The voice of their servant, Auntie Zhou, drifted over from the living room, followed by the shuffle of footsteps. Finally, there was what sounded like a fly buzzing incessantly around her ear.

"Master Liu is here."

As the humming congealed into these words, Mei awakened from her exhausted stupor. She opened her eyes and stared vacantly in front of her. The maid, Chuner, stood grinning at the foot of the bed. Mei frowned and shook her head as if to say, "Don't bother me," then turned over and pretended to be asleep. She had expected him to come. She really had been hoping someone would come to drive away her depression. If only it had not been him! All thought of sleep departed. Mei jumped up and ran to the door to lock it but changed her mind. She left it half opened as before, walked to the window, and sat down in her chair. She spoke softly but proudly to herself: "Will he dare?" The small hand on the belly of the Negro doll showed that it was precisely three o'clock. The oppressive heat of the July sun muted all sound. There was only the chirping of the cicadas in the *wutong* tree outside the window. Mei sat stiffly upright in her chair, as if awaiting some grave omen.

Suddenly the door creaked. Mei watched, startled. The face of Chuner, her thick lips parted, peered in and then quickly withdrew.

"Chuner!"

Mei's stern shout drew Chuner back inside. She stood fearfully in the doorway. Her thick lips, which lent an air of stupidity to her face, were half opened, almost as if to smile.

"Has Master Liu gone yet?"

"He's gone."

"Is my father asleep yet?"

"Not yet. Master Liu and the old master talked a long time. First the old master was happy; then he got angry."

Mei cocked her head and hesitated. She thought this very strange and

---

*   It is a common practice in parts of China to place straw mats on one's bed in summer to avoid the sticky heat of sleeping on sheets.

looked at Chuner's fat face with disbelief. She knew this tricky little girl would not stoop to lying, so maybe she was making a wild guess. But Chuner stepped closer and went on in a whisper, "Master Liu said to the old master that if he and the young mistress got married earlier, the old master could move into Master Liu's house. That way, if he got sick again in the middle of the night he wouldn't have to worry. Auntie Zhou told me your wedding will be next month!"

"Damn!"

Mei's color changed slightly, but she quickly recovered her air of indifference and scrutinized Chuner as if to test the reliability of her words. Then Mei laughed bitterly and asked, "And what did my father say?"

"The old master was very happy. Then I don't know what Master Liu said, but the old master started getting angry. The old master cursed the bastard student troublemakers and the *yamen* for not taking any action."

Mei closed her eyes and sneered. With the words "Button your lip," she ordered Chuner out, and holding her head in her hands, she sank into thought. She guessed what "Master Liu" must have said, but could her father really have agreed to carry it out next month? Mei was extremely upset. Although she had already decided on a way to deal with things, she had hoped they would not come to a head so soon.

That night Mei's father slept peacefully, and by the next day he had nearly recovered. While chatting with him, Mei tried to bring up the subject of her anxieties. Her father spoke to her with vehemence. "It was just some sort of bug, but everyone figured I was on my deathbed. Yuchun even wanted to rush the marriage without allowing time for the necessary arrangements. Heh! That youngster is really shrewd. I intend to live a few more years yet. I want to carry out your wedding with the full ceremony. With the students making such a fuss, who knows how much Yuchun will lose? Naturally, I would prefer that you wait until his business picks up before you get married. He sure knows how to talk. He said that I was getting old, that I was always sick, and that if you two got married soon, he'd have me live with you so he could look after me day and night. Ha! I, Dr. Mei, am not the type who follows his daughter to her husband's house just for a free meal ticket!"

Mei smiled. She knew her father intended to use all of this to get something out of the Lius. The severe criticism of "commercialized marriages" in her magazines immediately sprang to mind. But as long as her father's ideas helped further her own "delaying tactics" she was happy. She expressed the desire to "wait at least until I've graduated from high school," then quickly found a pretext to leave her father's presence.

"Worry about tomorrow when it comes. For the present, just walk the path that lies before you," Mei thought as she sat in her own room. She smiled as she picked up a copy of *Weekly Review** that Xu Qijun had left and began reading it enthusiastically.

Before she had finished a page, she heard the sound of voices coming from the living room. She threw down the magazine and ran out. In the anteroom off her father's bedroom she saw a handsome young man in a military uniform. It was Wei Yu. He had come to inquire about Dr. Mei's illness and say good-bye.

"I've already seen Uncle. Tomorrow I'm leaving for Lüzhou." Wei Yu spoke these words rapidly, then looked intently at Mei. His eyes appeared moist.

Mei forced a smile and, acting the hostess, invited him to come sit in the library. This tiny side room had once served as Dr. Mei's examining room. Then it had been used as the classroom for the children in the family. Recently, it had been abandoned altogether, and although it was still kept spotlessly clean, it already showed signs of disuse. Mei had hurriedly thought of this place so they would not be disturbed.

It took ten minutes for Mei to find out that Wei Yu's unit was starting out for Lüzhou and could end up going into battle. She also discovered that Wei Yu had been promoted to lieutenant. She stared at him. He spoke with exasperating slowness. A million questions lodged in Mei's throat, waiting for a pause to burst out.

"It's because we heard there would be fighting that a lot of the men

---

* Founded in Shanghai in 1919, this Kuomintang, or Nationalist Party, organ was one of the most important new journals to appear during the May Fourth period.

who managed the division's paperwork resigned. So they promoted me a grade. Of course, I don't know how to fight, but when you think about it, it's not so terrible. If I'm killed, that's okay. If I'm lucky enough not to be killed, I'm hoping the experience will improve my health. I think this should stir up my spirit. You see, Meimei, I'm wearing a uniform now. If I can't be a healthy person, I might as well die. This is my last act of courage, my last hope. But there's an eighty or ninety percent chance I'll die. If we lose the battle, I won't be able to escape, someone like me. . . ."

Wei Yu stopped abruptly. Although he felt the iron hand of fate tightly gripping him, the new books and magazines he had been reading of late kept him from letting the final words of self-denigration escape his lips. He cast his eyes downward, then glanced once more around the room. It was still the same old library. Events of ten years ago rushed into his mind. Back then his parents were still alive. Back then he had studied in this very room, sharing the same desk with Mei. Back then they had often pretended that they were bride and groom kneeling before the altar on their wedding day. It was also back then that their two hearts had become inextricably intertwined, inseparable for eternity. Now, now the two hearts were still the same, but everything around them had changed. He had to acknowledge the power of reality. He had to sever the feelings of love he had harbored for ten years. He could not hold back his tears.

Mei did not share his feelings of sorrow. She had been waiting patiently for Wei Yu to continue speaking. When it seemed likely that there would be no more, her questions began pouring out. "When will you be back? Do clerks also have to go to the front? It will take about ten days to get to Lüzhou, won't it? When you're traveling by land, they'll have to give you a sedan chair, won't they?"

This string of questions interrupted Wei Yu's train of thought. He smiled at Mei and replied as slowly as before, "There's no telling with the army. Maybe once we get there we won't fight. Right now no one knows. Even if we do fight, of course they won't send me to the front.

But if we lose I'll need two strong legs to escape. I'd rather get shot at! When will we be back? That's even harder to say."

For a moment it was silent. They exchanged glances. Then Wei Yu laughed bitterly and added, "This could be our last good-bye. I pray, Meimei, that you will have a peaceful and happy future."

Mei smiled knowingly and said with gravity, "I hope when you get to Lüzhou there is a battle. I hope you win. I know you are going to win. I have faith that this will be the beginning of your career. When that happens, when that happens, everything will be different. I'm waiting for that moment."

Smiling again, Mei stood up energetically, like a brave woman seeing her sweetheart off to war. Suddenly she remembered something. Staring strangely at him she whispered, "You probably won't get back this year. What about that matter of yours?"

As he replied, Wei Yu stood up and straightened his uniform. "If we don't return there is nothing they can do about it. They can't send her to Lüzhou, can they? Anyway, who says we'll stay in Lüzhou. When you're dealing with the army, who knows what will happen?"

A sudden gust of wind blew open the glass doors. Outside was a small courtyard with several stalks of bamboo and a flower bed covered with dense moss. Beside the flower bed stood a few broken flower pots filled with scraggly weeds. Mei walked woodenly over to close the doors, then turned and faced Wei Yu. He stood in the doorway, about to leave. She could not help smiling. It was a smile that said, "Our hearts are one," a comforting smile, an approving smile. It was also a smile of hope.

(Translated by Madeleine Zelin)

BA JIN
(1904–2005)

Born Li Feigan to a county magistrate family in Sichuan, Ba Jin was home-schooled due to his poor health. Influenced by the new ideas of anarchism and utopianism, he went to study in France in 1927. Lodging in the Latin Quarter in Paris, he wrote his first novel, Destruction (1929). In 1931 he published Family, the first in his Torrent trilogy, his best-known work: a saga of a family caught in the sweeping currents of change, a window into a nation facing the crossroads. Always sympathetic with the weak and the victimized, his novels and essays moved readers with a profound humanitarian spirit, which, however, did not sit well with prevailing Communist doctrines. He was disgraced during the Cultural Revolution and locked up in cow sheds to do hard labor. In his late years, Ba Jin wrote a series of soul-searching essays, reflecting on the human disaster that had befallen China and its people. Called by many "the conscience of twentieth century Chinese literature," he died in 2005.

Family (excerpts)

10

You can lock up a person physically, but you cannot imprison his heart. Although Juehui did not leave home for the next few days, his thoughts were always with his schoolmates and their struggle. This was something his grandfather could not have foreseen.

Juehui tried to envisage what stage the student movement had reached; he avidly searched the local paper for news. Unfortunately, there was very little. He was able to get hold of a mimeographed weekly, put out by the Students' Federation, which contained quite an amount of good news and a number of stirring articles. Gradually the tension was subsiding, gradually the governor was relenting. Finally, the governor sent his Department Chief to call on the students who had been injured in the riots, and issued two conciliatory proclamations. Moreover he had his secretary write a letter in his name apologizing to the Students' Federation and guaranteeing the safety of the students in the future.

Next, the local press carried an order by the city's garrison commander forbidding soldiers to strike students. It was said that two soldiers who confessed to having taken part in the theater brawl were severely punished. Juexin saw the proclamation posted on the streets, and he told Juehui about it.

With the news improving from day to day, Juehui, a prisoner in his own home, grew increasingly restless. He paced alone in his room, too fretful at times even to read. Or he lay flat on his bed, staring up at the canopy above.

"'Home. Home, sweet home!'" he would fume.

Hearing him, Juemin would smile and say nothing.

"What's so funny!" Juehui raged, on one of these occasions. "You go out every day, free as a bird! But just watch out. Some fine day you're going to end up like me yourself!"

"My smiling has nothing to do with you. Can't I even smile?" retorted Juemin with a grin.

"No, you can't. I won't let you smile! I won't let anyone smile!"

Juemin closed the book he had been reading and quietly left the room. He didn't want to argue.

"Home, a fine home! A narrow cage, that's what it is!" Juehui shouted, pacing the floor. "I'm going out. I must go out. Let's see what they're going to do about it!" And he rushed from the room.

Going down the steps into the courtyard, he spied Mistress Chen and Aunt Shen (the wife of his uncle Keding) sitting on the veranda outside his grandfather's room. Juehui hesitated, then made a detour around his brother Juexin's quarters and entered the large garden.

Passing through a moon-gate, he came to a man-made hill. The paved path he was following here forked into two branches. He chose the one to the left, which went up the slope. Narrow and twisting, it led through a tunnel. When Juehui emerged again on the other side, the path started downward. A delicate fragrance assailed his nostrils, and he struck off in the direction from which it seemed to be coming. Moving down slowly through the bushes, he discovered another small path to the left. Just as he was turning to it, the view before him suddenly opened up, and he saw a great sea of pink blossoms. Below was a plum tree grove with branches in full flower. Entering the grove, he strolled along the petal-strewn ground, pushing aside the low-hanging branches.

In the distance, he caught a glimpse of something blue shimmering through the haze of plum blossoms. As he drew nearer, he saw it was a person dressed in blue coming in his direction over the zigzag stone bridge. A girl, wearing a long braid down her back. Juehui recognized the bondmaid Mingfeng.

Before he could call to her, she entered the pavilion on the isle in the middle of the lake. He waited for her to emerge on the near side. But after several minutes there was still no sign of her. Juehui was puzzled. Finally, she appeared, but she was not alone. With her was another girl, wearing a short purple jacket. The tall girl's back was toward him as she chatted with Mingfeng, and he could only see her long plait, not her face. But as they came closer over the zigzag bridge leading from the near side of the isle, he got a look at her. It was Qianer, a bondmaid in the household of his uncle Ke'an.

As the girls neared the shore, he hid among the plum trees.

"You go back first. Don't wait for me. I still have to gather some blossoms for Madam Zhou," said Mingfeng's crisp voice.

"All right. That Madam Wang of mine is a great talker. If I'm out too long she'll grumble at me for hours." Going through the grove of plums, Qianer departed along the path by which Juehui had just come.

As soon as Qianer disappeared around a bend, Juehui stepped out and walked toward Mingfeng. She was breaking off a low-hanging branch.

"What are you doing, Mingfeng?" he called with a smile.

Concentrating on her task, Mingfeng hadn't seen him approach. She turned around, startled, on hearing his voice. She gave a relieved laugh when she recognized him. "I couldn't imagine who it was! So it's you, Third Young Master!" She went on breaking the branch.

"Who told you to gather blossoms at this hour of the day? Don't you know that early morning is the best time?"

"Madam Zhou said Mrs. Zhang wants some. Second Young Master is going to take them over." Mingfeng stretched for a branch that was heavily laden with blossoms, but she couldn't reach it, even standing on tiptoe.

"I'll get it for you. You're still too short. In another year or so you might make it," said Juehui, grinning.

"All right, you get it for me, please. But don't let Madam know." Mingfeng stepped aside to make room for Juehui.

"Why are you so afraid of Madam Zhou? She's not so bad. Has she scolded you again lately?" Juehui reached up and twisted the branch back and forth, twice. It snapped off. He handed it to Mingfeng.

"No, she doesn't scold me very often. But I'm always scared I'll do something wrong," she replied in a low voice, accepting the branch.

"That's called—Once a slave, always a slave! . . ." Juehui laughed, but he wasn't intending to deride Mingfeng.

The girl buried her face in the blossoms she was holding.

"Look, there's a good one," Juehui said cheerfully.

She raised her head and smiled. "Where?"

"Don't you see it? Over there." He pointed at a branch of a nearby tree, and her gaze followed his finger.

"Ah, yes. It has lovely blossoms. But it's too high."

"High? I can take care of that." Juehui measured the tree with his eye. "I'll climb up and break the branch off." He began unfastening his padded robe.

"No, don't," said Mingfeng. "If you fall you'll hurt yourself."

"It's all right." Juehui hung his robe over a branch of another tree. Underneath, he was wearing a close-fitting green padded jacket. As he started up the tree, he said to Mingfeng, "You stand here and hold the tree firm."

Setting his feet on two sturdy branches, he stretched his hand toward the blossom-laden branch he was after. It was out of reach, and his exertions shook the whole tree, bringing down a shower of petals.

"Be careful, Third Young Master, be careful!" cried Mingfeng.

"Don't worry," he responded. Cautiously maneuvering himself into another position, he was able to grasp the elusive branch. With a few twists, he snapped it off. Looking down, he saw the girl's upturned face.

"Here, Mingfeng, catch!" He tossed her the branch. When it was safely in Mingfeng's hand, he slowly climbed down the tree. "Enough," she said happily. "I've got three now; that's plenty."

"Right. Any more and Second Young Master won't be able to carry them all," laughed Juehui, taking up his robe. "Have you seen him around?"

"He's reciting by the fish pond. I heard his voice," Mingfeng replied, arranging the flowers in her hand. Observing that Juehui had only draped his robe over his shoulders, she urged, "Put it on. You'll catch cold that way."

As Juehui was putting his arms through the sleeves, the girl began walking off along the path. He called after her:

"Mingfeng!"

Stopping, she turned around and asked with a smile, "What is it?" But when he didn't answer, and only stood smiling at her, she again turned and walked away.

Juehui hastily followed, calling her name. Again she halted and turned. "Yes?"

"Come over here," he pleaded.

She walked up to him.

"You seem to be afraid of me lately. You don't even like to talk to me. What's wrong?" he asked, half in jest, toying with an overhanging branch.

"Who's afraid of you?" Mingfeng replied with a gurgle of laughter. "I'm busy from morning till night. I just haven't the time for talk." She turned to go.

Juehui held out a restraining hand. "It's true. You *are* afraid of me. If you're so busy, how do you have time to play with Qianer? I saw you two just now in the isle pavilion."

"What right have I to chat with you? You're a Young Master; I'm only a bondmaid," Mingfeug retorted distantly.

"But before we used to play together all the time. Why should it be any different now?" was Juehui's warm rejoinder.

The girl's brilliant eyes swept his face. Then she dropped her head and replied in a low voice, "It's not the same now. We're both grown up."

"What difference does that make? Our hearts haven't become bad!"

"People will talk if we're always together. There are plenty of gossipers around. It doesn't matter about me, but you should be careful. You have to uphold your dignity as one of the masters. It doesn't matter about me. I was fated to be just a cheap little bondmaid!" Mingfeng still spoke quietly, but there was a touch of bitterness in her voice.

"Don't leave. We'll find a place to sit down and have a long talk. I'll take the blossoms." Without waiting for an answer, he took the branches from her hands. Surveying them critically, he broke off two or three twigs and threw them away.

He set off along a small path between the plum grove and the edge of the lake, and she silently followed him. From time to time, he turned his head to ask her a question. She answered briefly, or responded with only a smile.

Leaving the grove, they crossed a rectangular flower terrace, then went through a small gate. About ten paces beyond was a tunnel. The tunnel was dark, but it was quite straight and not very long. Inside, you could hear the gurgling of spring water. On the other side of the tunnel, the path slanted upward. They mounted about two dozen stone steps, followed a few more twists and turns, and at last reached the top.

In the center of the small graveled summit was a little stone table with a round stone stool on each of its four sides. A cypress, growing beside the flat face of a large boulder, spread its branches in a sheltering canopy.

All was still except for the chuckling of a hidden brook, flowing somewhere beneath the rocks.

"How peaceful," said Juehui. He placed the blossoms on the table; after wiping the dust off one of the stone stools, he sat down. Mingfeng seated herself opposite him. They couldn't see each other clearly because of the blossoms heaped between them on the little table.

With a laugh, Juehui shifted the branches to the stool on his right. Pointing to the stool on his left, he said to Mingfeng, "Sit over here. Why are you afraid to be close to me?"

Silently, Mingfeng moved to the place he had indicated.

They faced each other, letting their eyes speak, letting their eyes say the many things words would not express.

"I must go. I can't stay too long in the garden. Madam will scold me if she finds out." Mingfeng stood up.

Taking her arm, Juehui pulled her down again to the seat. "It doesn't matter. She won't say anything. Don't go yet. We've just come. We haven't talked at all. I won't let you go!"

She shrank a bit from his touch, but made no further protest.

"Why don't you say anything? No one can hear us. Don't you like me anymore?" Juehui teased. He pretended to be very downcast.

The girl remained silent. It was as if she hadn't heard him.

"You're probably tired of working for our family. I'll tell Madam that you're grown up now, to send you away," Juehui said idly, with affected unconcern. Actually he was watching her reaction closely.

Mingfeng turned pale, and the light went out of her eyes. But her trembling lips did not speak. Her eyes glistened like glass, and her lashes fluttered. "You mean it?" she asked. Tears rolled down her cheeks.

Juehui knew his teasing had gone too far. He hadn't meant to hurt her. He was only testing her; and he wanted to pay her back for that cold remark. It had not occurred to him that his words could cause her so much pain. He was both satisfied and regretful over the results of his experiment.

"I'm only joking." He laughed. "You don't think I'd really send you away?" But his laughter was forced, for he had been very moved by her emotion.

"Who knows whether you would or not? You masters and mistresses are all as changeable as the winds. When you're displeased there's no telling what you'll do," sobbed Mingfeng. "I've always known that, sooner or later, I'd go the road of Xi'er, but why must it be so soon?"

"What do you mean?" Juehui asked gently.

"What you said. . . ." Mingfeng still wept.

"I was only teasing you. I'll never let that happen to you," he said earnestly. Taking her hand and placing it on his knee, he caressed it soothingly.

"But suppose that's what Madam Zhou wants," demanded Mingfeng, raising her tear-stained face.

He gazed into her eyes for a moment without replying. Then he said firmly, "I can take care of that, I can make her listen to me. I'll tell her I want to marry—" Mingfeng's hand over his mouth cut him short. He was quite sincere in what he was saying, although he hadn't really given the matter much thought.

"No, no, you mustn't do that!" the girl cried. "Madam would never agree. That would finish everything. You mustn't speak to her. I just wasn't fated. . . ."

"Don't be so frightened." He removed her hand from his mouth as he said this. "Your face is all streaked with tears. Let me. . . ." He carefully wiped her face with his handkerchief. This time she did not draw back. Wiping the tear-stains, he said with a smile, "Women cry so easily." He laughed sadly.

Mingfeng smiled, but it was a melancholy smile, and she said slowly, "I won't cry anymore after this. Working for your family I've shed too many tears already. Here together with you, I certainly shouldn't cry. . . ."

"Everything will be all right. We're both still young. When the time comes, I'll speak to Madam. I definitely will work something out, I mean it," he said comfortingly, still caressing her hand.

"I know your heart," she replied, touched. Somewhat reassured, she went on, half in a reverie, "I've been dreaming about you a lot lately. Once I dreamed I was running through the mountains, chased by a pack of wild animals. Just as they almost caught me, someone rushed down the slope and drove them away. And who do you think it was? You. I've always thought of you as my savior!"

"I didn't know. I didn't realize you had so much faith in me." Juehui's voice shook. He was deeply moved. "I haven't taken nearly good enough care of you. I don't know how to face you. Are you angry with me?"

"How could I be?" She shook her head and smiled. "All my life I've loved only three people. One was my mother. The second was the Elder Young Miss—she taught me to read and to understand many things; she was always helping me. Now both of them are dead. Only one more remains. . . ."

"Mingfeng, when I think of you I'm ashamed of myself. I live in comfort, while you have such a hard time. Even my little sister scolds you!"

"I'm used to it, after seven years. It's much better now, anyhow. I don't mind so much. . . . I only have to see you, to think of you, and I can stand anything. I often speak your name to myself, though I'd never dare say it aloud in anyone else's presence."

"You suffer too much, Mingfeng! At your age, you ought to be in school. A bright girl like you. I bet you'd be even better than Qin. . . . How wonderful it would be if you had been born in a rich family, or even in a family like Qin's!" Juehui said regretfully.

"I never hoped to be a rich young miss; I'm not that lucky. All I want is that you don't send me away, that I stay here and be your bondmaid all my life. . . . You don't know how happy I am just seeing you. As long as you're near me, my heart's at ease. . . . You don't know how I respect you. But sometimes you're like the moon in the sky. I know I can't reach you."

"Don't talk like that. I'm just an ordinary person, the same as everyone else." His low voice trembled and tears rolled from his eyes.

"Be quiet," she warned suddenly, grasping his arm. "Listen. Someone's down there."

They both listened. The sound, when it reached them, was very faint. Mingled with the babble of the hidden spring, it was difficult to distinguish clearly. They finally recognized it as the voice of Juemin singing.

"Second Young Master is going back to the house." Juehui rose and walked to the edge of the hilltop. He could see a small figure in gray flitting through the pink haze of the plum blossoms. Turning to Mingfeng he said, "It's Second Young Master, all right."

Mingfeng hastily rose to her feet. "I must go back. I've been out here too long. . . . It's probably nearly dinnertime."

Juehui handed her the plum blossoms. "If Madam Zhou asks why you're so late, make up an excuse—anything will do. . . . Say I asked you to do something for me."

"All right. I'll go back first, so we won't be seen together." Mingfeng smiled at him, and started down the slope.

He walked with her a few steps, then stood and watched her slowly descend the stone stairway and disappear around the face of a bluff.

Alone, he paced the hilltop, all his thoughts devoted to Mingfeng. "She's so pure, so good . . ." he murmured. Walking over to the little table, he sat down opposite the place she had just vacated, and, resting his elbows on the stone surface, supported his head in his hands and gazed off into the distance. "You're pure, truly pure . . ." he whispered.

After a while, he rose abruptly, as if awakening from a dream. He looked all around him, then hurried down the path.

ııııııııııııı

THE MOONLIGHT WAS lovely that night. Juehui couldn't sleep. At one in the morning, he was still strolling about the courtyard.

"Why aren't you in bed, Third Brother? It's cold out here." Juemin had come out and was standing on the steps.

"With a beautiful moon like this, sleep is a waste of time," Juehui replied carelessly.

Juemin walked down the steps into the courtyard. He shivered. "It's cold," he repeated, and raised his head to look at the moon.

There wasn't a cloud in the night sky. A full moon sailed through a limitless firmament, alone, chaste, its beams lulling all into slumber, coating the ground and the roof tiles with silver. The night was still.

"Lovely." Juemin sighed. "A perfect example of 'moonlight like frost.'" And he joined Juehui in his stroll. But the younger boy remained silent.

"Qin is really intelligent . . . and brave. A fine girl," Juemin couldn't refrain from commenting, a pleased smile on his face.

Juehui still said nothing, for his mind was occupied by another girl. He walked slowly behind his brother.

"Do you like her? Are you in love with her?" Juemin suddenly grabbed him by the arm.

"Of course," Juehui replied automatically. But he immediately amended, "Who are you talking about? Sister Qin? I don't really know. But I think *you* love her."

"That's right." Juemin was still gripping his arm. "I love her, and I think she could love me too. I haven't said anything to her yet. I don't know what to do. . . . What about you? You said you also love her."

From the sound of his voice and the way his fingers trembled on Juehui's arm, the younger boy could tell that his brother was highly agitated, even without seeing his face. Lightly he patted Juemin's hand and said with a smile, "Go to it. I'm not competing with you. I wish you success. I love Qin only like an elder sister."

Juemin did not reply. He stared at the moon for a long time. At last, when he had calmed down somewhat, he said to Juehui, "You're really a good brother. I was wrong about you; it got me all upset. I don't know what makes me so jealous lately. Even when I see Jianyun and Qin talking together, I feel annoyed. Do you think I'm silly? Are you laughing at me?"

"No, I'm not laughing at you," Juehui answered sincerely. "I sympathize with you. Don't worry. I don't think Jianyun will compete with you either." Then in another tone of voice, "Listen, what's that?"

A sound like quiet, subdued weeping spread softly, pervading every corner of the moonlit night. It was not a human voice, nor was it the cry of a bird or insect. The sound was much too light, too clear, for that. At times it seemed to rise in pitch, a persuasive plaint issued directly from the soul. Then it slowly faded again until it became almost inaudible, like the merest hint of a breeze. But one was still aware of a vibration in the atmosphere, charging the very air with sadness.

"What is it?" Juehui repeated.

"Big Brother playing a bamboo flute. The past few nights, he's been playing only when it's very late. I hear him every night."

"What's troubling him? He wasn't like this before. That bamboo flute has such a mournful sound!"

"I don't know exactly. I think it's probably because he's heard that Cousin Mei has come back to Chengdu. That must be it. He keeps playing those same mournful tunes, and always so late at night. . . . He probably is still in love with her. . . . I haven't been sleeping well the past few nights. I keep hearing his flute. It seems to carry a warning, a threat. . . . I'm in practically the same situation with Qin now as Big Brother was with Cousin Mei. When I hear that flute I can't help fearing I'll go the same road as he. I don't dare to even think about it. I'm afraid I couldn't live if it ever came to that. I'm not like him." Juemin's voice shook with emotion. He was almost in tears.

"Don't worry. You'll never go Big Brother's road," Juehui consoled him. "Times have changed."

He looked up again at the full moon, bathing the night with its limitless radiance. An irresistible strength seemed to well up within him as he thought of Mingfeng.

"You're so pure," he murmured. "You alone are as unsullied as the moon!"

24

One night, after the electric lights in the compound had been turned off, Mingfeng was called to the apartment of Madam Zhou. The fat face of the older woman was expressionless in the feeble glow of an oil lamp. Although she could not guess what Madam Zhou was going to say, all day Mingfeng had a premonition that something bad was about to happen to her. She stood before Madam Zhou with trembling heart and gazed at her unsteadily. They both were silent. The fat face seemed to swell gradually into a large, round object that wavered before Mingfeng's eyes, increasing her feeling of fear.

"Mingfeng, you've been with us for several years. I think you've worked long enough." Madam Zhou began very deliberately, though still speaking more quickly than most people. After these first few words, her speed increased, until the syllables were popping from her lips like little pellets.

"I'm sure you also are quite willing to leave," she continued. "Today, Venerable Master Gao instructed me to send you to the Feng family. You are going to be the concubine of the Venerable Master Feng. The first of next month is an auspicious day; they will call for you then. Today is the twenty-seventh. That still leaves four days. From tomorrow on, you needn't do any work. Take things easy for the next few days, until you go to the Feng family. . . .

"After you get there, be sure to take good care of the old man and the old lady. They say he's rather strange; his wife's temper is none too good either. Don't be stubborn; it's best to go along with their whims. They also have sons and daughters-in-law and grandchildren living together with them. You must respect them too.

"You've been a bondmaid in our family for several years, but you haven't gained anything from it. To tell you the truth I don't think we've treated you very well. Now that we've arranged this marriage for you I feel much better. The Feng family is very rich. As long as you remember to act according to your station, you'll never want for food or clothing. You'll be much better off than Fifth Household's Xi'er. . . .

"I'll think of you after you leave. You've looked after me all these years and I've never done anything to reward you. Tomorrow I'll have the tailor make you two new sets of good clothing and I'll give you a little jewelry." The sound of Mingfeng's weeping interrupted her.

Although every word cut the girl's heart like a knife, she could only let them stab. She had no weapon with which to defend herself. Her hopes were completely shattered. They even wanted to take away the love she depended upon to live, to present her verdant spring to a crabbed old man. Life as a concubine in a family like the Fengs could bring only one reward: tears, blows, abuse, the same as before. The only difference would be that now, in addition, she would have to give her body to be despoiled by a peculiar old man whom she had never met.

To become a concubine—what a disgrace. Among the bondmaids "concubine" was one of the worst imprecations they would think of. Ever since she was very small Mingfeng felt that it was a terrible thing to be a concubine. Yet after eight years of hard work and faithful service that was her only reward.

The road ahead looked very black. Even the thread of light which her pure love had brought her, even that was snapped. A fine young face floated before her. Then many ugly visages leered at her, horribly. Frightened, she covered her eyes with her hands, struggling against this terrifying vision.

Suddenly she seemed to hear a voice say, "Everything is decided by Fate. There is nothing you can do about it." An overwhelming disappointment took possession of her, and she wept brokenheartedly.

Words were flying from Madam Zhou so fast it was difficult for her to stop at once. But when she heard the girl's tragic weeping, she paused in surprise. She couldn't understand why Mingfeng was so upset, but she was moved by her tears.

"What's wrong, Mingfeng?" she asked. "Why are you crying?"

"Madam, I don't want to go!" sobbed Mingfeng. "I'd rather be a bondmaid here all my life, looking after you, and the young masters and the young mistresses. Madam, don't send me away, I beg you. There's still a lot I can do here. I've only been here eight years. I'm still so young, Madam. Please don't make me marry yet."

Madam Zhou's maternal instincts were seldom aroused, but Mingfeng's impassioned pleas struck a responsive chord. The older woman was swept by a feeling of motherly love and pity for the girl.

"I was afraid you wouldn't be willing," she said with a sad smile. "It's true, the Venerable Master Feng is old enough to be your grandfather. But that's what our Venerable Master has decided. I must obey him.

After you get there, if you serve the old man well, things won't be so bad. Anyhow you'll be much better off than married to some poor workingman, never knowing where your next meal is coming from."

"Madam, I'm willing to starve—anything but become a concubine." As Mingfeng blurted these words, the strength drained from her body, and she fell to her knees. Embracing Madam Zhou's legs, she begged, "Please don't send me away. Let me stay here as a bondmaid. I'll serve you all my life. . . . Madam, have pity, I'm still so young. Pity me. You can scold me, beat me, anything—only don't send me to the Feng family. I'm afraid. I couldn't bear that kind of life. Madam, be merciful, pity me. Madam, I've always been obedient, but this—I can't do it!"

Endless words were welling up from her heart into her throat, but something seemed to be stopping her mouth, and she could only swallow them down again and weep softly. The more she cried the more stricken she felt. The tragedy was too overwhelming. If only she could cry her heart out, she might have some relief.

Looking at the girl weeping at her feet, Madam Zhou was reminded of her own past. Sadly, maternally, she stroked Mingfeng's hair.

"I know you're too young," she said sympathetically. "To tell you the truth, I'm against your going to the Feng family. But our Venerable Master has already promised. He's the kind who never goes back on his word. I'm only his daughter-in-law. I don't dare oppose him. It's too late. On the first, you must go. Don't cry. Crying won't do any good. Just gather your courage and go. Maybe your life will be comfortable there. Don't be afraid. People with good hearts always get their just rewards. Get up now. It's time for you to be in bed."

Mingfeng hugged Madam Zhou's legs tighter, as if they were the only things that could save her. With her last strength she cried despondently, "Don't you have even a little pity for me, Madam? Save me. I'd rather die than go to the Feng family!"

Raising her tear-stained face, she looked into Madam Zhou's eyes and stretched forth her hands pleadingly. "Save me, Madam!" Her voice was tragic.

Madam Zhou shook her head. "There's nothing I can do," she replied sadly. "I don't want you to go, myself, but it's no use. Even I can't go against the decision of the Venerable Master. Get up now, and go to bed like a good girl." She pulled Mingfeng to her feet.

Mingfeng offered no resistance. All hope was gone. She stood dazedly before Madam Zhou, feeling that she was in a dream. After a moment, she looked around. Everything was dim and dark. She was still sobbing soundlessly. Finally, she brought herself under control. In a dull, melancholy tone she said, "I'll do what you say, Madam."

Madam Zhou rose wearily. "Good. As long as you're obedient I won't have to worry about you."

Mingfeng knew it was no use to remain any longer. She had never been so miserable in her life. "I'm going to bed, Madam," she said listlessly. She slowly walked from the room; her hand pressed to her breast. She was afraid her heart would burst.

Madam Zhou sighed as she watched the girl's retreating back, sorry that she was unable to help her. But, half an hour later, this comfortable, well-fed lady had forgotten all about Mingfeng.

The courtyard was dark and deserted. Feeble lamplight gleamed in Juehui's window. Originally Mingfeng had intended to return to the servants' room but now, seeing the light, she walked softly toward Juehui's quarters. The light was seeping through the tiny openings in the curtain, casting a pretty pattern on the ground. That curtain, the glass windows, that room, now seemed particularly adorable to Mingfeng. She stood on the stone porch outside the window and gazed unwinking at the white gauze curtain, holding her breath and being as quiet as possible so as not to disturb the boy inside.

Gradually, she imagined she could see colors on the white curtain; they became even more beautiful. Beautiful people emerged from the maze of color—boys and girls, very handsomely dressed, with proud and haughty bearing. They cast disdainful glances at her as they passed, then hurried on. Suddenly, the one she thought of day and night appeared in their midst. He gazed at her affectionately and halted, as if he wanted to speak to her. But crowds of people came hurrying and pushing from behind him, and he disappeared among them. Her eyes sought him intently, but the white gauze curtain, hanging motionless, concealed the interior of the room from view.

Mingfeng drew closer, hoping to get a look inside, but the window was higher than her head, and after two unsuccessful attempts, she stepped back, disappointed. As she did so, her hand accidentally bumped against the windowsill, making a slight noise. From within the room came a cough. That meant he wasn't asleep. She stared at the curtain. Would he push it aside and look out?

But inside it became quiet again, except for the low sound of a pen scratching on paper. Mingfeng rapped softly against the windowsill. She heard what sounded like a chair being shifted, then the scratching of the pen again, a bit faster. Mingfeng was afraid if she rapped any harder, she might be overheard. Juemin slept in the same room. Clutching a final hope, she again tapped, three times, and called softly, "Third Young Master." Stepping back, she waited quietly. She was sure he would come out this time. But again there was nothing but the rapid scratching of the pen and the low surprised remark, "Two a.m. already? . . . And I've a class at eight in the morning. . . ." And the sound of the writing resumed once more.

Mingfeng stood dully. Tapping again would be no use. He wouldn't hear it. She didn't blame him, in fact she loved him all the more. His words were still in her ears, and to her they were sweeter than music. He seemed to be standing beside her—so warm, so very much alive.

He needed a girl to love him and take care of him, and there was no one in the world who loved him more than she. She would do anything for him. But she also knew there was a wall between them. People wanted to send her to the Feng family, soon too, in four days. Then she would belong to the Fengs; she'd have no opportunity to see him again. No matter how she might be insulted and abused, he'd have no way of knowing. He wouldn't be able to save her. They'd be separated, forever separated. It would be worse than if they had been parted by death.

Mingfeng felt that a life of that kind was not worth living. When she had said to Madam Zhou, "I'd rather die than go to the Feng family," she had meant it. She was really considering death. The Eldest Young Miss had often told her that suicide was the only way out for girls who were the victims of Fate. Mingfeng believed this fully.

A long sigh from the room broke in on her wild thoughts. Mournfully, she looked around. All was still and very dark. Suddenly she remembered a similar scene of several months ago. Only that time he had been outside her window, and the conjecture he had overheard then had today become a reality. She recalled all the details—his attitude toward her, how she had said to him, "I'll never go to another man. I give my vow."

Something seemed to be wringing her heart, and she was blinded by tears. The lamplight from the window shone down on her head pitilessly. Eagerly she gazed at the beams, a hope slowly forming in her breast. She would cast all caution to the winds, rush into his room, kneel at his feet, tell him her whole bitter story, beg him to save her. She would be his slave forever, love him, take care of him.

But just then, everything went black. The lamp had been turned out. She stared, but she could see nothing. Rooted to the spot, she stood alone in the night, the merciless night that hemmed her in from all sides.

After a few moments, she finally was able to move. Slowly she groped her way through the disembodied darkness toward her own room. After a long time, she reached the women servants' quarters. She pushed open the half-closed door and went in.

A wick was sputtering feebly in a dish of oil. The rest of the room was all darkness and shadows. Beds on both sides of the room were laden with corpse-like figures. Harsh snores from the bed of the fat Sister Zhang struck out in every direction in a very frightening manner. They halted the startled Mingfeng in the doorway, and for a moment she peered anxiously around. Then with dragging feet she walked over to the table and trimmed the wick. The room became much brighter.

About to take off her clothes, Mingfeng was suddenly crushed by a terrible depression. She threw herself on her bed and began to cry, pressing her head against the bedding and soaking it with her tears.

The more she thought, the worse she felt. Old Mama Huang, awakened by the sound of her weeping, asked in a muzzy voice, "What are you crying about?"

Mingfeng did not answer. She only wept. After offering a soothing word or two, Mama Huang turned over and was soon fast asleep again. Mingfeng was left alone with her heartbroken tears. She continued to cry until sleep claimed her.

By the next morning Mingfeng had changed into a different person. She stopped smiling, she moved in a leaden manner, she avoided people. She suspected they knew about her; she imagined they were smiling disdainfully, and she hurried to get away. If she saw a few servants talking together, she was sure they were discussing her. She seemed to hear the word "concubine" everywhere, even among the masters and mistresses.

"Such a pretty girl," she thought she heard the Fifth Master say. "It's a shame to make her a concubine of that old man."

In the kitchen she heard the fat Sister Zhang angrily comment, "A young girl like that becoming the 'little wife' of an old man who's half dead! I wouldn't do it for all the money in the world!"

It got so that Mingfeng was afraid to go anywhere for fear of hearing contemptuous remarks. Except when she had to join the other servants for her two meals a day, she hid in her room or in the garden, alone and lonely. Once in a while, Xi'er or Qianer came to see her. But they were both very busy, and they could only steal out briefly for a comforting word or two.

Mingfeng wanted very much to speak to Juehui, and she was constantly seeking an opportunity. But lately he and Juemin were busier than usual. They left for school very early each morning and came home late in the afternoon. Sometimes they had dinner out. But even when they ate at home, they would go out again immediately after the evening meal and not return until nine or ten at night. Then they would shut themselves in their room and read, or write articles. On the one or two occasions she happened to meet Juehui, he gave a tender glance or a smile, but did not speak to her. Of course these were signs of his love, and she knew he was busy with serious affairs; even though he had no time for her, she did not blame him.

But the days were passing, quickly. She simply had to speak to him, to pour out her troubles, to seek his help. He didn't seem to have any inkling of what was happening to her, and he gave her no chance to tell him.

Now it was the last day of the month. Not many people in the compound knew about Mingfeng. Juehui was completely in the dark. He was all wrapped up in the weekly magazine. Even the hours he spent at home were devoted to study and writing; he had no contact with anyone who might have told him about Mingfeng.

To Juehui the thirtieth was the same as any other day. But for Mingfeng it was the day of reckoning: either she would leave him forever or serve him forever. The latter possibility was very slim, and Mingfeng knew it. Naturally she was hopeful that he would be able to save her and that she could remain his devoted servant always. But between them was a wall which could not be demolished—their difference in status.

Mingfeng knew this very well. That day in the garden when she had said to him, "No, no. I just wasn't fated," she already knew. He had replied that he would marry her. But his grandfather, Madam Zhou, and all the elders were arrayed against them. What could he do? Even Madam Zhou didn't dare go against a decision of the Venerable Master Gao. What chance would a grandson stand?

Mingfeng's fate was irrevocably decided. But she couldn't give up the last shred of hope. She was fooling herself, really, for she knew there wasn't the slightest hope, and never could be.

She waited to see Juehui that day with a trembling heart. He came home after nine in the evening. She walked to his window. Hearing the voice of his brother, she hesitated, afraid to go in but unwilling to leave. If she gave up this last opportunity, whether she lived or died, she would never be able to see him again.

At long last Mingfeng heard footsteps. Someone was coming out. She quickly hid in a corner. A dark figure emerged from the room. It was Juemin. She waited until he was some distance away, then hurried into the room.

Juehui was bent over his desk, writing. He did not look up as he heard her enter, but continued with his work. Mingfeng timidly approached.

"Third Young Master," she called gently.

"Mingfeng, it's you?" Juehui raised his head in surprise. He smiled at her. "What is it?"

"I have to speak to you." Her melancholy eyes avidly scanned his smiling face. Before she could go on, he interrupted:

"Is it because I haven't talked with you these last few days? You think I've been ignoring you?" He laughed tenderly. "No, you mustn't think that. You see how busy I am. I have to study and write, and I've other things to do too." Juehui pointed at a pile of manuscripts and magazines. "I'm as busy as an ant. It will be better in a day or two. I'll have finished this work by then. I promise you. Only two more days."

"Two more days?" Mingfeng cried, disappointed. As if she hadn't understood, she asked again, "Two more days?"

"That's right," said Juehui with a smile. "In two more days I'll be finished. Then we can talk. There's so much I want to tell you." He again bent over his writing.

"Third Young Master, don't you have any time now, even a little?" Mingfeng held back her tears with an effort.

"Can't you see I'm busy?" said Juehui roughly, as if reproving her for persisting. But when he observed her stricken expression and the tears in her eyes, he immediately softened. Taking her hand, he stood up and asked soothingly, "Has someone been picking on you? Don't feel badly."

He really wanted to put aside his work and take her into the garden and comfort her. But when he remembered that he had to submit his article by the next morning, when he recalled the struggle the magazine was waging, he changed his mind.

"Be patient," he pleaded. "In another two days we'll have a long talk. I definitely will help you. I love you as much as ever. But please go now and let me finish my work. You'd better hurry. Second Young Master will be back in a minute."

Juehui looked around to make sure that they were alone, then took her face in his hands and lightly kissed her lips. Smiling, he indicated with a gesture that she should leave quickly. He resumed his position at the desk, pen in hand, but his heart was pounding. It was the first time he had ever kissed her.

Mingfeng stood dazed and silent. She didn't know what she was thinking or how she felt. Her fingers moved up to touch her lips—lips that had just experienced their first kiss. "Two more days," she repeated.

Outside, someone was heard approaching, whistling. "Go, quickly," Juehui urged. "Second Young Master is coming."

Mingfeng seemed to awake from a dream and her expression changed. Her lips trembled, but she did not speak. She gazed at him longingly with the utmost tenderness, and her eyes suddenly shone with tears. "Third Young Master," she cried in an anguished voice.

Juehui looked up quickly, only to see her disappearing through the doorway.

He sighed. "Women are strange creatures." He again bent over his writing.

Juemin came into the room. The first words out of his mouth were, "Wasn't that Mingfeng who just left here?"

"Yes." Juehui continued writing. He did not look at his brother.

"That girl isn't the least bit like an ordinary bondmaid. She's intelligent, pure, pretty—she can even read a little. It's a shame that Ye-ye is giving her to that old reprobate for a concubine. It's a real shame!" sighed Juemin.

"What did you say?" Juehui put down his pen. He was shocked.

"Don't you know? Mingfeng is getting married."

"She's getting married? Who said so? She's too young!"

"Ye-ye is giving her to that shameless old scoundrel Feng to be his concubine."

"I don't believe it! Why, he's one of the main pillars of the Confucian Morals Society. He's nearly sixty. He still wants a concubine?"

"Don't you remember last year when he and a couple of his old cronies published a list of 'Best Female Impersonators' and were bitterly attacked by *Students' Tide*? His kind are capable of anything. He gets away with it too—he's got money, hasn't he? The wedding day is tomorrow. I certainly am sorry for Mingfeng. She's only seventeen."

"Tomorrow? Why wasn't I told before? Why didn't anyone tell me?" Juehui jumped to his feet and hurried out, clutching his hair. He was trembling all over.

"Tomorrow"! "Marry"! "Concubine"! "Old Feng"! The words lashed against Juehui's brain till he thought it would shatter. He rushed out; he thought he heard a mournful wail. Suddenly he discovered a dark world lying at his feet. All was quiet, as if every living thing had died. Where was he to go in this misty space between heaven and earth? He wandered about, tearing his hair, beating his breast, but nothing could bring him peace.

Suddenly a torturing realization dawned upon him. She had come to him just now in the utmost anguish, to beg for his help. Because she believed in his love and because she loved him, she had come to ask him to keep his promise and protect her, to rescue her from the clutches of Old Man Feng. And what had he done? Absolutely nothing. He had given her neither help nor sympathy nor pity—nothing at all. He sent her away without even listening to her pleas. Now she was gone, gone forever. Tomorrow night, in the arms of that old man, she would weep for her despoiled springtime. And at the same time she would curse the one who had tricked her into giving her pure young love and then sent her into the jaws of the tiger.

It was a terrifying thought. Juehui couldn't bear it. He had to find her, he had to atone for his crime.

He walked to the women servants' quarters and lightly tapped on the door. Inside it was pitch-dark. He called, "Mingfeng," twice, in a low voice. There was no answer. She must be asleep, he thought. Because of the other women, he couldn't very well go in.

Juehui returned to his room. But he couldn't sit still. Again he came out and went to the servants' quarters. Pushing the door open a trifle, he could hear only snoring inside. He walked into the garden and stood for a long time in the dark beneath the plum trees. "Mingfeng!" he shouted.

Only the echo replied. Several times he bumped his head against the low-hanging plum branches, scratching his forehead and drawing blood. But he felt no pain. Finally, disappointed, he slowly walked back to his own room. As he entered his room, everything began to spin.

Actually, the girl he sought was not with the women servants, but in the garden.

When Mingfeng left Juehui's room she knew that this time all hope was gone. She was sure he loved her as much as ever; her lips were still warm with his kiss, her hands still felt his clasp. These proved that he loved her; but they were also symbols of the fact that she was going to lose him and be cast into the arms of a lecherous old man. She would never see him again. In the long years ahead there would be only endless pain and misery. Why should she cling to a life like that? Why should she remain in a world without love?

Mingfeng made up her mind.

She went directly to the garden, groping her way through the darkness with a great effort until she reached her objective—the edge of the lake. The waters darkly glistened; at times feeding fish broke the placid surface. Mingfeng stood dully, remembering many things of the past. She recalled everything she and Juehui had ever said and done together. She could see every familiar tree and shrub—so dear, so lovely— knowing that she was going to leave them all.

The world was very still. Everyone was asleep. But they were all alive, and they would continue living. She alone was going to die.

In the seventeen years of her existence she had known nothing but blows, curses, tears, toil in the service of others. That plus a love for which she now must perish. Life had brought much less happiness to her than to others; but now, despite her youth, she would leave the world first.

Tomorrow, others had their tomorrow. For her there was only a dark empty void. Tomorrow birds would sing in the trees, the rising sun would gild their branches, countless pearls would bubble on the surface of the water. But she would see none of it, for her eyes would be closed forever.

The world was such an adorable place. She had loved everyone with all the purity of a young girl's heart, wishing them all well. She had served people without pause; she had brought harm to no one. Like other girls she had a pretty face, an intelligent mind, a body of flesh and blood. Why did people want to trample her, hurt her, deny her a friendly glance, a sympathetic heart, even a pitying sigh?

She had never owned nice clothes, nor eaten good food, nor slept in a warm bed. She had accepted all this without complaint. For she had won the love of a fine young man, she had found a hero whom she could worship, and she was satisfied. She had found a refuge.

But today, when the crisis came, reality had proved it was all an illusion. His love couldn't save her; it only added to her painful memories.

He was not for her. His love had brought her many beautiful dreams, but now it was casting her into a dark abyss. She loved life, she loved everything, but life's door was closing in her face, leaving her only the road to degradation.

Thinking of what this meant, she looked at her body in horror. Although she could not see clearly in the darkness, she knew it was chaste and pure. She could almost feel someone casting her into the mire. Painfully, pityingly, she caressed her body with soothing hands.

Mingfeng came to a decision. She would hesitate no longer. She stared at the calm water. The crystal depths of the lake would give her refuge. She would die unsullied.

When she was about to jump, a thought came to her, and she paused. She shouldn't die like this. She ought to see him once more, pour out her heart to him. Perhaps he could save her. His kiss still tingled on her lips, his face still shimmered before her eyes. She loved him so; she couldn't bear to lose him. The only beauty in her life had been his love. Wasn't she entitled even to that? When everyone else went on living, why did a young girl like her have to die?

She pictured an idyllic scene in which she chatted and laughed and played with rich girls her own age in a beautiful garden. In this wide world she knew there were many such girls and many such gardens. Yet she had to end her young life—and there was no one to shed a sympathetic tear, or offer a word or two of comfort. Her death would bring no loss to the world, or to the Gao family. People would quickly forget her, as if she had never existed.

Has my life really been so meaningless? she thought, stricken. Her heart filled with an unspeakable grief, and tears spilled from her eyes. Strength draining from her body, she weakly sat upon the ground. She seemed to hear someone call her name. It was his voice. She halted her tears and listened. But all was quiet; all voices were stilled. She listened, hoping to hear the call again. She listened for a long, long time. But there was no sound in the night.

Then she knew. He was not coming. There was a wall eternally between them. He belonged to a different sphere. He had his future, his career. He must become a great man. She could not hold him back, keep him always at her side. She must release him. His existence was much more important than hers. She could not let him sacrifice himself for her sake. She must go, she must leave him forever. And she would do so willingly, since he was more precious to her than life itself.

A pain stabbed through her heart, and she rubbed her chest. But the pain persisted. She remained seated on the ground, her eyes longingly roving over the familiar surroundings in the dark. She was still thinking of him. A mournful smile flitted across her face and her eyes dimmed with tears.

Finally, she could not bear to think any longer. Rising tottering to her feet, she cried in a voice laden with tenderness and sorrow, "Juehui, Juehui!"—and she plunged into the lake.

The placid waters stirred violently, and a loud noise broke the stillness. Two or three tragic cries, although they were very low, echoed lingeringly in the night. After a few minutes of wild thrashing, the surface of the lake again became calm. Only the mournful cries still permeated the air, as if the entire garden were weeping softly.

(Translated by Sidney Shapiro and Wang Mingjie)

DAI WANGSHU
(1905–1950)

Born in Hangzhou, Zhejiang, Dai Wangshu attended Shanghai University in 1923 and began publishing poetry in 1926. Politically active as a student, he also blazed a trail for Chinese poetry through his own work and by translating French symbolists, such as Charles Baudelaire and Paul Verlaine. His poem "Rainy Alley" (1927), in particular, with its mellifluous musicality and melancholic ambience, is credited with turning a new page in the annals of the new verse, winning him the title of "the poet of the rainy alley." In 1932 he went to study in France but was expelled in 1935 for supporting the Spanish left. Returning to China, he continued to be active both in literature and left-wing politics. In 1938 the Japanese occupation of Shanghai forced him to flee to Hong Kong, where he did anti-Japanese propaganda work and edited literary supplements for newspapers. He died of asthma on February 28, 1950, only a few months after being assigned a position in the new government of the People's Republic.

Rainy Alley

Holding up an oil-paper umbrella, alone
I loiter aimlessly in the long, long
and lonely rainy alley,
I hope to encounter
a lilac-like girl
nursing her resentment.

A lilac-like color she has
a lilac-like fragrance,
a lilac-like sadness,
melancholy in the rain,
sorrowful and uncertain;

She loiters aimlessly in this lonely rainy alley,
holding up an oil-paper umbrella
just like me,
and just like me
walks silently,
apathetic, sad and disconsolate.

Silently she moves closer,
moves closer and casts
a sigh-like glance,
she glides by
like a dream
hazy and confused like a dream.

As in a dream she glides past
like a lilac spray,
this girl glides past beside me;
she silently moves away, moves away,

up to the broken-down bamboo fence,
to the end of the rainy alley.

In the rain's sad song,
her color vanishes,
her fragrance diffuses,
even her
sigh-like glance,
lilac-like discontent
vanish.

Holding up an oil-paper umbrella, alone
aimlessly walking in the long, long
and lonely rainy alley,
I wish for
a lilac-like girl
nursing her resentment to glide by.

I Think

I think therefore I am a butterfly . . .
The soft call of a flower ten thousand years later,
Has passed through the dreamless, unwaking mist,
To make my multicolored wings vibrate.

—March 14, 1937
(Translated by Gregory Lee)

SHEN CONGWEN
(1902–1988)

Born in western Hunan, a frontier region of pristine natural beauty and extreme economic hardship, Shen Congwen was of Han, Tujia, and Miao descent. An autodidact who later became a well-respected historian, Shen joined the army at the age of fourteen and began publishing stories in 1924. His best-known novel, Border Town (1934), is a modernist pastoral portrayal of a young country girl and her ferryman grandfather. Written in a uniquely lucid and lyrical style, the novel, though widely acclaimed upon publication, did not sit well with the Communist conception of the peasants, seen through the narrow prism of class struggle. Shen was subsequently attacked by left-wing writers, and Border Town was banned in Mao's era. For decades he worked as a researcher at the Museum of Chinese History and died in 1988.

Border Town (excerpts)

Chapter 1

An old imperial highway running east from Sichuan into Hunan Province leads, after reaching the west Hunan border, to a little mountain town called Chadong. By a narrow stream on the way to town was a little white pagoda, below which once lived a solitary family: an old man, a girl, and a yellow dog.

As the stream meandered on, it wrapped around a low mountain, joining a wide river at Chadong some three *li* downstream, about a mile. If you crossed the little stream and went up over the heights, you could get to Chadong in one *li* over dry land. The water path was bent like a bow, with the mountain path the bowstring, so the land distance was a little shorter. The stream was about twenty *zhang* wide—two hundred feet—over a streambed of boulders. Though the quietly flowing waters were too deep for a boat pole to touch bottom, they were so clear you could count the fish swimming to and fro. This little stream was a major choke point for transit between Sichuan and Hunan, but there was never enough money to build a bridge. Instead the locals set up a square-nosed ferryboat that could carry about twenty passengers and their loads. Any more than that, and the boat went back for another trip. Hitched to a little upright bamboo pole in the prow was a movable iron ring that went around a heavily worn cable spanning the stream all the way to the other side. To ferry across, one slowly tugged on that cable, hand over fist, with the iron ring keeping the boat on track. As the vessel neared the opposite shore, the person in charge would call out, "Steady now, take your time!" while suddenly leaping ashore holding the ring behind. The passengers, with all their goods, their horses, and their cows, would go ashore and head up over the heights, disappearing from view. The ferry landing was owned by the whole community, so the crossing was free to all. Some passengers were a little uneasy about this. When someone grabbed a few coins and threw them down on the boat deck, the ferryman always picked them up, one by one, and pressed them back into the hands of the giver, saying, in a stern, almost quarrelsome voice, "I'm paid for my work: three pecks of rice and seven hundred coppers. That's enough for me. Who needs this charity?"

But that didn't always work. One likes to feel one's done the right thing, and who feels good about letting honest labor go unrewarded? So there were always some who insisted on paying. This, in turn, upset the ferryman, who, to ease his own conscience, sent someone into Chadong with the money to buy tea and tobacco. Tying the best tobacco leaves Chadong had to offer into bundles and hanging them from his money belt, he'd offer them freely and generously to anyone in need. When he surmised from the look of a traveler from afar that he was interested in those tobacco leaves, the ferryman would stuff a few into the man's load, saying, "Elder Brother, won't you try these? Fine goods here, truly excellent; these giant leaves don't look it, but their taste is wonderful— just the thing to give as a gift!" Come June, he'd put his tea leaves into a big earthenware pot to steep in boiling water, for the benefit of any passerby with a thirst to quench.

The ferryman was the old man who lived below the pagoda. Seventy now, he'd kept to his place near this little stream since he was twenty. In the fifty years since, there was simply no telling how many people he'd ferried across in that boat. He was hale and hearty despite his age; it was time for him to have his rest, but Heaven didn't agree. He seemed tied to this work for life. He never mulled over what his work meant to him; he just quietly and faithfully kept on with his life here. It was the girl keeping him company who was Heaven's agent, letting him feel the power of life as the sun rose, and stopping him from thinking of expiring along with the sunlight when it faded at night. His only friends were the ferryboat and the yellow dog; his only family, that little girl.

The girl's mother, the ferryman's only child, had some fifteen years earlier come to know a soldier from Chadong through the customary exchange of amorous verses, sung by each in turn across the mountain valley. And that had led to trysts carried on behind the honest ferryman's back. When she was with child, the soldier, whose job it was to guard the farmer-soldier colonies upcountry, tried to persuade her to elope and follow him far downstream. But taking flight would mean, for him, going against his military duty, and for her, leaving her father all alone. They thought about it, but the garrison soldier could see she lacked the nerve to travel far away, and he too was loath to spoil his military reputation. Though they could not join each other in life, nothing could stop them from coming together in death. He took the poison first. Not steely-hearted enough to ignore the little body growing within her, the girl hesitated. By now her father, the ferryman, knew what was happening, but he said nothing, as if still unaware. He let the days pass as placidly as always. The daughter, feeling shame but also compassion, stayed at her father's side until the child was born, whereupon she went to the stream and drowned herself in the cold waters. As if by a miracle, the orphan lived and matured. In the batting of an eye, she had grown to be thirteen. Because of the compelling deep, emerald green of bamboo stands covering the mountains on either side by the stream where they lived, the old ferryman, without a second thought, named the girl after what was close at hand: Cuicui, or "Jade Green."

Cuicui grew up under the sun and the wind, which turned her skin black as could be. The azure mountains and green brooks that met her eyes turned them clear and bright as crystal. Nature had brought her up and educated her, making her innocent and spirited, in every way like a little wild animal. Yet she was as docile and unspoiled as a mountain fawn, wholly unacquainted with cruelty, never worried, and never angry. When a stranger on the ferry cast a look at her, she would shoot him a glance with those brilliant eyes, as if ready to flee into the hills at any instant; but once she saw that he meant her no harm, she would go back to playing by the waterside as if nothing had happened.

In rainy weather and fair, the old ferryman kept at his post in the prow of the ferryboat. When someone came to cross the stream, he'd stoop to grasp the bamboo cable and use both hands to pull the boat along to the other shore. When he was tired, he stretched out to sleep on the bluffs by the waterside. If someone on the other side waved and hollered that he wanted to cross, Cuicui would jump into the boat to save her grandpa the trouble and swiftly ferry the person across, pulling on the cable smoothly and expertly without a miss. Sometimes, when she was in the boat with her grandpa and the yellow dog, she'd tug the cable along with the ferryman till the boat got to the other side. As it approached the far shore, while the grandfather hailed the passengers with his "Steady now, take your time," the yellow dog would be the first to jump on land, with the tie rope in his mouth. He'd pull the boat to shore with that rope clenched between his teeth, just as if it were his job.

When the weather was clear and fine and there was nothing to do because no one wanted to cross, Grandpa and Cuicui would sun themselves atop the stone precipice in front of their home. Sometimes they'd throw a stick into the water from above and whistle to the yellow dog to jump down from the heights to fetch it. Or Cuicui and the dog would prick up their ears while Grandpa told them stories of war in the city many, many years ago. Other times, they'd each press a little upright bamboo flute to their lips and play the melodies of bridal processions, in which the groom went to the bride's house and brought her home. When someone came to cross, the old ferryman would lay down his flute and ferry the person across on the boat by himself, while the girl, still on the cliff, would call out in a high-pitched voice, just as the boat took off:

"Grandpa, Grandpa, listen to me play. You sing!"

At midstream, Grandpa would suddenly break out in joyful song; his hoarse voice and the reedy sound of the flute pulsated in the still air, making the whole stream seem to stir. Yet the reverberating strains of song brought out the stillness all around.

When the passengers heading for Chadong from east Sichuan included some calves, a flock of sheep, or a bridal cortege with its ornate palanquin, Cuicui would rush to do the ferrying. Standing in the boat's prow, she'd move the craft along the cable languidly and the crossing would be quite slow. After the calves, sheep, or palanquin were ashore, Cuicui would follow, escorting the pack up the hill, and stand there on the heights, fixing her eyes on them for a long ways before she returned to the ferryboat to pull it back to the shore and home. All alone, she'd softly bleat like the lambs, low like a cow, or pick wildflowers to bind up her hair like a bride—all alone.

The mountain town of Chadong was only a *li* from the ferry dock. When in town to buy oil or salt, or to celebrate the New Year, the grandfather would stop for a drink. When he stayed home, the yellow dog would accompany Cuicui as she went to town for supplies. What she would see in the general store—big piles of thin noodles made from bean starch, giant vats of sugar, firecrackers, and red candles—made a deep impression on her. When she got back to her grandfather, she'd go on about them endlessly. The many boats on the river in town were much bigger than the ferryboat and far more intriguing, quite unforgettable to Cuicui.

Chapter 4

It was two years earlier: at festival time, on the fifth day of the fifth month, Grandpa found someone to replace him at the ferry and took the yellow dog and Cuicui into town to see the boat race. The riverbanks were crowded with people as four long red boats slipped across the river depths. The "Dragon Boat tide" that raised the waters, the pea-green color of the stream, the bright, clear day, and the booming of the drums had Cuicui pursing her lips in silence, though her heart swelled with inexpressible joy. It was so crowded, with everyone straining to see what was happening on the river, that before long, though the yellow dog remained at Cuicui's side, Grandpa was jostled away out of sight.

Cuicui kept watching the boat race, thinking to herself that her grandfather was bound to come back soon. But a long time passed and he failed to return. Cuicui began to feel a little panicky. When the two of them had come to town the day before with the yellow dog, Grandpa had asked Cuicui, "Tomorrow is the boat race: if you go into town by yourself to see it, will you be afraid of the crowd?" Cuicui replied, "Crowds don't scare me, but it's no fun to watch the race by yourself." At that, her grandfather thought it over and finally remembered an old friend in town. He went that night to ask the old man to come tend the ferryboat for the day so he could bring Cuicui to town. Since the other man was even more alone than the old ferryman, without a relative to his name—not even a dog—it was agreed that he'd come over in the morning for a meal and a cup of realgar wine. The next day arrived; with the meal finished and the ferry duty handed over to the other man, Cuicui and her family entered the town. It occurred to Grandpa to ask along the way, once again: "Cuicui, with so many people down there, and so much commotion, do you dare go down to the riverbank to watch the dragon boats alone?" Cuicui answered, "Of course I do! But what's the point of watching it alone?" Once they got to the river, the four vermilion boats at Long Depths mesmerized Cuicui. She forgot all about her grandfather. He thought to himself, "This will take some time; it'll be another three hours before it's over. My friend back at the ferry deserves to see the young people whoop it up. I ought to go back and trade places with him. There's plenty of time." So he told Cuicui, "It's crowded, so you stay right in this spot. I have to go do something, but I'll be sure to get back in time to take you home." Cuicui was spellbound by the sight of two boats racing prow-to-prow, so she agreed without taking in what her grandpa had said. Realizing that the yellow dog at Cuicui's side might well be more reliable than he, the old man returned home to the ferry.

When he arrived, Grandpa saw his old friend standing below the white pagoda, listening to the distant sound of the drums.

Grandpa hailed him to bring the boat over so the two could ferry across the brook and stand under the pagoda together. The friend asked why the old ferryman had returned in such a hurry. Grandpa told him he wanted to spell him awhile. He'd left Cuicui by the shore so his friend could also enjoy the excitement down at the big river. He added, "If you like the spectacle, no need to return, just tell Cuicui to come home when it's over. If my little girl is afraid to come by herself, you can accompany her back!" Grandpa's stand-in had long ago lost any interest in watching dragon boats; he'd rather stay here with the ferryman on the big bluffs by the stream and drink a cup or two of wine. The old ferryman was quite happy to hear that. He took out his gourd of wine and gave it to his friend from town. They reminisced about Dragon Boat Festivals past as they drank. Pretty soon the friend drank himself to sleep, out on the rock.

Having succumbed to the liquor, he could hardly return to town. Grandpa couldn't very well abandon his post at the ferry either. Cuicui, who was stranded at the river, began to worry.

The boat race achieved its final outcome and the military officers in town sent a boat into the Long Depths to release the ducks. Still Grandpa was nowhere to be seen. Fearing that her grandfather might be waiting for her somewhere else, Cuicui and the yellow dog made their way through the crowd, and still there was no trace of him. Soon it would be twilight. All the soldiers from town who'd come hefting benches to watch the commotion had shouldered them now and returned home, one by one. Only three or four ducks remained at liberty in the river. The number of people chasing them was dwindling too. The sun was setting, in the direction of Cuicui's home upstream. Dusk draped the river in a thin coat of mist. A terrible thought suddenly occurred to Cuicui as she surveyed this scene: "Could Grandpa be dead?"

Keeping in mind that Grandpa had asked her to stay in this spot, she tried to disprove the awful thought to herself by imagining that he must have gone into town and run into an acquaintance, maybe been dragged off to have a drink. That was why he hadn't come back. Because it really was a possibility, she didn't want to leave for home with the yellow dog when it wasn't completely dark yet. She could only keep on waiting for her grandpa there by the stone pier.

Soon two long boats from the other shore moved into a small tributary and disappeared. Nearly all the spectators had dispersed too. The prostitutes in the houses on stilts lit their lanterns and some of them were already singing to the sound of tambourines and lutes. From other establishments came the raucous shouting of men drinking during the guess-fingers game. Meanwhile, in boats moored below the stilt houses, people were frying up dishes for a feast; greens and turnips sizzled in oil as they were plopped into their woks. The river was already obscured by the misty darkness. Only a solitary white duck was still afloat on the river, with just one person chasing it.

Cuicui stayed by the dockside, still believing that her grandfather would come to take her home.

As the strains of song coming from the stilt houses grew louder, she heard talking on a boat below, and a boatman saying, "Jinting, listen, that's *your* whore, singing to some merchant from Sichuan while he downs his liquor! I'll bet a finger on it, that's her voice!" Another boatman replied, "Even when she sings drinking songs for other men, she's still thinking of me! She knows I'm in this boat!" The first added, "So she gives her body to other people, but her heart stays with you? How do you know?" The other said, "I'll prove it to you!" Whereupon he gave a strange whistle. The singing above stopped, and the boatmen had a good laugh. They had a good deal to say about the woman after that, much of it obscene. Cuicui was not used to such language, but she couldn't leave the spot. Not only that, she heard one of the boatmen say that the woman's father had been stabbed at Cotton Ball Slope—seventeen times. That uncomfortable thought suddenly seized her again: "Could Grandpa be dead?"

As the boatmen continued conversing, the remaining white drake in the pool swam slowly toward the pier where Cuicui stood. She thought to herself, "Come any closer and I'll catch you!" She kept waiting there quietly, but when the duck came within ten yards of the shore, someone laughed and hailed the sailors on the boat. A third person was still in the water. He grabbed the duck and was slowly making his way to shore, treading water. Hearing the shouting from the river, a man on the boat yelled back into the murky haze, "Hey, No. 2, you're really something! That's the fifth one you've bagged today." The one in the water replied, "This character was really clever, but I caught him anyway." "It's ducks for you today, and tomorrow women—I'll bet you'll be just as good at that." The one in the water fell silent and swam up to the pier. As he climbed up onshore, dripping wet, the yellow dog at Cuicui's side yapped at him as a warning. It was then that he noticed Cuicui. She was the only one on the dock now.

"Who are you?" he asked.

"Cuicui."

"And who might that be?"

"The granddaughter of the ferryman at Bixiju, Green Creek Hill."

"What are you doing here?"

"Waiting for my grandpa. He's coming to get me."

"It doesn't look like he's coming. Your grandfather must have gone into town for a drink at the army barracks. I'll bet he passed out and someone carried him home!"

"He wouldn't do any such thing. He said he'd come get me, so that's what he'll do."

"This is no place to wait for him. Come up to my house, over there where the lamps are lit. You can wait for him there. How about that?"

Cuicui mistook his good intentions in inviting her to his home. Recalling the revolting things the sailors had said about that woman, she thought the boy wanted her to go up into one of those houses with the singing girls. She'd never cursed before, but she was on edge, having waited so long for her grandfather. When she heard herself invited to go upstairs to his home, she felt insulted and said, softly:

"Damned lowlife! You're headed for the executioner!"

She said it under her breath, but the boy heard it, and he could tell from her voice how young she was. He smiled at her and said, "What, are you cursing me? If you want to wait here instead of coming with me, and a big fish comes up and bites you, don't expect me to rescue you!"

Cuicui answered, "If a fish does bite me, that's nothing to you."

As if aware that Cuicui had been insulted, the yellow dog began barking again. The boy lunged at the dog with the duck to scare him, then walked off toward River Street. The dog wanted to chase him, having now been insulted himself, when Cuicui yelled, "Hey, boy, save your barks for when they're needed!" Her meaning seemed to be, "That joker isn't worth barking at," but the young man thought he heard something else, to the effect that the dog should not bark at a well-meaning person. He was wreathed in smiles as he disappeared from view.

A while later, someone came over from River Street to fetch Cuicui, bearing a torch made from leftover rope and calling her name. But when she saw his face, Cuicui didn't recognize him. He explained that the old ferryman had gone home and could not come to retrieve her, so he'd sent a message back with a passenger for Cuicui to return home at once. When Cuicui heard that her grandfather had sent the man, she went home with him, skirting the city wall and letting him lead the way with his torch. The yellow dog sometimes went in front, sometimes in back. Along the way, Cuicui asked the man how he'd known she was still there by the river. He said No. 2 had told him; he worked in No. 2's household. When he got her home, he'd have to return to River Street.

Cuicui asked, "How did No. 2 know I was there?"

Her guide smiled and said, "He was out on the river catching ducks and he saw you by the dock on his way home. He asked you, innocently enough, to go home and sit awhile in his house until your grandpa came, but you swore at him! And your dog barked at him, having no idea who he was!"

Surprised at this, Cuicui asked, softly, "Who is No. 2?"

Now it was the worker's turn to be surprised: "You've never heard of No. 2? He's Nuosong! We call him No. 2 on River Street. He's our Yue Yun! And he asked me to take you home!"

Nuosong was not an unfamiliar name in Chadong!

When Cuicui thought of her curse words a while ago, she felt stunned and also ashamed. There was nothing she could say. She followed the torchbearer silently.

When they'd rounded the hill and could see the lamplight in the house across the stream, the ferryman spotted the torchlight where Cuicui was. He immediately set out with his boat, calling out in his hoarse voice, "Cuicui, Cuicui, is it you?" Cuicui didn't answer her grandpa, but only said, under her breath, "No, it's not Cuicui, not her, Cuicui was eaten by a big fish in the river long ago." When she was in the boat, the man sent by No. 2 left with his torch. Grandpa pulled on the ferry cable and asked, "Cuicui, why didn't you answer me? Are you angry at me?"

Cuicui stood in the prow and still said not a word. Her irritation at her granddad dissipated when she got home across the creek and saw how drunk the other old man was. But something else, which had to do with her and not her grandfather, kept Cuicui in silence through the rest of the night.

Chapter 5

Two years passed. It happened that during neither of those years'
Mid-Autumn Festivals, when the moon should have been at its fullest,
was there any moon to be seen. None of the exploits of young girls
and boys singing love songs to each other all night under the moonlight, customary in this border town, could take place. Hence the
two Mid-Autumn Festivals had made only a very faint impression on
Cuicui. But during the last two New Year's celebrations, she could see
soldiers and villagers put on lion dances and processions of dragon lanterns on the parade grounds to welcome in the spring. The sound of the
drums and gongs was exciting and raucous. At the end of the festival
on the evening of the fifteenth of the first month, the garrison soldiers
who had frolicked inside the lions and dragons traveled all over, bare-
chested, braving the fireworks. At the army encampment in town, at
the residence of the head customs inspector, and in some of the bigger
establishments on River Street, everyone cut thin bamboos or hollowed
out palm tree roots and stems, then mixed saltpeter with sulfur, charcoal, and steel powder to make thousand-pop firecrackers. Daring and
fun-loving soldiers, stripped to the waist, came waving their lanterns
and beating their drums as packs of little firecrackers dangling from
poles sent sparks down their backs and shoulders like rain showers.
The quickening beat of drums and gongs sent the crowd into a frenzy.
When the bursts of firecrackers were over, the crowd fired rockets
from great tubes anchored to the feet of long benches, setting them
off with fuses that extended into an open field. First came a white light
with a sizzle. Slowly, slowly, the sizzle changed into a great howl, like
a frightening clap of thunder and the roar of a tiger, as the white light
shot up two hundred feet into the air. Then it showered the whole sky
with multicolored sparks thick as droplets of rain. The soldiers bran-
dishing lanterns went around in circles, oblivious to the sparks. Cuicui
witnessed this excitement with her grandfather and it made an impression on her, but inexplicably, it was not as sweet and beautiful as that
left by the day of the dragon boats two years before.

Unable to forget that day, Cuicui had gone back to River Street with her grandpa the year before and watched the boats for some time. Just when everything was going fine, it suddenly began to rain, soaking everyone to the bone. To escape the rain, grandfather and grand-daughter, with the yellow dog, had gone up into Shunshun's stilt house, where they crowded into a corner. Someone passed by them carrying a stool; Cuicui recognized him as the man with the torch who had led her home. She said to her grandfather:

"Grandfather, that's the man who brought me home last year. Walking along the path with a torch like that, he was just like a highwayman!"

At first Grandpa said nothing, but when the man turned his head and approached, the ferryman grabbed him and said, grinning widely:

"Hey, there, you old highwayman, I asked you to stay for a drink but you wouldn't stay put! Were you afraid of poison? Did you think I dared to slay a true-born Son of Heaven?"

When the man saw that it was the ferryman, and then caught sight of Cuicui, he grinned. "Cuicui, how you've grown! No. 2 said a big fish might eat you if you stayed by the riverbank, but our river doesn't have any fish big enough to swallow you now!"

Cuicui said not a word. She puckered her lips and smiled. She heard this old highwayman speak No. 2's name, but the boy was nowhere to be seen. From the conversation between her grandfather and the other elder, Cuicui gathered that No. 2 was spending the Dragon Boat Festival two hundred miles downstream, at the Qinglang or Green Foam Rapids of the River Yuan. But this festival she got to see No. 1 and also the famous Shunshun. The old ferryman praised a fat duck that No. 1 brought home after catching it on the river, praised it twice, so Shunshun told him to give it to Cuicui. And when he learned how hard up their household was—too poor to wrap their own *zongzi* dumplings for the festival—he gave them a big lot of the three-cornered treats.

While that notable of the waterways conversed with her grandfather, Cuicui pretended to be looking at the events in the river, but really she was taking in every word. The other man said that Cuicui had grown quite beautiful. He asked her age, and whether she was promised to anyone. Her grandfather gleefully bragged about her, but seemed reluctant to broach the topic of her marriage prospects. He didn't breathe a word about that.

On the way home, Grandpa carried the white duck and other goods, while Cuicui led the way with a torch. The two made their way along the foot of the city wall, between the wall and the river. Grandpa said: "Shunshun is a good man, extremely generous. No. 1 is like him. The whole family is quite fine!" Cuicui asked, "Do you know everyone in the family?" Grandpa didn't see what she was driving at. The day had raised his spirits so much that he went ahead and asked, smiling, "Cuicui, if No. 1 wanted to take you as his wife and sent over a matchmaker, would you agree?" Cuicui replied, "Grandfather, you're crazy! Keep on like this and I'll get angry!"

Grandpa said no more, but clearly he was still mulling over this silly and inopportune idea. Cuicui, aggravated, ran up ahead, swinging the torch wildly from side to side.

"Don't be angry, Cuicui, I might fall into the river. This duck might get away!"

"Who wants that old duck?"

Realizing why she was angry, Grandpa began singing a shanty the oarsmen used to speed their rowing while they shot the rapids. His voice was rasping, but the words were clear as could be. Cuicui kept going as she listened, then suddenly stopped and asked:

"Grandfather, is that boat of yours going down the Green Foam Rapids?"

Grandpa didn't answer, he just kept on singing. Both of them recalled that Shunshun's No. 2 was spending the holiday on a boat at the Green Foam Rapids, but neither knew what the other was implying. Grandfather and granddaughter walked home in silence. As they neared the ferry, the man tending the boat for them brought it to the bank to await their arrival. They crossed the stream to go home, then ate the *zongzi*. When it came time for the man to go back to town, Cuicui was quick to light a torch for him so he could see his way home. As he crossed over the hill, Cuicui and her grandfather watched him from the boat. She said:

"Grandfather, look, the highwayman has gone back into the hills!"

As he pulled the boat along the cable, his eyes trained on the mist that had suddenly come up from the stream, Grandpa acted as if he'd seen something and softly sighed. He quietly tugged the boat toward home on the opposite bank and let Cuicui go ashore first, while he stayed by the boat. It was a festival day. He knew that country folk would still be returning home in the dark after seeing the dragon boats in town.

Chapter 6

One day the old ferryman got into an argument with a passenger, a seller of wrapping paper. The one refused to accept money proffered and the other insisted on paying. The old ferryman felt a little bullied by the merchant's attitude, so he put on a show of anger and forced the man to take back his money—pressed the coins right back into his hand. But when the boat reached the shore, the traveler jumped up onto the dock and cast a handful of coppers back into the boat, smiling gleefully before hurrying off on his way. The old ferryman had to keep steadying the boat till the other passengers made it ashore, so he couldn't pursue the merchant. Instead, he called out to his granddaughter, who was up on the hill:

"Cuicui, grab hold of that cheeky young paper-seller and don't let him go!"

Cuicui had no idea what was going on, but she went with the yellow dog to block the way of the first passenger off the boat. He laughed and said:

"Let me pass!"

As he spoke, a second merchant caught up with them and told Cuicui what it was all about. She understood and held on to the paper merchant's gown for dear life, insisting, "You can't go, you can't!" To show his agreement with his mistress, the yellow dog began barking at the man. The other traveling merchants were blocked for a while, but they all had a good laugh. Grandpa came up in an angry huff, forced the money back into the man's hand, and even stuck a big wad of tobacco leaves into the merchant's load. He rubbed his hands together and beamed: "Go on, now! Hit the road, all of you!" And at that, they all went on their way, chuckling.

"Grandfather, I thought you were quarreling with that man because he'd stolen from you!" Cuicui said.

Her grandfather replied:

"He gave me money, a lot of it. I don't want his money! I told him that and still he bickered with me about it. He just wouldn't listen to reason!"

"Did you give it all back to him?" Cuicui asked.

Grandpa shook his head and pouted. Then he winked and smiled knowingly, taking out from his belt the lone copper he had stuffed there. He gave it to Cuicui and said:

"He got some tobacco from me in return. He can smoke that all the way to Zhen'gan town!"

The pounding of faraway drums could be heard, and the yellow dog pricked up his ears. Cuicui asked Grandpa if he could hear it. He strained his ears and recognized the sound.

"Cuicui, the Dragon Boat Festival has come around again. Do you remember how last year Master Tianbao gave you a fat duck to take home? This morning First Master went off on business with his crew to east Sichuan. On the ferry he asked about you. I'll bet you forgot all about the downpour last year. If we go this time, we'll have to light a torch again to come home. Do you remember how the two of us came home, lighting our way with a torch?"

Cuicui was just then thinking about the other Dragon Boat Festival, two years ago. But when her grandfather asked, she shook her head, slightly annoyed, and said pointedly: "I don't remember it, not at all. I can't remember anything about it!" What she really meant was, "How could I have forgotten?"

Knowing full well what she really meant, Grandpa added, "The festival two years ago was even more interesting. You waited for me alone by the riverbank. It got dark and you were just about lost. I thought a big fish must have eaten you all up!"

Recalling this, Cuicui snickered.

"Grandfather, are you the one who thought a big fish might eat me? It was someone else who said that about me, and I told you! All you cared about that day was getting that old man from town to drink all the wine in your gourd! Some memory you have!"

"I'm old and my memory is completely gone. Cuicui, you've grown up now. You'll have no trouble going into town alone to see the boats race. No need to worry about a fish eating you."

"Now that I'm older, I ought to stay and mind the ferryboat."

"It's when you get really old that you stay with the ferryboat."

"When you get old, you deserve a rest!"

"Your grandfather isn't so old! I can still hunt tigers!" Grandpa said, flexing his biceps and making a muscle to show how young and strong he still was. "Cuicui, if you don't believe me, see if you can bite through this!"

Cuicui cast a sidelong glance at her grandpa, whose back was slightly hunched. She didn't reply. Far away, she heard the sound of *suona* horns. She knew what that meant. She could tell the direction it was coming from. She asked her grandpa to get in the boat with her and go to the other side, where their house was. To get a look at the bride's palanquin at the earliest point, Cuicui climbed the pagoda out back and looked over from above. Soon the wedding procession arrived: two men playing *suonas*, four strong peasant lads carrying an empty palanquin to collect the bride, a young man decked out in new clothes, who looked to be the son of a militia captain, two sheep and a young boy leading them, a vat of wine, a box of glutinous rice cakes, and a gift-bearer. When the troop boarded the ferryboat, Cuicui and her grandpa joined them. Grandpa tugged the boat line, while Cuicui stood by the ornately decorated bridal sedan chair, taking note of all the faces in the procession and the tassels on the palanquin. When they got to shore, the one who looked like the militia captain's son drew a red envelope with money in it from his embroidered waist pouch and gave it to the old ferryman. That was the custom in this locality, so Grandpa could not refuse the gift. But having the money in hand, Grandpa asked the man where the bride was from, her family name, and how old she was. When he had all this information and the *suona* players began their haunting melodies again after landing, the file of men crossed over the hill and went on its way. Grandpa and Cuicui remained in the boat, their emotions following the sounds of the *suonas* far into the distance.

Weighing the red money packet in his hand, Grandpa said, "Cuicui, the bride is from the Song Family Stockade and she's only fourteen."

Cuicui understood his meaning, but paid him no heed. She began quietly to pull the boat across.

When they reached the side where their house was, Cuicui rushed home to get their little twin-pipe bamboo *suona*. She asked Grandpa to play her the tune "The Mother Sees Her Daughter Off to Marriage." She lay down with the yellow dog in a shady spot on the bluffs in front of the house, where she could watch the clouds in the sky. The days were getting longer now. Before anyone noticed, Grandpa fell asleep. So did Cuicui and the yellow dog.

(Translated by Jeffrey C. Kinkley)

ZHOU ZUOREN
(1885–1967)

Born in Zhejiang, Zhou Zuoren followed the footsteps of his older brother Zhou Shuren, better known as Lu Xun: he attended the same schools, also studied in Japan, taught at Peking University, and partnered with Lu Xun on translation projects. But Zhou's literary reputation was always overshadowed by his brother's, and to make matters worse, his suspected Japanese "connections" in wartime led to his imprisonment for three years and censorship of his writing for decades. A most creative and prolific essayist, one who chronicled Chinese everyday life and commented on world affairs in a mild, quizzical tone, Zhou was forbidden to write after 1949 and resorted to translation in order to make a living. This important writer of the Republican era suffered more humiliation and persecution during the Cultural Revolution and died in 1967.

Reading in the Lavatory

In Chapter Four of Hao Yixing's *Notes from the Studio of Sun-Dried Books*, there is an item on reading in the lavatory:

> Legend tells of a pious Buddhist lady who chanted the sutras without cease, even in the lavatory. Though she reaped the reward for her piety in other ways, it was in the lavatory that she expired.

The idea is to warn against such behavior. Though the source of the story is the Buddha's object lessons for humanity, and it is not necessarily factual, yet we may take the point that unclean places are not suitable for chanting holy script. Ouyang Xiu's "Return to My Fields" records Qian Sigong's saying that he had been a lifelong reader: when sitting up he read the classics and histories, when lying down he read novels, and while in the lavatory he read ditties. Xie Xishen is also quoted as saying that Song Gongchui invariably took a book with him when he went to the lavatory, and his voice resounded far and near as he read from it. I can't help laughing at all this. When you go to the lavatory you have to pull down your trousers, and if you have a book in your hand, it is not only mucky, it is also very hard to manage. A person may be devoted to study, but need he go to such lengths? As for Xie Xishen's reference, quoted by Ouyang Xiu, to the three "on's" he most utilized for composing pieces, namely on the horseback, on the pillow, and on the lavatory, being the three places most conducive to thought, that is in contrast a very good crack: it is neither insincere nor superficial.

Master Hao writes a very good essay, but I can't entirely agree with him, because I am inclined to go along with reading in the lavatory. When I was small my grandfather told me the footmen in Peking had a saying: "The masters make fast work of their food, the underlings make fast work of their crap." Though there is an element of calculated interest in the footmen's words, I'm afraid they tell the truth. Granted that it is hard to be definite about the time spent in the lavatory, yet at all events it is unlikely to be very short. Moreover—which is not the case with a meal—however short it is, you can't help feeling it is time wasted, and want to find some way of utilizing it. For instance, the country folk where I come from like to take along a pipe when they go to the privy, and if there are people rinsing rice or washing clothes on the stone steps by the river, or someone passes by carrying a load, they can also engage in loud conversation, asking how many coppers the rice costs or where he is going to. Reading serves the same purpose, I would have thought, as smoking a pipe.

Having said that, one has to admit that some places are not terribly convenient for reading, and smoking a pipe is the only option. The privies by the river in a certain part of Zhejiang just mentioned are one example. Long ago, I once stayed in a bookshop in Nanjing kept by a friend from Hunan, called Liu. I was introduced to him by Zhao Boxian. The provincial examinations were being held that year, and he had opened a bookshop near the Floral Arch. I found it very uncomfortable living in the academy dormitory because I was unwell, so he invited me to stay with him. What with preparing medicine and making congee for me, catering to the book requirements of the gentlemen candidates for the examination, and on top of that secretly working for the revolution, he expended enormous energy, and I greatly admired him for it. I slept behind the bookcase at the rear of the shop, and took my medicine and consumed my congee there too. The trouble was, the convenience was outside. I had to go out of the shop and past two other shop fronts to an empty lot where there was a pile of rubbish against a wall. It was quite an ordeal for me to go there, partly it is true because my illness made walking difficult, but even if I had been in good health I suspect I wouldn't have been too keen. This is my second example. When I was in Japan in the summer of 1919, I went to visit a friend, and stayed in a mountain village called Kijo. Although the privy there was like most others in that it had a roof over the top, wooden sides, a door, and a window, the disadvantage was that it was some fifty yards from the house, stuck out in the middle of a field. At night you needed a lantern to light up your way, and an umbrella if it was raining. Unfortunately it seemed to be a particularly wet place: it rained for at least four out of the five days I was there. This is my third example. Lastly there are the latrines in Peking that consist only of a brick either side of a hole, and you just have to get on with it regardless of pouring rain, howling wind, or baking sun. Last year I went to Dingzhou to visit Fuyuan. The privies there are of the kind you find in the Ryukyus, where you perch over the edge of a pit with pigs grunting away beneath you. If you are not used to it, it is very unsettling, and you are hardly in the right frame of mind to read. This is my fourth example. According to the fourth century *Book of Anecdotes,* Shi Chang's toilet had a bed in it with silk drapes and beautiful cushions, and two maidservants standing by with sachets of perfume. This is too extravagant, and unsuitable too. Actually my point is a very simple one. All I require is a roof over my head, and walls, window, and door, and a light to turn on at night, or a candle if there is no electricity. I would have no objection to it being twenty or thirty steps from the house: that would require an umbrella, but fortunately it does not rain much in Peking. Given this kind of lavatory, I wouldn't have thought there could be any harm in taking a book along for a bit of a read.

Tanizaki Jun'ichirō's book *Setsuyo Zuilzitsu* has a chapter called "In Praise of Shade." The second section is on the good points of Japanese lavatories. In the monasteries of Nara and Kyoto, all the lavatories are old-fashioned. Situated in clumps of trees where you get the smell of green leaves and moss, they are dark but kept very clean. There are covered walkways joining them with the living quarters. To squat in the semidarkness, illuminated by the pale light from the paper screens, and lose oneself in thought, or to look through the window onto the temple gardens, is a wonderful experience. He goes on:

> I repeat, there must be a certain degree of obscurity, immaculate cleanliness, and a quietness in which you can hear even the whine of a mosquito clearly. Those are necessary conditions. I love to listen to the patter of rain in these lavatories. In Kanta especially, the lavatories have a long narrow slot at floor level for sweeping out the dust, which enables you to hear from right next to you the rain which drips from the eaves or tree leaves seep softly into the ground after washing the feet of the stone lanterns and moistening the moss on the stepping-stones. These lavatories are truly the best places for the sound of insects, the song of birds, as well as moonlit nights, best indeed for appreciating the character of all four seasons. I suspect that from ancient days our haiku poets

have derived countless material from these places. In this regard, it would be no exaggeration to say that the most romantic constructs of Japanese architecture are the lavatories.

Tanizaki is at bottom a poet, which explains why he writes so well, perhaps to the extent of dressing things up, but that is only in his wording: his viewpoint is sound enough. In the Warring States period of the late middle ages, the preservation and furtherance of culture in Japan rested entirely on the Gozan monasteries. That brought about a change in style and temper, seen for example in ink and wash paintings of dead trees, bamboos, and stones replacing the finely detailed academy style. Architecture naturally followed the same trend, represented in the teahouses. The romantic transformation of lavatories was an afterthought.

Buddhists seem to have always been very particular about the use of toilets. From my occasional dipping into the rules of conduct of both the Mahayana and Hinayana schools, I have been extremely impressed by the close attention of the old Indian sages to every aspect of life. In respect of toilet practices, the *Three Thousand Observances of the Bhiksu,* translated in the Han Dynasty, lists "twenty-five practices in the ablutions"; Chapter 6 of *Sarvastivada Vinaya Matrka* (the Song Dynasty translation), from "how to keep downwind" to "how to prepare toilet paper," consists of thirteen items; the Tang text by Yijing called *Report on Buddhism in the Southern Seas,* 2:18, has a chapter on "The Convenience." They all contain very precise instructions, some extremely solemn and at the same time funny. They really bowl you over when you read them. Then when we consider how the monk Lu Zhishen in the *Outlaws of the Marshes* was promoted from being in charge of growing vegetables to being in charge of ablutions, we can see that in Chinese monasteries they also used to take such matters seriously. But times have changed: it is no longer so. In 1921 I spent six months convalescing in the Western Hills, and stayed in the Ten Directions Hall of the Azure Clouds Temple. In all my walks I never discovered a halfway decent lavatory. It was as I wrote in my "Letters from the Hills":

My peregrinations have recently been extended to the springs east of here. It really is very nice there. I go there first thing in the morning before the day-trippers get there and linger awhile, enjoying the beauty of living waters. Sadly, though, it is not very clean. The path there is very smelly, because of the large quantities of what the *Pharmacopoeia* calls "human brown matter" spread about. China is a strange country: on the one hand people have a hard time finding nourishment, and on the other have no way of disposing of their waste products.

In this situation, to find an ordinary sort of lavatory in Chinese temples is a great good fortune; to hope to find somewhere you can lose yourself in thought or read a book is asking for the moon. Since the monks foul things up themselves, you can hardly blame the common folk.

But given a clean lavatory, it is still all right to read a book, though we can put writing out of our mind. And we needn't be particular about the kind of book—anything suited for dipping into is fine. My own rule is not to take rare books or hard-to-read books, though grammars are among my regulars. In my experience essays are best, and novels worst. As to declaiming, now that we no longer study the Eight Prose Masters there is of course no call for that.

1935

(Translated by David E. Pollard)

LIN YUTANG
(1895–1976)

Born to a Christian family in Fujian, Lin Yutang attended St. John's University in Shanghai. In 1919 he studied comparative literature at Harvard University and in 1924 received a Ph.D. from the University of Leipzig in Germany. A master of humor and a self-labeled "citizen of the world," Lin was a key figure in popularizing the Chinese way of life and philosophy in the West and the first Chinese writer to gain an international reputation through writing in English. In 1935, with the assistance of Pearl Buck and her editor at John Day, Lin published his best-selling English book, My Country and My People, *followed by* The Importance of Living *(1937) and* Moment in Peking *(1939). He moved to the United States in 1936 and lived there till 1954, when he was appointed the chancellor of the Nanyang University in Singapore. He died in Hong Kong in 1976.*

My Country and My People (excerpt)

Prologue

When one is in China, one is compelled to think about her, with compassion always, with despair sometimes, and with discrimination and understanding very rarely. For one either loves or hates China. Perhaps even when one does not live in China one sometimes thinks of her as an old, great big country which remains aloof from the world and does not quite belong to it. That aloofness has a certain fascination. But if one comes to China, one feels engulfed and soon stops thinking. One merely feels she is there, a tremendous existence somewhat too big for the human mind to encompass, a seemingly inconsequential chaos obeying its own laws of existence and enacting its own powerful life-drama, at times tragic, at times comical, but always intensely and boisterously real; then, after a while, one begins to think again, with wonder and amazement.

This time, the reaction will be temperamental; it merely indicates whether one is a romantic cosmopolitan individual or a conceited, self-satisfied prig. One either likes or dislikes China, and then proceeds to justify one's likes or dislikes. That is just as well, for we must take some sort of attitude toward China to justify ourselves as intelligent beings. We grope for reasons, and begin to tell one another little anecdotes, trifles of everyday life, escaped or casual words of conversation, things of tremendous importance that make us philosophers and enable us to become, with great equanimity, either her implacable critics, allowing nothing good for her, or else her ardent, romantic admirers. Of course, these generalizations are rather silly. But that is how human opinions are formed all over the world, and it is unavoidable. Then we set about arguing with one another. Some always come out from the argument supremely satisfied of their rightness, self-assured that they have an opinion of China and of the Chinese people. They are the happy people who rule the world and import merchandise from one part of it to another, and who are always in the right. Others find themselves beset with doubts and perplexities, with a feeling of awe and bewilderment, perhaps of awe and mystification, and they end where they began. But all of us feel China is there, a great mystical *Dasein*.

For China is the greatest mystifying and stupefying fact in the modern world, and that not only because of her age or her geographical greatness. She is the oldest living nation with a continuous culture; she has the largest population; once she was the greatest empire in the world, and she was a conqueror; she gave the world some of its most important inventions; she has a literature, a philosophy, a wisdom of life entirely her own; and in the realms of art, she soared where others merely made an effort to flap their wings. And yet, today she is undoubtedly the most chaotic, the most misruled nation on earth, the most pathetic and most helpless, the most unable to pull herself together and forge ahead. God, if there be a God, intended her to be a first-class nation among the peoples of the earth, and she has chosen to take a backseat with Guatemala at the League of Nations; and the entire League of Nations, with the best will in the world, cannot help her—cannot help her to put her own house in order, cannot help her to stop her own civil wars, cannot help her to save herself from her own scholars and militarists, her own revolutionists and gentry politicians.

Meanwhile, and this is the most amazing fact, she is the least concerned about her own salvation. Like a good gambler, she took the loss of a slice of territory the size of Germany itself without a wince. And while General T'ang Yülin was beating a world-record retreat and losing half a million square miles in eight days, two generals, an uncle and a nephew, were matching their strength in Szechuan. One begins to wonder whether God will win out in the end, whether God Himself can help China to become a first-class nation in spite of herself.

And another doubt arises in one's mind: What is China's destiny? Will she survive as she so successfully did in the past, and in a way that no other old nation was able to do? Did God really intend her to be a first-class nation? Or is she merely "Mother Earth's miscarriage"?

Once she had a destiny. Once she was a conqueror. Now her greatest destiny seems to be merely to exist, to survive, and one cannot but have faith in her ability to do so, when one remembers how she has survived the ages, after the beauty that was Greece and the glory that was Rome were long vanished, remembers how she has ground and modeled foreign truths into her own likeness and absorbed foreign races into her own blood. This fact of her survival, of her great age, is evidently something worth pondering upon. There is something due an old nation, a respect for hoary old age that should be applied to nations as to individuals. Yes, even to mere old age, even to mere survival.

For whatever else is wrong, China has a sound instinct for life, a strange supernatural, extraordinary vitality. She has led a life of the instinct; she has adjusted herself to economic, political, and social environments that might have spelled disaster to a less robust racial constitution; she has received her share of nature's bounty, has clung to her flowers and birds and hills and dales for her inspiration and moral support, which alone have kept her heart whole and pure and prevented the race from civic social degeneration. She has chosen to live much in the open, to bask in the sunlight, to watch the evening glow, to feel the touch of the morning dew, and to smell the fragrance of hay and of the moist earth; through her poetry, through the poetry of habits of life as well as through the poetry of words, she has learned to refresh her, alas! too often wounded, soul. In other words, she has managed to reach grand old age in the same way as human individuals do, by living much in the open and having a great deal of sunlight and fresh air. But she has also lived through hard times, through recurrent centuries of war and pestilence, and through natural calamities and human misrule. With a grim humor and somewhat coarse nerves, she has weathered them all, and somehow she has always righted herself. Yes, great age, even mere great age, is something to be wondered at.

Now that she has reached grand old age, she is beyond bodily and spiritual sorrows, and one would have thought, at times, beyond hope and beyond redemption. Is it the strength or the weakness of old age? one wonders. She has defied the world, and has taken a nonchalant attitude toward it, which her old age entitles her to do. Whatever happens, her placid life flows on unperturbed, insensible to pain and to misery, impervious to shame and to ambition—the little human emotions that agitate young breasts—and undaunted even by the threat of immediate ruin and collapse for the last two centuries. Success and failure have ceased to touch her; calamities and death have lost their sting; and the overshadowing of her national life for a period of a few centuries has ceased to have any meaning. Like the sea in the Nietzschean analogy, she is greater than all the fish and shellfish and jellyfish in her, greater than the mud and refuse thrown into her. She is greater than the lame propaganda and petulance of all her returned students, greater than the hypocrisy, shame, and greed of all her petty officials and turn-coat generals and fence-riding revolutionists, greater than her wars and pestilence, greater than her dirt and poverty and famines. For she has survived them all. Amid wars and pestilence, surrounded by her poor children and grandchildren, Merry Old China quietly sips her tea and smiles on, and in her smile I see her real strength. She quietly sips her tea and smiles on, and in her smile I detect at times a mere laziness to change and at others a conservatism that savors of haughtiness. Laziness or haughtiness, which? I do not know. But somewhere in her soul lurks the cunning of an old dog, and it is a cunning that is strangely impressive. What a strange old soul! What a great old soul!

II

But what price greatness? Carlyle has said somewhere that the first impression of a really great work of art is always unnerving to the point of painfulness. It is the lot of the great to be misunderstood, and so it is China's lot. China has been greatly, magnificently misunderstood. Greatness is often the term we confer on what we do not understand and wish to have done with. Between being well understood, however, and being called great, China would have preferred the former, and it would have been better for everybody all around. But how is China to be understood? Who will be her interpreters? There is that long history of hers, covering a multitude of kings and emperors and sages and poets and scholars and brave mothers and talented women. There are her arts and philosophies, her paintings and her theaters, which provide the common people with all the moral notions of good and evil, and that tremendous mass of folk literature and folklore. The language alone constitutes an almost hopeless barrier. Can China be understood merely through pidgin English? Is the Old China Hand to pick up an understanding of the soul of China from his cook and amah? Or shall it be from his Number One Boy? Or shall it be from his compradore and shroff, or by reading the correspondence of the *North-China Daily News*? The proposition is manifestly unfair.

Indeed, the business of trying to understand a foreign nation with a foreign culture, especially one so different from one's own as China's, is usually not for the mortal man. For this work there is need for broad, brotherly feeling, for the feeling of the common bond of humanity and the cheer of good fellowship. One must feel with the pulse of the heart as well as see with the eyes of the mind. There must be too a certain detachment, not from the country under examination, for that is always so, but from oneself and one's subconscious notions, and from the deeply embedded notions of one's childhood and the equally tyrannous ideas of one's adult days, from those big words with capital letters like Democracy, Prosperity, Capital, and Success and Religion and Dividends. One needs a little detachment, and a little simplicity of mind too, that simplicity of mind so well typified by Robert Burns, one of the most Scottish and yet most universal of all poets, who strips our souls bare and reveals our common humanity and the loves and sorrows that common humanity is heir to. Only with that detachment and that simplicity of mind can one understand a foreign nation.

Who will, then, be her interpreters? The problem is an almost insoluble one. Certainly not the sinologues and librarians abroad who see China only through the reflection of the Confucian classics. The true Europeans in China do not speak Chinese, and the true Chinese do not speak English. The Europeans who speak Chinese too well develop certain mental habits akin to the Chinese and are regarded by their compatriots as "queer." The Chinese who speak English too well and develop Western mental habits are "denationalized," or they may not even speak Chinese, or speak it with an English accent. So by a process of elimination, it would seem that we have to put up with the Old China Hand, and that we have largely to depend upon his understanding of pidgin.

The Old China Hand, or O.C.H.——let us stop to picture him, for he is important as your only authority on China. He has been well described by Mr. Arthur Ransome. But to my mind, he is a vivid personality, and one can now easily picture him in the imagination. Let us make no mistake about him. He may be the son of a missionary, or a captain or a pilot, or a secretary in the consular service, or he may be a merchant to whom China is just a market for selling sardines and "Sunkist" oranges. He is not always uneducated; in fact, he may be a brilliant journalist, with one eye to a political advisorship and the other to a loan commission. He may even be very well informed within his limits, the limits of a man who cannot talk three syllables of Chinese and depends on his English-speaking Chinese friends for his supplies of information. But he keeps on with his adventure and he plays golf and his golf helps to keep him fit. He drinks Lipton's tea and reads the *North-China Daily News*, and his spirit revolts against the morning reports of banditry and kidnapping and recurrent civil wars, which spoil his breakfast for him. He is well shaved and dresses more neatly than his Chinese associates, and his boots are better shined than they would be in England, although this is no credit to him, for the Chinese boys are such good bootblacks. He rides a distance of three or four miles from his home to his office every morning, and believes himself desired at Miss Smith's tea. He may have no aristocratic blood in his veins nor ancestral oil portraits in his halls, but he can always circumvent that by going further back in history and discovering that his forefathers in the primeval forests had the right blood in them, and that sets his mind at peace and relieves him of all anxiety about studying things Chinese. But he is also uncomfortable every time his business takes him through Chinese streets where the heathen eyes all stare at him. He takes his handkerchief and vociferously blows his nose with it and bravely endures it, all the while in a blue funk. He broadly surveys the wave of blue-dressed humanity. It seems to him their eyes are not quite so slant as the shilling-shocker covers represent them to be. Can these people stab one in the back? It seems unbelievable in the beautiful sunlight, but one never knows, and the courage and sportsmanship which he learned at the cricket field all leave him. Why, he would rather be knocked in the head by a cricket bat than go through those crooked streets again! Yes, it is *fear*, primeval fear of the Unknown.

But to him, it is not just that. It is his *humanity* that cannot stand the sight of human misery and poverty, as understood in his own terms. He simply cannot stand being pulled by a human beast of burden in a rickshaw—he has to have a car. His car is not just a car, it is a moving covered corridor that leads from his home to his office and protects him from Chinese humanity. He will not leave his car and his civilization. He tells Miss Smith so at tea, saying that a car in China is not a luxury but a necessity. That three-mile ride of an enclosed mind in an enclosed glass case from the home to the office he takes every day of his twenty-five years in China, although he does not mention this fact when he goes home to England and signs himself "An Old Resident Twenty-Five Years in China" in correspondence to the London *Times*. It reads very impressively. Of course, he should know what he is talking about.

Meanwhile, that three-mile radius has seldom been exceeded, except when he goes on cross-country paper hunts over Chinese farm fields, but then he is out in the open and knows how to defend himself. But in this he is mistaken, for he never has to, and this he knows himself, for he merely says so, when he is out for sport. He has never been invited to Chinese homes, has sedulously avoided Chinese restaurants, and has never read a single line of Chinese newspapers. He goes to the longest bar in the world of an evening, sips his cocktail, and picks up and imbibes and exchanges bits of sailors' tales on the China coast handed down from the Portuguese sailors, and is sorry to find that Shanghai is not Sussex, and generally behaves as he would in England. He feels happy when he learns that the Chinese are beginning to observe Christmas and make progress, and feels amazed when he is not understood in English; he walks as if the whole lot of them did not exist for him, and does not say "sorry" even in English when he steps on a fellow passenger's toes; yes, he has not even learned the Chinese equivalents of "*danke sehr*" and "*bitte schön*" and "*verzeihen Sie,*" the minimum moral obligations of even a passing tourist, and complains of anti-foreignism and despairs because even the pillaging of the Peking palaces after the Boxer Uprising has not taught the Chinese a lesson. There is your authority on China. Oh, for a common bond of humanity!

All this one can understand, and it is even quite natural, and should not be mentioned here were it not for the fact that it bears closely on the formation of opinions on China in the West. One needs only to think of the language difficulty, of the almost impossible learning of the Chinese writing, of the actual political, intellectual, and artistic chaos in present-day China, and of the vast differences in customs between the Chinese and the Westerners. The plea here is essentially for a better understanding on a higher level of intelligence. Yet it is difficult to deny the Old China Hand the right to write books and articles about China, simply because he cannot read the Chinese newspapers. Nevertheless, such books and articles must necessarily remain on the level of the gossip along the world's longest bar.

There are exceptions, of course—a Sir Robert Hart or a Bertrand Russell, for example—who are able to see the meaning in a type of life so different from one's own, but for one Sir Robert Hart there are ten thousand Rodney Gilberts, and for one Bertrand Russell there are ten thousand H. G. W. Woodheads. The result is a constant, unintelligent elaboration of the Chinaman as a stage fiction, which is as childish as it is untrue and with which the West is so familiar, and a continuation of the early Portuguese sailors' tradition minus the sailors' obscenity of language, but with essentially the same sailors' obscenity of mind.

The Chinese sometimes wonder among themselves why China attracts only sailors and adventurers to her coast. To understand that, one would have to read H. B. Morse and trace the continuity of that sailor tradition to the present day, and observe the similarities between the early Portuguese sailors and the modern O.C.H.'s in their general outlook, their interests, and the natural process of selection and force of circumstances which have washed them ashore on this corner of the earth, and the motives which drove, and are still driving, them to this heathen country—gold and adventure. Gold and adventure which in the first instance drove Columbus, the greatest sailor-adventurer of them all, to seek a route to China.

Then one begins to understand that continuity, begins to understand how that Columbus-sailor tradition has been so solidly and equitably carried on, and one feels a sort of pity for China; a pity that it is not our humanity but our gold and our capacities as buying animals which have attracted the Westerners to this Far Eastern shore. It is gold and

success, Henry James's "bitch-goddess," which have bound the Westerners and the Chinese together, and thrown them into this whirlpool of
obscenity, with not a single human, spiritual tie among them. They do
not admit this to themselves, the Chinese and the English; so the Chinese asks the Englishman why he does not leave the country if he hates
it so, and the Englishman asks in retort why the Chinese does not leave
the foreign settlements, and both of them do not know how to reply.
As it is, the Englishman does not bother to make himself understood
to the Chinese, and the true Chinese bothers even less to make himself
understood to the Englishman.

III

But do the Chinese understand themselves? Will they be China's best
interpreters? Self-knowledge is proverbially difficult, much more so in
a circumstance where a great deal of wholesome, sane-minded criticism is required. Assuredly no language difficulty exists for the educated Chinese, but that long history of China is difficult for him also
to master; her arts, philosophies, poetry, literature, and the theater are
difficult for him to penetrate and illuminate with a clear and beautiful understanding; and his own fellow men, the fellow passenger in a
streetcar or a former fellow student now pretending to rule the destiny
of a whole province, are for him, too, difficult to forgive.

For the mass of foreground details, which swamps the foreign
observer, swamps the modern Chinese as well. Perhaps he has even less
the cool detachment of the foreign observer. In his breast is concealed a
formidable struggle, or several struggles. There is the conflict between
his ideal and his real China, and a more formidable conflict between his
primeval clan-pride and his moments of admiration for the stranger.
His soul is torn by a conflict of loyalties belonging to opposite poles,
a loyalty to old China, half romantic and half selfish, and a loyalty to
open-eyed wisdom which craves change and a ruthless clean-sweeping
of all that is stale and putrid and dried-up and moldy. Sometimes it is
a more elementary conflict between shame and pride, between sheer

family loyalty and a critical ashamedness for the present state of things, instincts wholesome in themselves. But sometimes his clan-pride gets the better of him, and between proper pride and mere reactionism there is only a thin margin, and sometimes his instinct of shame gets the better of him, and between a sincere desire for reform and a mere shallow modernity and worship of the modern bitch-goddess there is also only a very thin margin. To escape that is indeed a delicate task.

Where is that unity of understanding to be found? To combine real appreciation with critical appraisal, to see with the mind and feel with the heart, to make the mind and the heart at one, is no easy state of grace to attain. For it involves no less than the salvaging of an old culture, like the sorting of family treasures, and even the connoisseur's eyes are sometimes deceived and his fingers sometimes falter. It requires courage and that rare thing, honesty, and that still rarer thing, a constant questioning activity of the mind.

But he has a distinct advantage over the foreign observer. For he is a Chinese, and as a Chinese, he not only sees with his mind but he also feels with his heart, and he knows that the blood, surging in his veins in tides of pride and shame, is Chinese blood, a mystery of mysteries which carries within its biochemical constitution the past and the future of China, bearer of all its pride and shame and of all its glories and its iniquities. The analogy of the family treasure is therefore incomplete and inadequate, for that unconscious national heritage is within him and is part of himself. He has perhaps learned to play English football, but he does not love football; he has perhaps learned to admire American efficiency, but his soul revolts against efficiency; he has perhaps learned to use table napkins, but he hates table napkins; and all through Schubert's melodies and Brahms's songs, he hears, as an overtone, the echo of age-old folk songs and pastoral lyrics of the Orient, luring him back. He explores the beauties and glories of the West, but he comes back to the East, his Oriental blood overcoming him when he is approaching forty. He sees the portrait of his father wearing a Chinese silk cap, and he discards his Western dress and slips into Chinese gowns and slippers, oh, so comfortable, so peaceful and comfortable, for in his Chinese gowns and slippers his soul comes to rest. He cannot understand the Western dog-collar anymore, and wonders how he ever stood it for so long. He does not play football anymore either, but begins to cultivate Chinese hygiene, and saunters along in the mulberry fields and bamboo groves and willow banks for his exercise, and even this is not a "country walk" as the English understand it, but just an Oriental saunter, good for the body and good for the soul. He hates even the word "exercise." Exercise for what? It is a ridiculous Western notion. Why, even the sight of respectable grown-up men dashing about in a field for a ball now seems ridiculous, supremely ridiculous; and more ridiculous still, the wrapping oneself up in hot flannels and woolen sweaters after the game on a hot summer day. Why all the bother? He reflects. He remembers he used to enjoy it himself, but then he was young and immature and he was not himself. It was but a passing fancy, and he has not really the instinct for sport. No, he is born differently; he is born for kowtowing and for quiet and peace, and not for football and the dog-collar and table napkins and efficiency. He sometimes thinks of himself as a pig, and the Westerner as a dog, and the dog worries the pig, but the pig only grunts, and it may even be a grunt of satisfaction. Why, he even wants to be a pig, a real pig, for it is really so very comfortable, and he does not envy the dog for his collar and his dog-efficiency and his bitch-goddess success. All he wants is that the dog leave him alone.

That is how it is with the modern Chinese as he surveys Eastern and Western culture. It is the only way in which the Eastern culture should be surveyed and understood. For he has a Chinese father and a Chinese mother, and every time he talks of China, he thinks of his father and his mother or of the memories of them. It was a life, their lives, so full of courage and patience and suffering and happiness and fortitude, lives untouched by the modern influence, but lives no less grand and noble and humble and sincere. Then does he truly understand China. That seems to me to be the only way of looking at China, and of looking at any foreign nation, by searching, not for the exotic but for the common human values, by penetrating beneath the superficial quaintness of manners and looking for real courtesy, by seeing beneath the strange women's costumes and looking for real womanhood and motherhood, by observing the boys' naughtiness and studying the girls' daydreams. This boys' naughtiness and these girls' daydreams and the ring of children's laughter and the patter of children's feet and the weeping of women and the sorrows of men——they are all alike, and only through the sorrows of men and the weeping of women can we truly understand a nation. The differences are only in the forms of social behavior. This is the basis of all sound international criticism.

LAO SHE
(1898–1966)

Born Shu Qingchun to an impoverished Manchu family in Peking, Lao She had a difficult childhood marked by violence, poverty, and exclusion. In 1900, his father was killed by the foreign soldiers who rampaged through the capital, and one-year-old Lao She survived by sleeping soundly under an overturned chest. Determined and diligent, Lao She eventually worked his way up and became a successful teacher and then administrator in the young republic, living a life of luxury and indulgence until he converted to Christianity and soon resigned from the government post. In 1924, through connections with British missionaries, he was offered a lectureship at the University of London, where for five years he taught Chinese and wrote fiction. Returning to China in 1929, he taught for a few years until he resigned and devoted himself exclusively to writing. In 1936 he published his magnum opus Luotuo Xiangzi (variously translated as Camel Xiangzi, Rickshaw Boy, or Rickshaw), followed by the novel Four Generations Under One Roof (1944). During the first seventeen years in new China, he was much admired as a writer, appointed to important government positions, and continuing to be productive, until the outbreak of the Cultural Revolution brought him down along with other literary giants of his generation. In 1966 he was said to have drowned himself in a lake, although his death remains a mystery.

Rickshaw (excerpts)

[In the first three chapters of the novel, Hsiang Tzu, a rickshaw puller in Peking, saved up enough money to buy a rickshaw and became his own man. But he was soon kidnapped by the army and lost his rickshaw. He managed to get away and stole three camels, which he sold for thirty-five dollars; hence his nickname "Camel Hsiang Tzu." With the money in his pocket, he now made it back to Peking hoping to restart his rickshaw career.]

Chapter Four

Hsiang Tzu lay for three days in a small inn in Hai Tien, his body shaking with chills and fever. He was delirious at times and had great purple blisters on his gums. Water was all he wanted, not food. Three days of fasting brought his temperature down and left his body flaccid as soft taffy. It was probably during these three days that, either by talking in his sleep or babbling deliriously, he let others find out about the camels. He was Camel Hsiang Tzu even before he recovered.

He had been simply Hsiang Tzu, as if he had no family name, ever since he came to the city. Now that Camel was put before Hsiang Tzu, no one would care what his family name was. Having or not having a family name didn't bother him, but to have sold three animals for only thirty-five dollars and then been stuck with a nickname to boot was nothing to brag about.

He decided to take a look around once he struggled to his feet, but he never expected his legs to be so weak. He collapsed feebly onto the ground when he got to the front door of the inn. He sat there, dizzily, for a long time, his forehead covered with cold sweat. He put up with it and then opened his eyes. His stomach rumbled; he felt a little hungry. He stood up very slowly and went over to a wonton peddler. Then, with a bowl of wonton soup, he sat down on the ground again. He took a mouthful and felt nauseated, but held the soup in his mouth awhile and forced it down. He didn't want any more. After a short wait it finally went straight down to his belly and he belched loudly twice. He knew he still had life in him.

He looked himself over after getting a little food in his stomach. He had lost a lot of weight and his ragged trousers couldn't have been dirtier. He was too tired to move but he had to get himself cleaned up immediately; he refused to enter the city looking like a wreck. Only he'd have to spend money to make himself clean and neat. It would take money to get his head shaved and buy a change of clothes and shoes and socks. He ought not to disturb the thirty-five dollars he had in hand. But after all, even if he didn't, wasn't it still a long way from enough to buy a rickshaw? He took pity on himself.

Although it wasn't so long ago that he had been captured by the soldiers, it was all like a nightmare when he thought about it now. This nightmare had aged him considerably; it was as if he'd taken on many years in a single breath. When he looked at his big hands and feet it was obvious they were his, but they looked like they might have been picked up any old place. He didn't dare think of all the hardship and danger he'd just gone through, but it was still there even though he didn't think about it. It was like knowing the sky is overcast during a succession of dark days, even though you do not go out to look at it. He knew his body was especially precious; he should not make himself suffer. He stood up, aware that he was still very weak, intending to go get properly dressed without another minute's delay—as if all he needed was to get his head shaved and his clothes changed to be strong again instantly.

It took a total of two dollars and twenty cents to get properly turned out. A jacket and trousers of fine-looking unbleached rough cloth cost one dollar, black cloth shoes were eighty cents, cotton socks were fifteen cents, and a straw hat cost twenty-five cents. He gave the tattered things he took off to a ragpicker in exchange for the usual two boxes of matches.

He headed down the highway with his two boxes of matches, his goal the Hsi Chih Gate. He had not gone very far before he felt unsteady and exhausted. But he gritted his teeth; he could not ride in a rickshaw. No matter how he looked at it he could not take a rickshaw. Couldn't any peasant make the trip? And besides, he was a rickshaw puller! What a joke to let his energy be drained by such a piddling sickness. He absolutely would not give in to weakness. Why, even if he had an accident and couldn't crawl, then he'd roll and roll all the way to the city. If he did not reach the city today it was all up with him; his body was the only thing he had confidence in, never mind being sick!

Wobbly and shaky, he lengthened his stride, but gold stars appeared before his eyes not far from Hai Tien. He leaned against a willow tree and pulled himself together. The turning earth and reeling sky made him dizzy for a while, but still he refused to sit down. The whirling earth and sky eventually slowed down and his heart seemed to come rolling back to its place again from somewhere far away. He wiped the sweat off his head and set out once more. He'd had his head shaved and gotten his clothes changed. Surely, he reasoned, this was enough to compensate for his weakness. Well, then, his legs had better do their duty and walk! He got almost to the northwest gate in one stretch.

When he saw the bustle of people and horses, heard the ear-piercing racket, smelled the dry stink of the road, and trod on the powdery, churned-up gray dirt, Hsiang Tzu wanted to kiss it, kiss that gray stinking dirt, adorable dirt, dirt that grew silver dollars! He had no father or mother, brother or sister, and no relatives. The only friend he had was this ancient city. This city gave him everything. Even starving here was better than starving in the country. There were things to look at, sounds to listen to, color and voices everywhere. All you needed was to be willing to sell your strength. There was so much money here it couldn't be counted. There were ten thousand kinds of grand things here that would never be eaten up or worn out. Here, if you begged for food, you could even get things like meat and vegetable soup. All they had in the village was cornmeal cakes. When he reached the west side of the Kao Liang Bridge he sat down next to the canal and dropped quite a few hot tears!

The sun was setting; the old willow branches bending above the canal had tiny glints of gold on their tips. There wasn't much water in the canal but there was a lot of trailing waterweed like an oily belt, narrow, long, and deep green, which gave off a slight rank smell of damp. The wheat on the north bank had already spit out its shoots. They were stunted and dry, with a layer of dust on their leaves. The pads of the water lilies along the southern embankment of the canal floated limply on the surface. Little bubbles were released around them at intervals. People were coming and going on the east side of the bridge. They all looked hurried in the light of the setting sun, as if they felt a kind of uneasiness as evening approached. It was all very enjoyable and precious to Hsiang Tzu. Only a little canal like this one could be considered a canal. These trees, the wheat, the water lily pads, the bridge, were the only real trees, wheat, water lilies, and bridge, because they were all part of Peking.

He was in no hurry sitting there. Everything he saw was familiar and dear. If he were to die while sitting there, he'd be content. He rested for some time and then crossed the bridge and bought a bowl of bean curd from a street vendor. Warmed by the scalding hot snow-white bean curd, the vinegar, soy sauce, chili pepper oil, and scallion tips gave off an absolutely wonderful smell that made Hsiang Tzu want to hold his breath. His hands couldn't stop trembling while he held the bowl and gazed at the dark green scallion tips. He took a mouthful. The bean curd opened a path in his body. He added two more spoonfuls of chili pepper oil. When he'd finished, sweat soaked his waistband. With his eyes half shut he held out the bowl. "Give me another bowlful!"

He felt like a man again when he stood up. The sun had sunk to its lowest point in the west. The evening clouds reflected in the canal made the water slightly red. His elation made him want to shout. He forgot all about being sick, forgot everything, as he rubbed the slick scar on his face, rubbed the coins in his pocket, and looked at the sunlight on the watchtower. Then, as if he had a conviction to act upon, he went determinedly into the city.

The gateway tunnel was jammed with every kind of cart and all sorts of people. Everyone wanted to get through it quickly but no one dared hurry. The cracking of whips, shouts, curses, honking of horns, ringing of bells, and laughter were blended into a continuous roaring by the megaphonelike tunnel, making a "weng weng." Hsiang Tzu's big feet cut forward and jumped backward while his hands fended off people to left and right. He pushed his way into the city like a great skinny fish which follows the waves and jumps for joy. He caught sight of Hsin Street; it was so broad and straight it made his eyes sparkle when they saw it just as brightly as the sunlight reflected off the roofs above him. He nodded his head.

His bedroll was still at the Jen Ho Rickshaw Agency; naturally he intended to hurry there. Although he did not always rent one of their rickshaws, he stayed at this agency because he had no home of his own. Liu, the owner, was a man who would soon be sixty-nine. He was old but not dignified. In his younger days he had served as a guard in the Imperial Treasury, operated a gambling house, trafficked in women, and practiced loan sharking. Liu had all the qualifications and abilities needed to carry on these enterprises: audacity, tact, skill, social contacts, reputation, and so forth. During the last days of the Qing Dynasty he had fought in mob wars, abducted women of good family, and "knelt on iron chains." Kneeling before the magistrate on iron chains, Liu never wrinkled his brow, never confessed, never once said, "Spare my life." The magistrate admired his unflinching fortitude under torture. This is called making a name for yourself.

As it happened, Liu came out into the new republic when he got out of jail. Liu could see that the police were becoming more and more powerful and the role of local bravo had already become a thing of the past. Even if those great old heroes Li K'uei and Wu Sung had still been alive, they wouldn't have been able to carry on either.

Liu opened a rickshaw agency. He had started out as a local bravo, or neighborhood bully, so he knew how to treat poor people: when to squeeze them and when to let up a little. He excelled in his genius for fast footwork. None of the rickshaw pullers dared try to outsmart him. One stare or guffaw from Liu would leave them completely stymied, as if they had one foot in heaven and one foot in hell. All they could do was let him persecute them.

Liu now had over sixty rickshaws. He did not rent out worn rickshaws—the very worst of his was almost new. He charged a somewhat higher rental fee but allowed two more rent-free days during the three yearly festivals than the other rickshaw agencies did. The Jen Ho Agency also had sleeping rooms, so unmarried men who pulled its rickshaws could stay there free, but they had to pay promptly for using the rickshaws. Anyone who couldn't pay up and tried to beg off would be thrown out the door like a broken teapot and have his bedroll confiscated. But if any of them had a serious problem or was ill, all he had to do was tell Liu about it. Liu would not sit idly by. He'd even go through fire and flood to help. This is called making a name for yourself.

Liu had the physiognomy of a tiger. He was nearly seventy but his back was still straight and he could still walk ten or twenty *li*. He had big round eyes, a big nose, a square chin, and a pair of tigerish canine teeth. His open mouth looked just like a tiger's. He was almost as tall as Hsiang Tzu. His head was shaved so it glistened and he had not grown a beard. He claimed to be a tiger, but alas he had no son, only a thirty-seven-or-so-year-old tiger daughter. Anyone who knew about old Liu also knew about Hu Niu, Tiger Girl. She, too, had grown up with the head and brains of a tiger and so she frightened men off. She was skillful at helping her father manage the business but no one dared ask for her as his wife. She was the same as a man in everything; she had a man's bluntness when swearing at someone and even added a few embellishments all her own. Under the rule of the Lius, the Jen Ho Agency was like a length of steel tubing: nothing out of place. This agency had a great deal of prestige and influence in the world of rickshaws. The methods of the Lius were often on the lips of rickshaw owners and pullers, the way scholars quote from the Confucian classics.

Until he bought his own rickshaw, Hsiang Tzu had pulled one of theirs. He had deposited his profits with Liu at interest, and when he finally had saved enough, he withdrew it all and bought his rickshaw. "Mister Liu," he'd said, "look at my new rickshaw!" He had taken his new rickshaw back to the Jen Ho Agency.

The old man had looked at it and nodded. "Not bad!"

"I'll still have to stay here. But whenever I work for a family, I'll go live there," added Hsiang Tzu rather proudly.

"Very well." Liu had nodded again.

And so, when Hsiang Tzu had a private job, he lived there. He lived at the agency when he was out of a private job and had to work the streets.

In the opinion of the other rickshaw men, it was unheard-of to have someone who no longer pulled a Jen Ho rickshaw go on living there. They wondered about it. The most far-fetched guess was that Hsiang Tzu was related to old Liu. Many others said old Liu probably had a high opinion of Hsiang Tzu and planned to fix Hu Niu up with a husband who would live there. Speculations like these were colored by a little envy, but perhaps things really would turn out like that. The Jen Ho Agency would certainly be left to Hsiang Tzu when old Liu died, that was what mattered. All they did was make foolish guesses about the situation. Naturally none of them dared be so rude as to say anything to Hsiang Tzu himself.

In fact, old Liu's good treatment of Hsiang Tzu was on quite another account. Hsiang Tzu was the sort of man who held fast to his old habits in a new environment. Suppose he joined the army; he certainly would not start right in pretending to be ignorant of what he was doing and cheat and swindle people the way most soldiers did as soon as he had put on his uniform. At the agency he started looking for something to do as soon as he came back each day and had wiped the sweat off his brow. He was never idle. He dusted off rickshaws, pumped up tires, spread the rain covers out to dry in the sun, and greased wheels. No one had to tell him to do these things; he did them voluntarily. Working made him very happy, as if it were the best of all amusements.

Ordinarily, there were about twenty men living at the agency. They either sat around talking or were dead asleep after putting away their rickshaws. Only Hsiang Tzu's hands were never idle. When he first came there everyone thought he was putting on a show for old Liu, trying to get himself in good like a stray dog. After a while they realized he was not putting up a false front in any way. He really was that forthright and natural, so there was simply nothing more to be said. Old Liu never praised him, never gave a sign he had noticed Hsiang Tzu; he simply made a mental note. He knew Hsiang Tzu was a good worker, so he was glad to have him around even if he wasn't pulling a Liu rickshaw. The courtyard and doorway, not to mention anything else, were always kept clean when Hsiang Tzu was there.

Hu Niu liked the big oaf even more. Hsiang Tzu always listened attentively when she spoke and never argued with her. The other rickshaw pullers were contrary because of all their miseries. She wasn't afraid of them in the least but preferred not to have much to do with them, so she saved all her comments for Hsiang Tzu. It was as if the Lius had lost a friend when Hsiang Tzu had a private job and was living out. And when he was there, even the old man's swearing seemed more to the point and a little kinder.

Hsiang Tzu entered the Jen Ho Agency carrying his two boxes of matches. It wasn't dark yet and the Lius were still eating dinner. Hu Niu put down her chopsticks when she saw him come in.

"Hsiang Tzu! Did you let a wolf catch you or did you go to Africa to dig in the gold mines?"

Hsiang Tzu said nothing; he grunted.

Liu's big round eyes gave Hsiang Tzu the once-over. He didn't say anything either.

Hsiang Tzu sat down facing them, his new straw hat still on his head.

"In case you haven't eaten, here's some." Hu Niu behaved as if she were taking care of a good friend.

Hsiang Tzu didn't move. His heart was suddenly full of a feeling of warm friendship he couldn't put into words. He had always regarded the Jen Ho Agency as his home. For private jobs his masters changed frequently, and when working the streets his passengers changed with every trip. This was the only place he was allowed to stay and there was always someone to chat with. He had just escaped with his life and come back to his friends and here they were, inviting him to have something to eat. While he wondered if they could be mocking him, he almost wept too.

"Just had two bowls of bean curd." He showed a little courtesy.

"What did you go away for? Where's your rickshaw?" Old Liu's eyes were still fastened on him.

"Rickshaw?" Hsiang Tzu spat.

"Come have a bowl of rice first. It won't kill you. What are two bowls of bean curd?" Hu Niu pulled at his sleeve like a wife fussing over a younger brother-in-law.

Hsiang Tzu did not take the rice bowl. He took out his money instead. "Sir, keep this for me. It's thirty dollars." He put the change back in his pocket.

Liu inquired with his eyebrows. Where did it come from?

Hsiang Tzu ate and told how he had been captured by the soldiers.

"Humph! You idiot!" Liu shook his head. "If you'd brought them to the city and sold them for the soup pot, they'd have been worth more than ten dollars a head. If it had been winter and they'd had their heavy coats, three head would have brought sixty dollars!"

Hsiang Tzu already regretted it; hearing this made him feel even worse. But, he went on to think, it was hardly virtuous to let three living animals have their throats cut for the soup pot. They had all escaped together so they should all live. That was all there was to say about it and he felt at peace in his mind.

Hu Niu cleared the table. Liu looked up as though he'd thought of something. Suddenly a laugh showed two teeth that looked more and more like tiger teeth the older he got. "Dolt! Did you say you were sick at Hai Tien? Why didn't you come straight back on the Huang Ts'un Road?"

"I had to go the long way around by the Western Hills. I was afraid that if I took the main road someone would catch me. I was pretty sure the villagers would grab me as a deserter if they thought things over."

Liu smiled and his eyes rolled back and forth. He had been afraid Hsiang Tzu was lying about the money. Maybe it was stolen. He wasn't going to hide anyone's loot for him. He had done every lawless thing there was to do when young, but he had to be careful now that he had taken up the role of reformed character. He knew what to watch out for, all right. There was only one flaw in Hsiang Tzu's story, but he had explained it away without mumbling. The old man relaxed. "Now what?" he said, pointing to the money.

"Whatever you say."

"Buy another rickshaw?" The old man stuck out his tiger teeth again as if to say, "You buy another rickshaw and still think you're going to stay at my place free again?"

"There isn't enough. I've got to buy a new one!" Hsiang Tzu did not look at Liu's teeth. He was concentrating on his own thoughts.

"Lend you the money? One percent interest. Anyone else gets charged two and a half."

Hsiang Tzu shook his head.

"Buying on installments from a dealer is not as good as giving me one percent."

"I won't buy one on installments either," Hsiang Tzu said intensely. "I'll save up until I get enough. Ready cash buys ready goods."

Old Liu stared at Hsiang Tzu as if he were trying to read a strange word he couldn't figure out and detested, but could hardly get angry at. He waited awhile and then picked up the money. "Thirty dollars? You're sure about the amount?"

"That's right." Hsiang Tzu stood up. "I'm going to bed. I've brought you a box of matches, sir." He put the box on the table and stood blankly for a moment. "There's no need to tell people about the camels."

[In chapters five through seventeen, Hsiang Tzu was seduced by Hu Niu and fooled into marrying her. Hu Niu's father disapproved of the marriage and disowned her, forcing the couple to move out and rent a room in a shabby mixed courtyard in the city. Hsiao Fu Tzu in the text below is the young daughter of the couple's neighbor Ch'iang, who was also a rickshaw puller. Earlier in desperation Ch'iang had sold his Hsiao Fu Tzu to a military officer, but she had come back and tried to feed the family by prostituting herself.]

Chapter Eighteen

There was simply no human sound at all in the mixed courtyard when June came. The children went out very early clutching their broken baskets to collect whatever they could. By nine that poisonous flower of a sun was already drying and splitting the skin on their skinny backs and they were forced to come home with what they had gathered and eat whatever the big people gave them. The somewhat older children, if they could scrape up the least amount of capital, would buy some bits of natural ice from an icehouse and, combining it with some they had scrounged, would go out and sell it all quickly.

If they hadn't got together this mite of capital, then they'd all go to the moat outside the city wall and take baths, stealing coal at the railway station outside of town without any extra trouble on the way. Or they'd go catch some dragonflies and cicadas to sell to the children of rich families.

The younger children didn't dare go so far. They all went to places nearby where there were trees and collected locust tree insects, digging their larvae out for fun.

After all the children had gone out, and all the men were gone too, the women would sit in their rooms with their backs bare, but none of them dared go outside. Not because of the way they looked, but because the ground in the courtyard was already hot enough to burn their feet.

Finally, when the sun was fast setting, the men and children came back in a continual stream. By this time there was shade from the wall and a little cool breeze in the courtyard. The hot air stored up in the rooms all day made them like the inside of a steamer basket. Everybody sat in the courtyard waiting for the women to get the cooking done. The courtyard was quite crowded then; it was just like a marketplace but one without merchandise. They had all been through one day's worth of heat and they were red-eyed and ill-tempered. Their bellies were empty again and their faces even more anxious and pale.

Let one word be spoken out of line and some of them wanted to beat the children, others wanted to beat their wives, and if they couldn't be beaten, at least they could be cursed at furiously. This sort of ruckus continued until everyone had eaten.

After eating, some of the children just lay down on the ground and went to sleep while others went out to the street to chase and frolic around. The adults all felt more cheerful after they had eaten their fill and those who enjoyed talking gathered in several groups to discuss the misfortunes of the day.

But those who had not yet eaten had no place to pawn anything or sell anything, assuming that they had anything to pawn or sell, because the pawnshops were already closed. The men paid no attention to how hot the rooms were. They dropped their heads down onto the *k'ang* and made not a sound or, perhaps, cursed loudly. The women held back their tears and tried to smooth things over. Then they went out and, after who knows how many rebuffs, finally managed to borrow twenty cents or so. Clutching this precious money, they went to buy cornmeal to make some mush for the family.

Hu Niu and Hsiang Tzu were not part of this pattern of living. Hu Niu was pregnant and this time it was true. Hsiang Tzu would go out bright and early but she always waited until eight or nine and then got up. It is a traditional and erroneous belief that it won't do to exercise when pregnant and Hu Niu really took it to heart. Besides, she wanted to take advantage of her condition to show off. Everyone else had to get up and get moving early. She was the only one who could calmly enjoy lying in bed as long as she liked. When evening came, she'd take a small stool to a place outside the front gate where there was a little cool breeze and sit there. She went in after almost everyone else in the place had gone to bed. She couldn't be bothered to gossip with them.

Hsiao Fu Tzu got up late too, but she had another reason. She feared the sidelong glances the men gave her, so she waited until they'd all gone to work and then, and only then, did she dare go outside her door. During the day, if she didn't visit Hu Niu, she'd go out walking because her advertisement was simply herself. In the evening, to avoid attracting the attention of the men who lived there, she would go out into the streets for another turn and sneak back when she figured they had all gone to bed.

Hsiang Tzu and Ch'iang were the exceptions among the men. Hsiang Tzu disliked entering this courtyard and feared going into his rooms even more. The endless griping of all the other men made him frantic and he longed to have a quiet place to sit by himself. At home, he felt more and more that Hu Niu was like a mother tiger. On top of that, the rooms were so hot and disagreeable that, with the tiger added in, it was as if he couldn't breathe when he got inside. Formerly, he'd come home early to avoid having her yell at him and scold him. Recently, with Hsiao Fu Tzu for company, she hadn't been keeping tabs on him so much, so he'd been coming home a little later.

Ch'iang hadn't been coming home much recently at all. He knew what his daughter was doing and he didn't have the nerve to come in the gate. But there was nothing he could do to keep her from doing it. He knew he didn't have the strength to take care of his children. It was better for him not to come back, and to pretend that out of sight is out of mind.

Sometimes he hated her. If Hsiao Fu Tzu had been a boy, he could guarantee that nothing this disgraceful would have been necessary. But this having a daughter! Why did it have to happen to him? Sometimes he pitied her. Here was his own daughter selling herself to feed her two little brothers! He could hate her or feel sorry for her but nothing else. When he was drinking and broke he didn't hate or pity her; he came back wanting money from her. At a time like that, he thought of her as something that could earn money. After all, he was the papa and to demand money from her was simply a matter of "calling things by their right names" and carrying out the correct relationship between father and child.

Sometimes he also thought about appearances. Didn't everybody hold Hsiao Fu Tzu in contempt? Her father couldn't forgive her either. He'd force her to give him the money and curse her too, as if he were cursing her for everyone to hear. He'd show them that he, Ch'iang, hadn't done anything wrong. It was Hsiao Fu Tzu who was born not caring about her reputation!

He'd rail at her and Hsiao Fu Tzu wouldn't even let out a deep breath. Hu Niu, on the other hand, would alternately swear and urge him to leave. Of course he'd take some money with him. It was only enough to keep him drunk because if he sobered up and looked at the money he'd just jump in the river or hang himself.

The heat on the fifteenth of June was enough to drive people mad. The sun had just risen and the ground was already afire. Puffs of gray dust, like clouds and yet not clouds, like mist and yet not mist, floated low in the air, making people exasperated. There was no breeze at all. Hsiang Tzu looked at the grayish-reddish sky and decided not to start work until late afternoon. He'd wait until after four o'clock to go out and keep going until dawn if he didn't make much. No matter what the night was like, it would be easier to put up with than the daytime.

Hu Niu nagged at him to get out of there. She was afraid it would hinder business if he was there because Hsiao Fu Tzu would probably bring home a "guest."

"You think it's better here? By afternoon even the walls are scorching!"

He said nothing, drank some cold water, and went out.

The willows along the street looked sick. Their leaves were all curled up and covered with dust; their branches, barely moving, drooped in utter dejection. There was not a spot of dampness anywhere in the main street. It was so dry it shimmered whitely. Then the dust from the dirt streets flew up and joined the dust in the sky to make a poisonous layer of gray dust that burned people's faces. It was dry everywhere, hand-scorching everywhere, depressing everywhere. The whole city was like a fired-up brick kiln, which made breathing difficult.

Dogs crawled along with their red tongues dragging. The nostrils of horses and donkeys flared out. The street vendors didn't dare yell and the asphalt pavements began to melt. It was so bad it seemed the sun would even melt the brass shop signs. The streets were very quiet, except for a monotonous banging and clanging from the metalworking shops, which annoyed people.

Rickshaw pullers were well aware that they wouldn't eat if they didn't get a move on, but they too were reluctant to look for business. Some parked their rickshaws in a shady place, put the top up, and took a nap in the rickshaw. Some burrowed into tea shops and drank tea. Others didn't take their rickshaws out at all; they just went out and looked around to see if there was any possibility of working. Those who were out working lost face quite willingly, even if they were the most prepossessing of fellows. They didn't dare run and just shuffled along with their heads down. Every well became their lucky star. It didn't matter how far they'd gone—when they saw a well they hurried over to it. They'd just take a long drink at the trough along with the horses and donkeys if there wasn't any freshly drawn water. And there were those who, coming down with cholera or befuddled by sunstroke, just went on and on until they collapsed and never stood up again.

Even Hsiang Tzu was a little scared! He realized, after pulling an empty rickshaw for a while, that he was surrounded by burning hot air and even the backs of his hands were sweating. But he still intended to take a fare if he got one in the hope that running might make a little breeze.

He did get a passenger, started off, and then realized that the temperature had reached a point that would not allow anyone to work. He'd run a little and then couldn't breathe. His lips were burning and seeing water made him want to drink it, although he wasn't really thirsty. That poisonous flower of a sun would split the skin on his hands and back if he didn't run. He got to his destination one way or another with his clothes glued to his body. He took his palm leaf fan and fanned himself. It was no use. The breeze was hot. He had already lost count of how many times he had had a drink of cold water and still he made for a teahouse. He felt somewhat better when he'd downed two pots of hot tea. The sweat came out of his body as soon as the tea went into his mouth. It was just as if the inside of his body was open at both ends and couldn't hold a drop of water. He didn't dare move.

He sat for a long time feeling very queasy. Since he didn't want to risk going out again and had nothing else to do, he began to think that the weather was determined to make things difficult for him. No, he would not give in to weakness. This wasn't his first day pulling a rickshaw and this wasn't his first nasty encounter with summer. He couldn't just fritter away an entire day this way.

He thought he'd go out but his legs were reluctant to move and his body was unusually weak. It was as if he'd spent too long in a hot bath and still didn't feel any better for it, even though he had sweated a lot. He sat a while longer and then couldn't put up with it anymore. Sitting here made him sweat too, so why not go out briskly and try anyway?

He realized his mistake as soon as he got outside. The layer of gray air had already scattered and the sky wasn't so depressing, but the sun was much worse than before. No one dared lift his head to look at it. All anyone knew was that the glare dazzled the eyes everywhere. The glare was all over. There was a whiteness shot through with red in the sky, on the rooftops, on the walls, and on the ground. The sun was a huge burning glass; it was as if every sunbeam had come through it and was heating things to their flash point. In this white glare every color stabbed the eyes and every smell had mixed in with it a fetid stench boiled out of the ground. There seemed to be no one in the streets, which had suddenly become a lot wider and without a breath of cool air. Their glitter made people afraid.

Hsiang Tzu didn't know what to do. He plodded on very slowly, pulling the rickshaw with his head down. He hadn't anywhere to go. He was confused. Covered with sticky sweat, he was giving off a sour smell. After he walked awhile his shoes and socks and feet were all stuck together, just as if he'd stepped in soppy mud. It was extremely uncomfortable.

He hadn't any intention of drinking more water but he went over to take a drink automatically whenever he saw a well. Not, however, to relieve his thirst. Apparently, it was to enjoy the bit of coolness when the well water went down his throat and into his stomach and produced a moment of sudden chill, gooseflesh, and a cold shiver. It was very pleasant. When he finished he'd hiccup repeatedly. The water wanted out!

He walked awhile and sat awhile. He was much too listless to look for business and still didn't feel hungry when noon came. He considered going to get something to eat as usual but felt nauseated when he saw the food. His stomach was full of almost every kind of water and sometimes made a little sloshing noise like the sound inside the belly of a donkey or horse which has just been watered.

When comparing the seasons, Hsiang Tzu had always believed that winter was more horrible than summer. It had never occurred to him that summer could be so unbearable. He'd been through more than one summer in this city all right, but couldn't recall ever being so hot. Was the weather hotter now than it used to be or was his body failing him? When he thought of that he was suddenly not so muddled and his heart seemed to have grown cold. His body, yes, his own body, wasn't making it! It frightened him, but there was nothing he could do to change things. There was no way he could drive Hu Niu away. He would turn into another Ch'iang or a man like that tall fellow he'd met or Hsiao Ma's grandfather. Hsiang Tzu was done for!

He got another fare shortly past noon. This was the hottest part of the day, and the hottest day of the year as well, but he decided to make the trip at a run. He didn't care how hot it was in the sun. If he managed it, and nothing happened to him, well then, that would prove there was nothing wrong with him. If he couldn't do it, what was there left to say? He might just as well trip and break his neck on the fiery ground!

He had gone only a little way when he became aware of a cool breeze just like cold winter air coming into a hot room through a slit in the door. He didn't dare believe it, so he looked at the willows along the road for confirmation. Yes indeed, they were all moving slightly.

Suddenly a great many people were out in the street. Those in the shops fought to get out and then held rush-leaf fans over their heads while they looked around. "There's a cool breeze! A cool breeze is coming!" Almost all of them wanted to shout and jump for joy. The willows suddenly seemed to have been transformed into angels bringing heavenly tidings. "The willow branches are waving! Lord of Heaven grant us a cool breeze!"

It was still hot but hearts were much calmer. A cool wind, even a little one, gives people lots of hope.

This cool wind passed by and the sunlight was not as strong; it was bright and then somewhat dimmer, as if a veil of flying dust floated in front of it. The wind suddenly rose and those willows, motionless most of the day, acted as if they'd had some pleasant news. Swaying and swinging, their branches looked like they'd grown another length. A gust of wind passed by and the sky darkened. All the gray dust flew high up into the sky and then settled back down and inky clouds were visible on the northern horizon.

There was no more sweat on Hsiang Tzu's body. He looked northward once, stopped the rickshaw, and put up the rain cover. He knew that summer rain comes when it says it's coming and doesn't waste time. He'd just got the cover on when there was another gust of wind. The black clouds were rolling onward and had already covered up half the sky. The hot air on the ground combined with the cold air above and the noisome dry dust. The air seemed cooler but it still was hot. The southern half of the sky was clear and sunny. The black clouds in the northern half were like ink.

Everybody was alarmed and frantic as if some great disaster loomed. Rickshaw pullers hurriedly put up rain covers, shopkeepers scurried to take down their signs, street vendors scrambled around stowing away their goods and mats, and pedestrians rushed by.

There was another blast of wind; when it had passed by, the shop signs, the mats, and the pedestrians all seemed to have been rolled up and carried off by the gust. All that was left were the willow branches following the wind in a mad dance.

The clouds had not yet covered the entire sky but it was already dark on the ground; the too hot, too bright, too clear noontime had abruptly been transformed into something that resembled a dark night. The wind brought the rain as it dashed wildly from east and west as if searching for something on the ground. Far off on the northern horizon there was a red flash as if the clouds had been split open and their blood gushed out. The wind diminished but it made a loud whistling noise that made people shiver. A blast of this kind passed by and nobody seemed to know what to do next. Even the willows were waiting for something apprehensively.

There was yet another flash, white and clear and right overhead. The fast-falling raindrops came with it and forced the dust to leap upward, giving the ground a rainish look of its own. Many huge raindrops pelted Hsiang Tzu on the back and he shivered twice.

The rain paused. Now the black clouds covered the entire sky. Still another blast of wind came, much stronger than the ones before, and the willow branches stretched out horizontally, the dust flew in all directions, and the rain fell in sheets. Wind, earth, and rain were all mixed up together; that gray, cold, roaring wind wrapped everything up inside itself and you couldn't tell what was a tree, what was ground, or what was cloud. It was a chaos of noise and confusion. The wind passed by, leaving behind only the driving rain to tear the sky, rend the earth, and fall everywhere. You couldn't see rain. There was only a sheet of water, a blast of wetness, and then innumerable arrowheads that spurted up from the ground and hundreds of torrents that fell from the roofs. In a few minutes the earth was indistinguishable from the sky as the rivers in the air flowed down and the rivers on the ground flowed across them to make a grayish dark turbid yellow, sometimes white, world of water.

Hsiang Tzu's clothes had been soaked beforehand. There wasn't a dry spot on him and his hair was wet under his straw hat. The water on the ground covered his feet. It was already hard to walk. The rain above pelted his head and back, swept across his face, and wrapped around his loins. He couldn't lift his head, couldn't open his eyes, couldn't breathe, and couldn't move forward. He was forced to stand in the middle of all that water without knowing where the road was or what front, back, left, and right were. All he was conscious of was the water that chilled him to the bone and sloshed over him. He was aware of nothing except a great vague hotness in his heart and the sound of rain in his ears. He wanted to put the rickshaw down but didn't know where to put it. He thought about running but the water held his feet. He could only keep moving, pulling the rickshaw with his head down one step at a time and more dead than alive. The passenger seemed to have died right there in the rickshaw. He let the rickshaw man risk his life in the rain without saying a word.

The rain let up some. Hsiang Tzu straightened up slightly and puffed once. "Sir, let's take shelter somewhere and then go on!"

"Make it snappy! What do you think you're doing just leaving me somewhere!" He stamped his feet and yelled.

For a moment Hsiang Tzu actually thought about leaving the rickshaw and going to find someplace out of the rain. But when he looked at how dripping wet he was, he knew he'd only get the shivers if he stopped. He ground his teeth and, paying no attention to whether the water was deep or shallow, began to run. He hadn't been running long when another flash came close behind another darkening of the sky and rain blurred his vision again.

When they finally arrived his passenger didn't give him a penny extra. Hsiang Tzu said nothing. He didn't care if he lived or not.

The heavy rain stopped and then resumed but fell much lighter than before. Hsiang Tzu ran straight home. He hugged the stove to get warm and shivered like the leaves on a tree in the wind and rain. Hu Niu steeped him a bowl of ginger and sugar water and he drank it all down in one draught like an idiot. When he finished he burrowed under his quilt and knew nothing more. His condition was like being asleep and yet not really sleeping. In his ears was the swishing sound of rain.

The black clouds began to look tired a little after four o'clock. Softly and weakly, they let loose paler flashes of lightning. In a while the clouds in the west broke up. The tops of the black clouds were edged with gold and a little whiteness came rushing underneath them. The lightning all went south, dragging the not so terribly loud thunderclaps along with it. After another interval, rays of sunlight came out through the spaces between the clouds in the west, making gold and green reflections on the water-covered leaves. In the east hung a pair of rainbows, their legs in the dark clouds, the tops of their bows in the blue sky. Soon the rainbows faded and there were no more black clouds in the sky.

The blue sky, as well as everything else that had been newly washed, looked like part of a charming world just risen from darkness. Even the "pond" in the mixed courtyard had a few dragonflies hovering over it.

But, except for the barefooted children who chased those dragonflies, no one in the place cared about taking pleasure in the clear sky that followed the rain.

A piece fell out of a corner in the rear wall in Hsiao Fu Tzu's room and she and her brothers hurriedly tore the matting off the *k'ang* and blocked up the hole. The courtyard wall had collapsed in several places but no one had time to do anything about it because they were all too busy taking care of their own rooms. Some had front steps that were too low and let the water in. They all had to race around with old bowls and dustpans bailing out the water. Some were on the roof looking for ways to patch it. Some had roofs that leaked like sprinkling cans and got everything inside soaking wet. They were busy moving things outside next to the cookstove to dry or hanging them on windowsills in the sun. They had huddled in their rooms while the rain was falling; rooms that might, when the moment came, collapse and bury them alive. They left their fate to Heaven. After the rain they tried to figure out how to repair their losses.

Although a heavy rain might lower the price of a pound of rice by half a cent, still, their losses were so great that such a trifling drop in price could not make up for them. They paid their rent but no one ever came to repair the place unless the dilapidation was so bad that no one could possibly live there. In that case, two masons would come along and fix up the wall haphazardly with mortar and broken bricks, preparing it for its next collapse. If the rent wasn't paid the whole family would be thrown out and have its goods confiscated. The walls were cracking, the roof might fall in and kill someone, and no one cared. A place like this was all their tiny income could afford. It was tumbledown, dangerous, and they deserved it!

The greatest loss of all resulted from the sickness brought on by the rainwater. All of them, young and old, were out in the streets looking for a deal all day and the furious rain of summer could pelt down on their heads at any time. They all sold their strength to make a living and were always covered with sweat. The fierce rain of the north was very hard and very cold. Sometimes there were hailstones as big as walnuts in it. If it did nothing else, the ice-cold rain striking at their open pores made them lie on the *k'ang* with a fever for a day or two.

The children got sick and there was no money for medicine. A spell of rain urged the corn and the *kaoliang* upward in the fields but it also sprinkled death onto many of the poor children in the city.

The adults got sick, and that was even worse. Poets chant about the lotus "pearls" and double rainbows that come after rain, but poor people suffer from hunger when the wage earners are sick. A spell of rain might well create a few more singsong girls and sneak thieves and put a few more people in jail. When adults get sick it's much better for boys and girls to become thieves and singsong girls than to starve! "The rain falls on the rich and on the poor, falls on the just and on the unjust." But the truth is that the rain is not evenhanded at all because it falls on an inequitable world.

Hsiang Tzu was sick and he certainly was not the only sick person in the place.

(Translated by Jean M. James)

BIAN ZHILIN
(1910–2000)

Born in Jiangsu, Bian Zhilin bought a copy of Bing Xin's A Maze of Stars *when he was fourteen, a chance encounter that kindled his passion for new poetry. In 1929 he entered Peking University and studied under Xu Zhimo, who quickly recognized Bian's poetic talent and helped him get published. Closely associated with the Crescent poets, who empha-sized metrics and prosody, Bian was most productive in the 1930s, when he wrote some of his best poems, including "Fragment" and "Dream of the Old Town," which combine techniques of Western modernism with the Chinese poetic tradition. In the tumultuous decades in Mao's China, Bian worked quietly as a professor and translator of Shakespeare.*

Evening

Evening sun leaning on West Hill,
    temple wall just standing, about to fall;
facing each other, what do they want to say?
    Why don't they say it, eh?

Haggard donkey, old man on its back,
    hurries home, clackety-clack,
hooves rapping on clay and stone—
    a dry and ragged tune!

A croak in midair—
    treetop, a crow there
soars up, but makes no sound,
      then lights and settles down.

          —1930

Dream of the Old Town

There are two kinds of sound in the small town,
equally desolate:
the fortune-teller's gong by day,
the watchman's clapper at night.

Unable to shatter dreams with his gong,
as if in a dream
the blind man walks the streets,
step by step.
He knows which slab of stone is low,
which slab of stone is high,
and the age of the daughter in each household.

His claps sending people deep into dreams,
as if in a dream
the watchman walks the streets,
step by step.
He knows which slab of stone is low,
which slab of stone is high,
and the door of which house is most tightly shut.

"Third watch already, listen,
Ah Mao's dad.

The baby makes such a row we can't sleep a wink,
always crying in his dreams.
Let's have his fortune told tomorrow."

It's deep in the night;
it's the quiet afternoon:
the watchman with his clapper crosses the bridge,
the fortune-teller with his gong crosses the bridge.
Ceaseless is the sound of water flowing under the bridge.

—August 11, 1933

Fragment

You stand on the bridge looking at the view—
the viewer on the balcony is viewing you.

The moon adorns your window—
you adorn someone else's dream.

—October 1935

Loneliness

Fearing loneliness the country boy
kept a cricket beside his pillow.
Toiling in the city after he grew up,
he bought a luminous watch.

As a child he used to envy the cricket
for having weeds on the tomb as its garden.
Now he has been dead for three hours,
yet the watch keeps on ticking.

—October 26, 1935
(Translated by Mary Fung and David Lunde)

XIAO HONG
(1911–1942)

Born to a wealthy landlord family in what she called "the easternmost and northernmost part of China," Xiao Hong (real name Zhang Naiying) lost her mother at the age of nine, became alienated from her father, and fled from home while still a teenager. Attending middle school in Harbin, she cohabited with a local teacher, became pregnant, and then was abandoned by the man. The Japanese occupation of Manchuria forced her to flee to Qingdao, where at the age of twenty-three she wrote her first novel, The Field of Life and Death (1935). Her fiery and strained romance with Xiao Jun, a noted left-wing writer, remains the stuff of legend in Chinese literature. Living a bohemian life beset by male cruelty, unwanted pregnancies, and ill health, she died at the age of thirty in Hong Kong, where she had completed Tales of Hulan River, a semi-autobiographical novel of poetic nostalgia and acute sensibility about her birthplace, Hulan.

Tales of Hulan River (excerpt)

Hulan River

1

After the harsh winter has sealed up the land, the earth's crust begins to crack and split. From south to north, from east to west; from a few feet to several yards in length; anywhere, anytime, the cracks run in every direction. As soon as harsh winter is upon the land, the earth's crust opens up.

The severe winter weather splits the frozen earth.

Old men use whisk brooms to brush the ice off their beards the moment they enter their homes. "Oh, it's cold out today!" they say. "The frozen ground has split open."

A carter twirls his long whip as he drives his cart sixty or seventy *li* under the stars, then at the crack of dawn he strides into an inn, and the first thing he says to the innkeeper is: "What terrible weather. The cold is like a dagger."

After he has gone into his room at the inn, removed his dogskin cap with earflaps, and smoked a pipeful of tobacco, he reaches out for a steamed bun; the back of his hand is a mass of cracked, chapped skin.

The skin on people's hands is split open by the freezing cold. The man who sells cakes of bean curd is up at dawn to go out among the people's homes and sell his product. If he carelessly sets down his square wooden tray full of bean curd it sticks to the ground, and he is unable to free it. It will have quickly frozen to the spot.

The old steamed-bun peddler lifts his wooden box filled with the steaming buns up onto his back, and at the first light of day he is out hawking on the street. After emerging from his house he walks along at a brisk pace shouting at the top of his voice. But before too long, layers of ice have formed on the bottoms of his shoes, and he walks as though he were treading on rolling and shifting eggs. The snow and ice have encrusted the soles of his shoes. He walks with an unsure step, and if he is not altogether careful he will slip and fall. In fact, he slips and falls despite all his caution. Falling down is the worst thing that can happen to him, for his wooden box crashes to the ground, and the buns come rolling out of the box, one on top of the other. A witness to the incident takes advantage of the old man's inability to pick himself up and scoops up several of the buns, which he eats as he leaves the scene. By the time the old man has struggled to his feet, gathered up his steamed buns— ice, snow, and all—and put them back in the box, he counts them and discovers that some are missing. He understands at once and shouts to the man who is eating the buns but has still not left the scene: "Hey, the weather's icy cold, the frozen ground's all cracked, and my buns are all gone!"

Passersby laugh when they hear him say this. He then lifts the box up onto his back and walks off again, but the layers of ice on the soles of his shoes seem to have grown even thicker, and he finds the going more difficult than before. Drops of sweat begin to form on his back, his eyes become clouded with the frost, ice gathers in even greater quantity on his beard, and the earflaps and front of his tattered cap are frosting up with the vapor from his breath. The old man walks more and more slowly, his worries and fears causing him to tremble in alarm; he resembles someone on ice skates for the first time who has just been pushed out onto the rink by a friend.

A puppy is so freezing cold it yelps and cries night after night, whimpering as though its claws were being singed by flames.

The days grow even colder:

Water vats freeze and crack;

Wells are frozen solid;

Night snowstorms seal the people's homes; they lie down at night to sleep, and when they get up in the morning they find they cannot open their doors.

Once the harsh winter season comes to the land everything undergoes a change: the skies turn ashen gray, as though a strong wind has blown through, leaving in its aftermath a turbid climate accompanied by a constant flurry of snowflakes whirling in the air. People on the road walk at a brisk pace as their breath turns to vapor in the wintry cold. Big carts pulled by teams of seven horses form a caravan in the open country, one following closely upon the other, lanterns flying, whips circling in the air under the starry night. After running two *li* the horses begin to sweat. They run a bit farther, and in the midst of all that snow and ice the men and horses are hot and lathered. The horses stop sweating only after the sun emerges and they are finally turned into their stalls. But the moment they stop sweating a layer of frost forms on their coats.

After the men and horses have eaten their fill they are off and running again. Here in the frigid zones there are few people; unlike the southern regions, where you need not travel far from one village to another, and where each township is near the next, here there is nothing but a blanket of snow as far as the eye can see. There is no neighboring village within the range of sight, and only by relying on the memories of those familiar with the roads can one know the direction to travel. The big carts with their seven-horse teams transport their loads of foodstuffs to one of the neighboring towns. Some have brought in soybeans to sell, others have brought sorghum. Then when they set out on their return trip they carry back with them oil, salt, and dry goods.

Hulan River is one of these small towns, not a very prosperous place at all. It has only two major streets, one running north and south and one running east and west, but the best-known place in town is the Crossroads, for it is the heart of the whole town. At the Crossroads there is a jewelry store, a yardage shop, an oil store, a salt store, a tea shop, a pharmacy, and the office of a foreign dentist. Above this dentist's door there hangs a large shingle about the size of a rice-measuring basket, on which is painted a row of oversized teeth. The advertisement is hopelessly out of place in this small town, and the people who look at it cannot figure out just what it's supposed to represent. That is because neither the oil store, the yardage shop, nor the salt store displays any kind of advertisement; above the door of the salt store, for example, only the word "salt" is written, and hanging above the door of the yardage shop are two curtains which are as old as the hills. The remainder of the signs are like the one at the pharmacy, which gives nothing more than the name of the bespectacled physician whose job it is to feel women's pulses as they drape their arms across a small pillow. To illustrate: the physician's name is Li Yung-ch'un, and the name of his pharmacy is simply "Li Yung-ch'un." People rely on their memories, and even if Li Yung-ch'un were to take down his sign, the people would still know that he was there. Not only the townsfolk, but even the people from the countryside are more or less familiar with the streets of the town and what can be found there. No advertisement, no publicity is necessary. If people are in need of something, like cooking oil, some salt, or a piece of fabric, then they go inside and buy it. If they don't need anything, then no matter how large a sign is hung outside, they won't buy anything.

That dentist is a good case in point. When the people from the countryside spot those oversized teeth they stare at them in bewilderment, and there are often many people standing in front of the large sign looking up at it, unable to fathom its reason for being there. Even if one of them were standing there with a toothache, under no circumstances would he let that dentist, with her foreign methods, pull his tooth for him. Instead he would go over to the Li Yung-ch'un Pharmacy, buy two ounces of bitter herbs, take them home, and hold them in his mouth, and let that be the end of that! The teeth on that advertisement are simply too big; they are hard to figure out, and just a little bit frightening.

As a consequence, although that dentist hung her shingle out for two or three years, precious few people ever went to her to have their teeth pulled. Eventually, most likely owing to her inability to make a living, the woman dentist had no recourse but to engage in midwifery on the side.

IN ADDITION TO the Crossroads, there are two other streets, one called Road Two East and the other called Road Two West. Both streets run from north to south, probably for five or six *li*. There is nothing much on these two streets worth noting—a few temples, several stands where flatcakes are sold, and a number of grain storehouses.

On Road Two East there is a fire mill standing in a spacious courtyard, a large chimney made of fine red brick rising high above it. I have heard that no one is allowed to enter the fire mill, for there are a great many knobs and gadgets inside which must not be touched. If someone did touch them, he might burn himself to death. Otherwise, why would it be called a fire mill? Because of the flames inside, the mill is reportedly run neither by horses nor donkeys—it is run by fire. Most folk wonder why the mill itself doesn't go up in flames since only fire is used.

They ponder this over and over, but are unable to come up with an answer, and the more they ponder it, the more confused they become, especially since they are not allowed to go inside and check things out for themselves. I've heard they even have a watchman at the door.

There are also two schools on Road Two East, one each at the southern and northern ends. They are both located in temples—one in the Dragon King Temple and one in the Temple of the Patriarch—and both are elementary schools.

The school located in the Dragon King Temple is for the study of raising silkworms, and is called the Agricultural School, while the one in the Temple of the Patriarch is just a regular elementary school with one advanced section added, and is called the Higher Elementary School.

Although the names used for these two schools vary, in fact the only real difference between them is that in the one they call the Agricultural School the silkworm pupae are fried in oil in the autumn, and the teachers there enjoy several sumptuous meals.

There are no silkworms to be eaten in the Higher Elementary School, where the students are definitely taller than those in the Agricultural School. The students in the Agricultural School begin their schoolwork by learning the characters for "man," "hand," "foot," "knife," and "yardstick," and the oldest among them cannot be more than sixteen or seventeen years of age. But not so in the Higher Elementary School; there is a student there already twenty-four years old who is learning to play the foreign bugle and who has already taught in private schools out in the countryside for four or five years, but is only now himself attending the Higher Elementary School. Even the man who has been manager of a grain store for two years is a student at the school.

When this elementary school student writes a letter to his family he asks questions like: "Has Little Baldy's eye infection gotten better?" Little Baldy is the nickname of his eldest son, who is eight. He doesn't mention his second son or his daughters, because if he were to include all of them the letter would be much too long. Since he is already the father of a whole brood of children—the head of a family—whenever he sends a letter home he is mainly concerned with household matters: "Has the tenant Wang sent over his rent yet?" "Have the soybeans been sold?" "What is the present market situation?" and the like.

Students like him occupy a favored position in the class; the teacher must treat them with due respect, for if he drops his guard, this kind of student will often stand up, classical dictionary in hand, and stump the teacher with one of his questions. He will smugly point out that the teacher has used the wrong character in a phrase he has written on the board.

AS FOR ROAD TWO WEST, not only is it without a fire mill, it has but one school, a Muslim school situated in the Temple of the City God. With this exception, it is precisely like Road Two East, dusty and barren. When carts and horses pass over these roads they raise up clouds of dust, and whenever it rains the roads are covered with a layer of mud. There is an added feature on Road Two East: a five- or six-foot-deep quagmire. During dry periods the consistency of the mud inside is about that of gruel, but once it starts to rain the quagmire turns into a river. The people who live nearby suffer because of it: When they are splashed with its water, they come away covered with mud; and when the waters subside as the sun reappears in the clearing sky, hordes of mosquitoes emerge and fly around their homes. The longer the sun shines, the more homogenized the quagmire becomes, as though something were being refined in it; it's just as though someone were trying to refine something inside it. If more than a month goes by without any rain, that big quagmire becomes even more homogenized in makeup. All the water having evaporated, the mud has turned black and has become stickier than the gummy residue on a gruel pot, stickier even than paste. It takes on the appearance of a big melting vat, gummy black with an oily glisten to it, and even flies and mosquitoes that swarm around stick to it as they land.

Swallows love water, and sometimes they imprudently fly down to the quagmire to skim their wings over the water. It is a dangerous maneuver, as they nearly fall victim to the quagmire, coming perilously close to being mired down in it. Quickly they fly away without a backward glance.

In the case of horses, however, the outcome is different: they invariably bog down in it, and even worse, they tumble down into the middle of the quagmire, where they roll about, struggling to free themselves. After a period of floundering they lie down, their energy exhausted, and the moment they do so they are in real danger of losing their lives. But this does not happen often, for few people are willing to run the risk of leading their horses or pulling their carts near this dangerous spot.

Most of the accidents occur during drought years or after two or three months without any rainfall, when the big quagmire is at its most dangerous. On the surface it would seem that the more rain there is, the worse the situation, for with the rain a veritable river of water is formed, nearly ten feet in depth. One would think this would make it especially perilous, since anyone who fell in would surely drown. But such is not the case. The people of this small town of Hulan River aren't so stupid that they don't know how brutal this pit can be, and no one would be so foolhardy as to try leading a horse past the quagmire at such times.

But if it hasn't rained for three months the quagmire begins to dry up, until it is no more than two or three feet deep, and there will always be those hardy souls who will attempt to brave the dangers of driving a cart around it, or those with somewhat less courage who will watch others make their way past, then follow across themselves. One here, two there, and soon there are deep ruts along both sides of the quagmire formed by the passage of several carts. A late arrival spots the signs of previous passings, and this erstwhile coward, feeling more courageous than his intrepid predecessors, drives his cart straight ahead. How could he have known that the ground below him is uneven? Others had safely passed by, but his cart flips over.

The carter climbs out of the quagmire, looking like a mud-spattered apparition, then begins digging to free his horse from the mud, quickly making the sad discovery that it is mired down in the middle of the quagmire. There are people out on the road during all of this, and they come over to lend a helping hand.

These passersby can be divided into two types. Some are attired in traditional long gowns and short overjackets and are spotlessly clean. Apparently none of them will move a finger to assist in this drama because their hands are much too clean. Needless to say, they are members of the gentry class. They stand off to the side and observe the goings-on. When they see the horse trying to stand up they applaud and shout, "Oh! Oh!" several times. But then they see that the horse is unable to stand and falls back down, again they clap their hands and again they shout several times, "Oh! Oh!" But this time they are registering their displeasure. The excitement surrounding the horse's attempts to stand and its inability to do so continues for some time, but in the end it cannot get to its feet and just lies there pitifully. By this time those who have only been watching the feverish activity conclude that this is about all that will happen, that nothing new will materialize, and they begin to disperse, each heading off to his home.

But let us return to the plight of the horse lying there. The passersby who are trying to free it are all common folk, some of the town's onion peddlers, food sellers, till masons, carters, and other workers. They roll up their trouser cuffs, remove their shoes, and seeing no alternative, walk down into the quagmire with the hope that by pooling their strength they will be able to hoist the horse out. But they fail in their attempts, and by this time the horse's breathing has become very faint. Growing frantic, they hasten to free the horse from its harness, releasing it from the cart on the assumption that the horse will be able to get up more easily once it is freed from that burden. But contrary to their expectations, the horse still cannot stand up. Its head is sticking up out of the mire, ears twitching, eyes shut, snorts of air coming from its nostrils.

Seeing this sad state of affairs, people from the neighborhood run over with ropes and levers. They use the ropes to secure the horse and the levers to pry it free. They bark out orders as though they were building a house or constructing a bridge, and finally they manage to lift the animal out. The horse is still alive, lying at the side of the road. While some individuals are pouring water over it and washing the mud off its face, there is a constant flow of people coming and going at the scene of the spectacle.

On the following day everyone is saying: "Another horse has drowned in the big quagmire!" As the story makes its rounds, although the horse is actually still alive, it is said to have died, for if the people didn't say so, the awe in which they held that big quagmire would suffer.

It's hard to say just how many carts flip over because of that big quagmire. Throughout the year, with the exception of the winter season when it is sealed up by the freezing weather, this big quagmire looks as though it has acquired a life of its own—it is alive. Its waters rise, then subside; now it has grown larger, in a few days it recedes again. An intimate bond between it and the people begins to form.

When the water is high, not only are horses and carts impeded, it is an obstacle even to pedestrians. Old men pass along its edge on trembling legs, children are scared out of their wits as they skirt around it.

Once the rain begins to fall, the water quickly fills the now-glistening quagmire, then overflows and covers the bases of neighboring walls. For people out on the street who approach this place, it is like being dealt a setback on the road of life. They are in for a struggle: sleeves are rolled up, teeth are ground tightly, all their energy is called forth; hands clutch at a wooden wall, hearts pound rapidly; keep your head clear, your eyes in focus . . . the battle is joined.

Why is it that this, of all walls, has to be so smooth and neatly built, as though its owners have every intention of not coming to anyone's aid in this moment of distress? Regardless of how skillfully these pedestrians reach out, the wall offers them no succor; clawing here and groping there, they grab nothing but handfuls of air. Where in the world is there a mountain on which wood like this grows, so perfectly smooth and devoid of blemishes or knots?

After five or six minutes of struggling, the quagmire has been crossed. Needless to say, the person is by then covered with sweat and hot all over. Then comes the next individual, who must prepare himself for a dose of the same medicine. There are few choices available to him—about all he can do is grab hold here and clutch there, till after five or six minutes he too has crossed over. Then, once he is on the other side he feels revitalized, bursts out laughing, and looks back to the next person to cross, saying to him in the midst of his difficult struggle: "What's the big deal? You can't call yourself a hero unless you've faced a few dangers in your life!"

But that isn't how it always goes—not all are revitalized; in fact, most people are so frightened that their faces are drained of color. There are some whose trembling legs are so rubbery after they have crossed the quagmire that they cannot walk for some time. For timid souls like this, even the successful negotiating of this dangerous stretch of road cannot dispel the mood of distress that has involuntarily settled upon them; their fluttering hearts seemingly put into motion by this big quagmire, they invariably cast a look behind them and size it up for a moment, looking as though they have something they want to say. But in the end they say nothing, and simply walk off.

ONE VERY RAINY DAY a young child fell into the quagmire and was rescued by a bean-curd peddler. Once they got him out they discovered he was the son of the principal of the Agricultural School. A lively discussion ensued. Someone said that it happened because the Agricultural School was located in the Dragon King Temple, which angered the venerable Dragon King. He claimed it was the Dragon King who caused the heavy downpour in order to drown the child.

Someone disagreed with him completely, saying that the cause of the incident rested with the father, for during his highly animated lectures in the classroom he had once said that the venerable Dragon King was not responsible for any rainfall, and for that matter, did not even exist. "Knowing how furious this would make the venerable Dragon King, you can imagine how he would find some way to vent his anger! So he grabbed hold of the son as a means of gaining retribution."

Someone else said that the students at the school were so incorrigible that one had even climbed up onto the old Dragon King's head and capped him with a straw hat. "What are the times coming to when a child who isn't even dry behind the ears would dare to invite such tremendous calamities down upon himself? How could the old Dragon King not seek retribution? Mark my word, it's not finished yet; don't you get the idea that the venerable Dragon King is some kind of moron! Do you think he'd just let you off once you've provoked his anger? It's not like dealing with a rickshaw boy or a vegetable peddler whom you can kick at will, then let him be on his way. This is the venerable Dragon King we're talking about! Do you think that the venerable Dragon King is someone who can easily be pushed around?"

Then there was someone who said that the students at that school were truly undisciplined, and that with his own eyes he had once seen some of them in the main hall putting silkworms into the old Dragon King's hands. "Now, just how do you think the old Dragon King could stand for something like that?"

Another person said that the schools were no good at all, and that anyone with children should on no account allow them to go to school, since they immediately lose respect for everyone and everything.

Someone remarked that he was going to the school to get his son and take him home—there would be no more school for him.

Someone else commented that the more the children study, the worse they become. "Take, for example, when their souls are frightened out of their bodies; the minute their mothers call for the souls to return, what do you think they say? They announce that this is nothing but superstition! Now, what in the world do you think they'll be saying if they continue going to school?"

And so they talked, drifting further and further away from the original topic.

Before many days had passed, the big quagmire receded once again and pedestrians were soon passing along either side unimpeded. More days passed without any new rainfall, and the quagmire began to dry up, at which time carts and horses recommenced their crossings; then more overturned carts, more horses falling into it and thrashing around;

again the ropes and levers appeared, again they were used to lift and drag the horses out. As the righted carts drove off, more followed: into the quagmire, and the lifting began anew.

HOW MANY CARTS and horses are extricated from this quagmire every year may never be known. But, you ask, does no one ever think of solving the problem by filling it in with dirt? No, not a single one.

AN ELDERLY MEMBER of the gentry once fell into the quagmire at high water. As soon as he crawled out he said: "This street is too narrow. When you have to pass by this water hazard there isn't even room to walk. Why don't the two families whose gardens are on either side take down their walls and open up some paths?"

As he was saying this, an old woman sitting in her garden on the other side of the wall chimed in with the comment that the walls could not be taken down, and that the best course of action would be to plant some trees; if a row of trees were planted alongside the wall, then when it rained the people could cross over by holding onto the trees.

SOME ADVISE TAKING down walls and some advise planting trees, but as for filling up the quagmire with dirt, there isn't a single person who advocates that.

Many pigs meet their end by drowning in this quagmire; dogs are suffocated in the mud, cats too; chickens and ducks often lose their lives there as well. This is because the quagmire is covered with a layer of husks; the animals are unaware that there is a trap lying below, and once they realize that fact it is already too late. Whether they come on foot or by air, the instant they alight on the husk-covered mire they cannot free themselves. If it happens in the daytime there is still a chance that someone passing by might save them, but once night falls they are doomed. They struggle all alone until they exhaust their strength, then begin to sink gradually into the mire. If, on the contrary, they continue to struggle, they might sink even faster. Some even die there without sinking below the surface, but that's the sort of thing that happens when the mud is gummier than usual.

What might happen then is that some cheap pork will suddenly appear in the marketplace, and everyone's thoughts turn to the quagmire. "Has another pig drowned in that quagmire?" they ask.

Once the word is out, those who are fast on their feet lose no time in running to their neighbors with the news: "Hurry over and get some cheap pork. Hurry, hurry, before it's all gone."

After it is bought and brought home, a closer look reveals that there seems to be something wrong with it. Why is the meat all dark and discolored? Maybe this pork is infected. But on second thought, how could it really be infected? No, it must have been a pig that drowned in the quagmire. So then family after family sautés, fries, steams, boils, and then eats this cheap pork. But though they eat it, they feel always that it doesn't have a fragrant enough aroma, and they fear that it might have been infected after all. But then they think: "Infected pork would be unpalatable, so this must be from a pig that drowned in the quagmire!"

Actually, only one or two pigs drown each year in the quagmire, perhaps three, and some years not a single one. How the residents manage to eat the meat of a drowned pig so often is hard to imagine, and I'm afraid only the Dragon King knows the answer.

Though the people who eat the meat say it is from a pig drowned in the quagmire, there are still those who get sick from it, and those unfortunates are ready with their opinions: "Even if the pork was from a drowned pig, it still shouldn't have been sold in the marketplace; meat from animals that have died isn't fresh, and the revenue office isn't doing its job if it allows meat like this to be sold on the street in broad daylight!"

Those who do not become ill are of a different opinion: "That's what you say, but you're letting your suspicions get the best of you. If you'd just eat it and not give it another thought, everything would be all right. Look at the rest of us; we ate it too, so how come we're not sick?"

Now and then a child lacking in common sense will tell people that his mother wouldn't allow him to eat the pork since it was infected. No one likes this kind of child. Everyone gives him hard looks and accuses him of speaking nonsense.

For example, a child says that the pork is definitely infected—this he tells a neighbor right in front of his mother. There is little reaction from the neighbor who hears him say this, but the mother's face immediately turns beet-red. She reaches out and smacks him.

But he is a stubborn child, and he keeps saying: "The pork is infected! The pork is infected!"

His mother, feeling terribly embarrassed, picks up a poker that is lying by the door and strikes him on the shoulder, sending him crying into the house. As he enters the room he sees his maternal grandmother sitting on the edge of the *k'ang*, so he runs into her arms. "Grannie," he sobs, "wasn't that pork you ate infected? Mama just hit me."

Now, this maternal grandmother wants to comfort the poor abused child, but just then she looks up to see the wet nurse of the Li family who shares the compound standing in the doorway looking at her. So she lifts up the back of the child's shirttail and begins spanking him loudly on the behind. "Whoever saw a child as small as you speaking such utter nonsense!" she exclaims. She continues spanking him until the wet nurse walks away with the Lis' child in her arms. The spanked child is by then screaming and crying uncontrollably, so hard that no one can make heads or tails of his shouts of "infected pork this" and "infected pork that."

IN ALL, THIS QUAGMIRE brings two benefits to the residents of the area: The first is that the overturned carts and horses and the drowned chickens and ducks always produce a lot of excitement, which keeps the inhabitants buzzing for some time and gives them something to while away the hours.

The second is in relation to the matter of pork. Were there no quagmire, how could they have their infected pork? Naturally, they might still eat it, but how are they to explain it away? If they simply admit they are eating infected pork, it would be too unsanitary for words, but with the presence of the quagmire their problem is solved: infected pork becomes the meat of drowned pigs, which means that when they buy the meat, not only is it economical, but there are no sanitation problems either.

2

Besides the special attraction of the big quagmire, there is little else to be seen on Road Two East: one or two grain mills, a few bean-curd shops, a weaving mill or two, and perhaps one or two dyeing establishments. These are all operated by people who quietly do their own work there, bringing no enjoyment to the local inhabitants, and are thus unworthy of any discussion. When the sun sets these people go to bed, and when the sun rises they get up and begin their work. Throughout the year—warm spring with its blooming flowers, autumn with its rains, and winter with its snows—they simply follow the seasonal changes as they go from padded coats to unlined jackets. The cycle of birth, old age, sickness, and death governs their lives as they silently manage their affairs.

Take, for example, Widow Wang, who sells bean sprouts at the southern end of Road Two East. She erected a long pole above her house on top of which she hangs a battered old basket. The pole is so tall it is nearly on a level with the iron bell at the top of the Dragon King Temple. On windy days the *clang-clang* of the bell above the temple can be heard, and although Widow Wang's battered basket does not ring, it nonetheless makes its presence known by waving back and forth in the wind.

Year in and year out that is how it goes, and year in and year out Widow Wang sells her bean sprouts, passing her days tranquilly and uneventfully at an unhurried pace.

But one summer day her only son went down to the river to bathe, and he fell in and drowned. This incident caused a sensation and was the talk of the town for a while, but before many days had passed the talk died away. Not only Widow Wang's neighbors and others who lived nearby, but even her friends and relatives soon forgot all about it.

As for Widow Wang herself, even though this caused her to lose her mind, she still retained her ability to sell bean sprouts, and she continued as before to live an uneventful and quiet life. Occasionally someone would steal her bean sprouts, at which time she would be overcome by a fit of wailing on the street or on the steps of the temple, though it would soon pass, and she would return to her uneventful existence.

Whenever neighbors or other passersby witnessed the scene of her crying on the temple steps, their hearts would be momentarily touched by a slight feeling of compassion, but only for a brief moment.

THERE ARE SOME PEOPLE who are given to lumping together misfits of all kinds, such as the insane and the slow-witted, and treating them identically.

There are unfortunates in every district, in every county, and in every village: the tumorous, the blind, the insane, the slow-witted. There are many such people in our little town of Hulan River, but the local inhabitants have apparently heard and seen so much of them that their presence does not seem the least bit unusual. If, unhappily, they encounter one of them on the temple steps or inside a gateway alcove, they feel a momentary pang of compassion for that particular individual, but it is quickly supplanted by the rationalization that mankind has untold numbers of such people. They then turn their glances away and walk rapidly past the person. Once in a while someone stops there, but he is just one of those who, like children with short memories, would throw stones at the insane or willfully lead the blind into the water-filled ditch nearby.

The unfortunates are beggars, one and all. At least that's the way it is in the town of Hulan River. The people there treat the beggars in a most ordinary fashion. A pack of dogs are barking at something outside the door; the master of the house shouts out: "What are those animals barking at?"

"They're barking at a beggar," the servant answers.

Once said, the affair is ended. It is obvious that the life of a beggar is not worth a second thought.

The madwoman who sells bean sprouts cannot forget her grief even in her madness, and every few days she goes to wail at the steps of the temple; but once her crying has ended, she invariably returns home to eat, to sleep, and to sell her bean sprouts. As ever, she returns to her quiet existence.

3

A calamity also struck the dyer's shop: Two young apprentices were fighting over a woman on the street, when one of them pushed the other into the dyeing vat and drowned him. We need not concern ourselves here with the one who died, but as for the survivor, he was sent to jail with a life sentence.

Yet this affair too was disposed of silently and without a ripple. Two or three years later, whenever people mentioned the incident they discussed it as they would the famous confrontation between the heroic general Yueh Fei and the evil prime minister Ch'in K'uai, as something that had occurred in the long-distant past.

Meanwhile the dyer's shop remains at its original location, and even the big vat in which the young man drowned is quite possibly still in use to this day. The bolts of cloth that come from that dye shop still turn up in villages and towns far and near. The blue cloth is used to make padded cotton pants and jackets, which the men wear in the winter to ward off the severe cold, while the red cloth is used to make bright red gowns for the eighteen- and nineteen-year-old girls for their wedding days.

In short, though someone had drowned in the dyer's shop on such and such a day during such and such a month and year, the rest of the world goes on just as before without the slightest change.

Then there was the calamity that struck the bean-curd shop: During a fight between two of the employees the donkey that turned the mill suffered a broken leg. Since it was only a donkey, there wasn't much to be said on that score, but a woman lost her sight as a result of crying over the donkey (it turned out to be the mother of the one who had struck the donkey), so the episode could not simply be overlooked.

Then there was the paper mill in which a bastard child was starved to death. But since it was a newborn baby, the incident didn't amount to much, and nothing more need be said about it.

4

Then too on Road Two East there are a few ornament shops, which are there to serve the dead.

After a person dies his soul goes down to the netherworld, and the living, fearing that in that other world the dear departed will have no domicile to live in, no clothes to wear, and no horse to ride, have these things made of paper, then burn them for his benefit; the townspeople believe that all manner of things exist in the netherworld.

On display are grand objects like money-spewing animals, treasure-gathering basins, and great gold and silver mountains; smaller things like slave girls, maidservants, cooks in the kitchen, and attendants who care for the pigs; and even smaller things like flower vases, tea services, chickens, ducks, geese, and dogs. There are even parrots on the window ledges.

These things are enormously pleasing to the eye. There is a court-yard surrounded by a garden wall, the top of which is covered with gold-colored glazed tiles. Just inside the courtyard is the principal house with five main rooms and three side rooms, all topped with green- and red-brick tiles; the windows are bright, the furniture spotless, and the air fresh and clean as can be. Flower pots are arranged one after another on the flower racks; there are cassias, pure-white lilies, purslanes, September chrysanthemums, and all are in bloom. No one can tell what season it is—is it summer or is it autumn?—since inexplicably the flowers of the purslanes and the chrysanthemums are standing side by side; perhaps there is no division into spring, summer, autumn, and winter in the netherworld. But this need not concern us.

Then there is the cook in his kitchen, vivid and lifelike; he is a thousand times cleaner than a true-to-life cook. He has a white cap on his head and a white apron girding his body as he stands there preparing noodles. No sooner has lunchtime arrived than the noodles have been cooked, and lunch is about to be served.

In the courtyard a groom stands beside a big white horse, which is so large and so tall that it looks to be an Arabian; it stands erect and majestic, and if there were to be a rider seated upon it, there is every reason to believe it could outrun a train. I'm sure that not even the general here in the town of Hulan River has ever ridden such a steed.

Off to one side there is a carriage and a big mule. The mule is black and shiny, and its eyes, which have been made out of eggshells, remain stationary. There is a particularly fetching little mule with eyeballs as large as the big mule's standing alongside it.

The carriage, with its silver-colored wheels, is decorated in especially beautiful colors. The curtain across the front is rolled halfway up so that people can see the interior of the carriage, which is all red and sports a bright red cushion. The driver perched on the running board, his face beaming with proud smiles, is dressed in magnificent attire, with a purple sash girding his waist over a blue embroidered fancy gown, and black satin shoes with snow-white soles on his feet. (After putting on these shoes he probably drove the carriage over without taking a single step on the ground.) The cap he is wearing is red with a black brim. His head is raised as though he were disdainful of everything, and the more the people look at him, the less he resembles a carriage driver—he looks more like a bridegroom.

Two or three roosters and seven or eight hens are in the courtyard peacefully eating grain without making a sound, and even the ducks are not making those quacking noises that so annoy people. A dog is crouching next to the door of the master's quarters, maintaining a motionless vigil.

All of the bystanders looking on comment favorably, every one of them voicing his praise. The poor look at it and experience a feeling that it must be better to be dead than alive.

The main room is furnished with window curtains, four-poster bed frames, tables, chairs, and benches. Everything is complete to the last detail.

There is also a steward of the house who is figuring accounts on his abacus; beside him is an open ledger in which is written:

"Twenty-two catties of wine owed by the northern distillery.

"Wang Family of East Village yesterday borrowed 2,000 catties of rice.

"Ni Jen-tzu of White Flag Hamlet yesterday sent land rent of 4,300 coppers."

Below these lines is written the date: "April twenty-eighth."

This page constitutes the running accounts for the twenty-seventh of April; the accounts for the twenty-eighth have evidently not yet been entered. A look at this ledger shows that there is no haphazard accounting of debts in the netherworld, and that there is a special type of individual whose job it is to manage these accounts. It also goes without saying that the master of this grand house is a landlord.

Everything in the compound is complete to the last detail and is very fine. The only thing missing is the master of the compound, a discovery which seems puzzling: could there be no master of such a fine compound? This is certainly bewildering.

When they have looked more closely the people sense that there is something unusual about the compound: How is it that the slave girls and maidservants, the carriage drivers and the groom, all have a piece of white paper across their chests on which their names are written? The name of the carriage driver whose good looks give him the appearance of a bridegroom is:

"Long Whip."

The groom's name is: "Fleet of Foot."

The name of the slave girl who is holding a water pipe in her left hand and an embroidered napkin in her right is:

"Virtuous Obedience."

The other's name is: "Fortuitous Peace."

The man who is figuring accounts is named: "Wizard of Reckoning."

The name of the maid who is spraying the flowers with water is: "Flower Sister."

A closer look reveals that even the big white horse has a name; the name tag on his rump shows that he is called:

"Thousand-Li Steed."

As for the others—the mules, the dogs, the chickens, and the ducks—they are nameless.

The cook who is making noodles in the kitchen is called "Old Wang," and the strip of paper on which his name is written flaps to and fro with each gust of wind.

This is all rather strange: the master of the compound doesn't even recognize his own servants and has to hang name tags around their necks! This point cannot but confuse and bewilder people; maybe this world of ours is better than the netherworld after all!

But though that is the opinion of some, there are still many others who are envious of this grand house, which is so indisputably fine, elegant, peaceful and quiet (complete silence reigns), neat and tidy, with no trace of disorder. The slave girls and maidservants are fashioned exactly like those in this world; the chickens, dogs, pigs, and horses too are just like those in this world. Everything in this world can also be found in the netherworld: people eat noodles in this world, and in the netherworld they eat them too; people have carriages to ride in this world, and in the netherworld they also ride them; the netherworld is just like this world—the two are exactly alike.

That is, of course, except for the big quagmire on Road Two East. Everything desirable is there; undesirable things are simply not necessary.

5

These are the objects that the ornament shops on Road Two East produce. The displayed handiwork is both dignified-looking and eye-catching, but the inside of the shop is a mass of confusion. Shredded paper is everywhere; there are rods and sticks all in a heap; crushed boxes and a welter of cans, paint jars, paste dishes, thin string, and heavy cord abound. A person could easily trip just walking through the shop, with its constant activity of chopping and tying as flies dart back and forth in the air.

When making paper human figures, the first to be fashioned is the head; once it has been pasted together it is hung on a wall along with other heads—men's and women's—until it is taken down to be used. All that is needed then is to put it atop a torso made of rods and sticks on which some clothes have been added, and you have the figure of a human being. By cutting out white paper hair and pasting it all over a sticklike papier-mâché horse, you have a handsome steed.

The people who make their living this way are all extremely coarse and ugly men. They may know how to fashion a groom or a carriage driver, and how to make up women and young girls, but they pay not the slightest attention to their own appearance. Long scraggly hair, short bristly hair, twisted mouths, crooked eyes, bare feet and legs; it is hard to believe that such splendid and dazzlingly beautiful lifelike human figures could have been created by those hands.

Their daily fare is coarse vegetables and coarse rice, they are dressed in tattered clothes, and they make their beds among piles of carriages, horses, human figures, and heads. Their lives seemingly are bitter ones, though they actually just muddle their way through, day by day, the year round, exchanging their unlined jackets for padded coats with each seasonal change.

Birth, old age, sickness, death—each is met with a stoic absence of expression. They are born and grow in accordance with nature's dictates. If they are meant not to grow old, then so be it.

‖‖‖‖‖‖‖‖‖‖‖‖

OLD AGE—GETTING OLD has no effect on them at all: when their eyesight fails they stop looking at things, when their hearing fades they stop listening, when their teeth fall out they swallow things whole, and when they can no longer move about they lie flat on their backs. What else can they do? Anyone who grows old deserves exactly what he gets!

Sickness—among people whose diet consists of a random assortment of grains, who is there who does not fall prey to illness?

Death—this, on the other hand, is a sad and mournful affair. When a father dies, his sons weep; when a son dies, his mother weeps; when a brother dies, the whole family weeps; and when a son's wife dies, her family comes to weep.

After crying for one, or perhaps even three days, they must then go to the outskirts of town, dig a hole, and bury the person. After the burial the surviving family members still have to make their way back home and carry on their daily routine. When it's time to eat, they eat; when it's time to sleep, they sleep. Outsiders are unable to tell that this family is now bereft of a father or has just lost an elder brother. The members of that particular family even fail to lock themselves in their home each day and wail. The only expression of the grief they feel in their hearts is joining the stream of people who go to visit the graves on the various festivals each year as prescribed by local custom. During the Qingming Festival—the time for visiting ancestral graves—each family prepares incense and candles and sets out for the family grave site. At the heads of some of the graves the earth has settled and formed a small pit, while others have several small holes in them. The people cast glances at one another, are moved to sighing, then light the incense and pour the wine. If the survivor is a close relative, such as a son, a daughter, or a parent, then they will let forth a fit of wailing, the broken rhythm of which makes it sound as though they were reading a written composition or chanting a long poem. When their incantation is finished they rise to their feet, brush the dirt from their behinds, and join the procession of returning people as they leave the grave sites and reenter the town.

When they return to their homes in the town they must carry on life as before; all year round there is firewood, rice, oil, and salt to worry about, and there is clothing to starch and mend. From morning till evening they are busy without respite. Nighttime finds them exhausted, and they are asleep as soon as they lie down on the *k'ang*. They dream neither of mournful nor of happy events as they sleep, but merely grind their teeth and snore, passing the night like every other night.

If someone were to ask them what man lives for, they would not be confounded by the question, but would state unhesitatingly, directly, and unequivocally: "Man lives to eat food and wear clothes." If they were then asked about death, they would say: "When a man dies that's the end of it."

Consequently, no one has ever seen one of those ornament craftsmen fashion an underworld home for himself during his lifetime; more than likely he doesn't much believe in the netherworld. And even if there were such a place, he would probably open an ornament shop when he got there; worse luck, he'd doubtless have to rent a place to open the shop.

6

In the town of Hulan River, besides Road Two East, Road Two West, and the Crossroads, there remain only a number of small lanes. There is even less worth noting on these small byways; one finds precious few of the little stalls where flatcakes and dough twists are made and sold, and even the tiny stands that sell red and green candy balls are mainly located where the lanes give out onto the road—few find their way into the lanes themselves. The people who live on these small lanes seldom see a casual stroller. They hear and see less than other people, and as a result they pass their lonely days behind closed doors. They live in broken-down huts, buy two pecks of beans, which they salt and cook to go with their rice, and there goes another year. The people who live on these small lanes are isolated and lonely.

A peddler carrying a basket of flatcakes hawking his product at the eastern end of the lane can be heard at the western end. Although the people inside the houses don't care to buy, whenever he stops at their gates they poke their heads out to take a look, and may on occasion even ask a price or ask whether or not the glazed or fried dough twists still sell for the same price as before.

Every once in a while someone will walk over and lift up the piece of cloth that covers the basket, as though she were a potential customer, then pick one out and feel to see if it's still hot. After she has felt it she puts it right back, and the peddler is not the least bit angry. He simply picks up his basket and carries it to the next house.

The lady of this second house has nothing in particular to do, so she too opens up the basket and feels around for a while. But she also touches them without buying any.

When the peddler reaches the third house, a potential customer is there waiting for him. Out from the house comes a woman in her thirties who has just gotten up from a nap. Her hair is done up in a bun on top of her head, and probably because it isn't particularly neat, she has covered it with a black hairnet and fastened it on with several hairpins. But having just slept on it, not only is her hair all disheveled, even the hairpins have worked their way out, so that the bun atop her head looks as though it has been shot full of darts. She walks out of her house in high spirits, throwing the door open and virtually bursting through the doorway. Five children follow in her wake, each one of them in high spirits; as they emerge they look every bit like a platoon marching in a column.

The first one, a girl of twelve or thirteen, reaches in and picks out one of the dough twists. It is about the length of a bamboo chopstick, and sells for fifty coppers. Having the quickest eye among them, she has selected not only the biggest one in the basket, but the only one in that size category.

The second child, a boy, chooses one that sells for twenty coppers.

The third child also chooses one that sells for twenty coppers; he too is a boy.

After looking them all over, the fourth child has no alternative but to choose one that sells for twenty coppers; and he too is a boy.

Then it is the fifth child's turn. There is no way of telling if this one is a boy or a girl—no hair on the head, an earring hanging from one ear, skinny as a dry willow branch, but with a large, protruding belly, it looks to be about five years old. The child sticks out its hands, which are far blacker than any of the other four children's—the hands of the other four are filthy black, all right, but at least they still look like human hands and not some other strange objects. Only this child's hands are indistinguishable. Shall we call them hands? Or what shall we call them? I guess we can call them anything we like. They are a mottled mixture of blacks and grays, darks and lights, so that looking at them, like viewing layers of floating clouds, can be a most interesting pastime.

The child sticks its hands into the basket to choose one of the fried dough twists, nearly each of which is touched and felt in the process, until the entire basket is soon a jumble. Although the basket is fairly large, not many dough twists had been put inside it to begin with: besides the single big one, there were only ten or so of the smaller ones. After this child has turned them all over, the ones that remain are strewn throughout the basket, while the child's black hands are now covered with oil as well as being filthy, and virtually glisten like shiny ebony.

Finally the child cries out: "I want a big one."

A fight then erupts by the front door.

The child is a fast runner, and takes out after its elder sister. Its two elder brothers also take off running, both of them easily outdistancing this smallest child. The elder sister, holding the largest dough twist in her hand, is unimaginably faster on her feet than the small child, and in an instant she has already found a spot where there is a break in the wall and has jumped through; the others follow her and disappear on the other side. By the time all the others have followed her past the wall, she has already jumped back across and is running around the courtyard like a whirlwind.

The smallest child—the one of indeterminate sex—cannot catch up with the others and has long since fallen behind, screaming and crying. Now and then, while the elder sister is being held fast by her two brothers, the child runs over and tries to snatch the dough twist out of her hand, but after several misses falls behind again, screaming and crying.

As for their mother, though she looks imposing, actually she cannot control the children without using her hands, and so seeing how things are going, with no end in sight, she enters the house, picks up a steel poker, and chases after her children. But unhappily for her, there is a small mud puddle in her yard where the pigs wallow, and she falls smack into the middle of it, the poker flying from her hand and sailing some five feet or so away.

With that this little drama has reached its climax and every person watching the commotion is in stitches, delighted with the whole affair. Even the peddler is completely engrossed in what is going on, and when the woman plops down into the mud puddle and splashes muck all over, he nearly lets his basket fall to the ground. He is so tickled he has forgotten all about the basket in his hands.

The children, naturally, have long since disappeared from sight. By the time the mother gets them all rounded up she has regained her imposing parental airs. She has each of them kneel on the ground facing the sun so that they form a line, then has them surrender up their dough twists.

Little remains of the eldest child's dough twist—it was broken up in all the commotion.

The third child has eaten all of his.

The second one has a tiny bit left.

Only the fourth one still has his clenched in his hand.

As for the fifth child, well, it never had one to begin with.

The whole chaotic episode ends with a shouting match between the peddler and the woman, after which he picks up his basket and walks over to the next house to try to make another sale. The argument between the two of them is over the woman's wanting to return the dough twist that the fourth child had been holding on to all that time. The peddler flatly refuses to take it back, and the woman is just as determined to return it to him. The end result is that she pays for three dough twists and drives the peddler with his basket out of her yard.

Nothing more need be said about the five children who were forced to kneel on the ground because of those dough twists, and as for the remainder of the dough twists that had been taken into the lane to be handled and felt by nearly everyone, they are then carried over into the next lane and eventually sold.

A toothless old woman buys one of them and carries it back wrapped in a piece of paper, saying: "This dough twist is certainly clean, all nice and oily." Then she calls out to her grandchild to hurry on over.

The peddler, seeing how pleased the old lady is, says to her: "It's just come from the pan, still nice and warm!"

7

In the afternoon, after the dough-twist peddler has passed by, a seller of rice pudding may come by, and like the other peddlers, his shouts from one end of the lane can be heard at the other end. People who want to buy his product bring along a small ceramic bowl, while others who are not interested in buying just sit inside their homes; as soon as they hear his shouts they know it is time to begin cooking dinner, since throughout the summer this peddler comes when the sun is setting in the west. He comes at the same time every day, like clockwork, between the hours of four and five. One would think that his sole occupation is bringing rice pudding to sell in this particular lane, and that he is not about to jeopardize his punctual appearance there in order to sell to one or two additional homes in another lane. By the time the rice-pudding peddler has gone, the sky is nearly dark.

Once the sun begins to set in the west the peddler of odds and ends, who announces his presence with a wooden rattle, no longer enters the lanes to peddle his wares. In fact, he does no more business on the quieter roadways either, but merely shoulders his load and makes his way home along the main streets.

The pottery seller has by then closed shop for the day.

The scavengers and rag collectors also head for home.

The only one to come out at this time is the bean-curd peddler.

At dinnertime some scallions and bean paste make for a tasty meal, but a piece of bean curd to go along with it adds a pleasant finishing touch, requiring at least two additional bowlfuls of corn-and-bean gruel. The people eat a lot at each sitting, and that is only natural; add a little hot-pepper oil and a touch of bean sauce to the bean curd and the meal is greatly enhanced. Just a little piece of bean curd on the end of the chopsticks can last a half bowlful of gruel, and soon after the chopsticks have broken off another chunk of bean curd, a full bowlful of gruel has disappeared. Two extra bowlfuls are consumed because of the addition of the bean curd, but that doesn't mean the person has overeaten; someone who has never tasted bean curd cannot know what a delightful flavor it has.

It is for this reason that the arrival of the bean-curd peddler is so warmly welcomed by everyone—men, women, young, and old alike. When they open their doors, there are smiles everywhere, and though nothing is said, a sort of mutual affinity quietly develops between buyer and seller. It is as though the bean-curd peddler were saying: "I have some fine bean curd here."

And it is as though the customer were answering: "Your bean curd doesn't seem half bad."

Those who cannot afford to buy the bean curd are particularly envious of the bean-curd peddler. The moment they hear the sound of his shouts down the lane drawing near they are sorely tempted; wouldn't it be nice to be able to have a piece of bean curd with a little green pepper and some scallions!

But though they think the same thought day in and day out, they never quite manage to buy a piece, and each time the bean-curd peddler comes, all his presence does for these people is confront them with an unrealizable temptation. These people, for whom temptation calls, just cannot make the decision to buy, so they merely eat a few extra mouthfuls of hot peppers, after which their foreheads are bathed in perspiration. Wouldn't it be wonderful, they dream, if a person could just open his own bean-curd shop? Then he could eat bean curd anytime he felt like it!

And sure enough, when one of their sons gets to be about five years of age, if he is asked: "What do you want to do when you grow up?"

He will answer: "I want to open a bean-curd shop." It is obvious that he has hopes of realizing his father's unfulfilled ambition.

The fondness these people have for this marvelous dish called bean curd sometimes goes even beyond this; there are those who would even lead their families into bankruptcy over it. There is a story about the head of a household who came to just such a decision, saying: "I'm going for broke; I'll buy myself a piece of bean curd!" In the classical language, the words "going for broke" would be the equivalent of giving up one's all for charity, but in modern speech most people would just say: "I'm wiped out!"

8

Once the bean-curd peddler packs up and heads for home, the affairs of another day have come to an end.

Every family sits down to its evening meal, then after they have finished, some stay up to watch the sunset, while the others simply lie down on their *k'angs* and go to sleep.

The sunsets in this place are beautiful to behold. There is a local expression here, "fire clouds"; if you say "sunset," no one will understand you, but if you say "fire clouds," even a three-year-old child will point up to the western sky with a shout of delight.

Right after the evening meal the "fire clouds" come. The children's faces all reflect a red glow, while the big white dog turns red, red roosters become golden ones, and black hens become a dark purple. An old man feeding his pigs leans against the base of a wall and chuckles as he sees his two white pigs turn into little golden ones. He is about to say: "I'll be damned, even you have changed," when a man out for a refreshing evening stroll walks by him and comments: "Old man, you are sure to live to a ripe old age, with your golden beard!"

The clouds burn their way in the sky from the west to the east, a glowing red, as though the sky had caught fire.

The variations of the "fire clouds" here are many: one moment they are a glowing red; a moment later they become a clear gold; then half purple, half yellow; and then a blend of gray and white. Grape gray, pear yellow, eggplant purple—all of these colors appear in the sky. Every imaginable color is there, some that words cannot describe and others that you would swear you have never seen before.

Within the space of five seconds a horse is formed in the sky with its head facing south and its tail pointing west; the horse is kneeling, looking as though it is waiting for someone to climb up onto its back before it will stand up. Nothing much changes within the next second, but two or three seconds later the horse has gotten bigger, its legs have spread out, and its neck has elongated . . . but there is no longer any tail to be seen. And then, just when the people watching from below are trying to locate the tail, the horse disappears from sight.

Suddenly a big dog appears, a ferocious animal that is running ahead of what looks like several little puppies. They run and they run, and before long the puppies have run from sight; then the big dog disappears.

A great lion is then formed, looking exactly like one of the stone lions in front of the Temple of the Immortal Matron. It is about the same size, and it too is crouching, looking very powerful and dominant as it calmly crouches there. It appears contemptuous of all around it, not deigning to look at anything. The people search the sky, and before they know it something else has caught their eye. Now they are in a predicament—since they cannot be looking at something to the east and something to the west at the same time—and so they watch the lion come to ruin. A shift of the eyes, a lowering of the head, and the objects in the sky undergo a transformation. But now as you search for yet something else, you could look until you go blind before finding a single thing. The great lion can no longer be seen, nor is there anything else to be found—not even, for example, a monkey, which is certainly no match for the glimpse of a great lion.

For a brief moment the sky gives the illusion of forming this object or that, but in fact there are no distinguishable shapes; there is nothing anymore. It is then that the people lower their heads and rub their eyes, or perhaps just rest them for a moment before taking another look. But the "fire clouds" in the sky do not often wait around to satisfy the children below who are so fond of them, and in this short space of time they are gone.

The drowsy children return home to their rooms and go to sleep. Some are so tired they cannot make it to their beds, but fall asleep lying across their elder sister's legs or in the arms of their grandmother. The grandmother has a horsehair fly swatter, which she flicks in the air to keep the bugs and mosquitoes away. She does not know that her grandchild has fallen asleep, but thinks he is still awake.

"You get down and play; Grandma's legs are falling asleep." She gives the child a push, but he is fast asleep.

By this time the "fire clouds" have disappeared without a trace. All the people in every family get up and go to their rooms to sleep for the night after closing the windows and doors.

Even in July it is not particularly hot in Hulan River, and at night the people cover themselves with thin quilts as they sleep.

As night falls and crows fly by, the voices of the few children who are not yet asleep can be heard through the windows as they call out:

> Raven, raven, working the grain-threshing floor;
> Two pecks for you, not a tiny bit more.

The flocks of crows that cover the sky with their shouts of *caw-caw* fly over this town from one end to the other. It is said that after they have flown over the southern bank of the Hulan River they roost in a big wooded area. The following morning they are up in the air flying again.

As summer leads into autumn the crows fly by every evening, but just where these large flocks of birds fly to, the children don't really know, and the adults have little to say to them on the subject. All the children know about them is embodied in their little ditty:

> Raven, raven, working the grain-threshing floor;
> Two pecks for you, not a tiny bit more.

Just why they want to give the crows two pecks of grain doesn't seem to make much sense.

9

After the crows have flown over, the day has truly come to an end.

The evening star climbs in the sky, shining brightly there like a little brass nugget.

The Milky Way and the moon also make their appearance.

Bats fly into the night.

All things that come out with the sun have now turned in for the night. The people are all asleep, as are the pigs, horses, cows, and sheep; the swallows and butterflies have gone to roost. Not a single blossom on the morning glories at the bases of the houses remains open—there are the closed buds of new blossoms, and the curled-up petals of the old. The closed buds are preparing to greet the morning sun of the following day, while the curled petals that have already greeted yesterday's sun are about to fall.

Most stars follow the moon's ascent in the sky, while the evening star is like her advance foot soldier, preceding her by a few steps.

As night falls the croaking of frogs begins to emerge from rivers, streams, and marshes. The sounds of chirping insects come from foliage in the courtyards, from the large fields outside the city, from potted flowers, and from the graveyard.

This is what the summer nights are like when there is no rain or wind, night after night.

Summer passes very quickly, and autumn has arrived. There are few changes as summer leads into autumn, except that the nights turn cooler and everyone must sleep under a quilt at night. Farmers are busy during the day with the harvest, and at night their more frequent dreams are of gathering in the sorghum.

During the month of September the women are kept busy starching clothes, and removing the covers and fluffing the matted cotton of their quilts. From morning till night every street and lane resounds with the hollow twang of their mallets on the fluffing bows. When their fluffing work is finished, the quilts are recovered, just in time for the arrival of winter.

Winter brings the snows.

Throughout the seasons the people must put up with wind, frost, rain, and snow; they are beset by the frost and soaked by the rain. When the big winds come they fill the air with swirling sand and pebbles, almost arrogantly. In winter the ground freezes and cracks, rivers are frozen over, and as the weather turns even colder the ice on the river splits with resounding cracks. The winter cold freezes off people's ears, splits open their noses, chaps their hands and feet. But this is just nature's way of putting on airs of importance, and the common folk can't do a thing about it.

This is how the people of Hulan River are: when winter comes they put on their padded clothes, and when summer arrives they change into their unlined jackets, as mechanically as getting up when the sun rises and going to bed when it sets.

Their fingers, which are chapped and cracked in the winter, heal naturally by the time summer arrives. For those that don't heal by themselves, there is always the Li Yung-ch'un Pharmacy, where the people can buy two ounces of saffron, steep it, and rub the solution on their hands. Sometimes they rub it on until their fingers turn blood-red without any sign of healing, or the swelling may even get progressively worse. In such cases they go back to the Li Yung-ch'un Pharmacy, though this time rather than purchasing saffron, they buy a plaster instead. They take it home, heat it over a fire until it becomes gummy, then stick it on the frostbite sore. This plaster is really wonderful, since it doesn't cause the least bit of inconvenience when it is stuck on. Carters can still drive their carts, housewives can still prepare food.

It is really terrific that this plaster is sticky and gummy; it will not wash off in water, thereby allowing women to wash clothes with it on if they have to. And even if it does rub off, they can always heat it once more over a fire and stick it back on. Once applied it stays on for half a month.

The people of Hulan River value things in terms of strength and durability, so that something as durable as this plaster is perfectly suited to their nature. Even if it is applied for two weeks and the hand remains unhealed, the plaster is, after all, durable, and the money paid for it has not been spent in vain.

They go back and buy another, and another, and yet another, but the swelling on the hand grows worse and worse. For people who cannot afford the plasters, they can pick up the ones others have used and discarded and stick them on their own sores. Since the final outcome is always unpredictable, why not just muddle through the best one can!

Spring, summer, autumn, winter—the seasonal cycle continues inexorably, and always has since the beginning of time. Wind, frost, rain, snow; those who can bear up under these forces manage to get by; those who cannot must seek a natural solution. This natural solution is not so very good, for these people are quietly and wordlessly taken from this life and this world.

Those who have not yet been taken away are left at the mercy of the wind, the frost, the rain, and the snow . . . as always.

(Translated by Howard Goldblatt)

PART TWO

1949–1976

CHRONOLOGY

Introduction to the Revolutionary Era

The founding of the People's Republic of China in October 1949 led to the creation of a socialist literary system. Borrowed from the Soviet model, Chinese bureaucracy established "central and provincial literary magazines, editorial boards of prescribed political composition, a National Publication Administration that reviewed publishing plans and rationed paper, and a Writers' Association that set down rules about writers' pay and privileges."* Mao's views on literature, which he had expressed explicitly in his famous Yan'an speech in 1942, provided the reigning ideology. Quoting Lenin, Mao had stated that literature and art are "the cogs and screws in the whole machine" of revolution; "therefore, the Party's literary and artistic activity occupies a definite and assigned position in the Party's total revolutionary work and is subordinated to the prescribed revolutionary task of the Party in a given revolutionary period." In other words: literature serves politics. Mao's speech became the blueprint for the party line on literature in new China.

Due to its subservience to politics, literature under communism has often, perhaps rightly, been dismissed as propaganda, as mere formulaic expressions that have little or no aesthetic value. But although literature was subordinate to politics in this so-called "Revolutionary Era," it is essential to recognize that there was, as Perry Link reminds us, a widespread assumption of literature's importance to the rest of life. Such an

---

* Perry Link, *The Uses of Literature: Life in the Socialist Chinese Literary System* (Princeton: Princeton University Press, 2000), p. 5.

assumption was predicated on faith in social engineering, which Mao and his followers believed capable of reshaping a person's moral character. Writers were therefore regarded as "engineers of the soul."

Literature occupying such a central position in the great Communist machine of social engineering comes at a price, as Chinese writers would soon find out. In 1956 and 1957, Mao, himself a highly accomplished poet, encouraged writers and intellectuals to speak their minds on public issues. Mao famously declared, "Let a hundred flowers blossom and a hundred schools of thought contend." In response, Wang Meng, Liu Bingyan, and others published critical pieces about bureaucratism, corruption, and inefficiency. Wang's story "The Young Man Who Has Just Arrived at the Organization Department" (1956), in particular, drew nationwide attention. Reneging on his own policy, Mao ordered a witch hunt, condemning those who had spoken out as "Rightists." The "hundred flowers" that had dared to bloom were now regarded as "poisonous weeds." The Rightists were publicly humiliated, deprived of their party memberships, and sent to the countryside for reform through hard labor.

The infamous Anti-Rightist Campaign, which claimed about half a million victims and left a deep and lasting psychic wound, was soon followed in 1958 by the "Great Leap Forward," a campaign aiming to boost China's economy. In order to overtake Britain in steel production in fifteen years, the whole country was mobilized: Families turned in their cooking pots, farming tools, doorknobs, or anything that could be melted down for iron. People's communes were established with the stated purpose of rapidly realizing a truly Communist society built on the Marxist notion, "From each according to his ability, to each according to his need." Zhao Shuli, a highly exalted writer in this period, captured well the spirit of communal sharing and collective responsibility in his story "The Unglovable Hands" (1960). The three-year-long utopian campaign ended in a disaster, with millions of people starved to death, housing turned into rubble, and the land savaged in the maniacal pursuit of useless, low-grade iron produced by uneducated peasants in their makeshift backyard furnaces.

No devastation, however, could surpass the catastrophe wreaked by the Cultural Revolution. Set in motion by Mao in 1966, this sweeping movement was allegedly intended to defend "true" Communist ideology from the threat of "backward" elements in Chinese society through violent class struggle. With youthful Red Guards spearheading the revolution, a spasm of violence spread into all walks of life and turned the country upside down: Millions were persecuted, homes ransacked, schools and universities closed, books burned, students sent down to the countryside to receive "reeducation" by the peasants, factories shut down. Factious battles broke out in the streets. The socialist literary system, which had held sway since 1949, also collapsed, and all branches of the writers' associations and their sponsored literary journals ceased to exist. In this turbulent period, the main literary output came from "the people" (workers, peasants, and soldiers) mobilized to compose, often collectively in committees, panegyrics for Mao the Great Helmsman and praises of the ongoing proletarian revolution. The few writers who did publish in these years wrote under strict guidelines and followed closely Mao's new mandates that literary works "should combine revolutionary realism and revolutionary romanticism" and "never forget the class struggle." These doctrines found exemplary expressions in the Model Modern Revolutionary Peking Operas, which replaced traditional opera plots with episodes in the struggle for Communist victory. In these modern operas, like *The Red Lantern*, social realism is combined with romantic characterization that exhibits the prescribed "three prominences": "among the masses, positive characters should stand out; among positive characters, the heroes should be apparent; and among heroes, there should be no doubt who the superheroes are."[*]

The death of Mao in September 1976 put an end to the ten-year turmoil that had rendered China a cultural wasteland. The ice in the frozen river might have cracked, but would take a long thaw before the currents of literary imagination could again run freely—or, at least, less impeded.

---

[*]   Link, p. 115.

MAO ZEDONG
(1893–1976)

Hundreds of millions once hailed him as the "Great Helmsman," to their ultimate sorrow. Mao Zedong, whose name is nearly synonymous with modern China, was also a writer. The eldest son of a rich farmer in Xiangtan, Hunan, Mao ruled the world's most populous country from 1949 to 1976 and brought about sweeping social movements, such as the Great Leap Forward and the Cultural Revolution, which devastated China. A master calligrapher, Mao composed in brushstrokes many poems in classical form, such as "Changsha," "Mount Liupan," and "Snow," included here. As a revolutionary politician and military strategist, he also penned numerous articles, pamphlets, and books. For decades, selections from Mao's work were taught in classrooms, making him the most-read writer in China. During the Cultural Revolution, Mao's Little Red Book of Sayings (also known as Quotations from Chairman Mao) was intended to be a sacred book to every Chinese. Unlike Charlie Chan's fortune-cookie aphorisms that dispense a mix of wisdom, humor, and racism, Mao's sayings were in essence policies to be implemented, principles to live by, and sentences to be carried out.

Changsha

—to the tune of "Chin Yuan Chun"

Alone I stand in the autumn cold
On the tip of Orange Island,
The Hsiang flowing northward;
I see a thousand hills crimsoned through
By their serried woods deep-dyed,
And a hundred barges vying
Over crystal blue waters.
Eagles cleave the air,
Fish glide in the limpid deep;
Under freezing skies
A million creatures contend in freedom.
Brooding over this immensity,
I ask, on this boundless land
Who rules over man's destiny?

I was here with a throng of companions,
Vivid yet those crowded months and years.
Young we were, schoolmates,
At life's full flowering;
Filled with student enthusiasm
Boldly we cast all restraints aside.
Pointing to our mountains and rivers,
Setting people afire with our words,
We counted the mighty no more than muck.
Remember still
How, venturing midstream, we struck the waters
And waves stayed the speeding boats?

—1925

Mount Liupan

—to the tune of "Ching Ping Yueh"

The sky is high, the clouds are pale,
We watch the wild geese vanish southward.
If we fail to reach the Great Wall we are not men,
We who have already measured twenty thousand *li*.

High on the crest of Mount Liupan
Red banners wave freely in the west wind.
Today we hold the long cord in our hands,
When shall we bind fast the Gray Dragon?

—1935

Snow

—to the tune of "Chin Yuan Chun"

North country scene:
A hundred leagues locked in ice,
A thousand leagues of whirling snow.
Both sides of the Great Wall
One single white immensity.
The Yellow River's swift current
Is stilled from end to end.
The mountains dance like silver snakes
And the highlands charge like wax-hued elephants,
Vying with heaven in stature.
On a fine day, the land,

Clad in white, adorned in red,
Grows more enchanting.

This land so rich in beauty
Has made countless heroes bow in homage.
But alas! Chin Shih-huang and Han Wu-ti
Were lacking in literary grace,
And Tang Tai-tsung and Sung Tai-tsu
Had little poetry in their souls;
And Genghis Khan,
Proud Son of Heaven for a day,
Knew only shooting eagles, bow outstretched.
All are past and gone!
For truly great men
Look to this age alone.

—1936

Quotations from Chairman Mao (excerpts)

A revolution is not a dinner party, or writing an essay, or painting a picture, or doing embroidery; it cannot be so refined, so leisurely and gentle, so temperate, kind, courteous, restrained, and magnanimous. A revolution is an insurrection, an act of violence by which one class overthrows another.

*

If there is to be a revolution, there must be a revolutionary party.

*

In class society everyone lives as a member of a particular class, and every kind of thinking, without exception, is stamped with the brand of a class.

*

War is the highest form of struggle for resolving contradictions.

*

Political power grows out of the barrel of a gun.

*

All reactionaries are paper tigers.

*

The people, and the people alone, are the motive force in the making of world history.

*

Serve the people.

*

Investigation may be likened to the long months of pregnancy, and solving a problem to the day of birth.

*

We have the Marxist-Leninist weapon of criticism and self-criticism. We can get rid of a bad style and keep the good.

*

In the world today all culture, all literature and art belong to definite classes and are geared to definite political lines. There is in fact no such thing as art for art's sake, art that stands above classes, art that is detached from or independent of politics. Proletarian literature and art are part of the whole proletarian revolutionary cause; they are, as Lenin said, cogs and screws in the whole revolutionary machine.

*

All our literature and art are for the masses of the people, and in the first place for the workers, peasants, and soldiers.

*

Let a hundred flowers blossom and a hundred schools of thought contend.

AI QING
(1910–1996)

Born Jiang Haicheng into a landlord family in Zhejiang, Ai Qing was brought up, as a fortune-teller suggested, by a peasant woman in order to avoid bad karma. Trained to be an artist, he went to France in 1929 to study painting. There he was influenced by French Symbolist poets and turned to writing. Returning to China in 1932, he joined the League of Left-Wing Writers. The following year he was arrested by the Nationalist regime for his radical politics, and in jail he composed his best-known poem, "Dayanhe—My Wet Nurse" (1933), a loving tribute to the working class as represented by the peasant woman who had raised him. After the outbreak of the Sino-Japanese War, he devoted himself wholeheartedly to the resistance movement and the Communist cause. Like most free thinkers of his generation, he was condemned in 1957 as a "Rightist" and exiled to remote regions for twenty years. In 1979 he was rehabilitated and allowed to write and publish. A major poet of twentieth century China, Ai was also the father of Ai Weiwei, the famous Chinese artist whose provocative work has made him a target of government censorship in recent years.

Wheelbarrow

In the land where the Yellow River once flowed
In the countless riverbeds now gone dry
A wheelbarrow
With its single wheel
Squeals, sending the cheerless sky into spasms
Across the silence and chill
From the foot of this mountain
To the foot of that mountain
Reverberates
The sorrow of the north country people

On the days of snow and ice
Between destitute little villages
A wheelbarrow
With its single wheel
Cuts deep ruts in the yellow soil
Across the vast and wild desert
From this path
To that path
Crisscrosses
The sorrow of the north country people

Dayanhe—My Wet Nurse

Danyanhe, my wet nurse,
Her name was the name of her native village.
She was a child bride
Dayanhe, my wet nurse.

I am the son of a landlord,
But also the son of Dayanhe
Brought up on Dayanhe's breast milk.
Raising me, Dayanhe raised her own family
And I was one raised on your milk
Dayanhe, my wet nurse.

Dayanhe, the snow today makes me think of you:
Your grass-covered snowbound grave
The dry weeds on the eaves of your shuttered house
Your mortgaged garden, ten feet square
Your stone bench by the door overgrown with moss
Dayanhe, the snowfall today makes me think of you.

With your thick palms, you cradled and caressed me
After you had stoked up the fire in the stove
After you had patted down coal ashes from your apron
After you had tasted the rice to make sure it was cooked
After you had set the bowls of soy paste on the black table
After you had mended your sons' clothes torn by mountain thorns
After you had bandaged your little child's hand cut by a firewood ax
After you had crushed one by one the lice on your children's shirts
After you had collected the first egg laid that day
With your thick palms, you cradled and caressed me.

I am the son of a landlord
After I had drunk dry your milk, Dayanhe
I was taken back home by my parents.
Ah, Dayanhe, why did you cry?

I was a guest in the house of my birth!
I touched the furniture of red lacquer and floral carving
I touched the gold patterns on my parents' bed

I stared dumbly at the "Family Happiness" sign on the eaves,
     unable to read the inscription
I put on new clothes and touched the silk and mother-of-pearl buttons
I looked at my sister, whom I barely knew, in mother's arms
I sat on a lacquered *k'ang* bench with a brazier underneath for warmth
I ate white rice that had been milled three times
Yet, I felt so uneasy! Because I
Was a newcomer in the house of my parents.

Dayanhe, to survive
After her milk had run dry
She began working with those arms that had cradled me
Smiling, she washed our clothes
Smiling, she carried a basket to the icy pond by the village
Smiling, she sliced turnips frozen in winter
Smiling, she stirred the grain hulls in the pig trough
Smiling, she fanned the flames under the stew pot
Smiling, she carried a winnowing basket of beans and wheat
     to bake them in the sun of the village square
Dayanhe, to survive
After her milk had run dry
She put those arms that had cradled me to work.

Dayanhe, who adored the child she had suckled
At New Year's, for him, she busied herself cutting rice candy
For him, who would sneak away to her house at the edge of the village
For him, who would walk up to her and call out "Mom"
Dayanhe, who would stick his bright red and green drawing
     of Guan Gong on the wall by the stove
Dayanhe, who would brag and boast to villagers about her foster child
Dayanhe once had a dream she could not tell anyone:
In the dream, she was enjoying the wedding banquet of the child she
   nursed

Sitting in a splendid hall adorned with silk garlands
And her beautiful daughter-in-law called her affectionately, "Mother"
. . . . . .
Dayanhe, who adored the child she had suckled!

Dayanhe did not awake from the dream.
When she died, the child was not at her side
When she died, the husband who beat her shed tears
Her five sons each cried bitter tears
When she died, she called out tenderly the name of her child
Dayanhe is dead
When she died, her child was not at her side.

Dayanhe, who left with tears!
Along with four decades of humiliation at the hands of the world
Along with countless sufferings as a slave
Along with a four-dollar coffin and a few bundles of rice straw
Along with a few-feet-square burial plot
Along with a handful of ashes from burning paper money
Dayanhe, who left in tears.

But these are what Dayanhe does not know:
Her drunkard husband is dead
Her eldest son became a bandit
Her second son died in the smoke of gunfire
Her third, fourth, and fifth
Live their days cursed by their teachers and landlords.
And I am writing condemnations of this unjust world.
When I returned to my village after years of wandering
On mountain ridges, in the fields
When I met my brothers, we felt closer than six or seven years ago.
This, this is what you, Dayanhe, resting quietly in your sleep
This is what you do not know!

Dayanhe, today, your child is in jail
Composing this hymn dedicated to you
To your spirit, a purple shade under the sallow earth
To your outstretched arms that once embraced me
To your lips that kissed me
To your gentle earth-colored face
To your breasts that once suckled me
To your sons, my brothers
To all of them on earth
Wet nurses like Dayanhe and their sons
To Dayanhe, who loved me as she loved her own sons.

Dayanhe,
I am your son
Brought up on your breast milk
I worship you
With all my heart!

> —On a snowy morning,
> January 14, 1933
> (Translated by Yunte Huang and Glenn Mott)

On a Chilean Cigarette Package

On a Chilean cigarette package
One sees a picture of the Goddess of Freedom.
Although she holds a torch in her hand,
She yet remains a dark shadow;

For serving as a trademark, an ad,
Let's give the goddess a space.

You can buy a pack with a few coins,
After you are through with it, in smoke it's gone.

You toss away the empty package on the sidewalk.
People step on it, people spit on it.
Be it a fact, or be it a symbol,
The Goddess of Freedom is but a pack of cigarettes.

—1954

(Translated by Julia C. Lin)

WANG MENG
(1934–)

Born in Hebei, Wang Meng is a living example of the trials and tribulations experienced by Chinese writers in the second half of the twentieth century. A radical idealist, Wang joined the Communist Party at the tender age of thirteen in 1948. The publication of his short story "The Young Man Who Has Just Arrived at the Organization Department" in 1956 caused a stir for its exposure of bureaucratic corruption. It was first lauded as a manifestation of Mao's Hundred Flowers spirit but soon condemned as an expression of a Rightist's discontent with the party. Wang was exiled to the countryside for twenty years until his rehabilitation in 1978. His tenure as the editor-in-chief of People's Literature *(1983–86) and then as minister of culture (1986–89) spans the decade-long period of cultural renaissance in post-Mao China. He remained an influential figure, until he was dismissed again by the government after Tiananmen for his liberal views. A prolific author of over sixty books, Wang embodies the tenacity of Chinese writers, whose spirit may best be captured by the title of his novel,* Long Live the Youth.

The Young Man Who Has Just Arrived at the Organization Department (excerpts)

Chapter 1

It was March, with a mixture of rain and snow in the air. Outside the door of the District Party Committee office a pedicab drew to a halt, and a young man jumped down. The driver looked at the large sign above the door and said politely to his passenger, "If you're coming here, there won't be any charge." One of the message center workers, a demobilized soldier called Old Lü, came limping out. After asking why the young man had come, he moved quickly to help unload his bags. This done, he went off to summon the Organization Department's office secretary, Chao Hui-wen. Chao Hui-wen grasped both of Lin Chen's hands tightly and said, "We've been waiting for you for a long time."

Lin Chen had met Chao Hui-wen while in the teachers' Party Branch in primary school. Two large eyes sparkled with friendliness and affection in her pale, beautiful face. Under those eyes, however, were dark circles caused by a lack of sleep. She led Lin Chen to the men's dormitory, placed his bags in order, and opened them. She also hung his damp blanket up to dry and made the bed. As she was doing these things she continually reached up to arrange her hair, just as any other capable attractive female comrade would do.

"We've been waiting for you for such a long time," she said. "Half a year ago we tried to have you assigned here, but the Cultural and Education Section of the District People's Council absolutely refused to agree. Later on the District Party Committee secretary went directly to the district chief and said he wanted you. He also made a fuss at the Education Bureau's personnel office. After all of this we finally got you transferred."

"I only learned about this the day before yesterday," Lin Chen replied. "When I heard that I was being transferred to the District Party Committee I didn't know what to think. What does this District Party Committee of ours do?"

"Everything."

"And the Organization Department?"

"The Organization Department does organizational work."

"Is there a lot of work?"

"At times we're busy. Sometimes we aren't."

Chao Hui-wen took a hard look at Lin Chen's bed and shook her head. "Young man," she said indignantly, in the manner of an older sister, "you haven't been keeping yourself clean. Look at that pillowcase! It's gone from white to black. And look at the top of your blanket. It's completely saturated with oil from your neck. Your sheet is so wrinkled it's like seersucker."

Lin Chen had the feeling that just as he was entering the doors of the District Party Committee and beginning his new life, he was also meeting a very dear friend.

Lin Chen was in an excited holiday mood as he rushed over to the office of the first vice director of the Organization Department to report his arrival. The vice director had a peculiar name—Liu Shih-wu.* As Lin Chen knocked nervously on his door, Liu Shih-wu was looking upward, a cigarette in his mouth, thinking about the work plans of the Organization Department. He welcomed Lin enthusiastically, but with a sense of propriety. After offering Lin a seat on the sofa, he himself sat down on the edge of his desk, pushing aside some of the papers that were piled high on the glass top. In a relaxed voice, he asked: "How are things going?" His left eye narrowed slightly. His right hand flicked his cigarette ash away.

"The secretary of the Party Branch told me to come here on the day after tomorrow, but since my work in the school was already finished I came today. Being sent to the Organization Department has made me anxious about my abilities. I'm a new Party member and I was formerly

---

*   Literally, the name means "Liu, the world and me."

a primary teacher. The work of a teacher in primary school is quite different from the organization work of the Party."

Lin Chen had prepared these words well in advance and spoke them very unnaturally, as if he were really a primary school student who was meeting his teacher for the first time. The room began to feel very warm. It was mid-March. Winter would soon be over. Yet, there was still a fire burning in the room. The frost on the window had melted and turned into dirty streaks. Beads of sweat formed on his forehead. He wanted to pull out a handkerchief and wipe them away, but he could not find one in his pockets.

Liu Shih-wu nodded his head mechanically and, without watching what he was doing, pulled a manila envelope out from a large pile of papers. Opening it, he removed Lin Chen's Party registration form and scanned it rapidly with a keen look in his eyes. Fine lines appeared across his broad forehead and he closed his eyes for a moment. Then, placing his hand on the back of his chair for support, he stood up—as he did so the jacket that had been lying across his shoulders slipped to the floor—and in a skilled effortless voice said, "Good. Fine. Excellent. The Organization Department is short of cadres now. You've come at the right time. No, our work is not difficult. With study and practice you'll be able to do it. That's the way it is. Also, you did a good job in your work at the lower level, right?"

Lin Chen sensed that this praise was given somewhat in jest, so he shook his head and replied apprehensively, "I didn't do my work well at all."

A faint smile appeared on Liu Shih-wu's unwashed face. His eyes sparkled with intelligence as he continued. "Of course, there is the possibility that you will have problems. It is possible. This is very important work. One of the comrades on the Central Committee has said that organization work is the housekeeping work of the Party. If the house is not properly cared for, the Party won't be strong." Without waiting for any questions Liu added an explanation. "What housework are we doing? We are developing and strengthening the Party, making the organization solid, and increasing the fighting power of the Party organization. We are establishing Party life on a foundation of collective leadership, criticism and self-criticism, and close ties with the masses. If we do this work well, the Party organization will be robust, lively, and will have the strength to fight. It will be up to the task of unifying and leading the masses. It will be better able to complete the work of socialist construction and fulfill the various duties of socialist transformation."

After each phrase Liu cleared his throat, except for those expressions which he knew well through repeated use. These he spoke so rapidly that he seemed to be saying one word. For example, when he said, "Let's anchor the life of the Party on . . ." it sounded as though he were saying, "Let's anchor the life of the Party on rata-tat-tat-tat." With the skill of someone manipulating an abacus, he handled concepts that Lin Chen thought were rather obscure and difficult to understand. Even though Lin listened with extreme intensity, he still could not grasp everything that Liu was saying.

Liu Shih-wu went on to assign Lin Chen his work. Then, just as Lin was opening the door to leave, he called to him, and in a completely different, easygoing manner asked, "How are you getting along, young man? Do you have a girlfriend?"

"No," Lin Chen replied, a touch of redness sweeping across his face.

"A big fellow like you still blushes?" Liu Shih-wu asked with a laugh. "Well, you're only twenty-two. There's no need to hurry. By the way, what's that book you have in your pocket?"

Lin Chen took the book out and read him the title, *The Tractor Station Manager and the Chief Agronomist.*

Liu reached for the book, opened it to the middle, and read a few lines. "Did the Central Committee of the Youth League recommend this book for you young people to read?"

Lin Chen nodded.

"Lend it to me so I can take a look."

Glancing at the papers piled high on the vice director's desk, Lin Chen asked in surprise, "Do you have time to read novels?"

Liu Shih-wu placed the book in the palm of his hand and gauged its weight. His left eye squinted slightly as he answered, "What do you mean? I'll read through a thin volume like this in half an evening. I read the four volumes of *And Quiet Flows the Don* in a single week. That's the way it is."

By the time Lin Chen went over to the main office of the Organization Department the sky had already cleared. Only a few clouds remained along the clear bright horizon. Sunlight streamed into the large court-yard of the District Party Committee. Everyone was busy. [. . .] Lin Chen stopped for a moment in the portico and looked at the dazzling courtyard. He was very happy about the beginning of his new life.

[. . .]

Chapter 3

Lin Chen had graduated from normal school in the autumn of 1953 and had been sent to serve as a teacher in the central primary school of this district. At that time he was an alternate Party member. Even after becoming a teacher he maintained the practices of his middle school student life. Early in the morning he lifted dumbbells. At night he wrote in his diary. Before every major holiday—May 1, July 1, etc.—he went about asking people for their opinions of him. Some people predicted that within three months he would be "converted" by the older adults whose lives were not so regulated. However, in a short time several teachers were praising him and saying with admiration, "This lad doesn't have any worries or family cares. All he knows is work."

Lin Chen proved himself worthy of such admiration. Because of his accomplishments as a teacher, during the winter recess of 1954 he received an award from the Bureau of Education.

People may have thought that the young teacher would continue on in this steady fashion, living his youthful years in contentment and hap-piness. But this was not to be. Simple, childlike Lin Chen had worries and concerns of his own.

After another year, Lin Chen was anxiously berating himself even more frequently. Was it due to the press of the high tide of socialism?

Was it the result of the convening of the All-China Conference of Young Socialist Activists? Or was it because he was getting older?

Lin Chen was now already twenty-two. He recalled how in his first year of middle school he had written an essay entitled "When I Am XX Years Old," and how in that essay he had written, "When I am twenty-two I want to . . ." Now he really was twenty-two and the pages of his life history still seemed to be blank. He had no meritorious achievements. He had not created anything. He had not braved any dangers or fallen in love. He had not written one single letter to a girl. He worked hard, but if the amount of work he did and the speed with which he did it were compared to the accomplishments of the young activists or the swiftness with which his life was flying by, of what possible comfort could this be to him? He set forth a plan to study this and study that, to do this and do that. He wanted to cover a thousand things in one day.

It was at this time that Lin Chen received his transfer notice. Now his history could read, "At twenty-two I became a Party worker." Was his real life going to begin from here? Suppressing his love for primary school teaching and the children, he kindled great hopes about his new job. After the secretary of the Party Branch discussed his transfer with him, he stayed up all night thinking about it.

Thus it was that Lin Chen excitedly climbed the stone steps of the District Party Committee, *The Tractor Station Manager and the Chief Agronomist* stuck in his pocket. He was filled with a sacred reverence for the life of a Party worker. . . .

[*Lin Chen's assignment in the Organization Department is in the Factory Organization Development Section. His section chief, Han Ch'ang-hsin, makes a very favorable first impression on him and he enthusiastically prepares for his first trip to a factory.*

[*Four days after his arrival, Lin Chen rides his bicycle to the T'ung Hua Gunnysack Factory to study Party recruitment work. What he finds leaves him shocked and confused. The factory director, a man named Wang Ch'ing-ch'üan, who is concurrently serving as Party Branch secretary, is domineering, dogmatic, and obviously not very interested in his duties. Worse yet, when Lin suggests to the Party member in charge of recruitment, Wei Ho-ming, that a* report on the situation be made to higher authorities, he is told that this has already been done several times with no effect. In Wei's words: "I don't know how many times I've talked to Han Ch'ang-hsin about this. Old Han didn't do anything. Instead, he turned around and gave me a lesson, telling me about the need to respect leadership and strengthen unity. Maybe I shouldn't be thinking like this, but I feel that we may have to wait until Factory Director Wang embezzles some money or rapes a woman before the higher echelons finally sit up and take notice!"

[Lin Chen cannot understand how such a situation can be permitted to exist, and he reports excitedly to Han Ch'ang-hsin about what he has learned. Han is unconcerned. He informs Lin that he knows all about Wang Ch'ing-ch'üan and tells him not to worry about matters that are beyond the scope of his duties. This fails to satisfy Lin Chen and he goes to talk to Han Ch'ang-hsin's superior, Liu Shih-wu. Liu openly acknowledges that Wang Ch'ing-ch'üan has made some serious errors, but he asks Lin to be patient, saying that conditions are not yet ripe for resolving the situation.

[Lin Chen's talk with Liu Shih-wu eases his mind temporarily, but subsequent visits to the gunnysack factory revive his indignation over Wang Ch'ing-ch'üan's performance. Thinking that he will hasten the "ripening of conditions" mentioned by Liu Shih-wu, he gives his approval to Wei Ho-ming's idea of organizing the workers into a discussion group that will submit complaints about Wang Ch'ing-ch'üan to higher authorities. However, after Wang learns of this plan and accuses Lin of encouraging antileadership activity, it is Lin, not Wang, who receives most of the criticism. At a meeting convened to discuss this matter, Han Ch'ang-hsin complains about Lin's "unorganized and undisciplined activity." Liu Shih-wu notes that Lin, as with most youth, is overly idealistic and reminds him pointedly that he is "definitely not the only person who has principles."

[After being subjected to such criticism, Lin Chen is uncertain about what he should do. Should he continue to struggle resolutely on behalf of his high standards? Or should he put aside this struggle temporarily and wait until he is more knowledgeable and more experienced? A chance meeting with Chao Hui-wen on the following Saturday evening helps him decide which path to follow.]

Chapter 7

On Saturday evening Han Ch'ang-hsin was getting married. Lin Chen went into the assembly hall, but he disliked the thick irritating smoke, the candy wrappers scattered about the floor, and the steady roar of loud laughter. Without waiting for the ceremony to begin, he made his departure.

The Organization Department office was dark. Lin Chen turned on the light and saw a letter on his desk. It was from his fellow teachers in the primary school. Enclosed inside was another letter signed by the children with their little hands. It read:

"Teacher Lin, how are you? We miss you very very much. All of the girls cried, but they are better now. We have been doing arithmetic. The problems are very hard. We think them over for a long time, but in the end we work them out."

As he read the letter Lin Chen could not refrain from smiling to himself. He picked up his pen, substituted a correct character for an incorrect one, and prepared to tell them in his reply not to use a wrong character when they wrote him again. It seemed as though he was watching Li Lin-lin, with the ribbon in her hair, Liu Hsiao-mao, who loved watercolor painting, and Meng Fei, the one who often held lead pencil tips in his mouth. Abruptly he lifted his head from the letter. Only the telephone, the ink blotter, and the glass desktop were there to be seen. The child's world that he knew so well was already far away. Now he was in an unfamiliar environment. He thought about the criticism leveled at him at the Party committee meeting two days earlier. Was it possible that it was actually he himself who was wrong? Was he really rude and childish, full of the cheap bravery of the young? Maybe he really ought to make an honest self-appraisal. Couldn't he do his own work well for two years or so and wait until he himself had "ripened" before intervening in all of these things?

An explosion of applause and laughter burst from the assembly hall.

A soft hand fell upon his shoulder. Startled, he turned his head and felt the glare of the light pierce his eyes. Chao Hui-wen was standing

silently beside him. All women comrades had a talent for walking without a sound.

"Why aren't you over there having a good time?" she asked.

"I'm too lazy to go. What about you?"

"I've got to be getting home," Chao Hui-wen replied. "How about
coming to my place and relaxing for a while? It's better than sitting here
brooding by yourself."

"I don't have anything to brood about," Lin Chen protested. He did,
however, accept Chao Hui-wen's kind invitation.

Chao Hui-wen lived in a small courtyard not far from the offices of
the District Party Committee. Her son was sleeping in a pale blue crib,
sucking contentedly on his fingers. She gave the baby a kiss and drew
Lin Chen to her own room.

"Doesn't his father come home?" Lin Chen asked cautiously.

Chao Hui-wen shook her head.

The bedroom looked as though it had been arranged very hastily. The
walls were completely bare and because of this they appeared exces-
sively white. A washstand huddled alone in a corner. On the windowsill
a flower vase held its empty mouth open like a fool. Only the radio on
the small table at the head of the bed seemed capable of breaking the
stillness of the room.

Lin Chen sat down on the rattan chair. Chao Hui-wen stood leaning
against the wall. Lin Chen pointed to the flower vase and said, "You
should put some flowers in it." Pointing to the walls, he asked, "Why
don't you buy some paintings and hang them up?" "Since I'm hardly ever
here, I haven't given it any thought," Chao Hui-wen replied. Indicating
the radio, she asked, "Would you like to listen? There's always good
music on Saturday evening."

The light on the radio came on and a dreamy gentle melody floated in
from afar. Slowly it became an emotional stimulant. The poetic theme
played by the violin seized Lin Chen's heart. He laid his chin on his
hands and held his breath. His youth, his aspirations, and his failures all
seemed to be transmitted through this music.

Chao Hui-wen leaned against the wall with her hands behind her back, oblivious to the whitewash rubbing off on her clothes. She waited until the movement was completed, and then, in a voice that was itself like music, she said, "This is Tchaikovsky's *Capriccio Italien*. It makes me think of a southern country and the sea. When I was in the Cultural Work Troupe I heard it often, and gradually I came to feel that the melody wasn't being played by someone else, but was boring its way out from my heart."

"You were in the Cultural Work Troupe?"

"I was assigned there after attending the Military Cadre School. In Korea I used my poor voice to sing for the soldiers. I'm a hoarse-voiced singer."

Lin Chen looked at Chao Hui-wen as if he were seeing her for the first time.

"What's wrong? Don't I look like a singer?" At this moment the program changed to "Theater Facts," and Chao Hui-wen turned the radio off.

"If you were in the Cultural Work Troupe, why do you hardly ever sing?"

Chao Hui-wen didn't answer. She walked over to her bed, sat down, and said, "Let's have a chat. Little Lin, tell me, what's your impression of our District Party Committee?"

"I don't know. That is to say, I'm not sure."

"You do have some differences of opinion with Han Ch'ang-hsin and Liu Shih-wu, don't you?"

"Maybe."

"When I first came I was that way too. Having transferred here from the military, I was making comparisons with military strictness and precision, and there were many things that I couldn't get used to. I made many suggestions and had one spirited argument with Han Ch'ang-hsin. But they made fun of me and said I was childish. They laughed at me for making so many suggestions before I was doing my own work well. Slowly I came to realize that I didn't have enough strength to struggle against the various shortcomings of the District Committee."

"Why not?" Lin Chen exclaimed, leaping to his feet as if he had been stabbed. His eyebrows came together in a deep frown.

"That was my mistake," Chao Hui-wen answered, taking a pillow and placing it on her lap. "At the time, I felt that with my own lack of experience and my own imperfection I certainly wasn't strong enough to be thinking about reforming comrades who were much more experienced than I was. Moreover, Liu Shih-wu, Han Ch'ang-hsin, and some other comrades actually do many things very well. If you scatter their shortcomings among our accomplishments it's like throwing dust into the clear air. You can smell it, but you can't grab hold of it. This is what makes it so hard."

"Right!" Lin Chen responded, smashing his right fist into the palm of his left hand.

[After this Chao Hui-wen and Lin Chen discuss what they see as the faults of several leading cadres, including Han Ch'ang-hsin and Liu Shih-wu. The plodding approach of these cadres toward their duties has troubled Chao Hui-wen for a long time and caused her many sleepless nights. Now at last she has an opportunity to vent her frustrations. Lin Chen is deeply moved by what she tells him.]

"Then . . . what's to be done?" he asked. Only now was Lin Chen beginning to realize how complicated everything was. It seemed that each and every shortcoming was attached to a whole series of causes that ran from the top to the bottom.

"That's true," Chao Hui-wen answered, deep in thought, her fingers tapping on her legs as if she were playing the piano. Looking into the distance, she smiled and said, "Thank you."

"Thank you?" Lin Chen thought that he had heard incorrectly.

"Yes. When I see you I seem to be young again. You often fix your eyes on something and don't move. You're always thinking, like a child who loves to dream. You get excited quite easily and blush at anything. Yet, you are also fearless, willing to struggle against every evil. I have a kind of woman's intuition that you . . . that a big change is on the way."

Lin Chen blushed deeply again. He had simply never thought about these matters and was completely embarrassed by his inability to do anything. "Well," he mumbled, "I hope that it's a genuine change and not just some blind confusion." Pausing a moment, he asked her, "You've thought about this for so long and have made such a clear analysis. Why have you kept everything to yourself?"

"I've always felt that there was nothing I could do," Chao Hui-wen answered. She put her hands across her chest and said, "I look and think, think, and look again. At times I think all night and can't fall asleep. I ask myself, 'You're doing routine office work. Can you understand all of these things?'"

"How can you think such thoughts? I feel that what you've been telling me is absolutely correct. You should tell this to the secretary of the District Party Committee. Or write it up and send it to the *People's Daily.*"

"Look, there you go again!" Chao Hui-wen's teeth glistened as she said this with a smile.

"How can you say, 'There I go again'?" Lin Chen stood up unhappily and scratched his head hard. "I've thought about this many times too. I feel that people should correct themselves through struggle instead of waiting until they're perfect before they enter the fray."

Suddenly Chao Hui-wen pushed open the door and went out, leaving Lin Chen alone in the empty room. He smelled the fragrance of soap and then in an instant she was back carrying a long-handled saucepan. She skipped in like one of those little girls who comb their hair into three braids, took the cover off the pan, and said dramatically, "Let's eat some water chestnuts. They're already well cooked. I couldn't find anything else good to eat."

"Ever since I was a child I've loved boiled water chestnuts," Lin Chen responded, happily taking the pan with his hands. He selected a large unpeeled one, took a bite, and spit it out with a frown. "This one is bad, both sour and rotten." As Chao Hui-wen laughed, Lin Chen angrily threw the squashed sour water chestnut to the floor.

When Lin Chen prepared to leave it was already late at night. The clear sky was completely covered with shy little stars. An old man singing, "Fried dumplings fresh from the pot," pushed his cart by. Lin Chen stood outside the doorway. Chao Hui-wen stood just inside, her eyes

sparkling in the darkness. "The next time you come there will be paintings on the wall," she said.

Lin Chen smiled understandingly and said, "I hope that you'll take up
singing again too." He gave her hand a squeeze.

Lin Chen breathed in deeply the fragrant air of this spring night. A
warm spring welled up within his heart.

[Shortly after his lengthy conversation with Chao Hui-wen, Lin Chen talks
to Wei Ho-ming and convinces him to send a letter describing conditions in the
gunnysack factory to the People's Daily. The letter is published with an editorial note advising the appropriate authorities to look into the matter. Now Liu
Shih-wu moves quickly. He initiates a thorough investigation, and as a result of
the findings, Wang Ch'ing-ch'üan is removed from his administrative posts in
both the factory and the Party.

[Lin Chen, however, is still not satisfied. When the standing committee of
the District Party Committee meets to discuss the situation in the gunnysack
factory, he tells the committee that Liu Shih-wu and Han Ch'ang-hsin should
bear responsibility for not solving the problems there sooner. "Indifference, pro-
crastination, and irresponsibility," he states, "are crimes against the masses." In
a loud voice he calls out, "The Party is the heart of the people and the working
class. We do not permit dust on the heart. We should not allow shortcomings in
Party organs." He persists until the District Party secretary tells him bluntly,
"Comrade, you get excited too easily. Reciting lyrics is not appropriate to the
conduct of organization work."

[This is a frustrating moment for Lin Chen. Once again his superiors have
ignored his views and called his idealism into question. But this is not the only
challenge Lin Chen faces as the story now moves to its conclusion. He must also
contend with the complex emotions that his relationship with Chao Hui-wen
has provoked.]

After the meeting adjourned, Lin Chen was so angry that he didn't eat
supper. He had never thought that the District Party secretary would
have such an attitude. His disappointment bordered on hopelessness.
When Han Ch'ang-hsin and Liu Shih-wu invited him to go for a walk, as
if they were unaware of his dissatisfaction with them, it made him even
more conscious of how impotent he was compared to them. He smiled

bitterly and thought to himself, "So you had the idea that speaking out before the standing committee would accomplish something!" Opening a drawer, he picked up the Soviet novel that Han Ch'ang-hsin had laughed at, and opened it to the first page. At the top was written, "The Model Life of Anastasia." "It's so hard," he said to himself.

Chapter 11

The next day after work Chao Hui-wen said to Lin Chen, "Come over to my place for supper. I'll make some dumplings." He wanted to decline, but she was already gone.

Lin Chen hesitated for some time, and then ate in the dining hall before going to Chao Hui-wen's home. When he arrived her dumplings were just ready. For the first time Chao Hui-wen was wearing a deep red dress. She had on an apron and her hands were covered with flour. Like an attentive housewife she told Lin Chen, "I used fresh beans in the dumplings."

"I . . . I've already eaten," Lin Chen stammered.

Chao Hui-wen did not believe him and rushed off to get chopsticks. But after Lin Chen repeated for a second and a third time that he really had eaten, she discontentedly began to eat by herself. Lin Chen sat nervously to one side, looking first one way and then the other, rubbing his hands together, and shifting his body. Those inexpressible feelings of warmth and anguish were once again welling up within his heart. His heart ached as if he had lost something. He simply did not dare look at Chao Hui-wen's beautiful face, shining red in the reflection of her red dress.

"Little Lin, what's wrong?" Chao Hui-wen asked, pausing from her meal.

"N . . . nothing."

"Tell me," she said, her eyes not moving from him.

"Yesterday I presented my opinions at the meeting of the standing committee. The District Party secretary didn't pay any attention to them at all."

Chao Hui-wen bit on her chopsticks and thought deeply for a moment. "That's not possible. Perhaps Comrade Chou Jun-hsiang just didn't want to give his views too lightly."

"Perhaps," Lin Chen replied, half believing, half doubting. Fearful of meeting Chao Hui-wen's concerned gaze, he lowered his head.

After eating several more dumplings Chao Hui-wen asked again, "Is there something else?"

Lin Chen's heart leaped. He raised his head and looked into her sympathetic, encouraging eyes. In a low voice he said, "Comrade Chao Hui-wen . . ."

Chao Hui-wen laid down her chopsticks and leaned back in her chair. She was a little taken aback.

"I want to know if you're happy," Lin Chen asked in a heavy, completely serious voice. "I saw your tears in Liu Shih-wu's office. Spring had just arrived then. Afterward I forgot about it. I've been going along living my own life, not caring about others. Are you happy?"

Chao Hui-wen looked at him with a touch of misgiving, shook her head, and said, "At times I forget too." Then, nodding her head, she smiled calmly and said, "Yes. Yes, I'm happy. Why do you ask?"

". . . I want so much to talk to you or listen to symphonies with you. You're wonderful, of course. But maybe there's something here that's bad or improper. I hadn't thought about this, and then all of a sudden I began to worry. Now I'm afraid that I'm disturbing someone."

Chao Hui-wen smiled and then frowned. She raised her slender arms and vigorously rubbed her forehead. After giving her head a toss, as if she were casting aside some unpleasant thought, she turned away and walked slowly over to the oil painting that had just recently been hung on the wall. She stood staring at it in silence. Its title was *Spring*. It depicted Moscow at the time when the first spring sun appears, with mothers and their children out on the streets.

After a few moments Chao Hui-wen turned back and sat down quickly on her bed, holding on to the railing with one hand. In an exceptionally quiet voice she said, "What are you saying? Really! I couldn't do anything so rash. I have a husband and a child. I haven't told you anything yet about my husband." She didn't use the more common term "loved one," but emphasized the word "husband." "We were married in 1952 when I was only nineteen. I really shouldn't have married so early. He had come out of the military and was a section head in a central ministry. Gradually he became rather slick, competing for position and material rewards, and failing to cooperate with others. As for us, all that seemed to be left was his return on Saturday evening and his departure on Monday. According to his theory love was either exalted or it was nothing. We quarreled. But I'm still waiting. He's now on assignment in Shanghai. After he returns I want to have a long talk with him. So, what is it that you want to say? Little Lin, you're my best friend. I have great respect for you. But you're still a child—well, perhaps that's not the proper term. I'm sorry. We both hope to lead a true, real life. We both hope that the Organization Department will become a genuine Party work organ. I feel that you're my younger brother. You wish that I would become more active, don't you? Life should have the warmth of mutual support and friendship. I've always been frightened by cold indifference. That's all there is to it. Is there anything more? Can there be anything more?"

[. . .]

Chao Hui-wen opened her briefcase, took out several sheets of paper and leafed through them. "I have some things that I want to show you this evening. I've already written up the problems that I've seen in the work of the Organization Department over the past three years and have put down my own thoughts about them. This . . ." She rubbed a piece of paper in embarrassment. "This is probably pretty laughable. I've set up a system for competing with myself, a way to let myself see if I've done better today than I did yesterday. I've drawn a table and if I make an error in my work—such as copying a name incorrectly on the notice of admission to the Party or adding up the number of new Party members wrong—I put down a black 'X.' If I go through a day without making any mistakes I draw a little red flag. If the red flags continue for a whole month without interruption, then I buy a pretty scarf or something else as a reward for myself. Maybe this is like it's done in kindergarten. Do you think it's funny?"

Lin Chen had been listening in a trance. "Absolutely not," he said solemnly. "I respect your seriousness about yourself. . . ."

When Lin Chen prepared to leave it was again already late at night. Again he stood outside the doorway. Chao Hui-wen stood just inside, her eyes sparkling in the darkness. "This is a beautiful evening, isn't it?" she asked. "Do you smell the sweet scent of the locust tree blossoms? Those common white flowers are more refined than peonies and more fragrant than peach or plum blossoms. Can't you smell them? Really! Good-bye. I'll be seeing you early tomorrow morning when we throw ourselves into our great but annoying work. Later, in the evening, look for me and we'll listen to the beautiful *Capriccio Italien*. After we're done listening I'll cook water chestnuts for you and we'll throw the peelings all over the floor."

Lin Chen stood leaning against the large pillar by the door of the Organization Department for a long time, staring at the night sky. The south wind of early summer brushed against him. He had arrived at the end of winter. Now it was already the beginning of summer. He had passed through his first spring in the Organization Department.

A strange feeling surged up in Lin Chen's heart. It was as if he had lost something valuable. It was like thinking about his inadequate accomplishments and slow progress over the past several months. But no, it was not really any of these. . . . Ah, people were so complicated! Nothing fit Liu Shih-wu's expression, "That's the way it is." No, nothing was the way it appeared, and because of this, everything had to be approached honestly, seriously, and conscientiously. Because of this, when unreasonable or unendurable things were encountered they were not to be tolerated. They were to be struggled against, one, two, or even three times. Only when a situation was changed could the struggle stop. There was definitely no reason to be disheartened or downcast. As for love, well . . . All that could be done was grit one's teeth and quietly suppress these feelings in the heart!

"I want to be more active, more enthusiastic, and certainly more strong," Lin Chen said quietly to himself. He lifted his chest and took a deep breath of the cool night air.

Looking through the window Lin Chen could see the green desk lamp and the imposing profile of the late-working District Party secretary. Determinedly and with impatience he knocked on the door of the leading comrade's office.

1956

(Translated by Gary Bjorge)

ZHAO SHULI
(1906–1970)

Founder of the Potato School of fiction, Zhao Shuli was best known for his realist stories about village life, rendered in clear, plain language, charged with light folk humor. Born into a hardscrabble peasant family in Shanxi, he was trained as a teacher but also had an interest in local folk theater. A political radical early in life, he joined the Communist Party in 1937. His works, including the short story "The Marriage of Xiao Erhei" (1943), his novella Rhymes of Li Youcai *(1943), and his novel* Sanli Wan *(1955), were all regarded as shining examples of literary outpouring in the wake of Mao's speech at the Yan'an Forum on Literature and Art in 1942. He became a target of political persecution during the Cultural Revolution, and after several years of imprisonment, public humiliation, and brutal abuse, Zhao died in 1970.*

The Unglovable Hands

The training corps of the Big Millstone Mountain Brigade, the White Cloud Ridge Commune, had been established when the brigade was still an advanced agricultural cooperative, and its goal was to teach skills to people who joined farm production for the first time. During that period of the advanced cooperative in 1956, a number of women and young students who had never participated in farming joined the workforce, but their work was below standard. Hence Director Ch'en Man-hung proposed that a training corps be established, that two old farmers of high productivity serve as instructors, that some low-yield land be set aside as the training fields to train the unskilled. After the proposal was approved by the Administration Committee, a few scores of low-yield *mu* on top of the Big Millstone Mountain and several parcels of orchard land in the gulch on the southern side were designated as such; Ch'en Ping-cheng, father of Director Ch'en Man-hung, and old orchard-hand Wang Hsin-ch'un were selected as instructors. Ch'en served as coordinator and Wang as vice coordinator, and the corps' members were assigned to various villagers as coaches. When commune members encountered unexpected difficulties with their work or when their coaches could not help them, they would then seek the advice of Ch'en or Wang. Even though the purpose of the corps was to train new workers, there were exceptions: (1) workers who had trouble with certain tasks might register for the classes when those tasks were taught; (2) those who could not perform certain tasks well or those recommended by the Evaluation Committee because of bad work attitudes were also included. Those in the last category, during this training period, would be denied full credit for each workday, which would be calculated on a 60 percent basis. It was a sort of token punishment for those who could have performed better but didn't.

Coordinator Ch'en Ping-cheng was already a man of seventy-six. In general, most men of his age should not participate in any major physical labor, but he was especially hale and hearty. As a young man, he could do the work of a man and a half; now in old age, he was the better of most young men in terms of strength. In the winter of 1958, when communes were established, the Big Millstone Mountain was classified as a brigade, and its leader was Ch'en Man-hung. The brigade soon had its Respect-Old-Folks Home, and the Evaluation Committee recommended that Ch'en Ping-cheng retire and live in the home. After three days in the home, the old man felt that light tasks such as stripping hemp stalks and picking cotton were not demanding enough to deplete his energy, so he asked to leave the home and to resume his job as coordinator of the training corps.

Old Man Ch'en Ping-cheng's skill as a farmer was considered first-rate, not only in the Big Millstone Mountain but also in the whole White Cloud Ridge area, which had cited him as an exceptional, exemplary worker. The stone dikes that he helped build never collapsed; the fire in the smoldering fertilizer pile that he had helped stack up never went out; and he was second to none in common tasks such as plowing, seeding, hoeing, and harvesting. When he taught in the training corps, he insisted not only on standards but also on proper style, claiming that if the style was not correct, the work would be below standard. For instance, in second-hoeing, he stressed that the tiller must bend his body to a certain degree, slant his body and feet to one side, and hold his feet steady. Also his hands must tightly hold on to the hoe, firmly strike the ground, and not allow the hoe to shake in any way. The standard was that the hoe must strike close to and around the seedling but not cover up any area yet undug. In piling dirt around the seedling, the tiller must, to the utmost extent possible, make a small mound with no more than three strikes of the hoe, and the top of the mound must be flat rather than pointed. As he lectured, he demonstrated to the trainees; sometimes he repeated the instructions more than ten times before he would allow them to do any work. Because of his many rules and regulations, they would remember one rule and forget another. Sometimes they stood too straight or moved forward incorrectly. Sometimes they hoed haphazardly, complicating simple chores. Old Man Ch'en Ping-cheng kept reminding one trainee, then another; he also frequently interrupted their work by giving another demonstration.

A man named Ho Ho-ho had spent half of his life hoeing without ever bending his back. When he hoed, the hoe itself bounced around wildly; if it happened to bounce onto the weeds, then he cut the weeds, but if it happened to hit the seedlings, then the crop was damaged. After the founding of the training corps, the brigade's Evaluation Committee wanted him to have some training in the corps. When he came,

Coordinator Ch'en Ping-cheng, as usual, taught him the proper hoeing style. The problem was that this man—nicknamed "Ha-ha-ha"—was indolent by nature. After bending down a little for hoeing, he would immediately straighten his back again. Old Man Ch'en Ping-cheng had his ingenuity. Next day he brought a spare hoe from his own home and shortened it to a length of three feet, telling Ho, "Your habit of not bending down can only be cured with this short-handled hoe." Once he had a new hoe, his problem was corrected. He had to bend his back when using this three-foot hoe; otherwise, he could not touch the ground. Later other teams heard of this new method; they all prepared a number of short-handled hoes for those not accustomed to bending their backs.

When the trainees became tired from style exercises, Coordinator Ch'en gave them a break. Eight or nine terraced paddy-fields below, Vice Coordinator Wang Hsin-ch'un taught his class the planting of seeds. During the break the two groups met; the two old men smoked tobacco and chatted; the trainees read their newspapers or had a good time together. When the two old men met, Ch'en would extend his hand for a handshake, and Wang would always try to avoid it. Though younger than Ch'en by more than ten years and friendly with Ch'en, Wang abhorred shaking Ch'en's hand, because when Ch'en shook his hand, he felt as though he were being squeezed by pliers.

One day during the break Ch'en invited Wang for a smoke. Ch'en had a flint. Wang said, "How nice it would be to have a fire!" A new trainee, a high school student, quickly proceeded to look for twigs. But all he could find were two dry, two-inch-long persimmon twigs. Wang smiled and said, "You don't have to look for firewood. Grandpa Ch'en has some." Puzzled, the trainee looked around him but could not see any. Old Man Ch'en added, "Yes, I have some." Leisurely he put down his flint; without looking he scratched the dirt around him for a while and, lo and behold, found two big handfuls of bark and twigs. Wang lit a match while Old Man Ch'en scratched around and got more wood, which he put on top of the pile. The trainee exclaimed in amazement, "This is very good," and began to do likewise. Old Man Ch'en tried to stop him: "Wait a minute; don't." But it was too late. The young man's middle finger had been pricked and he quickly withdrew his hand. Wang said, "Son, what kind of hands do you have? What type of hands does he have? His are like an iron rake; brambles or thorns—nothing could hurt them."

While rubbing his middle finger, the student looked at Ch'en's hands, which were different from those of ordinary people. The palms seemed to be square in shape, the fingers short, stubby, and bent; the backs and the palms of the hands were covered with calluses; and his round fingertips resembled half cocoons with nails attached to them. The hands looked like two small rakes made of tree branches. The student looked at the hands with contempt instead of admiration, as if he were saying, "How can you call them hands?"

The two old men sensed the young man's scornful attitude. Ch'en ignored him. Looking proud, Ch'en picked up his pipe to smoke. Old Man Wang, after lighting his pipe, said to the young man, "Young fellow, don't you slight his hands. Without them, the present training field would still remain uncultivated. This land belonged to landlord Wang Tzu-yü. According to old folks, these ten and more sections of land on top of the Big Millstone Mountain were left uncultivated since the third year of Emperor Kuang-hsü [1877] until the third year of Emperor Hsüan-t'ung [1910]. In those days neither his family nor mine had any land; he was a field hand working for Wang Tzu-yü, and I was herd boy. Later he came here to cultivate the land; after I grew up, I was elevated from herd boy to field hand and followed him to plant rice seeds in the marsh. All these fields were cultivated by him and our present brigade leader, digging them hoe by hoe and building dike after dike. Without his hands, this whole area would still be wasteland."

Even though the student was a little sorry that he had despised Ch'en's hands, he was unwilling to acknowledge his mistake openly. Instead, he said in a mocking tone, "No wonder we are such slow learners; it is all because we don't have his hands."

In a serious voice, Ch'en lectured the young man, "We want your hands to learn to work like mine, not to be like mine. If I wasn't the first one to dig these fields for planting, my hands wouldn't be like this. Now, folks of the older generation have already plowed the land with their hands; soon everything will be mechanized, and your hands won't have to become like mine."

Even though Old Man Ch'en did not wish others to have hands like his, he, nonetheless, was proud of them. His hands were not only firm and tough but also dexterous. He loved weaving and frequently wove thorn vines into all types of farming tools and sometimes made children's toys out of stalks of sorghum. When he made tools out of vines, he did not have to use an oxhorn wedge in splitting them. He divided a vine into three and used his index finger as the splitter—chi, chi, chi—the vine was split, and his hand was not even scratched. Yet he also did work of a very delicate nature. No one would guess that it was done by the same hands. The katydid cages that he made out of sorghum stalks featured a door, windows, upstairs and downstairs rooms, and on the two-inch-square windows he made many decorative patterns from different angles, with holes so tiny that even bees would have difficulty crawling through them.

After the periods of land reform, mutual assistance teams, and cooperatives, communes were established. Old Man Ch'en Ping-cheng's family income increased. In the winter of 1959, his children and grandchildren bought him a pair of knitted gloves to protect his hands. Upon receiving the gift, he said, "My hands have never enjoyed such luxuries before." As he tried them on, he found the palm not big enough, the fingers too tight and long. He barely drew them on before he stretched the palm into a square, stuffed the lower part of the fingers full, and left the upper part of the fingers empty. His son Ch'en Man-hung said, "After a while, they will fit you nicely." He put them on, opened and closed his hands a couple of times, then took them off and gave them to his daughter-in-law. "Please keep them for me."

"Dad, please wear them. Don't your hands get cold when you work in the field?"

"We are building a storage shed in the gulch and it's not convenient to move stones with them on." As soon as he said this, he left his gloves and walked away. Not long afterward, the work at the gulch was completed, but other work followed—cutting hay, cleaning sheep pens, storing turnips for winter, and thrashing corn, none of which went well with the use of gloves, and he soon forgot he had them.

One day the White Cloud Ridge held a goods exchange fair. His daughter-in-law said to him, "Now they don't really need you to teach them these odd skills, why don't you take the day off and visit the fair?" The old man agreed. He changed into his new cotton-padded jacket and tied a new sash around his waist. She then said, "This time you must wear your new gloves," and brought him his gloves. He drew them on and left.

The Big Millstone Mountain was a small village and had no consumer co-op. As the neighbors heard he was going to the White Cloud Ridge and saw him walking down the street in his new jacket and gloves, they asked him to buy things for them. One family wanted three ounces of oil; another family wanted two catties of salt. All those purchases would be more than his hands could carry, so he borrowed a basket from a neighbor. When he reached the White Cloud Ridge, he walked past half a street block and arrived at the consumer's co-op and purchased what he had been asked to buy. Then he walked to the commune and saw a carload of pitchforks being unloaded by a salesman. For two years new pitchforks had not been available in the area, and what the different brigades had was not enough to go around. He felt he could not miss the opportunity. Having no money, he remembered that his son, who was attending a meeting at the commune, might have some. So he went and told his son about the pitchforks. Man-hung said, "Yes, by all means. They are very precious. Go buy them quickly," and gave him fifty dollars. With the money he went to the mountain-goods section and looked over the pitchforks. Fastidious with tools, he could not bear to see any blemish on them. Removing his gloves and tucking them inside his sash, he picked up one pitchfork, put it on the floor to see if its three prongs were even and strong, and whether its head and handle were straight. Before he finished looking at one, more than ten people had gathered, everyone holding and examining a pitchfork. In no time, many more people came; even the brigade leader, who was conducting a meeting at the commune, temporarily halted the meeting to come over to buy some. No one was as fastidious as the old man; they merely asked the price and paid. Old man Ch'en Ping-cheng saw the situation getting out of hand. Forgetting his high standards, he chose five pitchforks at random, and the rest were grabbed by others. He paid, tied the pitchforks together, put them on his shoulder, carried his basket, and jostled his way out of the congested market section. With his hands full, he had no interest in wandering around the other half of the street block and went home by the same road he had taken.

Once he was outside the White Cloud Ridge village, the congestion was gone, and the road was much wider. Then he felt for his gloves. He could only find one. He put down his basket, the pitchforks, loosened his waist sash, but he could not find the other glove. He knew he must have lost it at the market. He thought, "All right, so be it. I don't use the gloves much anyway." He tied the sash back around his waist, carried the pitchforks on his shoulder with one hand and his basket with the other, and walked toward home. After he had taken a few steps he thought, "The kids bought them especially for me. Now that one glove is lost, and if I don't go back to look for it, I am not being nice to them." Turning back, he returned to the fair at the White Cloud Ridge. Fortunately, the salesman had found his glove and kept it on the counter. He returned it to him.

Some time later, Old Man Ch'en Ping-cheng was selected as the model worker of the year by the Evaluation Committee, and he had to attend the Convention of Model Workers at the county seat. It was another opportunity for him to wear his gloves. Besides his new cotton-padded jacket and his new sash, he wore his gloves.

The Big Millstone Mountain was about forty *li* from the county seat. Winter days are short, so Ch'en, after breakfast, left home and reached his destination at dusk. It was the registration day. Once in town, he registered for the convention, received his attendance permit, and started looking for a place to stay. He had not been in town for more than six months, and it had changed—the streets had been widened, the roads

were smooth, the dilapidated place where he had stayed while attending
the meetings before was replaced by rows of newly built brick and tile
houses. It was dark when he entered the hostel. Rows of rooms in the
rear section by the passageway were lit, indicating their occupancy;
some of the rooms on the first three rows were lit also. He went to the
reception desk, registered, and the receptionist took him to Room 5
of West Row Two. When he reached West Row Two, he saw that the
only light came from Room 6, while the rest of the rooms were dark.
He stepped on some objects, some of which were hard and others soft;
he had no idea what they were. The receptionist told him, "Be careful.
This row of rooms was just completed, no more than a week ago, and
there are still a few things here and there. Walk on this side; the other
side is a lime pit. Walk by the wall; there's some loose lumber around."
As they got to Room 5, the receptionist snapped on the light before
letting him into the room. What came into view were a clean room,
a good fire in the fireplace, a table by the window, two chairs, a stool,
two beds on each side of the room, an unpainted door and windows,
and recently whitewashed walls. The walls smelled damp as they were
heated by the fire. Looking at the beds, he asked, "Four in each room?"
The receptionist replied, "Yes."

"Will you have all the rooms occupied during the convention?"

"Almost. Some participants from far places have not yet arrived. Take
a little rest. Let me bring you some water to freshen you up." A while
later the receptionist brought in the water. The old man washed his
face, and people streamed in steadily, occupying all the rooms on West
Row Two. Besides the old man, Room 5 had three young men. The four
of them introduced themselves to one another.

The convention lasted for three and a half days. The old man either
listened to reports or prepared to make his own; like everyone else, he
was kept busy until the morning of the fourth day, when the county
Party chief made a summary report. In the afternoon those who lived
nearby went home; those who lived some distance away had to stay one
more night. Ch'en's home was forty *li* away—neither too far nor too
near. A young man could probably cover the distance and reach home

shortly after dusk. Since he was old, he did not want to walk in the dark and planned to spend an extra half day in town.

After lunch those who would stay the night all wanted to take a walk around town. The old man returned to West Row Two, Room 5, where his three roommates and another young man from Room 4 were playing poker. He said, "Don't you want to look around town?" One young man replied, "Grandpa, you just go ahead. We'll go later." The old man tied the sash around his waist, put on his gloves, and left. Since the courtyard was partially blocked by two big logs, he had to walk close by the wall of Room 3 after he passed the door of Room 4. He thought, "If only I could roll those logs aside, but to where?" Squatting by the door of Room 4, he sized up the situation, concluding that it would be best to roll the logs southward to face the lime pit. Once he made up his mind, he took off his gloves, put them on the steps, and proceeded to roll one of the logs. Cut off on both ends, this one log's middle section was unshapely, thick, short, bent, and flat. It was not easy to roll at all. It took him considerable strength to prop it up, but it turned over only once and was flat on the ground again. Seeking help, he first knocked on the door of Room 4, but no one answered. So he returned to Room 5 and said to the young people, "Comrades, would you please help me move the logs in the courtyard so people can walk more easily?"

"Surely, I tried to do that yesterday, but the logs won't budge," a young man replied, putting down his cards. The other three young men got up and stepped outside. The old man took off his new cotton-padded jacket, left it on his bed, and stepped out of the room.

The old man helped them move the logs. One young man said to him, "You just rest; let us do the work." The four young men took all the room around one short log. Unable to lay his hands on that one, he started to move the other log. After they had moved the short log, they saw him struggling with the other one. One young man stopped him. "Grandpa, please don't. We can do it." A second young man helped the first one lift it up. This log was a little longer than the first, and one end was thicker than the other. Though the person holding the thin end had no trouble lifting it, the man supporting the thick end did, murmuring continuously, "No, no." Then he let go. The young man at the other end was also about to drop the log when the old man said, "Let me do it." Immediately he bent down. Using his hands to support the log, and with his legs apart as if he were riding on a horse, he stiffened his shoulders and lifted it up. When the first young man saw the second one sticking up his thumb in admiration of the old man, he joined his friend, saying, "Grandpa, you are really marvelous. But you are an old man. Let us do it."

A receptionist carrying a kettle of hot water came by. When he saw what went on, he hurriedly said, "Thank you all. Let us do it."

"It's nothing."

"Before the convention started, the only cleanup work remaining was the courtyards of the first three rows of rooms. During the convention we had no time. We're waiting for tomorrow morning to start cleaning up when all the guests will have moved out. The few of us can finish the work in just a couple of days." Old Man Ch'en Ping-cheng said, "Why must you wait until we leave? The convention has ended. Isn't now a good time to help you clean up?"

"No, no, that would be too much trouble to impose on you all." Old Man Ch'en and the young people all said that they didn't mind, and comrades from other rooms, who had not left for town, all came out of their rooms saying that they too would like to help in the cleanup. Seeing this, the receptionist hurried to consult the manager. Even before the receptionist returned, everyone looked for cleanup tools. Since the first two rows had not been thoroughly cleaned up, the tools were piled up in the courtyards between the west-east rows. They found shovels, brooms, open baskets, and poles, and they immediately started to work. Old Man Ch'en wanted to haul the baskets for them, but everyone, upon seeing his white beard, insisted that he not do that type of heavy work. So he could only use a broom to sweep the courtyard along with the others. Model workers were truly model workers. When the people from the first three rows of rooms saw that the people on West Row Two were busy cleaning up, they immediately joined in the operation. In a short while, the receptionist and the manager came back. The manager advised everyone not to bother with the work; however, since he could not convince them, he called every staff member, including his assistant, the accountant, and the receptionists, to join in the task.

Everyone used shovels to remove leftover bricks or tiles, bark, wood shavings, and other miscellaneous items; Old Man Ch'en followed and swept after them. He started from the southwest corner of the courtyard in West Row Two and swept northward. When he reached the window of Room 6, he saw that there were mud cakes and wood shavings on the windowsill; he reached for the dirt with his broom. Because the windowsill was rather small, the broom was less than efficient; he put down his broom and brushed off the dirt with his ironlike hands. Then, looking toward the east, he saw every windowsill was similarly dirty. He started from Room 6 to Room 5, then to Room 4, and cleaned every windowsill before he returned to the west side to clean the courtyards.

Since there were many people, the work was done quickly. Within two hours, the six courtyards had been cleaned, and the garbage stood by both sides of the passageway; materials that could be used were left at the rear entrance of the storage room, to be hauled away by a truck that came by at night. After all the work had been completed, Old Man Ch'en felt satisfied, knowing that people could walk a lot more easily from then on.

The manager, his assistant, the accountant, and all the receptionists went to get water for the model workers to clean up. After that, some went into town; Old Man Ch'en once again put on his new cotton-padded jacket, tied the sash around his waist, and planned to put on his gloves—only to realize that they had been lost again. He casually asked his young friends, "When you cleaned, did you see my gloves?" One man answered, "No, we didn't see them. Where did you leave them?"

"On the windowsill of Room 4." Another man said, "Yes, I seemed to remember one glove in a pile of wood shavings, all smeared with mud, and I thought it was someone's discarded old glove."

"Yes, probably when I pulled down the wood shavings of Room 4 the shavings covered them and you didn't see them and threw them in with the garbage pile." The old man went to look for his gloves in the garbage pile by the passageway, but the garbage from the row of West Two alone filled up more than several dozen baskets. How could he find his gloves right away?

When a receptionist saw him, he asked, "Grandpa, what are you looking for?"

"My gloves."

"Are you sure they are in there?"

"Yes, I am."

"Then you go into town and have a good time. We will find them for you."

"Don't bother; they are not of much use to me," the old man said firmly.

The old man strolled around several blocks in town. Other than admiring some new buildings, he had little interest in anything else, thinking, "I don't buy or sell. Why must I linger by the stores?" So he returned to the hostel. It was not yet dusk, and his roommates had not yet returned. A receptionist opened the door for him and told him that his gloves had been found. He entered his room; the fire in the quiet fireplace was still strong; and his gloves had been washed by a receptionist and put on the back of a chair to dry.

He returned home the next day. After changing his clothes, he returned the gloves to his daughter-in-law. "You'd better keep them. My hands are unglovable."

1960

(Translated by Nathan K. Mao and Winston L. Y. Yang)

ANONYMOUS

One of the best-known Model Modern Revolutionary Peking Operas, The Red Lantern was produced in 1964, under the aegis of Jiang Qing, Chairman Mao's fourth wife. Formerly a play actress, Madame Mao tried to realize her political ambitions by controlling media and propaganda. Like the other two dozen or so Revolutionary Peking Operas produced during those tumultuous years, The Red Lantern fulfilled Mao's mandate that "art must serve the people" through a story about the Chinese Communist guerrilla war against Japan in the early 1940s in Manchuria. Adopting the sanctified doctrine of "combining revolutionary realism and revolutionary romanticism," the play was built on the traditional form of aria in Peking opera and the techniques of Western ballet. A Red classic, this play served as a lethal weapon of propaganda in Madame Mao's power struggle during the Cultural Revolution.

The Red Lantern: A Revolutionary Peking Opera in Eleven Acts (excerpt)

[The opera presents a page from the Chinese Communist guerrilla war against Japan in the early 1940s in northern China. In Acts I–IV, a Communist revolutionary railroad worker LI YÜ-HO lives with GRANDMA, who has accepted Li as her son, and a young girl, T'IEH-MEI, who calls him her father. All three of them work together to aid the guerrillas. An underground messenger jumps a train to deliver a secret codebook to Li, who is to transmit it to a guerrilla unit. A spine-less comrade, WANG, when threatened by the Japanese, betrays Li. Still unaware of the crucial turn of events, Li returns home after an unsuccessful attempt to deliver the codebook, as the curtain rises on Act V. The original libretto contains instructions for singing in various beats, which have been omitted in this excerpt.]

Act V: Relating the Story of a Revolutionary Family

Evening, at LI's *house. The audience can see both the living room and the area outside the door to the house. As the curtain rises,* GRANDMA LI *is in the room waiting for* LI YÜ-HO

GRANDMA: (*Sings*)

> The time grows late
> And Yü-ho has not yet returned.

(T'IEH-MEI *comes out of the back room. A siren sounds*)
T'IEH-MEI: (*Sings*)

> There's so much commotion in the streets,
> I worry about my father.

(LI YÜ-HO *enters holding his lunch box and a signal lantern. He knocks on the door*)
LI: (*Offstage*) T'ieh-mei!
T'IEH-MEI: Daddy is home.
GRANDMA: Hurry up, open the door.
T'IEH-MEI: (*Opens the door*) Daddy!
GRANDMA: Yü-ho!
LI: Mother!
GRANDMA: You're back. Did you make the connection? (*Takes his lunch box and the lantern*)
LI: No. (*Takes off his coat*)

GRANDMA: What happened?

LI: Mother! (*Sings*)

> At the porridge stall, as I contacted the knife-sharpener,
> Police car sirens sounded, and Japanese swarmed out to search.
> But the knife-sharpener covered me by luring away the wolves.
> Seizing the chance, I opened the lunch box and hid the secret
>   code.
> I hid it at the bottom of the porridge where it can't be found. . . .

T'IEH-MEI: Uncle Knife-Sharpener was wonderful!

GRANDMA: Yü-ho, so where is the secret code?

LI: Mother! (*Confiding in her, he continues singing*) To prevent any slip,
I've stored it in a safer place.

T'IEH-MEI: Daddy, you really are resourceful.

LI: T'ieh-mei, now you know all about it. It is more important than
our lives. We would rather have our heads cut off than reveal the
secret. You understand?

T'IEH-MEI: Of course I understand.

LI: So you do understand. Just look at this good child!

T'IEH-MEI: Oh, Daddy . . .

LI: Ah . . .

> (*It gradually gets dark.* GRANDMA LI *brings over a kerosene lamp*)

GRANDMA: Ah . . . look at you two.

LI: Mother, I have something to do. I have to go out again.

GRANDMA: All right. Be careful! Come back quickly.

LI: Okay. Don't worry.

T'IEH-MEI: Daddy, put this scarf around you. (*She puts a scarf around his
neck*) Daddy, be sure you come back early.

LI: (*Lovingly*) Don't you worry. (*He goes out the door, exits*)

> (T'IEH-MEI *closes the door.* GRANDMA LI *polishes the signal lantern
> with great care as* T'IEH-MEI *gazes at her intently*)

GRANDMA: Come, T'ieh-mei. Let me tell you the story about this red
lantern.

T'IEH-MEI: Ai. (*Very happily, she goes over to the table and sits down*)

GRANDMA: (*Seriously*) This red lantern has, for many years, lighted the paths upon which we poor people have trod. It has lighted the paths for us workers. In the past, your grandpa held it. Now your father holds it. My child, you already know what happened last night. At crucial junctures, we cannot part with it. You must remember: this red lantern is our family's treasured heirloom.

T'IEH-MEI: Oh, the red lantern is our family's treasured heirloom?

(GRANDMA LI *looks at* T'IEH-MEI *with confidence and trust, then she walks into the back room.* T'IEH-MEI *picks up the lantern, examines it carefully, and ponders it*)

T'IEH-MEI: (*Sings*)

I heard Grandma tell
About the red lantern,
Her words were few, but their meaning, profound.
Why don't my father and uncles
Fear any danger?
Because they want to save China, save the poor, and defeat the
Japanese devils.
I think: what they do everyone should try to do;
What they are we all should try to be.
Oh, T'ieh-mei!
You are seventeen, and no longer young.
Why don't you help Father to lighten his worries?
For instance, if Father carries a thousand-catty load,
You, T'ieh-mei, should bear eight hundred.

(GRANDMA LI *comes out of the back room*)

GRANDMA: T'ieh-mei, T'ieh-mei!

T'IEH-MEI: Grandma!

GRANDMA: My child, what are you thinking about?

T'IEH-MEI: Nothing.

(*A child's cry is heard from the neighbor's house*)

GRANDMA: (*Sighs*) Ai! They have nothing to eat again. We still have some cornmeal left. Hurry and take it over to them.

T'IEH-MEI: Yes, Grandma. (*She puts the cornmeal into a container*)

(HUI-LIEN *enters and knocks at the door*)

HUI-LIEN: Grandma Li!

T'IEH-MEI: Cousin Hui-lien is here.

GRANDMA: Hurry up, open the door for her.

T'IEH-MEI: Yes, Grandma. (*She opens the door.* HUI-LIEN *enters*)

GRANDMA: (*With concern*) Oh, Hui-lien, how is the baby?

HUI-LIEN: (*Sighs*) How can I afford to take the child to a doctor? These days, fewer and fewer people send me clothes for mending or washing. In our house we've been living from meal to meal, but now there's nothing left, nothing at all.

T'IEH-MEI: Cousin Hui-lien, here, take this. (*She hands her the cornmeal*)

HUI-LIEN: (*Extremely touched*) . . .

GRANDMA: Go ahead, take it. I was just sending T'ieh-mei to bring it over to you.

HUI-LIEN: (*Accepting the cornmeal*) You are so kind to us!

GRANDMA: Don't say that. The wall is the only thing separating us— otherwise we would be one family.

T'IEH-MEI: Grandma, we are one family even if we don't tear the wall down.

GRANDMA: T'ieh-mei is right.

(*The child cries again*)

AUNTIE T'IEN: (*Calling from offstage*) Hui-lien, Hui-lien!

(AUNTIE T'IEN *enters*)

T'IEH-MEI: Hi, Auntie.

GRANDMA: Auntie, come here and sit down.

AUNTIE T'IEN: I can't. The child is crying again. Hui-lien, go home and look after the child.

(*Seeing the cornmeal in* HUI-LIEN'*s hand, she is very touched*)

GRANDMA: Make some food for the child first.

AUNTIE T'IEN: But you yourselves don't have enough to eat.

GRANDMA: Ai! (*Warmly*) Between our two families, whatever is ours is also yours. So don't even think of it.

AUNTIE T'IEN: We have to get back.

GRANDMA: Don't worry. Take care!

(AUNTIE T'IEN *and* HUI-LIEN *exit*)

T'IEH-MEI: (*Closing the door*) Grandma, Cousin Hui-lien and her family have suffered too much!

GRANDMA: Yes. In the past, her father was a porter working on the railroad. He was crushed to death by a train. The Japanese devils not only didn't give them any compensation, they even seized her husband to work for them without pay. T'ieh-mei, our two families are working people sharing the same hatred and bitterness. We must take good care of them.

(FAKE LIAISON MAN, *an enemy agent in disguise, enters, knocks at the door*)

T'IEH-MEI: Who is it?

FAKE LIAISON MAN: Does Li Yü-ho live here?

T'IEH-MEI: Someone looking for Daddy.

GRANDMA: Open the door.

T'IEH-MEI: All right! (*She opens the door*)

(FAKE LIAISON MAN *enters the room and hurriedly closes the door behind him*)

GRANDMA: You are . . .

FAKE LIAISON MAN: I sell wooden combs.

GRANDMA: Do you have one made of peachwood?

FAKE LIAISON MAN: Yes, I do, but I want cash.

T'IEH-MEI: All right. Wait.

(FAKE LIAISON MAN *puts his pack down and turns around.* T'IEH-MEI *is about to get the signal lantern.* GRANDMA LI *stops her. Instead, she picks up the kerosene lamp to test the man.* T'IEH-MEI *suddenly understands*)

FAKE LIAISON MAN: (*Turns back, sees the lamp*) So I finally found you, thank Heavens. It wasn't easy, believe me!

(T'IEH-MEI's *surprise turns to anger; she is unable to control herself*)

GRANDMA: (*Realizes the plot, very calmly*) All right, my man. Come on, show us your wooden combs so we can choose one.

FAKE LIAISON MAN: What are you talking about, old lady? I came here to get the secret code.

GRANDMA: Child, what is he talking about?

FAKE LIAISON MAN: Don't interrupt, Grandma. The secret code is a very important document of the Communist Party. It has a great deal to do with the future of the revolution. Come on, give it to me, hurry up.

T'IEH-MEI: (*Angrily chasing him out*) Don't talk nonsense here. Get out.

FAKE LIAISON MAN: Don't, don't . . .

T'IEH-MEI: Get out!

(T'IEH-MEI *pushes the man out of the door, throws his pack at him, and slams the door with a bang*)

T'IEH-MEI: Oh, Grandma!

(GRANDMA *quickly stops* T'IEH-MEI *from talking.* FAKE LIAISON MAN *calls two plainclothes agents over to watch* LI's *house, and then exits*)

T'IEH-MEI: Grandma, I almost fell into his trap.

GRANDMA: My child, there must be someone who has turned traitor and betrayed us.

T'IEH-MEI: In that case, what shall we do?

GRANDMA: (*Whispers*) Hurry, tear off the signal.

T'IEH-MEI: What signal?

GRANDMA: That red butterfly on the window.

T'IEH-MEI: (*Understands*) Oh. (*About to tear it off*)

GRANDMA: T'ieh-mei, open the door and use it to block the light. You tear the signal off, I'll sweep the ground to cover you. Hurry, hurry!

(T'IEH-MEI *opens the door, and* LI YÜ-HO *enters in haste. He closes the door.* T'IEH-MEI *is frightened and* GRANDMA LI *drops her broom to the ground*)

LI: (*Sensing something wrong*) Mother, has something happened?

GRANDMA: There are "dogs" outside.

> (LI YÜ-HO *shows no fear. He quickly arrives at a conclusion about the enemy situation*)

GRANDMA: Oh, my son, my son!

LI: Mother, it is possible that I'll be arrested. (*Instructs his mother very cautiously*) The secret code is hidden under the stone tablet by the old locust tree on the western bank of the river. You must try your best to deliver it to the knife-sharpener. The password remains the same.

GRANDMA: The password remains the same.

LI: Right! You must be very careful.

GRANDMA: Don't you worry, son.

T'IEH-MEI: Daddy . . .

> (*Auxiliary warrant officer* HOU *of the Japanese military police enters, knocks on the door*)

HOU: Is Li *Shih-fu** home?

LI: Mother, they're here.

T'IEH-MEI: Daddy, you . . .

LI: T'ieh-mei, open the door.

T'IEH-MEI: Yes, Daddy.

HOU: Open the door!

> (T'IEH-MEI *opens the door, seizing that moment of activity to tear off the red butterfly*)

HOU: (*Entering*) Oh, you must be Li *Shih-fu*.

LI: Yes, I am.

HOU: Captain Hatoyama invites you to a party. (*He hands the "invitation" over*)

LI: Oh? Captain Hatoyama invites me to a banquet?

HOU: Correct.

LI: My goodness! What an honor! (*Scornfully he throws the invitation on the table*)

HOU: To make friends. Li *Shih-fu*, shall we?

---

* "Master" in Chinese.

LI: After you, please. (*To his mother, firmly and solemnly*) Mother, take care of yourself! I am going now.

GRANDMA: Just a minute. T'ieh-mei, bring some wine here.

T'IEH-MEI: Yes, Grandma. (*She goes to the back room to get wine*)

HOU: Hey! Old lady, there's lots of wine at the banquet, more than enough for him to drink.

GRANDMA: Ah . . . poor people are used to drinking their own wine, because drop by drop it soaks deep into their hearts. (*She takes the wine* T'IEH-MEI *has brought in and bids* LI YÜ-HO *farewell, dignified yet emotional*) Now, my son, this bowl of wine . . . you, you, you drink it down.

LI: (*Solemnly receives the wine*) Mother, with this wine at the bottom of my heart, I can cope with whatever wine they may offer me. (*Drinks it up in a gulp*) Mother, thank you, thank you, thank you! (*Heroically sings*)

Upon parting I drink a bowl of Mother's wine,
Courage fills this whole body of mine.
"To make friends with me"? Hatoyama invites me to dine;
I can handle him now, whatever his line.
Time is awry, storms descend without warning—Mother,
You must always be mindful of the changing weather.

T'IEH-MEI: Daddy! (*She throws herself onto the bosom of* LI YÜ-HO, *sobbing*)

LI: (*Continues singing his covert message, with intense affection and feeling*)

Little T'ieh-mei, watch the weather when going out to sell.
"Accounts," coming in and going out, you should remember well.
When tired, watch the door, beware of stray dogs roaming free;
When depressed, wait for the magpies to sing on the tree.
You should take over the family affairs
And share with Grandma her concerns and her cares.

T'IEH-MEI: Daddy! (*Sobs on her father's bosom*)

HOU: Li *Shih-fu*, shall we go?

LI: (*To* T'IEH-MEI) My child, don't cry. From now on, listen to your
     grandma.

T'IEH-MEI: Yes, Daddy.

GRANDMA: T'ieh-mei, open the door. Let your father go to the
     "banquet"!

LI: Mother, I am leaving now.

> (LI *holds his mother's hands tightly, and each encourages the other to*
> *keep struggling.* T'IEH-MEI *opens the door. A cold wind blows in. In*
> *heroic and majestic stride with head held high,* LI *goes out against*
> *the wind.* HOU *follows*)

> (T'IEH-MEI *picks up the scarf, chases her father, shouting, "Daddy!"*
> ENEMY AGENT A, B, *and* C *rush in, stopping* T'IEH-MEI)

AGENT A: Stop. Get back!

> (*He forces* T'IEH-MEI *back. The agents enter the house*)

T'IEH-MEI: Oh, Grandma . . .

AGENT A: Search! Don't move!

> (*The agents search and mess up the household. One of them finds a copy*
> *of an almanac, opens it up, and then throws it away*)

AGENT A: Let's go.

> (*Exit the* AGENTS)

T'IEH-MEI: (*Closes the door, pulls down the window curtain, looks about*)
     Grandma! (*She throws herself into her grandma's arms and sobs. A*
     little while later) Grandma, my daddy . . . will he return?

GRANDMA: Your father . . .

T'IEH-MEI: Oh, Daddy! . . .

GRANDMA: T'ieh-mei, your tears cannot save your father. Don't cry.
     Our family . . . It is time you should know about your family.

T'IEH-MEI: Know what?

GRANDMA: Sit down, child. Let Grandma tell you.

> (GRANDMA *gazes at the scarf, and all the past revolutionary events*
> *come back to her. Old hatred and new hatred bubble up in her mind.*
> T'IEH-MEI *moves a tiny stool and sits by her grandmother*)

GRANDMA: Child, your father . . . is he nice?

T'IEH-MEI: Daddy is nice.

GRANDMA: But your daddy is not your real father!

T'IEH-MEI: (*Shocked*) Ah? What did you say, Grandma?

GRANDMA: I am not your real grandmother either!

T'IEH-MEI: Ah? Grandma, Grandma, you must be crazy.

GRANDMA: No, I am not. My child, we three generations are not from one family. (*Stands up*) Your family name is Ch'en, mine is Li, and your father's is Chang. (*Sings*)

These past seventeen years have been stormy times, and I'm afraid to talk about the past.
I fear that you are too young and your will is not strong.
Several times I have tried but I just couldn't open my mouth.

T'IEH-MEI: Grandma, tell me. I won't cry.

GRANDMA: (*Sings*)

It looks as though your dad will never come home again this time.
And I, your grandmother, will be arrested and put in jail.
I see the heavy burden of the revolution soon falling on your shoulders.
I've told you the truth. Oh, T'ieh-mei!
Don't you cry, don't be sad!
You must stand firm, you must be strong!
Learn from your father, to have a red, loyal heart and a will as strong as steel.

T'IEH-MEI: Grandma, please sit down and tell me everything slowly.
(T'IEH-MEI *helps her grandmother sit down*)

GRANDMA: (*Sighs*) Hai! It is a long, long tale! In those early years, your grandfather worked as a repairman in the locomotive shop on the riverbanks in Hankow. He had two apprentices. One was your real father, Ch'en Chih-hsing.

T'IEH-MEI: My real father, Ch'en Chih-hsing?

GRANDMA: One was your present father, Chang Yü-ho.

T'IEH-MEI: Oh? Chang Yü-ho?

GRANDMA: At that time, the warlords fought each other and the whole
    country was in turmoil. Later (*She stands up*), Chairman Mao
    and the Communist Party led the people to revolt. In February
    of 1923, the railroad workers organized an all-China union at
    Chengchow. Wu P'ei-fu, that running dog of foreign devils,
    would not permit them to form a union. So the union head-
    quarters called a strike; all the workers of that line walked off
    their jobs. More than ten thousand workers along the riverbanks
    marched in demonstration. That evening, the weather was just
    as cold and the sky just as dark as today. I worried about your
    grandfather. I could neither sit still nor sleep. By the lamplight I
    mended old clothes. Suddenly I heard someone knocking at the
    door, shouting, "Mother Li, open the door, hurry!" So I quickly
    opened the door, and a man rushed in.

T'IEH-MEI: Who was he?

GRANDMA: He was your dad.

T'IEH-MEI: My dad?

GRANDMA: Your present dad. I saw he was wounded all over, holding
    this signal lantern in his left hand.

T'IEH-MEI: Signal lantern?

GRANDMA: He held a child in his right arm.

T'IEH-MEI: A child . . .

GRANDMA: A baby not quite a year old . . .

T'IEH-MEI: That child . . .

GRANDMA: It was no one else . . .

T'IEH-MEI: Who?

GRANDMA: It was *you*!

T'IEH-MEI: *Me?*

GRANDMA: Your daddy held you tightly in his arm; with tears in his
    eyes, he stood in front of me and cried, "Mother Li, Mother Li!"
    Then he just stared at me, unable to utter any words. I was so

upset I urged him to speak up, fast! He . . . he . . . he said, "My
Shih-fu and my brother Ch'en . . . they . . . they all sacrificed
their lives. This child is the only heir of my brother Ch'en . . . a
second generation of the revolution. I must raise her so that she
can continue with the revolution!" Then he repeatedly called out,
"Mother Li, Mother Li! From now on, I will be your own son,
and this child will be your own granddaughter." At that moment,
I . . . I . . . I took you over and held you tightly in my arms!

T'IEH-MEI: Oh, Grandma! (*She rushes to her grandmother's bosom*)

GRANDMA: Now, stand up, and stand straight! Listen to your grandma.
(*Sings*)

> During a labor strike your parents' blood the devils' hands did
> 　　stain;
> Since then Li Yü-ho has worked hard so the revolution may
> 　　obtain;
> He's vowed to carry on for those martyrs that the red lantern
> 　　may shine again;
> He wiped the blood off, buried the dead, and went back to the
> 　　fire line.
> Now the Japanese bandits have come to loot, kill, and burn;
> You've watched your father taken to jail, never to return.
> Note this "account" of blood and tears, note it down well,
> You must set a heroic goal, steel your will, get even with the
> 　　foe,
> For a blood debt can only be with blood redeemed.

T'IEH-MEI: (*Sings*)

> Hearing Grandma talk about revolution, oh, how sad yet heroic!
> I now realize I've grown up in the midst of these storms.
> Oh, Grandma, for seventeen years of rearing the debt I owe you
> 　　is deep as the ocean.
> From now on I'll aim high and keep my eyes clear.

I'll demand an eye for an eye; I must carry on the task left by the
   martyrs.
Now I raise the red lantern, let its light brighten all four corners.
   Daddy!
My father's will is, like the tall pine, unbending and strong.
A brave Communist he is, a pillar between the earth and the sky.
Daddy, I shall follow you forward without any hesitation.
Now the red lantern is raised high, its light, bright as day.
For my father to slaughter those beasts, it will light up the way.
Generation after generation, in the battlefield we shall remain
Until all the vicious wolves have been slain.

(T'IEH-MEI *and* GRANDMA *raise the red lantern high, striking a dra-
   matic stance. The lantern shines bright.*)
(*Stage dims*)
(*Curtain*)

                                (Translated by Richard F. S. Yang)

PART THREE

1976–Present

CHRONOLOGY

1976	End of the Cultural Revolution
1978	Deng Xiaoping assumes power
	Founding of the underground journal *Today*
1980	Reform and Opening Up
1983	Anti-Spiritual Pollution Campaign
1987	Anti-Bourgeois Liberalization Campaign
1989	Tiananmen Square Massacre
1997	Deng Xiaoping dies; Hong Kong returns to China
2000	Gao Xingjian is awarded the Nobel Prize in Literature
2012	Mo Yan is awarded the Nobel Prize in Literature

Introduction to the Post-Mao Era

The decade-long Cultural Revolution ended with Mao Zedong's death in 1976, but the damage done to Chinese literature by Maoism was hard to repair even as the country slowly returned to "normal." Major writers like Ba Jin, Mao Dun, Ding Ling, Wang Meng, and Ai Qing, who had endured years of persecution, were rehabilitated and allowed to write and publish again, but memories of the Mao years were impossible to erase. Deng Xiaoping, who had prosecuted the Anti-Rightist Campaign against intellectuals in 1957, came back to power in 1978. A pragmatist, Deng pushed for economic reforms and introduced the plan of Four Modernizations (industrial, agricultural, military, and scientific modernizations). When activists called for political modernization (democracy), they were thrown in jail.

But, as Václav Havel once said, "Life, with its unfathomable diversity and unpredictability, would not be squeezed into the crude Marxist cage." Literature, a great vehicle for channeling pent-up emotions, made a comeback in China as soon as the government loosened, however temporarily, its grip on cultural life. Leading the way was a short story titled "Scar" by Lu Xinhua, published in August 1978. An otherwise mediocre work, Lu's story about how a family was ruined by the Cultural Revolution hit a nerve among readers and gave birth to "scar literature," a label under which thousands of other works would be published in the next two years. It was in this period that a group of poets associated with the underground journal *Today*, founded by Bei Dao and others in 1978, burst onto the scene. They made a radical departure from the formulaic language of Mao's era. The poetry of Bei Dao, Gu Cheng, Shu

Ting, and Yang Lian was dense with symbolism, rebellious in emotions, and unconventional in technique. Due to its semantic opacity, a quality dreaded by a regime that favors literature with clear messages, the work of these poets was soon criticized by the literary establishment as being too *menglong* ("obscure" or "misty," leading to the nickname "Misty Poets"). Similar critique was also leveled at fiction influenced by Western modernism or having themes that were once taboos: absurdism in Gao Xingjian, existentialism in Bei Dao, black humor in Liu Suola, eroticism in Mo Yan, bestiality in Can Xue, and bold celebration of love in Wang Anyi.

The emergence of these new writers coincided with a "culture fever" gripping China. Economic reforms were under way, and intellectuals felt a strong urge to break through ossified official ideology and seek new ways of thinking. The ten-year catastrophe of the Cultural Revolution caused many Chinese to question the viability of traditional Chinese culture, which seemed to have provided a fertile ground for totalitarianism. Hungry for new ideas, China imported many works of Western literature, philosophy, and social science, from Martin Heidegger and Max Weber to Leo Tolstoy, Samuel Beckett, Sigmund Freud, and Walter Benjamin. The younger generation, in particular, were inspired by Western liberalism and felt disgruntled over the political reality in China. Their discontent was exacerbated by the increasing divide between the rich and the poor, a sentiment best captured by Cui Jian's pop song "Nothing to My Name" (1986).

The government, always weary of any sign of discontent, waged at least two campaigns—the Anti–Spiritual Pollution Campaign in 1983 and the Anti–Bourgeois Liberalization Campaign in 1987—in order to drive out "bad" influences and maintain the party's ideological control over the country. In June 1989, when student protests led to a nationwide call for democracy and political reform, the government resorted to the most drastic measure—a violent crackdown by guns and tanks, killing thousands of students and citizens in Beijing.

The Tiananmen Square massacre dealt a blow to China. Many writers went into exile abroad, part of a post-Tiananmen exodus of intellectuals, scientists, and students who had lost hope for their country. Those who stayed had to cope with a regime needing to repair its image in the world while tightening censorship and surveillance over what people say and write. Activists were jailed, books by Gao Xingjian and others were banned, and officials advocating liberal policies were sidelined.

Despite the setback and repression, Chinese writers continued to write, as they had always done in the tumultuous twentieth century. A new generation of poets came of age, including Che Qianzi, Yu Jian, Xi Chuan, and Zhang Zao. These poets, after the spiritual baptism of June 4, wrote with more abandon and less fettered imaginations. Commercialization of publishing houses also led to a boom in Chinese fiction, which began to draw worldwide readership with new talents such as Ma Yuan, Yu Hua, Su Tong, and Chi Zijian. The winning of the Nobel Prize in Literature by Gao Xingjian in 2000 and then by Mo Yan in 2012 symbolically signaled the rise of Chinese literature in the world, just as the return of Hong Kong to Chinese rule in 1997 indicated the ascension of China as a new world power.

Yet when Premier Zhu Rongji was cornered by foreign journalists in 2000 for comments on Gao Xingjian, now a French citizen, winning the Nobel Prize, the premier diplomatically congratulated France and refused to acknowledge Gao as a Chinese writer. Fifteen years later, Gao's books are still banned from bookstore shelves in mainland China. For official China to reject or repress the best of its national literature, that is a typical, ironic tale of modern China.

BEI DAO

(1949–)

Born in the year that saw the founding of the People's Republic, Bei Dao, the foremost poet in contemporary China, often characterizes himself as someone who has truly been raised "under the red flag." A concrete mixer and blacksmith during the Cultural Revolution, Bei Dao, whose real name is Zhao Zhenkai, became disillusioned with Communist ideology and turned to poetry. On a snowy day in December 1978, in a suburb of Beijing, he and his friends founded an underground literary journal, Today, dedicated to a new poetry of fresh imagery and symbolic density. Their style was soon dismissed by literary orthodoxies as being "obscure" or "misty." After June 4, 1989, Bei Dao lived abroad in exile for many years, without a passport or homeland, as a true citizen of the world, until he was offered a prestigious teaching position at the Chinese University of Hong Kong. A Guggenheim Fellow and honorary member of the American Academy of Arts and Letters, Bei Dao is also a highly accomplished prose writer, translator, and photographer.

The Answer

Debasement is the password of the base,
Nobility the epitaph of the noble.
See how the gilded sky is covered
With the drifting twisted shadows of the dead.

The Ice Age is over now,
Why is there ice everywhere?
The Cape of Good Hope has been discovered,
Why do a thousand sails contest the Dead Sea?

I came into this world
Bringing only paper, rope, a shadow,
To proclaim before the judgment
The voice that has been judged:

Let me tell you, world,
I—do—not—believe!
If a thousand challengers lie beneath your feet,
Count me as number one thousand and one.

I don't believe the sky is blue;
I don't believe in thunder's echoes;
I don't believe that dreams are false;
I don't believe that death has no revenge.

If the sea is destined to breach the dikes
Let all the brackish water pour into my heart;
If the land is destined to rise
Let humanity choose a peak for existence again.

A new conjunction and glimmering stars
Adorn the unobstructed sky now:
They are the pictographs from five thousand years.
They are the watchful eyes of future generations.

Let's Go

Let's go—
Fallen leaves blow into deep valleys
But the song has no home to return to.

Let's go—
Moonlight on the ice
Has spilled beyond the riverbed.

Let's go—
Eyes gaze at the same patch of sky
Hearts strike the twilight drum.

Let's go—
We have not lost our memories
We shall search for life's pool.

Let's go—
The road, the road
Is covered with a drift of scarlet poppies.

Notes from the City of the Sun

Life

The sun has risen too

Love

Tranquillity. The wild geese have flown
over the virgin wasteland
the old tree has toppled with a crash
acrid salty rain drifts through the air

Freedom

Torn scraps of paper
fluttering

Child

A picture enclosing the whole ocean
folds into a white crane

Girl

A shimmering rainbow
gathers brightly colored feathers

Youth

Red waves
drown a solitary oar

Art

A million scintillating suns
appear in the shattered mirror

People

The moon is torn into gleaming grains of wheat
and sown in the honest sky and earth

Labor

Hands, encircling the earth

Fate

The child strikes the railing at random
at random the railing strikes the night

Faith

A flock of sheep spills out of the green ditch
the shepherd boy plays his monotonous pipe

Peace

In the land where the king is dead
the old rifle sprouting branches and buds
has become a cripple's cane

Motherland

Cast on a shield of bronze
she leans against a blackened museum wall

Living

A net

The Red Sailboat

Ruined walls broken ramparts all around
how can the road extend beneath our feet
not morning stars but streetlights that have slid
into your pupils pour forth
I don't want to comfort you
the trembling maple leaf
is scrawled with spring lies
the sunbird from the tropics
hasn't perched on our trees
and the forest fire behind
is only sunset in a cloud of dust

If the earth is sealed in ice
let us face the warm current
and head for the sea
if the reef is our future image
let us face the sea
and head for the setting sun
no, longing for a conflagration
is longing to turn into ash
but we seek only a calm voyage
you with your long floating hair
I with my arms raised high

(Translated by Bonnie S. McDougall)

City Gate Open Up (excerpt)

Light and Shadow

1

I returned to the city of my birth at the end of 2001, after a long, unforeseen parting of thirteen years. As the plane descended, the myriad lights of the houses and buildings rushed into the portholes, whirling and spinning. I suffered a momentary shock: Beijing looked like a huge, glittering soccer stadium. It was a cold midwinter night. After I went through customs, three strangers with a raised sign that read "Mr. Zhao" were waiting for me. Though of different height and size, they weirdly resembled one another against the glow of the arc lights, as if shadows from some other world. The welcoming ceremony was brief and silent; not until we were all seated in a sleek black sedan did they begin to speak, though it was difficult to distinguish between courtesies or threats, the lights outside like the tide keeping me distracted.

When I was a child, nights in Beijing were dark, pitch-dark, a darkness a hundredfold darker than today. So, for instance, Zheng Fanglong lived next door to my family in a two-room residence with only three fluorescent lights: eight watts in the sitting room, three watts in the bedroom, and a shared three-watt bulb that hung from a small porthole between the kitchen and bathroom. In other words, whenever the whole family celebrated New Year's or decided to live large on any ordinary day, they never used more than fourteen watts—those brilliant, bulb-lined full-length mirrors weren't fashionable yet.

Perhaps this is an extreme example for Sanbulao (Three Never Old) Hutong No. 1, but for the rest of Beijing I fear the situation was even worse. My classmates often lived with their family in one room with one light, and were commonly forced to observe "blackouts"—but once the light-string was pulled . . . *What about homework? . . . Quit your lip-flapping, there's always tomorrow.*

The lightbulbs were ordinarily bare, shadeless, a dim yellow softness—

a shade only made a mysterious halo and washed out the numerous sub-tleties of darkness, projecting a single spotlight upward. Back then girls didn't wear makeup, or even dress up, though they were strikingly beau-tiful, which certainly had something to do with the quality of the light. The spread of fluorescent lights was a disaster, painfully dazzling the eyes, blotting out the sky as it enveloped the earth without impediment or pause. As the nighttime illumination on a chicken farm pushes hens to lay more eggs, fluorescent lights create the illusion of daylight, except humans cannot lay eggs and so they become more agitated, heart vexed thoughts confused. What's unfortunate is that kind of feminine beauty can't exist anymore—to apply makeup on those ashen, worn-out faces is useless. And yet the ones who suffer the most under fluorescent lights are children. With nowhere to hide in that space erased of imagination, they prematurely step into the savageness of a public square.

Our physics teacher once said that when one enters the dark, visual acuity expands twenty-thousand-fold for a brief moment. So in this way the darkness allows one to see things as clear as a flame. Light originally signified humankind's first evolutionary milestone, but surpassing this milestone only produced an open-eyed blindness. To think that the male beast once possessed the keen vision of a wolf, swiftly adapting focus: *woosh . . . see the flame . . . woosh . . . see the flock of sheep . . . woosh . . . see the matchless beauty of the she-wolf.*

In those days there were plenty of "four eyes"*—besides lighting conditions, this must have had something to do with study habits. Stu-dents would argue vigorously over why, in the unlit darkness of the countryside, were there so few "four eyes." Although the school pro-vided night-study rooms (i.e., space with sufficient lighting), it couldn't prevent the all-hour overachievers and hardcore intellectuals, like my good friend Cao Yifan, from some light reading—nestling into his quilt with *Dream of the Red Mansion* and flashlight in hand, he long ago joined the ranks of "four eyes."

Back then streetlamps in Beijing were scarce; many hutong alleys

---

*   A Chinese nickname for those who wear glasses.

and lanes didn't have a single one, and even if there were some lamps each one was separated by thirty to fifty meters of darkness and only illuminated the small area immediately below it. Adults often exploited the story of the forehead-tapping beggar to frighten us. The forehead-tapping beggar used a certain enchanting drug to abduct children. The tale itself became an enchanting drug, bewildering countless children, the teller always conveying the fuzziest of details, and so, for one, what exactly did the head-tapping trick entail to instantly stupefy a child into mechanically following the villain away? Didn't Taiwan unleash this kind of advanced weaponry a long time ago? While we couldn't be sure if such a crime actually occurred, oil and vinegar spiced up the oral legend which stretched through hutong history into my childhood.

For the night traveler, streetlamps are more for steeling nerves than for illumination. The night traveler rides her bike, whistles a faint melody, *ding-ding* rings her bell. If every streetlamp is out, or some kid has shattered them with a slingshot, she panics, cursing eight generations of ancestors.

As streetlamps were scarce, one needed to provide another light source to bike at night. Toward the end of the fifties there were still bicyclists who used paper lanterns, as depicted in Hou Baolin's masterful piece of comic *xiangsheng* cross-talk "Night Traveler." Most used a kind of square flashlight that was strapped onto the handlebars. The next grade up was a dynamo-powered light that generated electricity at the spinning hub. If the bicycle's speed was uneven, the light flickered on and off, a visible part of Beijing's nightscape.

At the end of the 1950s, modern streetlights were installed along Chang'an Avenue, the thoroughfare of "eternal peace." Walking along the long avenue as dusk settled and the lights flickered on filled oneself with pride, mind clear eyes ablaze, as if devouring communism with a glance. In stark contrast, the lights in hutong neighborhoods were extremely dim. Once you strayed from the broad open road, you'd be lost again in Beijing's endless hutong maze.

When I was a child I'd play the shadows game with my little brother and sister—intercepting the light with hands overlapped and fingers intertwined to cast animals of all kinds onto the walls, weak or ferocious, from the chase to the fight. No one chose to be a rabbit, the weak meat for the strong, behind the succession of shadows lurked a will to power, the shadowteers believing they were masters of the ten thousand manifestations.

For children, darkness is for hide-and-seek. Retreat from the realm of light into countless hiding places, deep into the nooks and corners. When we moved into Three Never Old Hutong Alley No. 1, there was still a rock garden in the courtyard—strange, otherworldly forms of Taihu stone terrified people at night; whatever shapes one said they appeared as, they thus appeared. The courtyard was the perfect place to play hide-and-seek. Both sides trembled with fear—who could be sure one wouldn't encounter the ghost of the famous former resident, the voyager Zheng He, or one of his handmaidens? Hearing the high-pitched, trilling calls pierced our quivering hearts: "Saw you a long time ago, *yalayala*! Don't play dumb, come out come out—" And then a shrill scream right behind our backs, bodies tingling with goose bumps.

Darkness was also for telling stories, particularly ghost stories. Adults told them to children, children retold them to each other. In a country that doesn't believe in God, to use ghosts to frighten children and to frighten oneself truly reinforces Confucian orthodoxy. Chairman Mao made appeals for don't-be-afraid-of-ghosts stories to be told in school, at once confounding the people. First off, the bold are few in this world; furthermore, to not be afraid of ghosts requires a troubling explanation: one must first prove the existence of ghosts to prove one shouldn't be afraid of them.

During the "Revolution" we'd make revolution by day and tell ghost stories by night, as if ghosts and revolution didn't contradict one other at all. In my first year of high school at Beijing No. 4, I lived in the dormitory. Often, once the lights were switched off for the night, one student would inevitably start to vocalize some spooky music. At the decisive moment, another would smoothly push over a bed rail or toss a metal washbasin to the ground. After this special effects assault, the self-professed bold ones could never withstand any test of fear.

As fluorescent lights became common after 1970, Beijing suddenly turned bright and ghosts no longer manifested themselves. Fortunately, the power consistently went out. Once it did, houses here and there would glow with candles, as if remembering and mourning a lost childhood.

2

Waking up, ceiling bright with the reflected light of a heavy snowfall. Warm air from the heater stirs the curtains as the window frame blurs with the light pouring in, making it seem as if a train is slowly, ever so gently, moving forward, taking me to a faraway place. I linger in bed until my parents rush me out.

A heavy snow turns the city into a mirage, as if one stares into a mirror of self-reflection. Soon the mirror will smash and shatter, in a flash, mud splashes everywhere. On the road to school wrapped in a padded cotton coat, I grab a handful of wet snow, roll it into a ball, and throw it at the old locust tree by the hutong gate. Alas, it misses its target. I burst into the classroom as the school bell rings. Once again, it is as if the windows of the room were those of a train leaving the platform, gradually accelerating. In the gloominess, the teacher's silhouette turns, chalk dust flies up, the numerals on the blackboard seem to fade. The teacher raises her pointer at me and shouts, "*Hai!* Yes, YOU, are you deaf?"

As soon as the end-of-school bell rang, spring arrived. The eaves once white with snow were soaked black with water, the sky curved down, endless branch-tips were tinted green, bees buzzed in the sunlight, a steady hum, the shadows of girls dashed around like kites whose strings no one could catch, fluff from willow trees fluttered down, irritating people. I started to write, first plagiarizing Liu Baiyu's *Red Agate Essays*, then Wei Wei's *Who Are the Most Beloved People?* Liu Baiyu wrote of watching the sunrise from a plane above Moscow. This passage I evidently couldn't plagiarize. I was puzzled: Why Moscow? I strolled to Houhai Lake to watch the sunset. What precisely is this red agate over there? The setting sun looked like a two-*fen* piece of fruit candy. Swallows flew back and forth across the lake; the Western Hills folded up and down in layers. Upon the glittering waves a foul stench rose up from the foam.

On a windless day, a cloud paused, motionless, casting its shadow upon a playground. Some muscular upperclassmen swung themselves mechanically on some parallel bars, their shadows like a metronome. Beneath a horizontal bar, I positioned my feet, took a breath, and prepared to stretch upward. Grip fixed, the plan was to do six consecutive reps to pass. After two, my spirit and strength were already depleted, legs kicked out, forehead just reaching the iron bar. It seemed as if I was exhausting all my energy to climb into the sky and peek at the freely drifting clouds.

The summer sun cut the streets into two halves. In the shade it was as cool as water as I passed like a fish through the crowd. I abruptly changed tactics and walked to the side of scorching sun, alone but proud, stepping on my own shadow, face dripping with sweat, my whole body soon drenched. When I reached my destination, I treated myself to a popsicle.

I like wandering the streets aimlessly, without a thought or care. At the heart of the grown-up world, there is a kind of subconscious sense of security. Just don't look up, and everything one sees is below chest-level—no need to suffer if you're ugly, no need to be distracted by the pleasures angers sorrows joys of the world. When enveloped by a thronging crowd, sky a dark screen, tightly squeezed without a trace of wind, one must struggle and strive to break free from the siege. One benefit of being young is having a unique point of view: a deformed face reflected in a nickel-plated doorknob, the stream of human figures mirrored in glass display windows, countless feet trample cigarette butts, a candy wrapper rises and falls along a sidewalk curb, sunlight on the spokes of bicycle wheels, the taillights of a bus blinking on and off. . . .

I like rainy days, the way the boundary between light and shadow fades, a harmony of milk and water, like the color palette of a dilettante painter. Birds and clouds descend to lightning-rod heights, empty crows' nests in the branches of tall trees, bright-colored umbrellas meet by chance like drifting duckweed, raindrops make tracks on glass, handwriting on bulletin boards smudges their judgments, the reflected light in puddles scatters beneath my feet.

Yifan and I would often walk over to Dongan Market. In the 1960s, Dongan Market was renovated into a shopping mall, its name changed from "East Peace" to Dongfeng "East Wind" Market, its former ambience wholly destroyed. Before, all the small vendors displayed their wares in charming disorder, and anything you wanted you could find. In my memory, that place is a maze of lights: a cross-luster of electric lamps, gas lamps, kerosene lamps, and candles all melding into a bewitching haze. Beneath such illumination, the faces of the shop vendors and customers appeared utterly mysterious. If one could but fix that moment onto a scroll it could represent the perfect scene of daily life at the time. Once in a while, a thread of sunlight leaked inside, barely shifting—that most ancient hour hand.

3

Every child naturally harbors many illusions. The play of light and shadow, the space of imagination, even the body's biology all shape these illusions. As children grow up, most of them are forgotten—time society customs systems of knowledge together forge this forgetting as one enters adulthood.

The three years between the ages of ten to thirteen were difficult for me—that breaking point of the advancing body and mind when puberty begins. Deprivation was daily existence. In a photograph from that time I look like a starving African boy with eyes glazed in a fixed stare, the trace of a sly, strange smile at the corners of my mouth.

I must have been in the throes of a consummate illusion. Before my eyes I saw grotesquely shaped trees, brilliant flowers about to drop petals, smoke suspended midair, water flow backward, crooked houses, stairs roll out, clouds turn into monsters, inscrutable shadows, stars so big and bright. . . . When I finally saw Van Gogh's starry sky I felt no surprise. For me, such visions are the normal result of a deprived existence.

I'd walk the streets with dazed eyes glazed, talking to myself, straight ahead no turns. In class, especially, as I could barely hear a word of what the teacher was saying, I'd immerse myself in my illusionary world. The teacher would ask a question, my reply would be nonsense. During parent-teacher conference, the teacher transferred all her worries to my mother and father. As my mother was a doctor, she didn't make a to-do over nothing. But I was put under close surveillance.

Waking up in the middle of the night, I see my shoes shuffling along, making a circle before returning to their original place. An enormous ship suddenly rushes in through the window, a stranger's face appears in the glass, a forest lit from behind erupts in flames. . . .

One evening I returned home alone and found a white cloud motionless above the gate of Three Never Old Hutong No. 1. Not huge, a bit curved in the canopy-shape of a large umbrella, the cloud was incredibly low, even a little lower than our four-story home. Some years later I learned about UFOs and was instantly enlightened. Beneath that cloud it was as if I was put under an enchanting spell—mind a confusion of tangled threads, body completely rigid. Time seemed to have stopped. I finally took a step forward, and quick as a wing-flap ran into the house.

(Translated by Jeffrey Yang)

GU CHENG
(1956–1993)

The son of a noted writer and party member, Gu Cheng began writing poetry in his teens. Often associated with Bei Dao and other Misty Poets, Gu was known for his work's radiant innocence with a touch of melancholia. He was always seen wearing a stovepipe hat, cut from a leg of blue jeans, supposedly an amulet to dispel evil spirits and safeguard the dreams in his head. He searched for a simple, utopian life in poetry and reality, until his tragic death, some say a murder-suicide, on a small island in New Zealand in 1993. His two-line poem, "A Generation," with its imagistic brevity and ironic twist, defines the dreams and disillusionment of more than one generation in post-Mao China, and has become a rallying cry of rebellion against ideological orthodoxy and political repression.

A Generation

the black night gave me black eyes
still I use them to seek the light

—April 1979

Nameless Flowers

On the way back from mowing, in drizzling rain, I saw wet little flowers.

Wildflowers,
stellar spots,
like lost buttons
litter the roadside.

They lack the chrysanthemum's
golden locks,
don't have the peony's
tender looks;

they have only small flowers,
and frail leaves,
wafting faint fragrance
into the gorgeous spring.

My poems,
like nameless flowers,
follow the seasons' winds and rains,
quietly opening
    in the lonely world of men.

—June 1971

Farewell, Cemetery

In Chongqing's Shapingba Park, facing distant Geleshan Martyrs Cemetery, among weeds and scattered trees, is a Red Guard cemetery. Following no footprints, my poem and I happened upon it. What more can we say. . . .

1 A Faded Path Has Brought Me Among You

a faded path
has brought me
among you
like a stray ray of sunlight
standing with the tall grass
and short trees
I don't speak for history
or that voice from on high
I come
only because of my age

staggered you
sank into the earth
crying tears of joy
clutching imaginary guns
in clean fingers
that had known only textbooks
and heroes' stories
maybe out of some
common custom
on the last page of each book
you drew yourselves

no longer depicted
in the pages of my heart
it has turned against the tide
now wet with leaf-tip blue dew
when I open it

I can't use a pen
can't use a brush
I can only use my life's

softest breaths
to paint some
image worthy of conjecture

2 Geleshan's Clouds Are Cold

Geleshan's clouds
are cold
as bloodless hands
reaching for the cemetery
amid fire and molten lead
silent parents
with the same hands
caress their dear children
the slogans they left you
never forgot
maybe they were just what
called death down upon you

you poured a shared belief
into your final breaths
you are not far apart
on one side are fresh flowers
lively Sundays
Young Pioneers
on the other side, beggar-ticks
ants and lizards
you were so young
your hair was jet-black
death's night
has eternalized your purity

I wish
I were a Young Pioneer

a fresh hanging fruit
and I wish I were you
a newlywed photo
forever frozen
in a happy moment
but I go on living
in gravity-bound thought
like a rowboat
slowly approaching
the dusk riverbank

3 I Have No Brother, But I Believe . . .

I have no brother
but I believe you were
my brother
in the whirs of cicadas
on top of a sandpile
you gave me
a clay tank
a paper airplane
you taught me
to join words in clever ways
you were a giant
though just in sixth grade

I have a sister
but I believe you were
my sister
in the pale green morning
you'd slightly turn
then jump so high
those rubber band chains
that shot you toward the sky

were stretched too tight
I had shortened them some
to bind up my socks

and he?
who was he
who tore off the reed sparrow's
gold-button wings
sprinkling the ground with blood
who wrapped the antennae of the long-horned beetle
in gauze and flame
made it unsteadily
climb onto the sill
for its pulp-gulping crime
who was he?
I don't know

4 You Lived Among Tall Mountains

you lived among tall mountains
lived among walls
every day walking the requisite path
never having seen the ocean
not knowing love
knowing no other land
knowing only that somewhere
in some mute fog
an "evil" floated
thus, down the center of every desk
a battle line was drawn in chalk
you were leaving
laughing
to hide strange flashing feelings
as if to hide the glow of the moon

behind silhouettes of trees
in the statutes you found
only callousness and hatred
as spectacular as fireworks
so, one morning
you polished up your belt buckles
with rough leaves
and left

everyone knows
it was the sun
that led you off
riding on marching songs
to look for paradise
until, halfway along
you got tired
tripped into a bed whose headboard
was studded with bullet holes and stars
you seemed to have played in a game
that could start all over

5 Don't Question the Sun

don't question the sun
it can't be responsible for yesterday
yesterday belonged to
another star
that has burnt away
in terrible yearning
these days in the temples
there are only potted plants
and airs of silence
as solemn
as white icebergs
sailing warm currents

when did the bazaar
and the rebuilt merry-go-round
start to turn again
carrying the dancing and
silent youths
toothless children
the elderly
maybe there must always be
lives doomed to be
shed by the world
like the feathers dropped daily
in the camps of white-breasted geese

tangerine, pale green
sweet and bitter
lights come on
in the humid twilight
time has a new lease on life
I'm going home
to rewrite my life
and I haven't forgotten
to carefully circle the tombs
the empty eggshell moon
will wait here
for the fledglings to return

6 Yes, I Too Am Going

yes, I too am going
to another world
stepping over your hands
despite the fallen leaves
and a thin film of snow
I keep on walking
huge rocks beside me, dark woods

and an exquisite
gingerbread town
I go to love
to seek out kindred spirits
because of my age

I believe
you are lucky
that the earth doesn't flow
those proud smiles
cannot float up through the red
clay and disperse
November's drizzle
as it seeps down to you
will filter out
life's doubts
eternal dreams
are purer than life

I have left the cemetery
leaving only the night and
the blind canes still groping
your headstone inscriptions
groping
your entire lives
farther, and farther, cemetery
may you rest in peace
may that faded path
by some pale green spring
be quietly erased

—*January 1980*

I'm a Willful Child

—I want to draw windows all over the land, let eyes used to darkness get used to the light.

maybe
I'm a child who's been spoiled by his mother
I am willful

I wish
every moment
were colorful as crayons
I wish
I could draw on dear paper
awkward freedom
draw an eye
that would never cry
a sky
feathers and leaves that belong to the sky
pale green evening and apples

I want to draw morning
draw dew
all the smiles in sight
I want to draw all the youngest
unsuffering loves
draw my imaginary
lover
she has never seen storm clouds
her eyes are the color of the clear sky
she's always watching me
always, watching
will never turn away

I want to draw distant landscapes
draw a clear horizon and waves
draw scores of happy streams
draw hills
sprouting pale down
I'll bunch them together
let them love each other
let them acquiesce
let every subtle tremor of spring
be the birth of a tiny flower

and I want to draw the future
I've never seen her, and cannot
but know she is beautiful
I'll draw her fall windbreaker
draw flaming candles and maple leaves
draw the many hearts snuffed out
for love of her
draw marriage
draw one after another early-rising holidays—
stick candy wrappers at the top
and pictures from storybooks

I'm a willful child
I want to erase all unhappiness
I want to draw windows
all over the land
let eyes used to darkness
get used to the light
I want to draw the wind
draw mountain ranges each higher than the last
draw the Eastern peoples' yearning
draw the ocean—
an endlessly happy sound

finally, in the paper's corner
I want to draw myself
draw a koala
deep in a Victoria forest
sitting on a calm branch
slow
with no home
no faraway heart
just so many
berrylike dreams
and great big eyes

I am wishing
wanting
but don't know why
I have no crayons
haven't had one colorful moment
I have only I
my fingers and the pain of creating
just these tattered sheets
of dear paper
let them go look for butterflies
let them from this day on
be gone

I am a child
spoiled by an imaginary mother
I am willful

—*March 1981*

(Translated by Aaron Crippen)

MO YAN

(1955–)

Born Guan Moye in rural Shandong, Mo Yan worked in the wheat and sorghum fields for ten years after primary school, an experience upon which the future Nobel laureate in literature would continuously draw for inspiration in writing. Like the fertile soil of Oxford, Mississippi, for William Faulkner, the pristine land of Gaomi County would provide a backdrop, a Chinese Yoknapatawpha, for Mo Yan's stories, in which hardscrabble peasants and other lowly characters, while barely making a living, battle against enemies and with each other in the brutal game of life and death. After years of farming, Mo Yan joined the army in 1976 and attended the Military Art Academy in 1984. His debut story "A Crystal Carrot" (1985) brought him national attention, followed by Red Sorghum (1986), a novel about three generations of love and horror, a hallucinatory, myth-laden tale told through a discrete series of flashbacks. While his pen name "Mo Yan" literally means "don't speak" in Chinese, Mo has been a prolific writer firing verbal cannons at sordid Chinese reality, rendered in a Rabelaisian carnivalesque language. In 2012 he was awarded the Nobel Prize in Literature.

Red Sorghum (excerpts)

On her sixteenth birthday, my grandma was betrothed by her father to Shan Bianlang, the son of Shan Tingxiu, one of Northeast Gaomi Township's richest men. As distillery owners, the Shans used cheap sorghum to produce a strong, high-quality white wine that was famous throughout the area. Northeast Gaomi Township is largely swampy land that is flooded by autumn rains; but since the tall sorghum stalks resist waterlogging, it was planted everywhere and invariably produced a bumper crop. By using cheap grain to make wine, the Shan family made a very good living, and marrying my grandma off to them was a real feather in Great-Granddad's cap. Many local families had dreamed of marrying into the Shan family, despite rumors that Shan Bianlang had leprosy. His father was a wizened little man who sported a scrawny queue on the back of his head, and even though his cupboards overflowed with gold and silver, he wore tattered, dirty clothes, often using a length of rope as a belt.

Grandma's marriage into the Shan family was the will of heaven, implemented on a day when she and some of her playmates, with their tiny bound feet and long pigtails, were playing beside a set of swings. It was Qingming, the day set aside to attend ancestral graves; peach trees were in full red bloom, willows were green, a fine rain was falling, and the girls' faces looked like peach blossoms. It was a day of freedom for them. That year Grandma was five feet four inches tall and weighed about 130 pounds. She was wearing a cotton print jacket over green satin trousers, with scarlet bands of silk tied around her ankles. Since it was drizzling, she had put on a pair of embroidered slippers soaked a dozen times in *tong* oil, which made a squishing sound when she walked. Her long shiny braids shone, and a heavy silver necklace hung around her neck—Great-Granddad was a silversmith. Great-Grandma, the daughter of a landlord who had fallen on hard times, knew the importance of bound feet to a girl, and had begun binding her daughter's feet when she was six years old, tightening the bindings every day.

A yard in length, the cloth bindings were wound around all but the big toes until the bones cracked and the toes turned under. The pain was excruciating. My mother also had bound feet, and just seeing them saddened me so much that I felt compelled to shout: "Down with feudalism! Long live liberated feet!" The results of Grandma's suffering were two three-inch golden lotuses, and by the age of sixteen she had grown into a well-developed beauty. When she walked, swinging her arms freely, her body swayed like a willow in the wind.

Shan Tingxiu, the groom's father, was walking around Great-Granddad's village, dung basket in hand, when he spotted Grandma among the other local flowers. Three months later, a bridal sedan chair would come to carry her away. After Shan Tingxiu had spotted Grandma, a stream of people came to congratulate Great-Granddad and Great-Grandma. Grandma pondered what it would be like to mount to the jingle of gold and dismount to the tinkle of silver, but what she truly longed for was a good husband, handsome and well educated, a man who would treat her gently. As a young maiden, she had embroidered a wedding trousseau and several exquisite pictures for the man who would someday become my granddad. Eager to marry, she heard innuendos from her girlfriends that the Shan boy was afflicted with leprosy, and her dreams began to evaporate. Yet, when she shared her anxieties with her parents, Great-Granddad hemmed and hawed, while Great-Grandma scolded the girlfriends, accusing them of sour grapes.

Later on, Great-Granddad told her that the well-educated Shan boy had the fair complexion of a young scholar from staying home all the time. Grandma was confused, not knowing if this was true or not. After all, she thought, her own parents wouldn't lie to her. Maybe her girlfriends had made it all up. Once again she looked forward to her wedding day.

Grandma longed to lose her anxieties and loneliness in the arms of a strong and noble young man. Finally, to her relief, her wedding day arrived, and as she was placed inside the sedan chair, carried by four bearers, the horns and woodwinds fore and aft struck up a melancholy tune that brought tears to her eyes. Off they went, floating along as though riding the clouds or sailing through a mist.

Grandma was light-headed and dizzy inside the stuffy sedan chair, her view blocked by a red curtain that gave off a pungent mildewy odor. She reached out to lift it a crack—Great-Granddad had told her not to remove her red veil. A heavy bracelet of twisted silver slid down to her wrist, and as she looked at the coiled-snake design her thoughts grew chaotic and disoriented. A warm wind rustled the emerald-green stalks of sorghum lining the narrow dirt path. Doves cooed in the fields. The delicate powder of petals floated above silvery new ears of waving sorghum. The curtain, embroidered on the inside with a dragon and a phoenix, had faded after years of use, and there was a large stain in the middle.

Summer was giving way to autumn, and the sunlight outside the sedan chair was brilliant. The bouncing movements of the bearers rocked the chair slowly from side to side; the leather lining of their poles groaned and creaked, the curtain fluttered gently, letting in an occasional ray of sunlight and, from time to time, a whisper of cool air. Grandma was sweating profusely and her heart was racing as she listened to the rhythmic footsteps and heavy breathing of the bearers. The inside of her skull felt cold one minute, as though filled with shiny pebbles, and hot the next, as though filled with coarse peppers.

Shortly after leaving the village, the lazy musicians stopped playing, while the bearers quickened their pace. The aroma of sorghum burrowed into her heart. Full-voiced strange and rare birds sang to her from the fields. A picture of what she imagined to be the bridegroom slowly took shape from the threads of sunlight filtering into the darkness of the sedan chair. Painful needle pricks jabbed her heart.

"Old Man in heaven, protect me!" Her silent prayer made her delicate lips tremble. A light down adorned her upper lip, and her fair skin was damp. Every soft word she uttered was swallowed up by the rough walls of the carriage and the heavy curtain before her. She ripped the tart-smelling veil away from her face and laid it on her knees. She was following local wedding customs, which dictated that a bride wear three layers of new clothes, top and bottom, no matter how hot the day. The inside of the sedan chair was badly worn and terribly dirty; like a coffin, it had already embraced countless other brides, now long dead. The walls were festooned with yellow silk so filthy it oozed grease, and of the five flies caught inside, three buzzed above her head while the other two rested on the curtain before her, rubbing their bright eyes with black sticklike legs. Succumbing to the oppressiveness in the carriage, Grandma eased one of her bamboo-shoot toes under the curtain and lifted it a crack to sneak a look outside.

She could make out the shapes of the bearers' statuesque legs poking out from under loose black satin trousers and their big, fleshy feet encased in straw sandals. They raised clouds of dust as they tramped along. Impatiently trying to conjure up an image of their firm, muscular chests, Grandma raised the toe of her shoe and leaned forward. She could see the polished purple scholar-tree poles and the bearers' broad shoulders beneath them. Barriers of sorghum stalks lining the path stood erect and solid in unbroken rows, tightly packed, together sizing one another up with the yet unopened clay-green eyes of grain ears, one indistinguishable from the next, as far as she could see, like a vast river. The path was so narrow in places it was barely passable, causing the wormy, sappy leaves to brush noisily against the sedan chair.

The men's bodies emitted the sour smell of sweat. Infatuated by the masculine odor, Grandma breathed in deeply—this ancestor of mine must have been nearly bursting with passion. As the bearers carried their load down the path, their feet left a series of V imprints known as "tramples" in the dirt, for which satisfied clients usually rewarded them, and which fortified the bearers' pride of profession. It was unseemly to "trample" with an uneven cadence or to grip the poles, and the best bearers kept their hands on their hips the whole time, rocking the sedan chair in perfect rhythm with the musicians' haunting tunes, which reminded everyone within earshot of the hidden suffering in whatever pleasures lay ahead.

When the sedan chair reached the plains, the bearers began to get a little sloppy, both to make up time and to torment their passenger. Some brides were bounced around so violently they vomited from motion sickness, soiling their clothing and slippers; the retching sounds from inside the carriage pleased the bearers as though they were giving vent to their own miseries. The sacrifices these strong young men made to carry their cargo into bridal chambers must have embittered them, which was why it seemed so natural to torment the brides.

One of the four men bearing Grandma's sedan chair that day would eventually become my granddad—it was Commander Yu Zhan'ao. At the time he was a beefy twenty-year-old, a pallbearer and sedan bearer at the peak of his trade. The young men of his generation were as sturdy as Northeast Gaomi sorghum, which is more than can be said about us weaklings who succeeded them. It was a custom back then for sedan bearers to tease the bride while trundling her along: like distillery workers, who drink the wine they make, since it is their due, these men torment all who ride in their sedan chairs—even the wife of the Lord of Heaven if she should be a passenger.

Sorghum leaves scraped the sedan chair mercilessly when, all of a sudden, the deadening monotony of the trip was broken by the plaintive sounds of weeping—remarkably like the musicians' tunes—coming from deep in the field. As Grandma listened to the music, trying to picture the instruments in the musicians' hands, she raised the curtain with her foot until she could see the sweat-soaked waist of one of the bearers. Her gaze was caught by her own red embroidered slippers, with their tapered slimness and cheerless beauty, ringed by halos of incoming sunlight until they looked like lotus blossoms, or, even more, like tiny goldfish that had settled to the bottom of a bowl. Two teardrops as transparently pink as immature grains of sorghum wetted Grandma's eyelashes and slipped down her cheeks to the corners of her mouth.

As she was gripped by sadness, the image of a learned and refined husband, handsome in his high-topped hat and wide sash, like a player on the stage, blurred and finally vanished, replaced by the horrifying picture of Shan Bianlang's face, his leprous mouth covered with rotting tumors. Her heart turned to ice. Were these tapered golden lotuses, a face as fresh as peaches and apricots, gentility of a thousand kinds, and ten thousand varieties of elegance all reserved for the pleasure of a leper? Better to die and be done with it.

The disconsolate weeping in the sorghum field was dotted with words, like knots in a piece of wood: A blue sky yo—a sapphire sky yo—a painted sky yo—a mighty cudgel yo—dear elder brother yo—death has claimed you—you have brought down little sister's sky yo—

I must tell you that the weeping of women from Northeast Gaomi Township makes beautiful music. During 1912, the first year of the Republic, professional mourners known as "wailers" came from Qufu, the home of Confucius, to study local weeping techniques. Meeting up with a woman lamenting the death of her husband seemed to Grandma to be a stroke of bad luck on her wedding day, and she grew even more dejected.

Just then one of the bearers spoke up: "You there, little bride in the chair, say something! The long journey has bored us to tears."

Grandma quickly snatched up her red veil and covered her face, gently drawing her foot back from beneath the curtain and returning the carriage to darkness.

"Sing us a song while we bear you along!"

The musicians, as though snapping out of a trance, struck up their instruments. A trumpet blared from behind the chair:

"Too-tah-too-tah-"

"Poo-pah-poo-pah-" One of the bearers up front imitated the trumpet sound, evoking coarse, raucous laughter all around.

Grandma was drenched with sweat. Back home, as she was being lifted into the sedan chair, Great-Grandma had exhorted her not to get drawn into any banter with the bearers. Sedan bearers and musicians were low-class rowdies capable of anything, no matter how depraved.

They began rocking the chair so violently that poor Grandma couldn't keep her seat without holding on tight.

"No answer? Okay, rock! If we can't shake any words loose, we can at least shake the piss out of her!"

The sedan chair was like a dinghy tossed about by the waves, and Grandma held on to the wooden seat for dear life. The two eggs she'd eaten for breakfast churned in her stomach; the flies buzzed around her ears; her throat tightened, as the taste of eggs surged up into her mouth.

She bit her lip. Don't throw up, don't let yourself throw up! she commanded herself. You mustn't let yourself throw up, Fenglian. They say throwing up in the bridal chair means a lifetime of bad luck. . . .

The bearers' banter turned coarse. One of them reviled my great-granddad for being a money-grabber, another said something about a pretty flower stuck into a pile of cow shit, a third called Shan Bianlang a scruffy leper who oozed pus and excreted yellow fluids. He said the stench of rotten flesh drifted beyond the Shan compound, which swarmed with horseflies. . . .

"Little bride, if you let Shan Bianlang touch you, your skin will rot away!"

As the horns and woodwinds blared and tooted, the taste of eggs grew stronger, forcing Grandma to bite down hard on her lip. But to no avail. She opened her mouth and spewed a stream of filth, soiling the curtain, toward which the five flies dashed as though shot from a gun.

"Puke-ah, puke-ah. Keep rocking!" one of the bearers roared. "Keep rocking. Sooner or later she'll have to say something."

"Elder brothers . . . spare me . . ." Grandma pleaded desperately between agonizing retches. Then she burst into tears. She felt humiliated; she could sense the perils of her future, knowing she'd spend the rest of her life drowning in a sea of bitterness. Oh, Father, oh, Mother. I have been destroyed by a miserly father and a heartless mother!

Grandma's piteous wails made the sorghum quake. The bearers stopped rocking the chair and calmed the raging sea. The musicians lowered the instruments from their rousing lips, so that only Grandma's sobs could be heard, alone with the mournful strains of a single woodwind, whose weeping sounds were more enchanting than any woman's. Grandma stopped crying at the sound of the woodwind, as though commanded from on high. Her face, suddenly old and desiccated, was pearled with tears: she heard the sound of death in the gentle melancholy of the tune, and smelled its breath; she could see the angel of death, with lips as scarlet as sorghum and a smiling face the color of golden corn.

The bearers fell silent and their footsteps grew heavy. The sacrificial choking sounds from inside the chair and the woodwind accompaniment had made them restless and uneasy, had set their souls adrift. No longer did it seem like a wedding procession as they negotiated the dirt road; it was more like a funeral procession. My grandfather, the bearer directly in front of Grandma's foot, felt a strange premonition blazing inside him and illuminating the path his life would take. The sounds of Grandma's weeping had awakened seeds of affection that had lain dormant deep in his heart.

It was time to rest, so the bearers lowered the sedan chair to the ground. Grandma, having cried herself into a daze, didn't realize that one of her tiny feet was peeking out from beneath the curtain; the sight of that incomparably delicate, lovely thing nearly drove the souls out of the bearers' bodies. Yu Zhan'ao walked up, leaned over, and gently—very gently—held Grandma's foot in his hand, as though it were a fledgling whose feathers weren't yet dry, then eased it back inside the carriage. She was so moved by the gentleness of the deed she could barely keep from throwing back the curtain to see what sort of man this bearer was, with his large, warm, youthful hand.

I've always believed that marriages are made in heaven and that people fated to be together are connected by an invisible thread. The act of grasping Grandma's foot triggered a powerful drive in Yu Zhan'ao to forge a new life for himself, and constituted the turning point in his life—and the turning point in hers as well.

The sedan chair set out again as a trumpet blast rent the air, then drifted off into obscurity. The wind had risen—a northeaster—and clouds were gathering in the sky, blotting out the sun and throwing the carriage into darkness. Grandma could hear the *shh-shh* of rustling sorghum, one wave close upon another, carrying the sound off into the distance. Thunder rumbled off to the northeast. The bearers quickened their pace. She wondered how much farther it was to the Shan household; like a trussed lamb being led to slaughter, she grew calmer with each step. At home she had hidden a pair of scissors in her bodice, perhaps to use on Shan Bianlang, perhaps to use on herself.

The holdup of Grandma's sedan chair by a highwayman at Toad
Hollow occupies an important place in the saga of my family. Toad
Hollow is a large marshy stretch in the vast flatland where the soil
is especially fertile, the water especially plentiful, and the sorghum
especially dense. A blood-red bolt of lightning streaked across the
northeastern sky, and screaming fragments of apricot-yellow sunlight
tore through the dense clouds above the dirt road, when Grandma's
sedan chair reached that point. The panting bearers were drenched
with sweat as they entered Toad Hollow, over which the air hung
heavily. Sorghum plants lining the road shone like ebony, dense and
impenetrable; weeds and wildflowers grew in such profusion they
seemed to block the road. Everywhere you looked, narrow stems
of cornflowers were bosomed by clumps of rank weeds, their purple, blue, pink, and white flowers waving proudly. From deep in the
sorghum came the melancholy croaks of toads, the dreary chirps of
grasshoppers, and the plaintive howls of foxes. Grandma, still seated
in the carriage, felt a sudden breath of cold air that raised tiny goose
bumps on her skin. She didn't know what was happening, even when
she heard the shout up ahead:

"Nobody passes without paying a toll!"

Grandma gasped. What was she feeling? Sadness? Joy? My God, she
thought, it's a man who eats fistcakes!

Northeast Gaomi Township was aswarm with bandits who operated
in the sorghum fields like fish in water, forming gangs to rob, pillage,
and kidnap, yet balancing their evil deeds with charitable ones. If they
were hungry, they snatched two people, keeping one and sending the
other into the village to demand flatbreads with eggs and green onions
rolled inside. Since they stuffed the rolled flatbreads into their mouths
with both fists, they were called "fistcakes."

"Nobody passes without paying a toll!" the man bellowed. The bearers stopped in their tracks and stared dumbstruck at the highwayman of
medium height who stood in the road, his legs akimbo. He had smeared
his face black and was wearing a conical rain hat woven of sorghum
stalks and a broad-shouldered rain cape open in front to reveal a black

buttoned jacket and a wide leather belt, in which a protruding object was tucked, bundled in red satin. His hand rested on it.

The thought flashed through Grandma's mind that there was nothing to be afraid of: if death couldn't frighten her, nothing could. She raised the curtain to get a glimpse of the man who ate fistcakes.

"Hand over the toll, or I'll pop you all!" He patted the red bundle.

The musicians reached into their belts, took out the strings of copper coins Great-Granddad had given them, and tossed these at the man's feet. The bearers lowered the sedan chair to the ground, took out their copper coins, and did the same.

As he dragged the strings of coins into a pile with his foot, his eyes were fixed on Grandma.

"Get behind the sedan chair, all of you. I'll pop if you don't!" He thumped the object tucked into his belt.

The bearers moved slowly behind the sedan chair. Yu Zhan'ao, bringing up the rear, spun around and glared. A change came over the highwayman's face, and he gripped the object at his belt tightly. "Eyes straight ahead if you want to keep breathing!"

With his hand resting on his belt, he shuffled up to the sedan chair, reached out, and pinched Grandma's foot. A smile creased her face, and the man pulled his hand away as though it had been scalded.

"Climb down and come with me!" he ordered her.

Grandma sat without moving, the smile frozen on her face.

"Climb down, I said!"

She rose from the seat, stepped grandly onto the pole, and alit in a tuft of cornflowers. Her gaze traveled from the man to the bearers and musicians.

"Into the sorghum field!" the highwayman said, his hand still resting on the red-bundled object at his belt.

Grandma stood confidently; lightning crackled in the clouds overhead and shattered her radiant smile into a million shifting shards. The highwayman began pushing her into the sorghum field, his hand never leaving the object at his belt. She stared at Yu Zhan'ao with a feverish look in her eyes.

Yu Zhan'ao approached the highwayman, his thin lips curled resolutely, up at one end and down at the other.

"Hold it right there!" the highwayman commanded feebly. "I'll shoot if you take another step!"

Yu Zhan'ao walked calmly up to the man, who began backing up. Green flames seemed to shoot from his eyes, and crystalline beads of sweat scurried down his terrified face. When Yu Zhan'ao had drawn to within three paces of him, a shameful sound burst from his mouth, and he turned and ran. Yu Zhan'ao was on his tail in a flash, kicking him expertly in the rear. He sailed through the air over the cornflowers, thrashing his arms and legs like an innocent babe, until he landed in the sorghum field.

"Spare me, gentlemen! I've got an eighty-year-old mother at home, and this is the only way I can make a living." The highwayman skillfully pleaded his case to Yu Zhan'ao, who grabbed him by the scruff of the neck, dragged him back to the sedan chair, threw him roughly to the ground, and kicked him in his noisy mouth. The man shrieked in pain; blood trickled from his nose.

Yu Zhan'ao reached down, took the thing from the man's belt, and shook off the red cloth covering, to reveal the gnarled knot of a tree. The men all gasped in amazement.

The bandit crawled to his knees, knocking his head on the ground and pleading for his life. "Every highwayman says he's got an eighty-year-old mother at home," Yu Zhan'ao said as he stepped aside and glanced at his comrades, like the leader of a pack sizing up the other dogs.

With a flurry of shouts, the bearers and musicians fell upon the highwayman, fists and feet flying. The initial onslaught was met by screams and shrill cries, which soon died out. Grandma stood beside the road listening to the dull cacophony of fists and feet on flesh; she glanced at Yu Zhan'ao, then looked up at the lightning-streaked sky, the radiant, golden, noble smile still frozen on her face.

One of the musicians raised his trumpet and brought it down hard on the highwayman's skull, burying the curved edge so deeply he had to strain to free it. The highwayman's stomach gurgled and his body, racked by spasms, grew deathly still; he lay spread-eagled on the ground, a mixture of white and yellow liquid seeping slowly out of the fissure in his skull.

"Is he dead?" asked the musician, who was examining the bent mouth of his trumpet.

"He's gone, the poor bastard. He didn't put up much of a fight!"

The gloomy faces of the bearers and musicians revealed their anxieties.

Yu Zhan'ao looked wordlessly first at the dead, then at the living. With a handful of leaves from a sorghum stalk, he cleaned up Grandma's mess in the carriage, then held up the tree knot, wrapped it in the piece of red cloth, and tossed the bundle as far as he could; the gnarled knot broke free in flight and separated from the piece of cloth, which fluttered to the ground in the field like a big red butterfly.

Yu Zhan'ao lifted Grandma into the sedan chair. "It's starting to rain," he said, "so let's get going."

Grandma ripped the curtain from the front of the carriage and stuffed it behind the seat. As she breathed the free air she studied Yu Zhan'ao's broad shoulders and narrow waist. He was so near she could have touched the pale, taut skin of his shaved head with her toe.

The winds were picking up, bending the sorghum stalks in ever deeper waves, those on the roadside stretching out to bow their respects to Grandma. The bearers streaked down the road, yet the sedan chair was as steady as a skiff skimming across whitecaps. Frogs and toads croaked in loud welcome to the oncoming summer rainstorm. The low curtain of heaven stared darkly at the silvery faces of sorghum, over which streaks of blood-red lightning crackled, releasing earsplitting explosions of thunder. With growing excitement, Grandma stared fearlessly at the green waves raised by the black winds.

The first truculent raindrops made the plants shudder. The rain beat a loud tattoo on the sedan chair and fell on Grandma's embroidered slippers; it fell on Yu Zhan'ao's head, then slanted in on Grandma's face.

The bearers ran like scared jackrabbits, but couldn't escape the pre-noon deluge. Sorghum crumpled under the wild rain. Toads took refuge under the stalks, their white pouches popping in and out noisily; foxes hid in their darkened dens to watch tiny drops of water splashing down from the sorghum plants. The rainwater washed Yu Zhan'ao's head so clean and shiny it looked to Grandma like a new moon. Her clothes too were soaked. She could have covered herself with the curtain, but she didn't; she didn't want to, for the open front of the sedan chair afforded her a glimpse of the outside world in all its turbulence and beauty.

ıllıllıllıllıllıll

I T WAS RAINING as she sat in the bridal sedan chair, like a boat on the ocean, and was carried into Shan Tingxiu's compound. The street was flooded with water, peppered by a layer of sorghum seeds. At the front door she was met by a wizened old man with a tiny queue in the shape of a kidney bean. The rain had stopped, but an occasional drop splashed onto the watery ground. Although the musicians had announced her arrival with their instruments, no one had emerged to watch the show; Grandma knew that was a bad sign. Two men came out to help her perform her obeisances, one in his fifties, the other in his forties. The fifty-year-old was none other than Uncle Arhat Liu, the other was one of the distillery hands.

The musicians and bearers stood in the puddles like drenched chickens, somberly watching the two dried-up men lead my soft-limbed, rosy-cheeked grandma into the dark wedding-chamber. The men exuded a pungent aroma of wine, as if they had been soaked in the vats.

Grandma was taken up to a *k'ang* in the worship hall and told to sit on it. Since no one came up to remove her red veil, she took it off herself. A man with a facial tic sat curled up on a stool next to her. The bottom part of his flat, elongated face was red and festering. He stood up and stuck a clawlike hand out toward Grandma, who screamed in horror and reached into her bodice for the scissors; she glared intently at the man, who recoiled and curled up on the stool again. Grandma didn't set down her scissors once that night, nor did the man climb down from his stool.

Early the next morning, before the man woke up, Grandma slipped down off the *k'ang*, burst through the front door, and opened the gate; just as she was about to flee the premises, a hand reached out and grabbed her. The old man with the kidney-bean queue had her by the wrist and was looking at her with hate-filled eyes.

Shan Tingxiu coughed dryly once or twice as his expression softened. "Child," he said, "now that you're married, you're like my own daughter. Bianlang doesn't have what everybody says. Don't listen to their talk. We've got a good business, and Bianlang's a good boy. Now that you're here, the home is your responsibility." Shan Tingxiu held out to her a ring of bronze keys, but she didn't take them from him.

Grandma sat up all the next night, scissors in hand.

On the morning of the third day, my maternal great-granddad led a donkey up to the house to take Grandma home; it was a Northeast Gaomi Township custom for a bride to return to her parents' home three days after her wedding. Great-Granddad spent the morning drinking with Shan Tingxiu, then set out for home shortly after noon.

Grandma sat sidesaddle on the donkey, swaying from side to side as the animal left the village. Even though it hadn't rained for three days, the road was still wet, and steam rose from the sorghum in the fields, the green stalks shrouded in swirling whiteness, as though in the presence of immortals. Great-Granddad's silver coins clinked and jingled in the saddlebags. He was so drunk he could barely walk, and his eyes were glassy. The donkey proceeded slowly, its long neck bobbing up and down, its tiny hooves leaving muddy imprints. Grandma had only ridden a short distance when she began to get light-headed; her eyes were red and puffy, her hair mussed, and the sorghum in the fields, a full joint taller than it had been three days earlier, mocked her as she passed.

"Dad," Grandma called out, "I don't want to go back there anymore. I'll kill myself before I go back there again. . . ."

"Daughter," Great-Granddad replied, "you have no idea how lucky you are. Your father-in-law said he's going to give me a big black mule. I'm going to sell this runty little thing. . . ."

The donkey nibbled some mud-splattered grass that lined the road.

"Dad," Grandma sobbed, "he's got leprosy. . . ."

"Your father-in-law is going to give me a mule. . . ."

Great-Granddad, drunk as a lord, kept vomiting into the weeds by the side of the road. The filth and bile set Grandma's stomach churning, and she felt nothing but loathing for him.

As the donkey walked into Toad Hollow, they were met by an overpowering stench that caused its ears to droop. Grandma spotted the highwayman's bloated corpse, which was covered by a layer of emerald-colored flies. The donkey skirted the corpse, sending the flies swarming angrily into the air to form a green cloud. Great-Granddad followed the donkey, his body seemingly wider than the road itself: one moment he was stumbling into the sorghum to the left of the road, the next moment he was trampling on weeds to the right. And when he reached the corpse, he gasped, "Oh!" several times, and said through quaking lips, "Poor beggar . . . you poor beggar . . . you sleeping there? . . ." Grandma never forgot the highwayman's pumpkin face. In that instant when the flies swarmed into the air she was struck by the remarkable contrast between the graceful elegance of his dead face and the mean, cowardly expression he'd worn in life.

The distance between them lengthened, one *li* at a time, with the sun's rays slanting down, the sky high and clear; the donkey quickly outpaced Great-Granddad. Since it knew the way home, it carried Grandma at a carefree saunter. Up ahead was a bend in the road, and as the donkey negotiated the turn, Grandma tipped backward, leaving the security of the animal's back. A muscular arm swept her off and carried her into the sorghum field.

Grandma fought halfheartedly. She really didn't feel like struggling. The three days she had just gotten through were nightmarish. Certain individuals become great leaders in an instant; Grandma unlocked the mysteries of life in three days. She even wrapped her arms around his neck to make it easier for him to carry her. Sorghum leaves rustled. Great-Granddad's hoarse voice drifted over on the wind: "Daughter, where the hell are you?"

[. . .]

|||||||||||||||||

THE MAN PLACED Grandma on the ground, where she lay as limp as a ribbon of dough, her eyes narrowed like those of a lamb. He ripped away the black mask, revealing his face to her. It's him! A silent prayer to heaven. A powerful feeling of pure joy rocked her, filling her eyes with hot tears.

Yu Zhan'ao removed his rain cape and tramped out a clearing in the sorghum, then spread his cape over the sorghum corpses. He lifted Grandma onto the cape. Her soul fluttered as she gazed at his bare torso. A light mist rose from the tips of the sorghum, and all around she could hear the sounds of growth. No wind, no waving motion, just the white-hot rays of moist sunlight crisscrossing through the open cracks between plants. The passion in Grandma's heart, built up over sixteen years, suddenly erupted. She squirmed and twisted on the cape. Yu Zhan'ao, getting smaller and smaller, fell loudly to his knees at her side. She was trembling from head to toe; a redolent yellow ball of fire crackled and sizzled before her eyes. Yu Zhan'ao roughly tore open her jacket, exposing the small white mounds of chilled, tense flesh to the sunlight. Answering his force, she cried out in a muted, hoarse voice, "My God . . ." and swooned.

Grandma and Granddad exchanged their love surrounded by the vitality of the sorghum field: two unbridled souls, refusing to knuckle under to worldly conventions, were fused together more closely than their ecstatic bodies. They plowed the clouds and scattered rain in the field, adding a patina of lustrous red to the rich and varied history of Northeast Gaomi Township. My father was conceived with the essence of heaven and earth, the crystallization of suffering and wild joy.

The braying donkey threaded its way into the sorghum field, and Grandma returned from the hazy kingdom of heaven to the cruel world of man. She sat up in a state of utter stupefaction, her face bathed in tears. "He really does have leprosy," she said. As Granddad knelt down, a sword appeared in his hand, as if by magic. He slipped it out of its scabbard; the two-foot blade was curved, like a leaf of chive. With a single swish, it sliced through two stalks of sorghum, the top halves thudding to the ground, leaving bubbles of dark-green liquid on the neat, slanted wounds.

"Come back in three days, no matter what!" Granddad said.

Grandma looked at him uncomprehendingly. He dressed while she tidied herself up, then put his sword away—where, she didn't know. Granddad took her back to the roadside and vanished.

Three days later, the little donkey carried Grandma back, and when she entered the village she learned that the Shans, father and son, had been murdered and tossed into the inlet at the western edge of the village.

(Translated by Howard Goldblatt)

SHU TING
(1952–)

A Fujian native, Shu Ting, real name Gong Peiyu, was the leading woman poet in the 1980s. Like many of her generation during the Cultural Revolution, she was sent to the countryside to "receive reeducation by the peasants" in 1969, when she was still a high school student. In 1972, she returned to the city and worked at factories. The publication in 1979 of her poem "To an Oak," which freely expresses romantic love, made her an instant celebrity in a nation still reeling from a decade-long cultural and spiritual devastation. Often associated with the Misty Poets, Shu Ting crafted a lyrical voice of a woman, weary of ideological weight and restraint, looking for beauty and truth in the apolitical and ordinary.

To an Oak

If I love you—
I won't be like the trumpet creeper
Flaunting itself on your tall branches,
If I love you—
I won't be like the lovesick bird,
Repeating to the green shade its monotonous song;
Nor like a brook,

Bringing cool solace the year round;
Nor like a perilous peak,
Adding to your height, complementing your grandeur;
Nor even sunlight,
Nor even spring rain.
No, these are not enough!
I must be a kapok tree by your side;
In the image of a tree standing by you,
Our roots clasped underground,
Our leaves touching in the clouds.
With every breeze
We salute each other,
But no one
Will understand our language.
You have your trunk of steel and iron branches,
Like knives, like swords,
And like spears.
I have my huge, red flowers,
Like heavy sighs,
And like valiant torches.
We share the burdens of cold, storms, lightning;
We share the joys of mists, vapors, rainbows.
We may seem forever severed,
But are lifelong companions.
This is the greatest of love;
This is constancy:
Love—
I love not just your robust form,
I also love the ground you hold, the earth you stand on.

—March 27, 1977

A Roadside Encounter

The phoenix tree suddenly tilts
The bicycle bell's ring hangs in air
Earth swiftly reverses its rotation
Back to that night ten years ago

The phoenix tree gently sways again
The ringing bell sprinkles floral fragrance
      along the trembling street
Darkness gathers, then seeps away
The dawning light of memory merges
      with the light in your eyes

Maybe this didn't happen
Just an illusion spawned by a familiar road
Even if this did happen
I'm used to not shedding any tears.

—March 1979

Assembly Line

On the assembly line of time
Nights huddle together
We come down from the factory assembly lines
And join the assembly line going home
Overhead
An assembly line of stars trails across the sky
By our side
A young tree looks dazed on its assembly line

The stars must be tired
Thousands of years have passed
Their journey never changes
The young trees are ill
Dust and monotony deprive them
Of grain and color
I can feel it all
Because we beat to the same rhythm

But strangely
The only thing I do not feel
Is my own existence
As though the woods and stars
Maybe out of habit
Maybe out of sorrow
No longer have the strength to care
About a destiny they cannot alter

—January–February 1980

Where the Soul Dwells

all roads lead to you
none of them reach you

your words are compiled into dictionaries
those who keep copies of your silence
have their own renditions in their hearts

you locked the door
then threw away the key
you never walk down that street, yet each time
you look up you see a window open

catcalls and applause
sedimentary rocks are soft
before they turn into amber
    amid the lush foliage
that cicada of yours

shrills

—1986
(Translated by Eva Hung)

LIU SUOLA
(1955–)

Born in Beijing to a family of high-ranking Communist cadres, Liu Suola, who also goes by Sola in English, tasted the bitterness and brutality of the Chinese revolution early in life when her parents were taken away in a political purge and exiled to a rural pig farm for twenty years. Music became her consolation, and Liu studied composition at the Central Conservatory of Music from 1977 to 1981. The publication in 1985 of her first novella, You Have No Choice, spiced with dark humor and Existentialist ennui, made her a pioneer of avant-garde Chinese fiction. She lived in England and the United States from 1988 to 2002, composing music, hopping blues clubs in Memphis, and jamming with jazz musicians in the Mississippi Delta. An internationally renowned vocalist, composer, and writer, Liu was cited by the New York Times for her ability to "wander from echoes of Chinese opera to simple folklike melodies." The novella In Search of the King of Singers (1987), which follows, gives us a glimpse into that inspirational wandering.

In Search of the King of Singers (excerpts)

If anybody had wanted to find out where the two of us were on this earth then, they would have to use a magnifying glass to enlarge the map twenty times; still, they probably wouldn't have been able to locate our whereabouts. It was a tiny little place, not far from the primeval forest, but it wasn't shown on the map, though the primeval forest was. We circled around and around, and nearly walked our legs off. I grumbled and grumbled, but B just kept quiet. The skin on our noses had peeled off I don't know how many times, but the King of Singers still eluded us. B, do you really have to see him, to plead with him? Why are you so sure he's better than you are, in what way is he better? I've never come across a mountain as difficult to climb as this one—the soil slips and gives way for no reason. You walk and you walk, you only want to push on. A tree crashes to the ground. What a pain in the ass you are! The plants up in the mountain were so weird I dared not touch them. My shoelaces came undone as we walked, I stooped to tie them and found several leeches clinging to my shoes. What a pain in the ass you are!

B had his run of luck while he was still at the university. The scores he composed were published in magazines, as if they were recipes. Some called him avant-garde; he went mad when he heard this. I'd say he was a fool, just as he was a fool when he courted me. At the time, people said he was fooling around with me; when he got a bit of fame they said I was fooling around with him. If it were possible I'd quite like to go back to the past. The problem arose not because of that outdated label, "avant-garde," it started with the quest for the King of Singers. He considered this more important than getting the Nobel Prize, though of course Nobel simply didn't care a fig for composers. At first I thought it was good fun and went around with him for a bit; but, after a few months, I began to find the whole thing more and more absurd. They said the King of Singers was up in the north; we went to the coldest places—even our snot froze into icicles—only to learn that the King of Singers was in fact down in the south, in places where leeches thrive. We didn't know where in this world leeches thrive. As we crossed the primeval forest, the leeches even bit B's vital parts, but the King of Singers was still nowhere to be found. The strangest thing was the illiterate village people all said they'd seen him, and what they said sounded convincing: he was dressed in black and his head was shaven. You'd ask them where he was, they'd say he'd just left. So we trailed after him, like two lousy wriggling worms.

After much difficulty we made it to the top of the mountain. A bunch of bare-bottomed kids surrounded us, jumping and shouting. A group of farmhouses made of bamboo and straw came into sight. A bare-breasted woman was sitting on the balcony of one of these houses, her skin like the old trees in the forest. On seeing B, she disappeared into the dark room behind her. These were all two-story farmhouses. Animals and men lived together there—animals downstairs, men upstairs. Gesticulating all the while, I asked one naked child whether he'd seen a man passing through here, dressed in black, his head shaven, singing about whatever he saw.

The kids all laughed and there was quite a hullabaloo. B took out a handful of sweets and passed them around. One of the kids pointed at a place halfway down the mountain and shouted something, and the rest joined in. But we had just come from there! Desperate, I shouted, "An old man down there said he's at the top of the mountain, said he lives at the top, how could he be down there?" The kids started to play among themselves; a dog strolled over, stretching himself lazily in front of us. I screamed and shouted. One of the kids looked up at me, and then looked at the place halfway down the mountain. I flung my knapsack to the ground; a dark cloud drifted slowly across the sky, darkening the village. I sat glumly on the ground; the cloud passed, the colors of bamboo and straw returned to the village. I started to cry.

I wasn't keen to see the King of Singers; I only wanted to help B by fulfilling the duties of a girlfriend. I was dying to fulfill my duties. Perhaps love was a transparent vacuity; it needed to be embellished by something solid and colorful. I was obsessed with this kind of fanatic embellishment, but the King of Singers seemed to be sneering at me for my vacuity. There was a foreign magazine on the ideal home. It had photographs of every single thing a home needed, from shorts to fur coats, from cutlery to bedroom items. The magazine was on sale at a special department store for forty-five yuan. I was a student and couldn't afford it. Even now I wouldn't want to fork out so much money for a lousy magazine, but at that time I really hankered after it. I kept thinking about it whenever I felt bored. It was only after B had proposed the plan to go in quest of the King of Singers that I put it out of my mind. But as I sat crying at the top of the mountain, I thought about that magazine again. I wanted the food pictured there, wanted one of the dresses they featured, wanted to abandon myself to three days of sleep on the huge bed, to spray myself all over with French perfume, to get a new haircut and have a manicure. . . . Oh, the city, the city, the city!

To people in the city, B was an odd fish, he was too full of enthusiasm. He tried endlessly to improve himself and was too busy to think about life. As far as I was concerned, he hadn't yet attained complete success, but he'd rushed off to complete, to perfect, his self. I felt, however, that the self and success were two totally different things. Composing music was no religion. All that talk about character and spirit, the heart and the soul, enlightenment and inspiration; about true music being pure, lofty, and sublime, and so on and so forth. . . . As I saw it, B was full of talent, full to bursting; but he insisted upon seeing himself as a monk and looking up to the King of Singers as Buddha. At the university, this King of Singers had been my sworn enemy; B was gripped tightly in the King's clutches, a glazed look in his eyes. I could feel that he couldn't concentrate even when he was kissing me. But now it seemed that it wasn't such a good thing after all for the King of Singers to have acquired this disciple. B hadn't given any concerts since his university days, when he received recognition from the public, and no more was heard of his work. He spent all his time on this quest for the King of Singers. Orchestral music had brought him fame but, years later, he dressed himself in rags and mixed with country people, his whereabouts completely unknown.

We went our separate ways a long time ago. I looked upon this quest for the King of Singers with increasing despair. That day when I sat crying at the top of the mountain, B came over to help me up; I didn't move. He dropped his hands to his sides and squatted on the ground. Still crying, I started to splutter, I didn't know what I was saying.

Words just tumbled out of my mouth, like tiny smoke rings smokers make by pouting their lips and tapping their cheeks. One sentence tumbled out after another. I kept feeling that we were like two somnambulists who had climbed up a high mountain. The wind at the top blew away all sound, so that you suspected this was really a world without sound and that there was no King of Singers after all. Then the wind stopped, I heard a few dogs bark. Several months later, when I was in the amusement park wearing a long dress made of pure Hangzhou silk and laughing merrily in one of those electric whirling chairs, I suddenly remembered that the wind up in the mountain could blow away all sound. Yet, amid the sound of the swirling wind around the whirling chairs, I could hear pop music. It was loud and triumphant, powerful enough to drown everything.

After I left B and returned to the city, I felt an urgent need to cast off my old self. I got in the bathtub and soaked for so long that I nearly fainted from exhaustion. I did everything I had wanted to do when I was on the mountain. Then I frittered away my days in shops, amusement parks, exhibition halls, and social gatherings. Everyone wanted to know whether we'd actually managed to achieve anything. I exaggerated and dramatized my experience. I became a heroine and a superwoman in people's eyes. But I saw another "me" on the mountain, one who soon drooped under the light of the sun, like wild tropical flowers that bloom but for a while. I simply don't know what I've been doing these few years. I haven't seen my Buddha.

Everybody in the city had paired me off with B and reacted to our breaking up with amazement and disapproval. They thought it was temporary, a matter of getting back to the city at different times. I knew, however, that this was a choice for life. He wanted to find his King of Singers; I wanted simply to be a singer. People kept coming to consult me about B's works. This made me see our differences even more clearly. I didn't think much about whether I'd been right or wrong, but I did miss the time we'd spent together. I dreamed that he had married a country girl; she had a sad, supple, beautiful singing voice. I cried in my dream. When I woke up, I rushed to the theater to sign payment receipts.

[. . .]

I was lying in bed going over the innumerable letters that had arrived, mostly from my fans. At first I was surprised that I should have made such a hit singing popular songs; later, I came to feel I deserved it. But when I opened a large envelope, I found inside it only a slip of paper with the words: "Your songs are crap." I crumpled up the paper and threw it away, then picked it up again and smoothed it out. I knew what kind of a singer I was, I knew where I stood. I'd never done anything seriously in my life. Easy come, easy go; always doing things by halves. I was like a sick bird that soared high into the sky one moment and came straight down the next, that hiccupped at the sun and farted at the stars. Everything I did was for fun. When I came back from the mountain, I suddenly wanted to have a go at this business called singing—not arias, of course. It so happened that a friend of mine wanted me as a partner, I agreed, so singing became my profession. There are all kinds of fairy tales in this world. Standing on the stage and relying on the lighting, the colors, and the microphone to make people think you're a somebody is one such fairy tale. Cut a leech in half and you have two leeches. Two times two makes four; four times four, sixteen—one has to come up with a few tricks in order to survive. I was pleased with myself for my ability to earn good money, when in fact I had been made a fool of by the King of Singers.

The phone rang. Knowing full well who it was, I picked it up and said straightaway:

"It's about time you rang!"

"Are you still in bed? I only slept two hours yesterday I'm ready to drop I've got so many things to do my clothes were all moth-eaten I'd forgotten about the mothballs I sunned my clothes all day yesterday my costume now has a large hole in it how sad how sad how sad and I went out to fix up two shows just the taxis cost me a fortune well, shall we go?"

"Pick me up in half an hour. I'm still in bed."

"You sleep too much. Be quick. I'll come right away."

Before I could reply, she hung up.

Mimi was like this: impatient, always on the move. She had five phones in that small flat of hers—just so she could pick up the phone anytime, anywhere, she said. She even had a phone in the bathroom, and she would read fashion magazines and talk on the phone while sitting on the loo.

When I had the time, I loved reading fashion magazines about fashion trends abroad. I had quite a collection of such magazines. One day my girlfriends came and divided them up among themselves. Collecting fashion magazines was like going in search of the King of Singers: labor in vain, that's what it was! In the end, I thought better of it and simply went and bought myself a pile of cheap sportswear—it was still fun, I thought. But Hanna, wrapped in that expensive dress of hers that was worth over a hundred U.S. dollars, never stopped telling me I was too sloppy. Hanna was a beautiful woman with a slim figure, poised and elegant. She had just come back from England, and was so loaded with good breeding and good manners that she seemed to find it hard even to laugh in public. She spoke with a perfect accent, was impeccably dressed, and showed a proper disdain for discotheques. This "aristocratic air" of hers threw Weiwei completely off her stride, and she worried endlessly that she might be shown up for her "vulgarity." Weiwei was as clever as a rat, but she had a face like a cat. With an impressive flow of Peking dialect at her command, with the slang and colloquialisms of different countries at her disposal, Weiwei did exactly what she felt like in front of anybody and everybody, in defiance of good manners. Yet, when Hanna was around, even if the whole world was dancing to the beat of disco music, she'd only dare to wriggle her shoulders stealthily when Hanna was not looking.

Hanna loved lecturing me. "You can't see beyond your nose! Don't you know there're other countries in this world—Paris, New York, London? Of course, New York doesn't count. Americans are so common," she said with a wave of her hand. "Here the most you can do is to sing, or interpret B's symphonies for people. Now that you've broken up with B, why don't you marry into Europe? But don't go to America, Americans are so common." She paused. "This quest for the King of

Singers—it's unthinkable, simply suicidal. You've seen nothing of the world. Go abroad, go abroad! But don't go to the States, Americans are so common!"

True, we had seen nothing of the world. I rather feared B would have to spend the rest of his life in the wild mountains. I too was entangled in this absurd business of his: I could neither follow him, nor leave him. Hanna had married a descendant of an English aristocrat. People said her lucky star was smiling on her; she was the "aristocrat" among us. Perhaps the family she married into could be counted one of the true aristocratic families in the world, that was perhaps why she could speak with such absolute certainty about the Americans all being "common." But, when she fell asleep, that wonderful heritage which could be traced back to her father and her grandfather would manifest itself, making her snore and mumble in her sleep. What was more, that faint trace of a mustache around her mouth, and her gnarled knuckles, all reminded her mercilessly that she was her father's daughter. Her eyes were dark and bright, but they only shone when she forgot that she was her husband's wife and her mother-in-law's daughter-in-law. I knew how absolutely charming she was when she opened her mouth wide to laugh, twisting her nose and baring her teeth, and she had in her a real treasure of sophisticated vulgar language. Her husband had certainly fallen in love with these wonderful qualities of hers, only to discover that they were all gone after he married her.

I was too lazy to argue with Hanna about my future. She said I made life difficult for myself and that I was simpleminded; I just stuck to my own opinions. The word loneliness might be rubbish, yet it never stopped niggling me, shamelessly, stubbornly. I thought about finding myself a new partner, but I couldn't forget B. I could have married a good husband, yellow or white or black, it would be fine by me as long as he loved me; but I felt completely at a loss, not knowing what to ask for. My private life was a complete mess.

[. . .]

I really wanted to know how many of the virtues of an Oriental woman I possessed and how many of the "obsessions" of a modern woman I had in me. "Don't model yourself on what you see in films and pack your bags and go and stay in a hotel the minute you get home," as one model husband said to his disgruntled wife. All the women in the world were competing against one another in madness. I had packed my bags, stayed in hotels, but I still became B's official representative. I wanted to leave him, yet I also wanted to do something for him; I knew I wasn't capable of being his able and virtuous wife, yet I also knew that there was something in his innermost being which held my soul in tether. There's a fairy tale about a pair of shoes. Whoever put them on would find himself at a loss as to where he'd go and what would become of him. It was said that the shoes were put away by a goddess. I suspected that the goddess was a shoemaker. She must have gone home and produced innumerable pairs modeled on them. They were now sold at a high price in shoe shops, throwing everyone into confusion.

All right, I'd be B's representative and hold a concert for him. B wanted to channel art toward purity and sincerity, but was utterly forgotten by the people. Holding a concert for him now was like excavating an ancient tomb. Everyone likes to sing the praises of dead geniuses.

I was helping in this excavation and working a lot harder than when I dug holes in the ground to plant trees. I was excavating the B in my heart and his colleagues as well. Real musicians are the biggest block-heads in the world. Equipped only with the twelve notes of the scale, they hover above a stretch of marshes. The rest of us can only look up at them from the marshes. But, even more pitiful are those who tend to think too much in words. I've never come across that type; I only know that the marshes are full of the bubbles they've thrown up. May music bless us and keep us.

There were people who loved to argue about what sort of art was the greatest. I wouldn't dare participate in such lofty debates. Before I put *that type* of shoes on, I could say anything I liked. Now giving my views on this subject was suicidal. A long time ago I had a dream about my former self, what I used to be, and what I grew out of. It was a thick white bean-curd-like lump. It lay on a stretch of salt-soaked wilderness.

Nothing could grow there. But soon the sun, rain, tides, mountains, and rocks came one after another to change it. And then there were flowers, plants, and trees to decorate it, the spirit of heaven and earth to nourish it, and the practical education of the human world to shape it. So it became me, lying on a huge warm and comfortable bed. This I knew with certainty. But I could never make out when I had mistakenly bought those shoes and let them gain possession of my feet, leading me I knew not whither.

What was B's former self? What did he grow out of?

"All my life I have wanted to do this." He looked at me but was not talking to me.

"All my life I have wanted to see this King of Singers." He did not look at me but could only be talking to me.

"You really believe that those prehistoric cave paintings were done by extraterrestrial visitors?" After all it wasn't you and it wasn't me, though of course it could be you or it could be me.

"Do you believe that without the mountains the sky would fall?" How could that happen? Even without anything to hold it up, the sky wouldn't fall.

"Every year the King of Singers holds a gathering with his disciples." I know, it's the same old story again, a gathering with his disciples in the wildest and most primitive region. "All the people go there to hear the King of Singers; the singing spirits dance as they sing, the singing spirits of the entire world are there." It would have to be an enormous stretch of wilderness, wider even than the sea, or the singing spirits would all fall into the sea. "The entire wilderness is packed full of singing spirits, they sing and dance, sing and dance." Sing and dance, sing and dance. "For five days and five nights nonstop. It's earthshaking." Like a landslide and a tidal wave. "All those who love the King of Singers go there to see him; they go in groups, carrying torches, bringing provisions. It will take days or weeks, or months, or years." I know there were people who set off on this journey from time immemorial. "They sing all the way." Yes. "They do sing all the way." Yes. "Thousands of years have gone by like this." Yes. "Would you go too?" Yes.

Did I buy those shoes then? What made me do it? It was midnight now, a whole pile of B's scores were lying in front of me. "Don't you know by now that B's music is in a class of its own?" I had never studied them carefully in the past. I read over these scores under the lamplight, and listened to the tape recordings. The scores were filled with notes like the prehistoric cave-paintings, like those mountains taller than the sky. The mountains collapsed, becoming the wilderness. The wilderness collapsed, becoming the sea. The sea collapsed, becoming—I switched off the light—the place which gave us birth and nurtured us.

The mountains in the south were shrouded in thick, eerie mists; people there seldom saw the sun. Like a rising tide, waves of mists rose from the valley, obscuring the fields and villages at the foot of the mountain. All the mountains were alive and exhaling steam, steam which carried with it monotonous, long-drawn-out calls that echoed everywhere. People said these were the voices of the "singing spirits"— the followers of the King of Singers—calling to one another. Trees in the burnt-out wasteland, deeply scorched, stretched out their long fingernails to clutch at the soil. Crash. Crash. Everywhere huge boulders collapsed and came rolling down from on high, swallowing all living things.

"Is this rosin the fragrance of pine? Just pine. No fragrance." A "singing spirit" was holding a piece of rosin in his hands and sniffing at it again and again. He hunkered down on his haunches and walked about, trying to amuse the others.

In the rainy season the turbid water of the rising river was filled with desire.

"Come on, get drunk, drink yourself to death." A man gave B a bowl of wine. A fish, stuffed with vegetables and chilies, was being roasted in the fire.

The "singing spirits" had bright, childlike eyes, eyes that made you want to cry.

This one made a move to leave as soon as he saw us.

"No more for me, I'm going back," he said to the host, his mouth full of fish.

"Wait, do please sing us a song first," I said. "Wouldn't you like to have your voice here?" I showed him the cassette recorder. B just sat there, poking the fire.

"It couldn't stay long there." He pointed at his throat and went over to the side of the mat to get his shoes.

I stood up. "Where are you from?"

"Don't eat the grain I sow, or the eagles will come and eat you whole." He looked at me and winked mischievously.

Like one bewitched, I put on my shoes and followed him out of the bamboo hut, out of the stockaded village. Though it was past midnight, one could still hear the clopping of cows' hooves and the screeching of rusty wheels. The children were all asleep; the river continued to rise.

He walked so fast that I soon lost him in the fog. Through the fog there appeared pairs of dark bright eyes, thick dark brows, and long thick eyelashes. It was a group of women, short and small-built. They were carrying heavy bundles of firewood and examining me quizzically with raised heads.

"What do you want?"

"I want to record his voice." I pointed at the thick fog ahead.

"The temperature of your tongue is different from his. The two of you can't have children."

"I want to record him."

"Hens hide their heads, pigs lie on the ground, bulls point their horns at the sky, people sleep with their legs crossed. . . ." They disappeared, laughing loudly.

I ran back to the hut.

"Is this rosin the fragrance of pine? Just pine. No fragrance."

The "singing spirits" had bright, childlike eyes, eyes that made you want to cry.

There was nothing transcendental about B's music. One would probably have to break away from one's body before one could "transcend." When I was traveling in the long-distance bus, I kept getting the feeling that my head was weighing me down. I only wanted to find some way of holding my head up, and didn't care a damn about worry, resentment, music, or happiness. Perhaps that was what transcendence means? B's music made me think immediately of the mountains; the mountains made me think of the bus; the bus made me think of the heavy feeling in my head. What if I held my head up and simply walked? I would end up huffing and puffing, no doubt. Oh, the mountains, the mountains!

Hanna said that "B, the young composer" should be printed in large archaic calligraphy on the program—how daunting, I thought! B wasn't around, so it was impossible to ask him to write his own introduction and provide a synopsis of his career. I had to make use of my feeble command of the language and write about him. In the style of pop-music lyrics, I wrote: "B is a man. Years have passed since he went away and disappeared into the foggy highlands of the south. Praise him, damn him. It's up to you. He can't hear you anyway."

It was the middle of the night. When I switched off the cassette recorder, there was no sound, only a cat scratching the floor upstairs. From out of nowhere came a sweet fragrance. Strange, for I never kept any plants. I switched on the light and looked around. The smell was coming from the cupboard. But there were only a few bottles and glasses, a tray and an opened packet of tea leaves there. It was the tea leaves. When I drank the tea during the day, it had no fragrance at all, and now, in the dark of night, it gave off a fragrance that filled the entire room. Hell, it was really late. All of a sudden, I felt extremely sad. Soon it'd be another day. Day is the space for facts and people. I could only think about the next step, the next step, and the next step. It's often said that man relies on his hands and a dog on its hind legs. I never could understand what connection there is between a man's hands and a dog's hind legs. After all, every living thing wants to triumph over something and possess something. What is it that I want to triumph over? What is it that I want to possess? Do I want to triumph over the King of Singers? Impossible! Do I want to possess B? Equally impossible! Why did I organize this concert, then? I had to. For B, for myself; not for B, nor for myself.

Who was the fool who said reality was what women chased after? He'd certainly lost his head over a woman. Perhaps reality is what women are after in the first place, but then they learn pretense in order to attract men. Men learn pretense too in order to chase after women. In the end nobody cares about reality at all. Was it men or women who first chased after reality? Was it men or women who first invented pretense? One can never be sure which comes first, like the chicken-and-egg question. But pretense is spreading, everyone is doing things that distort reality. I've left B; I hated the King of Singers. Yet here I am, organizing a concert for B, that's pretense enough. But what about B? He has left the city and gone to the wilderness, his mind filled with music scores and composition techniques, to become a disciple of the King of Singers. Isn't that pretense too? Heavens! He must be very lonely, since he'll be the only pretender in the wilderness, unless he's forgotten all about musical notation and composition techniques. He wasn't born a saint. Nurture and formal education turned him into a favorite with the people. Will he count at all, there in the wilderness? He's left this place, where attention was paid him, where people called him a "composer"; what would the King of Singers call him? A sham, perhaps, or a loafer living off music, or a bullshitter, or . . . unless he's forgotten everything here. What value will these scores have then? Won't they be mere rubbish? We've raised him to the status of a great composer, but he might long have forgotten what composition means. Why bother to invite the reporters; what have reporters got to do with him? He's gone chasing after reality, and here I am creating for him the biggest unreality of all.

Morning had come. A pigeon flew onto my balcony. It stood on the window ledge cooing; its red eyes were fixed on me and its concentrated stare made me uneasy, like the stare of a third-rate secret agent. I got up, opened the window, and scattered some beans on the window ledge. Go on, go and eat your beans. I began to plan what to wear and how to make myself presentable in order to pull a few more strings and fix up a few more performances. Money, the concert, B. B thought he could get away from material things by running away, but in fact he'd left behind him a long rope, one end of which was still fastened to him. The other end was fastened to the music that was created out of money. I always sang about "the birds, fishes, the wind," but that pigeon irritated me no end. To make money with lyrics like "I love pigeons" was as synthetic as margarine, protein substitutes, nylon and polyester. "Don't lose your natural self." I made myself smart and trendy, there was nothing wrong with that, but there was less and less of the natural woman in me.

[. . .]

When the plane took off, I felt a great relief. I was finally on my way to a big show and I had also signed a recording contract. The profit would be considerable, certainly enough to hold the concert for B. I could leave all trivial matters behind. The plane carrying this lump of chaos that was me glided through the atmosphere. "Render therefore unto Caesar the things which are Caesar's; and unto God the things that are God's." No matter where the shoes led you, surely there would have to be an end somewhere, wouldn't there? This smartly dressed lump of chaos in a plane, was it flying back to its original form, or on its way to completing its rebirth? Who could tell? Once you started walking in this pair of shoes, you found yourself in a complete muddle. Confusion and clarity, clarity and confusion; contradiction and paradox, paradox and confusion—these would entangle you and throw you into turmoil; only the pair of shoes knew for certain; they'd tell you all hesitation was futile.

The plane made its way through masses of clouds. I'm glad I'm a human being so I can sit so high up in the sky, and yet it's also human beings alone that can sit so high up in the sky without being able to touch the clouds. But birds are not happy either: though they can fly, they're held tightly in their own physical substance. This is the misfortune of those whose original form is clearly defined. The basest swallow and the noblest phoenix have a clearer conception of their own value than a lump of chaos. But neither heaven nor earth could do anything to disperse solid physical substance, or make it undergo various transformations. Chaos often envies clarity: little does it know that after it has been dispersed by an air stream, it can merge with the upper atmosphere and fly even higher than the birds, or dissolve into the mire and descend to the depths where ghosts and spirits dwell. Chaos doesn't know itself for what it is, and it never knows what it should or should not do, whether it's right or wrong; it always envies clarity but is always dispersed by the air stream.

I pretended to be a career woman and sat there with a rapt look on my face. Was B dependent on me for help? One moment I'd say yes, another, no. The B I knew was a living person and I rushed about on behalf of this living person. Everyone needs some sort of support to keep going. If B wasn't dependent on me and if I wasn't organizing this concert for him, I didn't know what I should do. Surely B depended on me. As the plane flew higher and higher, so did my aspirations. How I wished I could move the King of Singers. But what for? To give B back to me?

The plane landed. My self-confidence was greater than that of all the passengers put together. I quickly got myself a taxi, asked the driver to take me to the hotel as quickly as he could, had the receptionist arrange a room for me as quickly as he could, took a hot shower as quickly as I could, dried myself as quickly as I could, slipped on my comfortable pajamas as quickly as I could, settled myself in bed as quickly as I could, and went over my songs.

I hadn't been in bed long when I noticed it was dinnertime. I changed and went down to the restaurant, which faced the hotel lobby on one side and the garden on the other. The garden was neither Chinese nor Western. It was vulgar, delicately refined, confused, glamorous, mean, and sumptuous all at once. The waiter came over to me and asked in English, "Tea?" I said yes in Chinese. A look of contempt flashed over his face. I said, "Could you take my order, please?" "Sorry, just a moment." He then went straight over to a foreigner and asked respectfully, "Tea?" All the foreigners around me had been served, but I was still waiting "just a moment."

A compatriot with a big nose was sitting by himself at a table across from me. He too seemed to have been kept waiting for a long while. He came over and said: "I know you. You've performed here, haven't you? I really enjoyed it."

"Thank you."

"You see the way Chinese treat Chinese?" He looked at the waiter. "You won't find this anywhere else in the world. No self-respect at all!"

I smiled a forced smile.

"I like the way you sing."

"Thank you."

"And your songs too."

"Thank you."

"They're really marvelous."

"Thank you."

"Natural."

"Thank you."

"You are casual, unpretentious, not stagy. Some singers are too much like actresses I don't like it songs must be sung with feeling must be sung naturally properly a singer must take the audience through many different emotions must express his distinctive personality in the singing must convey sentiments that are moving you want to make people feel as moved as you are you have to exert an influence over the audience you have to be natural to be real to reveal your true feelings to . . ."

In the valleys late autumn set in. Mountain winds entangled themselves with the evening light; tree branches disturbed the peace and quiet of the night. Still searching and still unsuccessful, we were each deep in our own thoughts. Lying on the ground beneath a starry sky, with the winds blowing around us, we felt relaxed, numb. The winds dispersed one's spirit like an anesthetic; it was as if they wanted to take your physical substance and dissolve it into the vastness and haziness of the surroundings. Breath melted, conversations melted, gestures melted, leg wounds melted, desires melted, feelings too melted. The solid physical substance moved near the stars one moment, fell to the ground the next; the four limbs reached out into their surroundings one moment, retracted the next and disappeared. Perhaps all original forms were making themselves visible at this moment. The stars, trees, weeds, stones, human beings, hares, wolves, pheasants—none of these could actually talk, each was a particle in the air and each had simply borrowed a physical body in order to wander about the earth. Why do human beings insist they can talk? Why is it said that stars can talk?

And why is it said too that wolves, hares, pheasants, and even the sea can talk?

At that time, there were only two colors on earth: darkness was trying with all its might to hold the atmosphere in its grasp, while a silver color poured down trying to save the living. All of a sudden, a strange sound came on the wind, came moving through the air currents. It seemed to have come from under the earth, it also seemed to have come from the sky. It seemed as if hundreds and thousands of spirits were there matchmaking for all things and for heaven and earth, bringing enlightenment to all living creatures and awakening them from oblivion and ignorance.

"Do you hear it?" B asked me.

"Yes."

"He has finally come." B's eyes brightened with excitement.

We followed the sound and walked toward that place, we kept walking toward that place. The sound came intermittently, so did the silver color in the sky. B, you've finally found what you wanted. You're going to win. You feel great, don't you? You've found what you wanted. We can go home now.

A cliff appeared before us. At the top of the cliff a huge rock jutted out, forming a platform. A group of singing spirits were sitting in a circle; others were climbing up the cliff from the foot of the mountain. Those on the platform were swaying their bodies and calling sonorously, their eyes fixed on the moon. The slow crescendo of their calling was like the rising tide swallowing the dark night. There was no leader here and no audience; everyone was enveloped in the solemn atmosphere, the naked bodies reflecting the silver light.

I was still standing there stunned when I discovered that B was taking off his clothes. He stripped himself naked and ran toward the cliff. I wanted to shout after him, but was afraid that I might destroy the harmony of the night. B had gone over and climbed up onto the platform. He now stood among the singing spirits, and called sonorously to the moon.

None of the singing spirits looked at him; no one paid him any attention. All the silver light of the universe was gathering there on the platform. A group of dark naked bodies were swaying and dancing: it was impossible to tell B from the others. Fatigue, cold, damp, and the insects began to attack me. I stood in the shadows, enveloped by darkness. I did not have the courage to go naked to that platform where the light was, and I could not go back. The singing spirits never stopped swaying, never stopped calling. Everything was singing, was the spirit of the universe. This lasted until the darkness gradually faded and the calling of the singing spirits, and their human forms, gradually disappeared into the clouds. Then the fog rose, everything was enveloped in white. Suddenly, the light of dawn and B appeared together before me. He was the only one on the platform who was still looking at a moon that had long lost its luster. Down in the valley, the sun had risen; people were up and about. Up here, everything was still enveloped in white.

"Well, here comes your food. Time I went and had mine." Noticing my strange look, Big-Nose returned, embarrassed, to his table.

I wanted to say, "Sorry, I was distracted." But I said nothing and just leaned slightly forward; the words wouldn't come.

IT WAS A huge stadium. Since the show featured all the top performing artists, it was completely sold out, and the stadium was now packed. The singers, male and female, were all gorgeously dressed, everything they were wearing was a masterpiece created by a top craftsman. A female singer was noisily complaining about her pleated skirt not being properly ironed. A big-eared, fatheaded male singer, who'd just had plastic surgery to give him double-fold eyelids, kept rolling his eyes at people. Electronic sounds darted back and forth, whistling through the auditorium. Flashes of laser light dazzled the eyes. The footlights kept on changing color. I sat alone on the floor in a corner backstage, my head buried between my knees. I felt more nervous than I ever had before, not knowing what this performance would bring. Perhaps it was

time to seek my fortune with cards or by divination; but at this moment
I wouldn't have taken anybody's word for anything. I had a protective
talisman from Lin Xi—he had given it to me as a gift specially for this
occasion, wishing me success. Gu Peng had given me a photo which
he took of me five years ago, you could read that face at a glance. I had
even brought B's photo along. I took all these things from my pocket. At
first I had wanted to go onstage wearing this coat with large pockets.
I had bought it from a peasant in the mountains. It was made of coarse
hand-woven cotton, printed and dyed with large decorative patterns
by the peasants. I took all my things from the pockets to reduce my
burden. Then, after careful consideration, I took off the coat too. My
trousers were also made of homespun cloth. With the coat off, I was
left with a printed short-sleeve jacket—the type worn by peasants. The
only fancy thing I had on was a gold chain with a purple spar on it. It
was my turn now. I went out in my short-sleeve jacket and the trousers made of homespun cloth. The minute I went onstage, there was a
commotion in the audience; I couldn't help but take a step back. Electronic music roared like thunder in my ears. I looked at the vast crowd
before me, but felt only emptiness in my heart. I forced a wry smile,
then I drifted toward the microphone. Still the same songs, the same
stereotyped songs that earned loud applause. People never seem to tire
of these songs. They're so easy to learn. All you need to make a living
as a singer is to control the tone color, stay in tune, and sway a bit with
the music. I swayed gently and looked around me. There was no one I
knew. Everyone was smiling; everyone was enraptured. When the first
song came to an end, there was applause and loud whistling. Same for
the next one. How long would I have to sway like this? How long would
I have to smile like this? My throat went dry. My eyes swept over the
audience, but I saw no one I knew, no one whatsoever; there would be
no miracles. Amid the applause, I retreated backstage, but was invited
by the announcer to take a curtain call. I took a deep bow, hoping that
the audience would stop applauding. After all, I only wanted to make
some money for B's concert. The songs I sang were all "crap." But people were still whistling and applauding, and the electronic music rang

out again. I gestured to the band and they stopped playing, looking at me in bewilderment. The audience too suddenly became quiet. I walked up to the microphone and said, "Please switch off the overhead lights; please switch off the footlights too. Thank you." There was darkness everywhere. Then I said, "Please give me a spotlight over there." A beam of white light appeared to my left. "Thank you, thank you." There was complete silence. I really wanted to walk naked into the white light, as B had done, but I hesitated. I didn't move. Standing in the dark, outside the white light, I felt surrounded once more by the cold, the damp, and the insects. I saw innumerable singing spirits calling to the moon. I would never walk into that beam of silver light; I would always have to stand on the outside, in the dark; I would never be a singing spirit, never see the King of Singers; all I could do was stand here, waiting, waiting. B, will you appear again with the light of day?

September 17, 1985

(Translated by Martha Cheung)

YANG LIAN

(1955–)

Born in Switzerland to parents who were Chinese diplomats, Yang Lian grew up in Beijing and began writing in his late teens as the tumultuous Cultural Revolution was winding down. A participant in the Beijing Democracy Wall Movement in 1978, Yang was also an important contributor to the underground journal Today. *In 1983, Yang published his long poem "Norlang," which taps deep into the mythological past and present of China, searching for a reality beyond what is dictated by ideology. His work soon became a target of criticism during the Anti-Spiritual Pollution Campaign launched by the government. Winner of the Nonino International Literature Prize in 2012 and the International Capri Prize in 2014, Yang has lived in self-imposed exile in Europe since 1988.*

Norlang

*A Tibetan male deity. There is a waterfall and a snowcapped mountain on the
high plateau between Sichuan and Gansu, named after this god.*

Suntide

The plateau like a raging tiger
     burns at the shore of creation's torrent
Light! There is only light;
      the setting sun floods
      in a perfect sphere
      earth hangs in space

The pirate sail opens to the arm,
      rock to chest
      eagle to heart
The shepherd's solitude swallowed
      in the endlessly undulating brush
The prayer-flag fluttering
      a sad, shrill faith
      slowly rising through the azure

For which departed cloud
      do you stand in silent tribute now?
Crawling beneath the feet of the ages,
      enduring the demands of the dusk
A myriad tombstones like plows
      drop anchor at the wasteland's end
Abandoned by each other, forever abandoned:
      returning copper to earth,
      letting the fresh blood rust

Are you still pouring tears
          upon every thunderclap?
Each year the west wind wakes the gold-panner's fate
          from the gravelly deeps
The cliffside trail has collapsed
          there is no path along the precipice
          the sundial in the cave is black
And the heavens of the ancient shaman once again reveal
          the riddle of the seven lotus flowers

Light! Sacred crimson glaze
          fire-worship
          fire-dance
Lave the soft moans
          bestow upon the firmament
          the tranquillity of a shattered urn
Are you finally roused by this vast moment?
—the sun waits
          in ecstasy
          for the meteoric
          apocalypse

Golden Tree

I am god of the waterfall,
          I am god of the snow mountain
Mighty master of the crescent moon
Leader of all rivers
The sparrow makes his nest in my bosom
The dense grove conceals
          the path to the secret pool
My passion like a herd of bucks
          newly come of age

My desire like the spring season
Condenses tumult

I am a golden tree
Gold-harvest tree
Fierce challenge rises from the abyss
Casts aside the admonitions of timid bystanders
Until my wave
  fills it to the brim

Roaming woman
  surface glistening
Who is she
  this woman that compels me to drink?

My gaze holds back the night
Twelve horns hold back the pomegranate wind
Every place I come to
  is without shadow
Every berry touched is a bright star
  in the center of the universe
  rising
Possessing you
  I
  the true man

Blood Sacrifice

Cluster the crimson pattern on the white skull,
  make an offering to sun and war
With blood of sacrificial infant
  blood of circumcision
Nourish my never-broken life

Obsidian knife rips earth's chest
        heart raised high
Countless banners like the drumbeat of a wrestling master
        raging in the sunset
I live, I smile,
        I lead you proudly to conquer death
—sign your name in blood for history
        adorn the ruins
        the ceremony

And so,
        wipe out your sorrows!
        Let the precipice
        seal in the mountain spirit
The vulture dives and dives again
        like a gusting tempest
        pecking eye sockets clean
On the bitter sacrificial altar
        the racing
        falling bodies
        bloom
Long-lost hopes return
        on the sharp edge of starvation
        casting screams and eulogies
Where have you learned to discover
        the solitary grandeur of the arched horizon?
Therefore
        let the blood flow
        the glory of meeting death
        is stronger than death

Pay tribute to me! Forty virgins will sing
        for your good fortune

Burned bodies like bronze bells
  parade at the fast and during the watch
That nobly abject
  innocently criminal
  purely filthy
  tide
Vast memory
  my mystery accompanies
  the shuddering ecstasy
  continuously becoming
  being born
The pagoda towers aloft
  guiding the mountain dusk
  on a heavenward path
You are free—
  from the pool of blood
  approach the divine

Gatha

Despairing of expectation
Expectant with despair

Expectation is endless despair
Despair is perfect expectation

Expectation may never begin
Despair may never end

The summons may only sound once
The greatest resonance is stillness

Midnight Celebration

A form based on a folk-elegy of Sichuan, using the original section headings

1. INTROIT

Lead:

Midnight had fallen, brilliant darkness unfolds its tiger skin, radiates a brilliant green. Distance. The fragrance of the grass touches our hearts, the dew dampens the heavens. Who has gathered us together?

Chorus:

Oh, so many! So many!

Lead:

The constellations have tilted, imperceptibly sleep fills with the wind soughing in the pines, blowing through strange arms. We are squeezed tightly together, dreaming of a bonfire, big and bright. The children also sleep.

Chorus:

Oh, so many! So many!

Lead:

Our souls tremble, they thirst, searching for a space amid the pitch-black leaves. Behind the vertiginous silence there is a sound, slowly melting into moonlight. Is this then the light we have been searching for?

Chorus:

Oh, so many! So many!

2. PIERCING THE FLOWER

This is the proclamation of Norlang:
The one road is a transparent road

The only road is a supple road
I say this: follow that stream of praise
The sunset has precipitated
 the flow of blood has melted
Guide of the waterfall
 of the snow mountain
Women
 smiling
 rippling
 naked
 alluring
Come from every corner,
 dancing
 to bathe
Transcend illusion
 partake of my purity

3. CODA

Now
 the plateau like a raging tiger
 receives the infinite caress of transparent fingers
Now
 the tousled forest spreads its ravaged beauty,
 resplendent, stark beauty
Announcing
 to the mountain torrent
 to the gravel-heaped destruction of the village
 the harmony of the universe
Tree roots
 like thick ankles
 keep stubbornly walking
The homeless children
 smile

Pride identity
    rise up from within death
    the lily plays the music of my divinity
My light
    illumines you
    even in your meteoric
    fall
A golden summons
    returns anguish to the sea
    the never-tranquil sea
Over the black night
    over oblivion
    over the twittering, faint cry of dream talk
Now
    in the center of the universe
    I say: live on—
Heaven and earth have begun.
    Birds are calling. All
    nearly
    a revelation

        (Translated by Alisa Joyce,
            with John Minford)

Burial Ground

from the Poem-cycle *Banpo*

1

DEATH AND MASKS

Good-bye, storms; good-bye, sun—

Planetary masquerade, you'll never find me
However your sudden backward glance may seem to catch my eye

Don't worry, we can't hurt each other now
Jeers and curses, tears and lies, after my death
Bother me no more than the maggots in my ears

Look! Living steles walk on the yellow earth
Grow tall and black like a raven sky
I lie underground, my contempt for the gods complete

For men, I need only one mask: tears, laughter
You'll never find me, you can't kill me again
Here, I feel safe at last—thank you

2

FUNERAL PROCESSION

North of the village, the road vanishes, calm begins;
       Who am I?
North of the village,
       A muddy stream of people draped in tenebral night;
       Whose are these two hands that raise me?
Avoided by the sun, surging like the tide;
       Who takes this last step for me?
Dirge;
       Who gives me this somber, ancestral cadence?
Earth;
       Who are these travelers by my side,
          with their faces like stone?
Suddenly distant, stranger!
       Who digs my grave?

Gathered together in haste, roaming far away;
   Who shares this warm darkness with me?
Body silent, soul raging;
   Whose is the wailing that surrounds me?

The road vanishes, calm begins; in the anticipated distress,
   Whose name shall I question first?
History, humble funeral rites of mighty mankind;
   Whom shall I raise with my hands?
Robbing eyes of water, seeping breathing eagles;
   For whom have I taken this last step?
Within the yellow earth and without;
   Whom shall I bid follow the somber, ancestral cadence?
Earth, long forged into a cauldron of torture;
   Whose crimes shall I declare?
O wind, the grassland is scorched black!
   For whom shall I dig a grave?
From one mistake to the next, from one home to another;
   Whom shall I meet again in the warm darkness?
Heart, a black cat, claws hope;
   Whom shall I surround with my wailing?

3

DESCENT

She was her mother's dear child
Softly drifting down like a snowflake
She was the glimmering evergreen in her own dreams
The sun's patterned kerchief was torn
Removed an expanse of damp shade
Who knows why

The trembling earth failed to catch her
A tiny petal of white
She fell into a cold gray urn
Buried with strung stone beads and ear pendants
Buried with unfinished dreams
Who knows why

(Translated by Pang Bingjun and John Minford,
with Sean Golden)

The Book of Exile

You are not here   Marks of this pen
Just written are swept off by a wild wind
Emptiness like a dead bird soars across your face
Funereal moon is a broken hand
Turning back your days
Back to the page when you do not exist
In writing   You
Bask in your deletion

Like another's voice
Bits of bones are spat carelessly in a corner
Hollow sound of water brushing water
Carelessly enters breathing
Enters a pear and ceases to look at others
Skulls all over the ground are you
In words and lines you grow old in a night
Your poetry invisibly traversing the world

—January 13, 1990

Masks and Crocodile (selections)

1

    Masks are born of faces
        copy faces
    but ignore faces

masks   are born on blank pages
 cover the blankness
but still there is only blankness

2

    This word has your face
        intricately carved
woodenly polished a thousand times

    finally   forgotten torn down
      spread out all bloody
      you hear God retching

3

    Faces crumble silently
     nightmares in the flesh
inch by inch chisel you away

      shipwrecks
    and fallen-out teeth
chatter with mud and slime
               (Translated by Mabel Lee)

CAN XUE
(1953–)

With a declared ambition to out-Kafka Kafka, Can Xue, born in Hunan to parents both condemned as "Rightists" in Mao's era, is a contemporary writer with a unique style and exceptional talent. Despite only an elementary school education, she taught herself English and read foreign literature voraciously. After years of manual labor, first as a factory worker and then as a seamstress, she began writing at the age of thirty. In 1985 she published her first story, "Yellow Mud Street," followed by a collection of short stories two years later. Sensitive, sharp, and absurdist, her work quickly drew national and international attention. A member of China's Writers Association, she now lives in Beijing.

Hut on the Mountain

On the bleak and barren mountain behind our house stood a wooden hut.

Day after day I busied myself by tidying up my desk drawers. When I wasn't doing that I would sit in the armchair, my hands on my knees, listening to the tumultuous sounds of the north wind whipping against the fir-bark roof of the hut, and the howling of the wolves echoing in the valleys.

"Huh, you'll never get done with those drawers," said Mother, forcing a smile. "Not in your lifetime."

"There's something wrong with everyone's ears," I said with suppressed annoyance. "There are so many thieves wandering about our house in the moonlight, when I turn on the light I can see countless tiny holes poked by fingers in the window screens. In the next room, Father and you snore terribly, rattling the utensils in the kitchen cabinet. Then I kick about in my bed, turn my swollen head on the pillow, and hear the man locked up in the hut banging furiously against the door. This goes on till daybreak."

"You give me a terrible start," Mother said, "every time you come into my room looking for things." She fixed her eyes on me as she backed toward the door. I saw the flesh of one of her cheeks contort ridiculously.

One day I decided to go up to the mountain to find out what on earth was the trouble. As soon as the wind let up, I began to climb. I climbed and climbed for a long time. The sunshine made me dizzy. Tiny white flames were flickering among the pebbles. I wandered about, coughing all the time. The salty sweat from my forehead was streaming into my eyes. I couldn't see or hear anything. When I reached home, I stood outside the door for a while and saw that the person reflected in the mirror had mud on her shoes and dark purple pouches under her eyes.

"It's some disease, " I heard them snickering in the dark.

When my eyes became adapted to the darkness inside, they'd hidden themselves—laughing in their hiding places. I discovered they had made a mess of my desk drawers while I was out. A few dead moths and dragonflies were scattered on the floor—they knew only too well that these were treasures to me.

"They sorted the things in the drawers for you," little sister told me, "when you were out." She stared at me, her left eye turning green.

"I hear wolves howling." I deliberately tried to scare her. "They keep running around the house. Sometimes they poke their heads in through the cracks in the door. These things always happen after dusk. You get so scared in your dreams that cold sweat drips from the soles of your feet. Everyone in this house sweats this way in his sleep. You have only to see how damp the quilts are."

I felt upset because some of the things in my desk drawers were missing. Keeping her eyes on the floor, Mother pretended she knew nothing about it. But I had a feeling she was glaring ferociously at the back of my head, since the spot would become numb and swollen whenever she did that. I also knew they had buried a box with my chess set by the well behind the house. They had done it many times, but each time I would dig the chess set out. When I dug for it, they would turn on the light and poke their heads out the window. In the face of my defiance they always tried to remain calm.

"Up there on the mountain," I told them at mealtime, "there is a hut."

They all lowered their heads, drinking soup noisily. Probably no one heard me.

"Lots of big rats were running wildly in the wind." I raised my voice and put down the chopsticks. "Rocks were rolling down the mountain and crashing into the back of our house. And you were so scared cold sweat dripped from your soles. Don't you remember? You only have to look at your quilts. Whenever the weather's fine, you're airing the quilts; the clothesline out there is always strung with them."

Father stole a glance at me with one eye, which, I noticed, was the all-too-familiar eye of a wolf. So that was it! At night he became one of the wolves running around the house, howling and wailing mournfully.

"White lights are swaying back and forth everywhere." I clutched Mother's shoulder with one hand. "Everything is so glaring that my eyes blear from the pain. You simply can't see a thing. But as soon as I return to my room, sit down in my armchair, and put my hands on my knees, I can see the fir-bark roof clearly. The image seems very close. In fact, every one of us must have seen it. Really, there's somebody squatting inside. He's got two big purple pouches under his eyes too, because he stays up all night."

Father said, "Every time you dig by the well and hit stone with a screeching sound, you make Mother and me feel as if we were hanging in midair. We shudder at the sound and kick with bare feet but can't reach the ground." To avoid my eyes, he turned his face toward the window, the panes of which were thickly specked with fly droppings.

"At the bottom of the well," he went on, "there's a pair of scissors which I dropped some time ago. In my dreams I always make up my mind to fish them out. But as soon as I wake, I realize I've made a mistake. In fact, no scissors have ever fallen into the well. Your mother says positively that I've made a mistake. But I will not give up. It always steals into my mind again. Sometimes while I'm in bed, I am suddenly seized with regret: the scissors lie rusting at the bottom of the well, why shouldn't I go fish them out? I've been troubled by this for dozens of years. See my wrinkles? My face seems to have become furrowed. Once I actually went to the well and tried to lower a bucket into it. But the rope was thick and slippery. Suddenly my hands lost their grip and the bucket flopped with a loud boom, breaking into pieces in the well. I rushed back to the house, looked into the mirror, and saw the hair on my left temple had turned completely white."

"How that north wind pierces!" I hunched my shoulders. My face turned black and blue with cold. "Bits of ice are forming in my stomach. When I sit down in my armchair I can hear them clinking away."

I had been intending to give my desk drawers a cleaning, but Mother was always stealthily making trouble. She'd walk to and fro in the next room, stamping, stamping, to my great distraction. I tried to ignore it, so I got a pack of cards and played, murmuring, "One, two, three, four, five . . ."

The pacing stopped all of a sudden and Mother poked her small dark green face into the room and mumbled, "I had a very obscene dream. Even now my back is dripping cold sweat."

"And your soles too," I added. "Everyone's soles drip cold sweat. You aired your quilt again yesterday. It's usual enough."

Little sister sneaked in and told me that Mother had been thinking of breaking my arms because I was driving her crazy by opening and shutting the drawers. She was so tortured by the sound that every time she heard it, she'd soak her head in cold water until she caught a bad cold.

"This didn't happen by chance." Sister's stares were always so pointed that tiny pink measles broke out on my neck. "For example, I've heard Father talking about the scissors for perhaps twenty years. Everything has its own cause from way back. Everything."

So I oiled the sides of the drawers. And by opening and shutting them carefully, I managed to make no noise at all. I repeated this experiment for many days and the pacing in the next room ceased. She was fooled. This proves you can get away with anything as long as you take a little precaution. I was very excited over my success and worked hard all night. I was about to finish tidying my drawers when the light suddenly went out. I heard Mother's sneering laugh in the next room.

"That light from your room glares so that it makes all my blood vessels throb and throb, as though some drums were beating inside. Look," she said, pointing to her temple, where the blood vessels bulged like fat earthworms. "I'd rather get scurvy. There are throbbings throughout my body day and night. You have no idea how I'm suffering. Because of this ailment, your father once thought of committing suicide." She put her fat hand on my shoulder, an icy hand dripping with water.

Someone was making trouble by the well. I heard him letting the bucket down and drawing it up, again and again; the bucket hit against the wall of the well—boom, boom, boom. At dawn, he dropped the bucket with a loud bang and ran away. I opened the door of the next room and saw Father sleeping with his vein-ridged hand clutching the bedside, groaning in agony. Mother was beating the floor here and there with a broom; her hair was disheveled. At the moment of daybreak, she told me, a huge swarm of hideous beetles flew in through the window. They bumped against the walls and flopped onto the floor, which now was scattered with their remains. She got up to tidy the room, and as she was putting her feet into her slippers, a hidden bug bit her toe. Now her whole leg was swollen like a thick lead pipe.

"He"—Mother pointed to Father, who was sleeping stuporously— "is dreaming it is he who is bitten."

"In the little hut on the mountain, someone is groaning too. The black wind is blowing, carrying grape leaves along with it."

"Do you hear?" In the faint light of morning, Mother put her ear against the floor, listening with attention. "These bugs hurt themselves in their fall and passed out. They charged into the room earlier, at the moment of daybreak."

I did go up to the mountain that day, I remember. At first I was sitting in the cane chair, my hands on my knees. Then I opened the door and walked into the white light. I climbed up the mountain, seeing nothing but the white pebbles glowing with flames.

There were no grapevines, nor any hut.

(Translated by Ronald R. Janssen and Jian Zhang)

WANG ANYI
(1954–)

Born in Nanjing and brought up in Shanghai, Wang Anyi is the daughter of two writers who were labeled "Rightists" in Mao's era. At the age of sixteen, she was sent to the countryside in Anhui, a remote region plagued by famine. Two years later, she joined a local troupe as a cellist. Returning to Shanghai in 1978, she began writing fiction. Her love trilogy, Love on a Barren Mountain *(1986),* Love in a Small Town *(1986), and* Love in a Beauteous Valley *(1987), all novels of daring exploration of a once-taboo topic—sexual awakening—propelled her into the national limelight. Currently the vice chairperson of China's Writers Association, she teaches creative writing at Fudan University.*

Love in a Small Town (excerpt)

They had been together since they were very young, dancing in the same ballet troupe. They both danced in "The Red Detachment of Women"; she was in the "Dance of the Little Soldiers" and he the "Dance of the Children Brigade." She excelled on pointe because of the amount of training she had in the propaganda team at school; she had worn through several pairs of ordinary cloth shoes practicing her pointe work, and when she finally switched over to flat-topped ballet shoes, she felt ever so light and sure-footed, as if she had been doing weight-training and had just discarded the sandbags tied to her feet. His waist and legs were particularly pliant and strong because he used to study with a teacher who was also knowledgeable in the martial arts; he could do *tours jetés*, somersaults, anything required of him. Bending backward, he could stretch till his head touched his feet; in his *balancé* to the back, the tip of his foot would touch the back of his head. He was really good. She was then only twelve, and he a few years older, just sixteen.

Two years have passed. The excitement over "The Red Detachment of Women" has subsided, and the troupe is rehearsing "On the Yimeng Mountains." A teacher from the Dance Department of the Provincial Performing Arts School has come to conduct a day's class with the troupe, and in just one day's time has found out that they have destroyed their physiques through incorrect training. They don't have muscles, just flesh with neither flexibility nor strength. The teacher even pulls her to the middle of the studio, and turning her around, points out to everyone her typically deformed legs, hips, and shoulders. And the problems are indeed serious; she has thick legs, thick arms, a thick waist, and very broad hips. Her breasts are twice the normal size, protruding like small hills, hardly like a fourteen-year-old's. The whole troupe, under the prompting of the Provincial School dance teacher, scrutinizes her body, and it makes her feel awful. Naturally she is ashamed, and to overcome this sense of shame she puts on a proud and disdainful look, holding her head high, throwing her chest out, and looking at others out of the corners of her eyes as though they were beneath her.

At this time she is half a head taller than him. Something must have gone wrong with his body; he has just stopped growing, and though he is eighteen, he still looks very much a child. He can only perform children's roles, and yet when he is in costume as a child, his face is obviously that of a grown-up. In fact he looks much older than his real age. If he weren't such a good dancer, the leaders of the troupe would probably have to think twice about retaining him.

Though neither of them is a principal dancer, they both work hard. In the early mornings and late evenings they are the only people in the studio. Even in cold weather they strip down to flimsy practice clothes, and they don't have to come near to smell each other's sweat and odor, at once sweet and repellent. His odor is strong, hers no less so. Her roommates, young girls with limited knowledge of such matters, all say she has B.O. and refuse to sleep in the bed next to hers. She doesn't care, and even thinks: "Well, even if it is B.O., you haven't got it. It's the things few people have that are really precious!" But this is just a thought. She nevertheless feels a little sad, and a little inferior. What she doesn't know is it has nothing to do with B.O., just a strong natural odor. Sometimes when they take a break during practice to catch their breath, they will look at each other and, breathing deeply, she will say out of curiosity: "Oh, you smell like watermelon." Then he will lower his head to one side, raise his arm and sniff at his armpit, and reply with a laugh: "My sweat is sweet; that's why in summer all the mosquitoes come after me." And sure enough, there are tiny brown scars all over his fair skin; traces of summer left there, never to go away. And then he will exclaim in a surprised tone: "You smell like steamed dough!" She too will raise her arm and sniff at her armpit, and reply: "My sweat is sour; mosquitoes don't like me." And her dark skin really is smooth, without even the tiniest mark. They will both laugh, a little short of breath, and then resume their practice.

They mostly practice on their own, but sometimes they also help each other out. Her legs are not very turned out, and he helps her loosen up. She lies on her back on the floor, draws her feet up toward her buttocks, and he pushes her knees down until they touch the floor on either side. When she finally gets up, a damp human shape is left on the red-painted floor, its legs bent outward exactly like a frog's. It takes a while for this silhouette to evaporate. He practices pirouettes around and around the silhouette, as if encircled by an invisible wall, stopping only when the silhouette disappears into the floorboards.

He wishes that he could grow a few centimeters taller, and has the notion that the elasticity of the tendons is crucial to this, so he tries hard to loosen up. He stands on one leg with his back against the wall and, stiffening the other leg, asks her to push it toward his head. She pushes hard, her face against the curve of his calf. He always stands against the wall at one end of the bar as they do this, and with time there appears on the whitewashed wall a yellowish human form standing on one leg, never to go away. When she stands at that end with one leg on the bar to loosen up, she is face-to-face with this one-legged man, and she thinks it's fun to trace a line from one foot mark to the other.

They practice diligently, he no taller for it, and she much rounder and fleshier. She's tall, all right, yet far from slim. Time passes, and they are one year older.

THIS IS A SMALL TOWN bounded by three or four rivers, with a very narrow road leading to the railway. The best things about it are its trees—elms, willows, poplars, cedars, peach, plum, apricot, date, and persimmon—all fresh and green. If you travel on a ferry coming down-river, you'll see this green delta with its luxuriant vegetation a long way off; as you come closer, you will see the houses of gray and red bricks; and coming still closer, you will hear the watermen singing their work songs in a quite unaffected manner. People in this town are used to drinking river water, and get diarrhea every time they drink well water. The watermen's business is to deliver river water to the town folks. The water is transported in oil drums on large carts, and spills over now and then as the carts jolt along the bumpy paths. Ruts left by the cartwheels, some shallow, some deep, crisscross the paths along the banks. As the carts rumble from one rut to another, the wheels hit against the sides of the ruts and the waterman's voice lingers on one trembling note very rhythmically. Just as one cart trembles off into the distance, another announces itself as it comes along, and so it continues, as much a part of the town as the luxuriant woods. And then the ferry resumes its jour-ney, leaving behind several dozen passengers and a dozen or so peddlers carrying baskets on shoulder poles. They cross the wobbly gangway to the bank, and then follow the earthen path to the main street.

Most streets in town are paved with stone slabs, polished by the feet of pedestrians, baked warm in the sun. It's really comfortable walking on them wearing cloth-soled shoes and feeling the heat under your feet. The shoulder poles bob up and down as the peddlers' feet flap on the stone slabs, each step evoking an echo. When the peddlers reach the main street, they put down their baskets, filled with chives, the first harvest of the year, so fresh that the morning dew is still shining on them. That day, nine out of ten households in town eat dumplings stuffed with chives, and the fragrance fills the streets. The baskets, emptied of chives, are filled up with fried snacks, and leisurely the peddlers carry them away.

A horse cart rattles along the street, heading south to buy hay. On the cart a bedsheet is hoisted as a sail. The old horse labors on, head down, while an unbridled pony gallops alongside, joyfully shaking its head and flicking its tail, lifting its slim legs ever so high. At times it runs ahead, at times it lags behind, and at times it heads off in all directions. It knocks over an old lady's black-jelly stall, but nobody minds. They all make way for it and let it get on with its antics.

On some walls the whitewash has peeled off, leaving bare the gray bricks underneath. Big posters are pasted on these walls, billing films shown in the cinema and plays put on in the theater. A cinema ticket costs ten cents, a theater ticket thirty cents. In the cinema things are just projected onto the screen, though the actors are really good; in the theater you see real people performing, but they are less accomplished, so the pricing is fair. In the evenings both play to a full house, just the right number of people to fill up both places, so it's quite perfect.

At night, when all the peddlers are gone and all the shops are shut, the street is pitch-black; only the stones shine in the crystal-clear moonlight. Doors are shut, then windows are shut, and then even the lights are extinguished. Children begin to dream about the days when they will be grown-ups; old-timers sit thinking, or relive the memories of their younger days. Those who are neither old nor young have another kind of pleasure, moving in the dark, planting the seeds of life. This time next year, the town will hear the wailing of new inhabitants.

Now, there is nothing but pitch-black silence.

In the cinema, only the screen is lit up, and human images move on

it, enacting the joys and sorrows of life. In the theater, the stage glitters
and dazzles, and real people take on fictional roles.

THEY NEVER STOP practicing; they can't even if they want to. If they
stopped, she would get even fatter and thicker, and he, because his body
has refused to grow even one centimeter taller, cannot afford to gain the
slightest weight, as that would make him look even shorter. And so they
continue to practice relentlessly.

But actually it's not all hard work; sometimes it can even be fun.
Her figure has developed in such a way that she looks awful whatever
she wears, and is clumsy whatever she does. It's only when she takes
her clothes off, leaving only the leotard, that her proportions become
more pleasing. When she is engaged in dance movements, movements
uncalled-for in daily life, a good feeling surges inside her. She looks into
the mirrors around her, and thinks to herself: "It's unfair to say I'm
ugly, and it's unfair to say I'm clumsy." Drops of sweat roll down her
satin-smooth skin, like pearls. Her hair, all wet, sticks to her long thick
neck. It grows down low, extending almost to the point where the neck
is joined to the back. The short hairs on her neck are always getting wet,
then drying off, and as a result become all curly. When the sun shines
on this curly hair, in profile she looks like a little lamb.

He too looks more lithe when he's in practice clothes. Besides, since
he's technically superior to most people, what does it matter if his
physique isn't perfect? When he tries out some really difficult steps,
he experiences a sense of elation. He takes off his vest, revealing his
extremely white but coarse back. Acne spreads profusely all over his
face and his body; it is as though the nutrition he absorbs must have an
outlet, and since he gains neither height nor weight, all the nutrition and
energy go toward nurturing his spots, which are like small red beans, a
sign of his youthful vigor. When the spots gradually subside, they leave
behind small brown hollows like wells. His back, in particular, is full of
such hollows, and strongly resembles the rough surface of a rock. Each
brown well is filled with a drop of sweat, clear and transparent.

Sweating is like taking a shower; it cleanses the dirt from even the deepest recesses of the body. After sweating, one feels extremely relaxed and carefree.

There is only a small room with a cement floor for having a wash-down. It's right next to the pantry, and the pantry is right next to a water pump, so they can mix the right amount of hot and cold water and then carry it into the washroom and put it on a small cement platform. Under the platform there is a drain, and at the back of the door hooks for hanging clothes. That's all there is for furnishing. Both men and women use this room, and if the door is closed, one has to shout: "Anyone in there?" and the person inside shouts back: "Occupied." If it's a woman's voice from inside, the man outside turns back and waits till she finishes, and vice versa. Otherwise the person inside unhooks the lock and stands behind the door, and then locks up again when the person outside has entered.

When the weather is hot, this room is quite crowded, and arguments frequently arise. But in winter it's deserted. Since it is a windowless, north-facing room with no sunlight all day and nothing to keep it warm, it can be very cold. The unpainted wooden door is half open, revealing the naked cement floor, whitened with constant washing. If it weren't for the little pools of water left on the floor by the two of them taking turns to shower every day, the room would be even more desolate. He always lets her have her wash first, while she is still sweating from the exercise, so that she won't feel too cold, but still she dares not stay too long, for she will soon feel the piercing cold. While he is waiting, to keep his body warm he continues practicing, doing *grand jetés* around the room. Every time he comes to the north windows he seems to hear the sound of water splashing in the washroom. He can't help but see in his mind's eye water flowing down her smooth, broad back, then diverging into two streams, running down her elephantine legs until it reaches the ground and runs over the cement floor.

One day she didn't shift her feet throughout her wash-down, and when he carried his water into the room he saw that amid the little pools of water on the floor there were two footprints, completely dry, left there by a pair of feet wearing soft rubber slippers. He stared at the footprints, and gradually he traced a pair of ankles, calves, knees, thighs, and up he went, until it seemed that the whole person was standing in front of him. Before he realized it, his water had turned cold.

The next day he bought her an apple-green plastic bucket, remembering that she had complained about the basin being too small, saying even two basins of water weren't enough for a good wash. A bucketful should be quite enough, he thought.

Maybe with more water she enjoys her wash more, and no more dry footprints appear on the wet floor. All the footprints are drowned.

The bucket, filled with boiling water, flattens into an oval as she carries it in her hand. Sunlight shines through the apple-green sides, turning the water a tender shade of green, with a layer of pale green steam hovering over it. The water in the bucket shakes as she enters the small, dark room and disappears behind the unpainted and half-rotted wooden door. The room is extremely dark, with neither window nor lamp; only a narrow band of light seeps through from underneath the door. But there is some light on the bucket of water, luminous, a most tender green. The water is scalding. A dry, stiff towel gets soaked in no time. She lifts this towel, saturated with hot water, and puts it over her shoulder. She can feel the water running down her chest and back, like hundreds of needles pricking her skin. She sucks in her breath with a "schusch" and repeatedly dips the towel into the bucket, and splashes water over her body. The water in the bucket gradually diminishes, and the light dims. Now she starts to put on her clothes. She pushes the door open; the sunlight hurts her eyes like the touch of a passionate and violent lover. She is so happy! The sight of him sweating and still engaged in a continuous series of *grand jetés*, a dirty knee-band wrapped around his blackened leg, moves her to pity, and she generously lends him the bucket.

The next day, she takes the bucket he has returned to fetch water, but finds that he has not cleaned it after he used it. There is a little grayish water left at the bottom of the bucket, and on the sides a film of grayish particles. She is just about to tell him off, and then stops herself and stands in a daze. She tilts the bucket and looks around inside it. There are tiny particles in the greyish water too, and she can't help speculating what they might be—can these be flecks of his skin? She knows that not only sweat comes from the skin, but also that tiny flecks of skin are sloughed off; not dust or dirt, just flecks of skin. When she thinks of this she can't help resenting it. She fills the bucket with clean water, pours it away, and then half fills it again before she starts cleaning the sides. The plastic bucket seems rough to the touch somehow; something which she can't wash away titillates her palm. No matter how dark the room is, every time she scoops water up in her palms she sees tiny particles in it, particles swimming about like playful fish. On this day, even after her wash-down, she still feels unclean, and her back feels itchy. So she keeps moving her shoulders and back muscles about in some rather unseemly gestures. Her roommates resent her the more for it; some probably suspect that she has lice or something, though she washes every day, while they only go to the public bath once a week.

The women's public bath is exactly like the men's. It's a big pool, and bathers lower themselves into it much as dumplings are put into boiling water to cook. By afternoon the water becomes murky. Since the theatrical troupe enjoys a special status in town, on Saturday mornings, before the villagers come into town, the public bath is open to the troupe for two hours so the actors and actresses can have their wash first. The girls all bring their own washbasins and scoop water from the pool to wash themselves. When they are done, they walk out with their hair wet and hanging down, their faces glowing, and their dirty clothes in the basins which they balance on one hip much as the renowned ancient beauty Xishi did after she finished washing silk by the river. At the door of the public bathhouse the villagers are queuing, their faces dirty, their eyes gluey, and their bodies shivering. They look at the girls in wonder and admiration, trying hard to imagine what a blessed, royal life they lead.

On winter afternoons, there are always men and women walking about the streets, their faces glowing from the heat of the public bath.

The men and women with glowing faces, carrying baskets on shoulder poles or in their hands, or pulling carts, are satisfied, and hurry along the roads leading out of town. One of these roads leads to the pier, another goes north across the floodgate. In the evening the sun gradually sinks behind the three high red flags cut in the earth on top of the floodgate, and turns these discolored flags a deep red. This is the noisiest hour here below the gate; carts rumble past, interspersed with the solitary ringing of bicycle bells, and women wearing homemade shoes walking on the dusty cement road leave behind clear imprints of the even or uneven sewing on their soles. They hurry on while the sun is still shining. When they reach a dirt track, their footprints are lost in the shifting dust.

It is the dry season; it hasn't rained for three consecutive months. On the main road the loosened earth is a full inch thick, completely covering your feet as you walk. The fields are cracked, the ponds dry, the water from the wells murky, and the water level of the river below the dam has gone down, laying bare dark green moss. The setting sun is fiery. After sinking behind the floodgate it stays, as if by magic, behind a small green wood in the distance. Every small wood is a village you can see but can't reach, like a mirage.

Deep in the night when all is quiet the dogs start barking in the distance. The dogs in town don't bark, but then hundreds of cats create a commotion. At times like this their screeching shakes the whole town; they seem to be crying, or laughing, or panting, or sighing, and no one is able to sleep. Some bachelor jumps out of bed, grabs a shoulder pole, and hits at two cats blindly, trying to separate them, but they seem to have been glued together since birth. On closer look he finds they're two silent dogs. The cats have all gone and are continuing their heartrending cries elsewhere. The next morning the bachelor gets up with bloodshot eyes, curses the cats, then curses the dogs, and then looks up at the sky. It doesn't look like it's going to rain; he curses heaven. Lastly, he thinks of the couple from out of town who are staying in the secondary school; they actually wear pants with stripes and floral patterns. Though they only do it in the house, at bedtime, still, pants are pants; how can you have stripes and flowers on them? It's just not right.

|||||||||||||||

THEY HAVE WORKED diligently through a severe winter, and have now seen the coming of a dry spring. Her body is so rotund that it's impossible for it to grow anymore; it's like a ripened fruit, but the proportions are wrong. And his body seems as stubborn as his will; it is fixed, refuses to grow. Though she looks like an adult, she is still very childish. She never hides her feelings. She will be laughing one minute, crying the next, as changeable as the summer weather, and yet you don't feel that she's abnormal or affected, simply naive. When a group of girls goes on and on teasing a boy in the courtyard, and finally gets him to say: "At night my dad bites my mum's mouth," the others all laugh to themselves but pretend not to have heard and change the subject, while she falls about with laughter, completely losing control of herself. It's not only that she doesn't cover up for herself, she nullifies the others' efforts at evasion. They all turn red and try to stop her, but then she says, seemingly very knowledgeable: "The child knows nothing." The others just don't know what to make of her, and can only call her "Silly girl!" But she won't even put up with that, saying in protest: "Who says I'm silly? I know everything." All they can do is ignore her. As she grows more and more like a woman, her childishness and clumsiness become more apparent.

She still asks him to help her turn out her legs and loosen her joints, just as she used to when she was young. Though this task has become more and more difficult for him, he can't turn her down, and it has become a torture for him.

She lies before him, her legs bent in front of her chest, and slowly parts them to either side. He can't control the turmoil in his heart. He is panting loudly, almost suffocating with the effort to suppress himself. Sweat pours down from his head, his face, his shoulders, his back, and from the inside of his thighs. As though to compensate for his childlike body, he has matured mentally with unusual speed, and he feels like a completely adult man. When he helps her to loosen up, an evil thought takes hold of him; he wants to hurt her, so he pushes hard. She screams; a scream like the siren on a ferry.

It frightens him; his hands weaken, letting go of her knees. She brings her knees together, and holds them in her arms in front of her chest, still screaming. Then she starts to revile him, using a whole series of dirty words which only men would have used, such as "fuck you." She doesn't really know what it means, just that it's a strong word and gives vent to her anger. This, however, works on his imagination and makes him more agitated, so he throws the same vulgarity back at her, only he means it. She still doesn't understand its meaning, and still lies on the floor holding her knees in her arms. Nor does she hold them properly; she holds on to one knee and stretches the other leg, and then she holds on to the other knee while stretching the first one. Every time she stretches or bends her legs, her well-developed waist and chest vibrate in response. As he swears back at her, her anger mounts, and a string of dirty words such as "fuck your brother-in-law" come out of her mouth, illogical and unfit for any ear. He gets worked up, and counterattacks in even coarser language, meaning every word of it. She won't let him speak anymore, just continues her abuse in a loud, shrill voice, trying to drown him out. His voice is deep and strong; it comes through gradually. When she thinks she has won and stops to catch her breath, his voice is still resounding in the room. Only then does she realize that he has not stopped cursing, but has kept up with her. His voice is like the bass in an orchestra; it may not carry much of the melody, but it always has a part to play. She doesn't even have time to catch her breath before she starts cursing afresh, trying to best him. He doesn't give up, and follows her shrill clamor with his deep, deliberate voice until she is finally exhausted and starts to cry, rolling all over the floor. He then stops, and stares at her gloomily.

Her whole body is blackened with dirt, and she rubs her eyes with her blackened hands so that her tears become black too, and roll all over her dirty face. Suddenly he feels sad. He takes her bucket, fills it with warm water, and tells her to have a wash. She refuses to listen and goes on crying; this show of sympathy makes her cry even more pitifully and she feels even more heartbroken. All he can do now is go forward and pull her up. Though she's heavy and is deliberately clinging to the floor, he is extremely strong, and has no trouble getting her on her feet and pushing her into the washroom. When he hears her locking up and then sobbing in the midst of splashing water, his heart is suddenly filled with love and tenderness.

Her heart feels lighter as she splashes water on her body and feels the dirt and sweat wash away like a layer of unwanted skin. By now her tears have dried, but she goes on sobbing as though in protest. Yet at the same time a strange feeling of warmth fills her heart, gradually spreading throughout her body, like the gentle touch of someone very intimate. She is almost happy, but she doesn't want to stop sobbing, for this too seems a consolation.

From this day on they stop talking to each other; they are enemies.

Though they don't talk, they still practice. He practices on his own, she on her own; he doesn't help her turn out, she doesn't help him loosen up his legs, they just practice by themselves. They both look very grave, overserious, as though attending a solemn occasion. There is no more conversation or laughter in the studio. When they laughed in the studio there used to be a slight echo, but now the only sound is the thump of their feet as they land on the floor, and the echo sounds empty, emphasizing the solitude and the monotony.

In contrast to this hushed atmosphere are the excitement and tension in their hearts. In her heart she is still contending fiercely with him, cursing him with hundreds of dirty words she doesn't understand. After that, she feels she is the one who has been abused, she who is pitiful and helpless, so she is even more self-pitying than ever. Every movement is carried out in a long-suffering and dignified manner, and she doesn't realize her own affectation. All she feels is that there seems to be a fresh goal in practicing, that it has become more meaningful. It is no longer just self-entertainment nor just self-improvement, it seems to have taken on the added dimension of a performance. Thus she practices harder than usual, and becomes extremely demanding of herself. When she fails to execute a step she just lets go of her body and lets it flop heavily to the ground. The pain often makes her want to cry out, but she always holds back. She will struggle to get up and make a second, hopeless attempt. It seems that by doing so she hopes someone will be moved; actually she moves herself to the point of tears.

He, in the meantime, is also torturing himself, bending and folding his body into inconceivable shapes. He bends down, his head touching his feet, but he isn't satisfied with that. He sticks his head out between his feet and holds it erect so he can look at the world from the usual angle. The shape of his body becomes most perplexing; one can't even tell his trunk from his legs. But as a result of this 360-degree inversion, his eyes survey the world with greater equanimity. He can hold this position for twenty minutes. He seems to hate his body and is intent on punishing it; as if his body has an existence independent of and antagonistic to his soul, which is meting out the punishment. The punishment is so harsh that it becomes a little pretentious. Each, for untellable reasons neither of them understands, strives for excellence. Thus it comes to the time of the first spring rain.

The rain comes like this:

The prelude is hot, July-like weather. People haven't even had time to take off their sweaters before it becomes so hot that they don't want to keep their T-shirts on. Skirts appear in the courtyard, yet they don't have the courage to go outside; they just flaunt themselves ruefully on the premises of the theatrical troupe. All of a sudden the sky darkens; it remains dark for a whole day before it pours down, each drop of rain the size of a bean. Cool air descends as though time has reversed its journey. In a split second the colorful skirts are gone and the quilts laid out to air in the courtyard all collected, exposing the wet cement floor. The floor is uneven, the depressions hold water, and rain falling on these small pools ripples successive circles outward. It is now evening, and a rainy evening gives one a feeling of warm desolation, or is it a cool warmth? The rain flows down along the tiles on the roof of the studio, clumsily following a circuitous route to the eaves. Soon there is a curtain of water hanging from the eaves.

There is a curtain of water in front of every house. People leave their doors half open and, leaning on the doorframes, separated by the water curtains, start chatting. The talk is all about the drought and the rain this spring. They eat as they chatter on, a big bowl of rice in the left hand, a pair of warped wooden chopsticks in the right, picking up the rice in the congee with the chopsticks. The congee looks a little brownish red because of the sodium added, and seems the more tasty for it. There are a few salted beans and pickles in the bowl, smelling of mold; but once you're used to it the smell becomes quite delectable. The rain falling on the pebbled pavement makes a surprisingly loud noise, drowning out any other sound, so people have to shout. There is one house with its door locked; whoever lives there hasn't come home yet, and the clothes hanging out in front of the house have not been taken in. There is a pair of pants with floral patterns, all wet, and the flowers look exceptionally colorful.

It has turned cool again, and sweaters are called for. Villagers who have no sweaters wear quilted jackets, nearly all of them black. After the rain the streets actually seem a little desolate and cold. The pebbled pavement has been thoroughly washed; the earth looks darker and the pebbles brighter, as though outlined in ink. The water in the river has risen, and looks crystal clear, covering the moss on the banks. The cement path beneath the dam appears whiter than before, but the dirt track looks darker. The scattered woods are all fresh and green, like villages made up of trees. In some village, a child has died during the heavy downpour; he was going to the lake for weeds to feed the pigs, and slipped when he was walking by a catchwater. The story has spread over several miles and then vanished, as if scattered by the wind. The townsfolk still say that the rain has been timely, making the weather more pleasant, and the villagers are also singing its praises, for the green wheat in the fields has all brightened up.

THEY STILL DON'T TALK to each other, as though they're deadly enemies. Others all notice it and think it strange. Yet after a while they become used to it and are no longer surprised. But after they've been used to it for a while, they once more feel that there's something strange about it. Since the animosity has lasted so long, there must be an unusual reason, and they can't just let the two of them be enemies forever. They have asked her, but she won't talk; they have asked him, and he won't talk either. They go back to question her again, and because they seem so serious, she can't help taking it seriously too, reacting in a stiff and stubborn manner. Her reaction draws even more attention, as they think that she is about to open up her heart, and they become even more persistent in their questioning. This rouses her feeling of having been wronged, which is further exaggerated because of their seriousness, and she bursts into tears. The fact that she is crying strengthens the confidence of others to get at the root of the matter, but she shakes her head in tears: "I don't want to say anything; I have nothing to say." It is the truth, but it sounds as though there is much behind it. They keep on questioning her, but then she refuses to speak anymore, just keeps crying as if she's heartbroken. She is crying partly because she feels she has been wronged, but more because she is puzzled and embarrassed, as she knows for a fact that nothing has happened. Nothing has actually happened, and yet the situation looks so serious; she feels responsible, and therefore a little afraid. Her reaction at least partially satisfies the others. They feel that now they are justified in going to question him again.

Cornered, all he can do is hit back at them verbally. He is all tensed up, cursing ferociously; he doesn't know what he is saying or why he is saying it. He feels rather ridiculous but he simply can't stop. Everyone is shouting at him, telling him to stop, telling him to apologize to her. Apologize for what? They all seem to know; the two of them are the only ones who don't understand, and yet actually the two of them are the ones who do. But they don't realize this; they think that they understand nothing, and feel that they have been wronged, the victims of a terrible joke.

They are surrounded by the others, and the leader of the dance section grabs each by one hand, trying hard to make them shake hands and be friends again. Both of them are struggling fiercely and it takes the combined effort of everyone to hold them. She is crying, he cursing; both are angry and frustrated because they are struggling to no end. At last their hands touch; they are still struggling to avoid touching one another, but now the aversion seems a little false. Their hands touch, and they suddenly seem moved, the struggle to free themselves has obviously weakened. Their hands are at last brought forcibly together by the section leader, palm to palm. He has never felt more strongly about her body before, nor she his. Their hands touch for a split second, like lightning, and in the midst of everyone's resounding laughter their hands part, and they both turn to escape. But that split second seems so long, long enough for them to experience and savor for a lifetime. It is as though in that split second when they touch, he realizes that this is the hand of a woman, and she that this is the hand of a man. They escape, so ashamed that they can't look each other in the face, let alone talk to each other.

So it is that they still don't talk to each other. But now their silence has everyone's approval, and they are left alone. They practice as usual, and as hard. She throws herself violently on the floor; the physical pain gives her such a wonderful sense of satisfaction that she has become almost addicted to it. The more painful it is, the more she sympathizes with herself, and the more determined she becomes. He tries his utmost to twist his body into unrecognizable shapes, for that is the only way he can calm down; he is proud of his severity with himself. When either one of them leaves the studio, the other's determination and confidence in this self-torture will disappear, the physical tension and excitement vanish all of a sudden. They torture themselves because they want to show something off. It is a pity that they are concentrating so hard on themselves that they can't spare ten percent, or even one percent, of their attention for the other's performance. Their effort is completely wasted. Their need for the other person originates in themselves. There is satisfaction and meaning in hardship and endurance only if the other person is present. Yet ultimately both are showing off to themselves, hoping thereby to gain their own trust and sympathy.

But young and ignorant as they are, it is only natural that they don't realize this. They simply take delight in practice, and feel that they need each other's presence during practice. Because of this inexplicable need, they have a tacit understanding: they won't practice alone, but if one of them comes to the studio, the other will turn up unbidden, and once there, neither will leave without the other.

After three heavy downpours, the weather becomes hotter every day; it is summer. The cicadas sing from before daybreak until night. The sun penetrates the thin tiles of the studio roof and the heat surrounding the room pours in through the open door and windows. Every day they give the floor a thorough wash with their sweat, and the red paint gradually fades, revealing the original pale color. It is wonderful to feel the sweat exuding through every pore. Her wet leotard sticks to her body. She is practically naked, the hints are so blatant, though not the tiniest part of her body is bare. These hints, much more strongly than nakedness, stimulate thoughts and desires. She is not well proportioned; every part of her body is exaggerated or distorted, like the creation of a cartoonist. The curves thrust in and out without restraint. Yet once you are accustomed to it, normal well-proportioned bodies actually seem flat and dull.

He is wearing nothing but a pair of athletic shorts and a shabby kneeband around his left knee. He is so thin that his bones seem to stick out of his pale, coarse skin; as he dances, one can see his bones moving under his skin. His ribs are clearly visible, two neat columns of them, giving the impression that the skin here has disappeared. His ribs, strong as steel, obstruct the flow of his sweat, which either streams down from rib to rib, or gets caught between the ribs, casting a pattern of shadows on his body. Her body is as smooth and shiny as velvet, with sweat pouring down. The two of them, dripping wet, now turn their attention to each other and really see each other for the first time. Before this the one has never looked at the other; each only saw, admired, and loved himself or herself. Now, while they try to catch their breath, they suddenly have a chance to look at each other, and in the other's dripping body they seem to see their own naked image. They feel shy, and can't help avoiding each other's eyes. They are still resting; it is too hot and the cicadas are too noisy.

At midday, the only noise is that of the cicadas' song. Every front door along the street is open, yet no sound comes from the houses.

People don't even snore during their afternoon naps; just trickles of saliva, still warm, shine and even steam on the pillows. The shopping hall in the department store looks especially deserted; there are only flies buzzing and tracing out circles in the air. The shop assistants are bent over the counters, fast asleep, the glass surface of the counters cooling their faces, and their faces warming and moistening the glass. Occasionally an untimely customer will hesitate in the shopping hall and glide noiselessly across the marble floor. No ferry calls at the pier; under the red-hot sun the river reflects a blinding light. Naked children walk a long distance along the banks and put their feet into the river to test the water; it's boiling. There are several water-carts lying around, with planks raised, and the watermen sleeping underneath them.

She tries a *grand jeté* in which one foot is supposed to touch the back of her head, but she fails, and falls heavily onto the floor. It seems as if it is the floor which rises up to meet her and strikes her a heavy blow. The feel of the warm floorboards suddenly makes her weak. She turns over, and, lying on her back, arms outstretched, stares at the triangular roof of the studio. A thick strut points down at her body as though it is going to fall. The shady ceiling is wide and deep, a sanctuary. She feels calm and untroubled. Her eyes follow the ceiling's dark edge downward, and come up against the unexpected glare of the sun; the sun's rays are particularly bright just beneath the eaves and it makes her sad, almost hopeless. She lies on the floor, motionless, time flowing by her side, and stopping by her side. There is a tall old scholar tree in the courtyard, its leaves casting pale shadows on the window. She almost catches a glimpse of that ever-singing cicada spreading and folding its wings.

Just at this moment, two steely thin legs appear by the crown of her head; the leg bones stick out and all the muscles seem to recede rapidly toward the back. She cranes her neck backward to look at these legs; there are some sparse, coarse hairs pitch-black against his snowy skin. She stares at them quietly, and finds them ridiculous. But now the leg bones are leaning toward her. He is squatting in front of her looking into her eyes. He asks all of a sudden:

"Want me to give you a hand?"

"No!" She wants to shout, but her voice is hoarse and she can't raise it. With a quick push she sits up, but his hands are already under her arms, and before she can steady herself he has pushed her up to a standing position. She wobbles, but his hands grip her armpits like iron wrenches and force her to stand steadily. With his hands still under her arms, she feels the burning heat there, while other parts of her body have cooled down. The heat from these two places is overwhelming. She doesn't feel hot anymore, and the sweat flows down pleasantly, like a song. When she is firmly on her feet he takes his hands away and lowers them until they reach his thighs. His palms and wrists are all wet from the sweat in her armpits, and the warmth of her armpits envelops his hands. Now his hands, hanging by his side, seem lonely and desolate. He can't help stretching his fingers, trying to catch something, but there is nothing there.

She is back on her feet now, and walks straight toward the bar, where she starts to do *balancé*, the tip of her foot drawing empty semicircles in the air. Bright sunlight catches on her foot and throws half a halo in midair. The movements of her protrusive, almost deformed buttocks seem so extraordinarily displeasing to the eye that he really wants to kick at them. She is conscious of his stare, and it makes her happy. His eyes are warmly fondling her thick legs, legs which have lost their elegant curve, and yet have an innocent appeal in their ugliness. She continues her series of *balancés,* and feeling her tendons stretch and relax she is so lighthearted and so happy that she can't hold back the urge to glance at him. To her surprise he has already gone back to his own routine. Her spirits plummet; though her legs are still swinging back and forth, her heart is not in it anymore. He is doing a side-split, and as his legs form a straight line on the floor, he bends his torso slowly to the front, with his arms touching the ground, parallel to his legs, and his hands clasping his flexed feet. He senses her attacking him with her stare, aimed at his weakest and most sensitive spot. He can't help shivering, and folding up his limbs he crouches on the floor. She has withdrawn her stare. Dispirited, he curls up on the floor for a long while before standing up again. Plucking up his spirits, he walks to her side. He stands there struggling with himself, blushing. Finally he mumbles:

"What is it that you dislike about me?"

She doesn't expect him to speak, let alone about something so serious, so she too is embarrassed. She gradually lowers her leg, her face turning red. She answers: "Nothing," and laughs as though it is funny.

"We'd better stop this," he says. "We should help each other out."

"That's all right with me," she replies, her heart pounding. She feels this is something unusual.

And so they begin to talk to each other again. Yet somehow they feel that it was more wonderful when they were not on speaking terms. As soon as they talk to each other, the tension is gone, and then the sense of excitement, the inexplicable agitation and curiosity in anticipating the outcome of these events, and the secret flow of ideas by tacit understanding are completely gone too. But still, they both feel that a weight has been lifted from their minds. The tension was just too great, and too dangerous. They did not realize what kind of danger it was, but they both felt the sense of adventure.

Their relationship has returned to normal, but they no longer have a clear conscience. Each seems to be harboring secret designs; they avoid each other and no longer help each other practice. They talk, but only briefly and awkwardly. When he wants to tell her that the canteen has started serving and that if she's late she won't get any good dishes, he means well, of course, but his words sound like a warning: "Meal's served!" And she answers angrily: "Who needs to be told!" When she has finished showering and wants to tell him it's his turn, she speaks as though it's an ultimatum: "I've finished, I'm telling you." And he replies, seemingly irritated: "Who needs to be told you've finished!" It seems that this is the only way in which they can talk to each other; they have forgotten how pleasant and natural conversing with each other used to be. Though they use angry words, they don't really quarrel because neither of them wants to do so. They don't want to be enemies again. Coming out of that embarrassing situation wasn't easy, and they treasure the breakthrough. But they both seem a little regretful that the embarrassment is over. Originally they thought that something extraordinary was going to happen, and they were full of expectations, a little afraid, a little hesitant. But now everything has returned to normal; nothing extraordinary will ever happen, or rather, something started to happen and then stopped, so that their expectations have fallen through and they feel strangely resentful of each other. The stiff way in which they talk to each other is thus not all pretense, there is some real cause for it. She frequently glares at him sideways for no reason at all, the whites of her eyes showing even more distinctly against her dark complexion, which makes the glare more effective. He looks as though he is always brooding; his face seems overcast, and since his complexion is pale this sense of gloom is all the more obvious. Sometimes it really scares her, and she dares not give full rein to her temper.

But still, they are on speaking terms again. Ever since they started talking again they seem less dedicated in their practice. Self-torture has lost its meaning, and when they look for a new way to communicate and to fight they can't find it. They are both at a loss. For a period of time they seem to have lost their goal in life and have become dispirited. Besides, the weather is extraordinarily hot. In the midday sun someone breaks an egg on a paving stone in the street and watches it cook. Almost a hundred people come to watch, their faces all sweaty and oily, but they are so amazed by the sight that they completely forget about the heat. Only the children keep on crying loudly because the prickly heat on their heads, all pus now, is hurting terribly. At night, though the sun is gone, the earth pants for breath from the heat it has soaked up, and exhales it in gasps, steaming the bamboo beds and straw mats lying all over the streets. Actually it is as hot outdoors as it is indoors; so hot that even mosquitoes don't come out.

Yet in the countryside the crops are growing particularly luxuri-antly; the leaves of the beans are a delightful green and tender pods have appeared. Old villagers, like dogs, stick their tongues out in the heat but they still keep saying: "It's hot when it should be hot and cold when it should be cold; that's the way for the weather to be." The melons are growing nicely too. A small watermelon—thin-skinned, with red pulp and black seeds—only costs three cents. A peddler carries them through the lanes and streets, shouting as he goes along. Even in the early morning one feels greasy because of the heat, so someone in the troupe beckons the peddler into the courtyard and everyone sits around his basket eating melons. After they have eaten their fill they ask the accountant to pay the peddler and charge it to the "heat-prevention" account.

The peddler takes a rest in a shady corridor at the back of the kitchen, where there is actually a little breeze. He feels good and it makes him talkative, so he starts telling stories about the melon fields. These are all scandalous stories, such as the one about a farmer catching a couple fornicating while he was keeping watch in the melon fields, or a young girl who wet her pants from eating too many melons. Someone reports this to the troupe leader, and the peddler nearly has to forfeit his earnings from the melons. Yet on the whole he has had an easy day; he has sold two basketfuls of melons without having to endure much of the heat. Now that he has finished a good day's work he ambles out of town leisurely, carrying his empty baskets on a shoulder pole. On his way back there is a well every mile or so, the water is sweet and cool, and a drink of it drives the heat away. The peddler thinks: There's no reason why people living on the main street should suffer so—crowding together under this heat, without even the shade of a tree where they can catch the breeze, and working strict hours whether the sun is high up in the sky or not. But the girls in town are really nice, with such fair complexions and soft skin; the men in town are fortunate indeed.

The townsfolk, on the other hand, pity the villagers who cannot even find a place to hide under the burning sun. Their shoulders and legs are covered in blisters, and their skin peels off layer after layer. The sun also makes the color of their clothes fade and they never wear anything the least colorful. What a monotonous life! But the melons are really something. The inexplicable thing is why the couple at the middle school keep their door shut even in this burning weather. It would be understandable if it were only at night, but is it necessary to keep the door shut in the middle of the day too? Not unless they can't hold out until

nightfall; imagine doing that when the sun is high, it must be excruci-
atingly hot! And yet though they are at it day and night, there is never
any sign of them having a baby. The woman looks like an unmarried
girl, her tummy flat, her waist and buttocks narrow, and her skin soft
and supple.

Even after the hottest period is over and the calendar says that it is
autumn, the heat lasts another eighteen days.

AFTER THESE EIGHTEEN burning days, the theatrical troupe sends some
of its members to a major company in a southern seaside city to learn
new routines. Since only principal dancers and actors are allowed to
go, the two of them are left behind, still practicing every day, and still
doing things the wrong way. She has grown even taller and bigger, and
in comparison he, who has not grown at all, looks as though he has
actually shrunk. She feels that she is becoming too big, that her body
has become a burden. When she takes a wash and looks at her unusually
full breasts, she is shocked and worried. She doesn't know why they
have grown so big, and she doesn't know what will happen if they go
on developing. She even suspects that this may be a strange illness. The
thought makes her head swell, and she is so scared that she wants to cry.
She studies every single part of her body, all so big, and she becomes
afraid of herself. She knows that she is too big, but there is no way
she can make herself smaller. In the company of the troupe's slim and
refined girls she can't help feeling lowly and inferior because of her size.
Besides, she never thinks before she speaks and so her words always
seem incoherent or out of place. Her intelligent companions all call her
Big Soppy. Fortunately she is someone who doesn't think much, so her
feelings of inferiority and fear do not affect her health in the slightest.
She is energetic, and her appetite is huge. At night when she climbs into
bed, she hugs herself with her own arms, feeling extremely fond of herself. And then she falls soundly asleep, like a baby, without the least care
in the world. In her sleep she frequently makes noises with her mouth,
the sounds of a pampered child.

The burden for him is his maturity. At heart he seems a fully grown man, filled with shameless desire so mean and base that it frightens him. At first he did not know which part of his body was the seat of such desire; if he did, he would surely be determined to destroy that part of himself. And then one night he wakes up at an inappropriate time, and it suddenly dawns on him where his sin originates; to him it is all sin. But by this time he has realized how impossible it is to destroy that part of himself, and what's more, because it is such an important part he begins to treasure his desires as well. He does not understand why this is so.

And now the ones who had gone to learn new routines have come back, wearing stylish clothes and carrying the latest in traveling bags. They get off the ferry, step onto the unsteady gangway, and make their way to the bank. Both of them have come to welcome the returning team. She has not succeeded in pushing her way to the front, and so has not been able to lay her hands on a single bag, but she's excited and happy all the same. She either walks in front of the group as if she is clearing the way for an army, or walks at the back as though to make sure that everything is all right, all the while babbling about irrelevant things. No one answers her; no one hears her. Yet if it were not for her and her prattle the occasion would not have been so lively.

He walks in the center of the group, next to the principal dancer who always plays the male lead in dance dramas. The principal dancer puts one arm around his shoulders. Though he never attracts much attention he and the principal dancer are the best of friends, and the latter confides in him. On the way from the pier to the theater, the principal dancer says to him:

"You'll get a new role."

The role is the young Red Army soldier in the *pas de deux* "Hard Times." It is impossible to find someone as small as him and technically as brilliant. In other troupes this role is always danced by a woman. The role seems custom-made for him; it suits him so perfectly that no questions are raised and he is cast for it. It is all smooth sailing except for one thing—there are many lifts in the dance, and in one particular section the old soldier is required to carry the young one on his back while performing difficult steps, showing his robustness and strength. At this point his major defect is revealed. Though he looks small he is incredibly heavy. The "old soldier" just does not have the strength to carry him; he bends under his weight, unable to perform a single step. Moreover, neither of them has had practice in lifts in *pas de deux*, and as a result they do not know how to make the lifts easier. He clings to his partner's back with all his might, and though he feels embarrassed and apologetic it doesn't help. When he clumsily jumps off his partner's back time and again, his partner can't help complaining:

"You really are too heavy."

He turns red, countering: "You're just chicken!"

Anger darkens his partner's face, and a confrontation seems unavoidable. The principal dancer tries to smooth things over, saying:

"I'll have a go."

The principal dancer walks through the steps carrying him on his back, but though he succeeds in doing this he can't catch his breath afterward. Then all the others come up to him and take turns walking around with him on their backs, laughing. Finally he has had enough, and struggles to get back on the ground, giving the person under him a hard push. This at last puts an end to the joke on him.

In the evening he skips dinner, staying in the studio to improve his *balloné*. He knows that the initial jump is all-important: if he could get on to his partner's back with ease, what follows would be no problem at all. But if he were to exhaust himself trying to cling to his partner and fail to coordinate his breathing with the steps, there'd be trouble. Besides, he also wishes that he could take things more easily.

After a short while, she too comes to practice. She practices every day after dinner as if she thinks it's good for digestion. Thus she can eat more; she loves eating and has a great appetite. Today she is wearing a new peach-colored leotard, one of those the travelers have brought back with them for distribution to the troupe. This is one of the regular leotards used by the big companies, with a very low neckline, especially at the back where it reaches almost down to the waist. The elasticized welts around the legs are too tight, and cut deeply into her thighs.

All of a sudden he asks her amicably to help him rehearse the lifts in the dance. She has not heard him speak so mildly to her for a long time, and besides, she has had a stupid urge to show off since that afternoon, so she readily consents. First of all he takes her through the paces; but that afternoon she had stood on one side watching them rehearse and taken note of every movement, so now she does every step correctly. He then goes to the electrician for a tape recorder and the music tape, speedily locates that section of the music, and starts the tape. He climbs onto her back, and strangely, she doesn't feel burdened at all. On the contrary, the exuberant music makes her very happy. He performs his movements on her back, feeling secure; he had not thought that her back would be so broad, firm, and strong. They go through the paces like a dream, and at the end of it she's panting only a little, as is normal. Before he speaks she says eagerly:

"Let's do it one more time!"

This time they take it from the top. She has learned all the old soldier's steps and her rendering is none too bad; she actually expresses the heightened emotions rather well. When it comes to the lift, he gets on to her back with perfect ease. She has strong, powerful arms. Since she makes light of the burden, his confidence increases and his movements become bolder and more adroit, thus making it even easier for her. Gradually they become familiar with the way each other moves, and he finds that the understanding between them is better than what he had achieved with his original partner. After going through the dance five or six times, they become at ease with the movements and dance without hesitation, forgetting the technical difficulties and the need for mental preparation before the lift. Every gesture of the arm and every movement of the leg seem second nature to them. And the music is uplifting; every repetition makes it more intimate and more beautiful. She has forgotten that her role is that of an old Red Army soldier, and thinks that she is just playing herself; he has also forgotten that his role is a young soldier, and thinks that he is just playing himself. Every movement has become their own, an expression of their feelings and instincts. They have forgotten themselves in the dance; their images flash across one mirror onto another until they are surrounded by images of themselves. They actually feel that they are beautiful, and they never feel better about themselves than when they dance. Besides, there is also the music.

As he climbs on her back once again he smells the heavy odor of sweat; he feels the firmness of her back on his chest, exposed by the low-cut leotard, naked, warm, and wet. His equally warm, wet chest rubs against her back, making a noise, and the friction hurts a little. He can feel the strong movements of her waist with his knees and her rounded muscular shoulders and thick neck with his hands. As she pants, her neck alternately tenses up and relaxes. Her hair, soaked in sweat, is plaited and fixed to the back of her head with hairpins. The tip of her plait brushes against his nose, and he can smell the strong odor of oil and sweat while a cool hairpin pricks his cheek. All his senses are aroused, freed from the dance techniques, and he tenses up once again. But this is a different kind of tension; instead of suppressing all physical and emotional sensations, now every sense and every feeling is strained, fine-tuned, and activated. Dancing has become for him just mechanical movements, unworthy of the slightest attention. He is carried on the back of a burning body; a burning body is moving energetically under him. Even the tiniest breath is communicated to his most sensitive nerve, igniting his hope, which is erupting like lightning and fire.

The light and heat are passed on to her. She cannot feel anything besides the scorching brazier of red-hot coal on her back. The heat has become unbearable; and yet when he gets down and the burning sensation disappears, she feels an emptiness on her back and yearns for him to be up there again. When he gets back up on her back she feels that her heart and lungs are all on fire and wishes to roll on the ground to extinguish the flames scorching her body. But the music and the dance won't let her lie down. She seems to be controlled by a mighty and invisible will, repeating the routine over and over again, lifting him onto her back, then casting him to the ground. Suddenly she feels completely at ease; her panting stops and her breathing is synchronized with the tempo of her movements. Her body moves of its own accord.

The movements of their bodies are perfectly coordinated. He feels easy and confident jumping onto her back, never making the slightest mistake, as though that is the place where he truly belongs and the jumps which he performs on the ground are just expressions of his impatience to be up there again. Her mind is only at ease when he is on her back; the heavy burden pressed tightly against her gives her great pleasure. They seem glued together in all their movements, inseparable and intimate. He rolls on her back, jumping up and getting off, and the friction is dear to him, quenching the thirst of his flesh and soul. And the weight of his whole body, with all the rolling, jumping, and rubbing, is but a caress to her. His movements obviously hurt her; her back bends under the weight and her legs shake, but the dance goes on without a single missed step. The music is repeated continuously, interminably, and becomes more and more exuberant, never allowing a moment's rest.

It is now late into the night, and someone roars at the studio, cursing them for disturbing his sleep; someone else opens and shuts a window with a loud bang. But they are oblivious to all these noises. The music envelops their world, an exuberant world totally out of control.

Finally someone turns off the electricity mains. The light suddenly goes off and the music stops; around them all is dark. The lights in the courtyard are turned off too, and there is no moon in the sky. It is pitch-black, like the bottom of an abyss. He was on her back when their movements stopped with the music, frozen. Thirty seconds pass before he lands on the floor. Without uttering a single word, they run away in fear. The strange thing is they manage not to run into each other or fall down in this darkness, but just disappear like puffs of smoke.

(Translated by Eva Hung)

ZHAI YONGMING
(1955–)

Born in Chengdu, Sichuan, Zhai Yongming is a leading female poet in contemporary China. She began writing when working in the fields after high school. In 1984 the publication of her poem cycle "Woman" brought her to national prominence. She lived in the United States for several years and once worked as a coat-check girl. After returning to China, in 1998 she opened the White Night bar and hosted a salon, à la Gertrude Stein in Paris, that has become a center for literary and art events in her native city.

Premonition

The woman in black appears in the dead of night
And wears me out with one furtive glance
It dawns on me all fish will die this season
And every road cuts across the path of birds in flight

Darkness drags off mountains like a corpse
Barely audible are the heartbeats of nearby thickets
With human eyes
Those giant birds look down at me from the sky
In a barbarous air mum over its secret
Winter heaves with a masculine consciousness of brutality

I've been unusually calm
Like the blind, so that I see the night in the daytime
With an infant's innocence, my fingerprints
Reveal no more proof of sorrow
Footsteps! A voice is growing old
The dream seems to know, inside my own eyes
I see an hour that forgot to blossom
Weighing down the twilight

Moss in mouth, they beg at meanings
That fold smiles tacitly back into their bosoms
As night shivers in spasm, like a cough
Stuck in the throat, I have left this dead cavern.

Hypnosis

she tells me   one's life
is sealed
in sleep

her gestures   tone of voice
and the whole world's life
exhaust me profoundly
for a moment

her breath of orchid   into
my pineal gland
dozing off
I see the butterfly from a previous existence

returning   or not
the first half of my life
battles in my sleep   she discovers

my soul
has taken   the melatonin of *fin-de-siècle*

The Language of the '50s

Born in the '50s   we speak
Just this language
Nowadays   it's become comic routines
Served on plates   course after course
At banquets

Those red flags, leaflets
Violent images   those
Belts buckled with clenched fists
And bloodthirsty slogans   all stiff and fallen
Those victimizers and victims
Will never return
The love of an entire generation   castrated
Will not return

Born in the '50s   but
We no longer speak those words
Just as we don't ever again say "love"
All articulations, phrases, and tones
Agile as they age at dinner tables

They don't understand   their youthful hair
Sparkling under the sun like soap bubbles
Floating around me
They lower their heads in concert
Thumbs busier than other fingers
Texting   QQ   and a hieroglyphic alphabet:

Born in the '50s
We too must learn   the language flying in the air
All those lost words
Only lived at certain times
Like grapes, goji berries, and dates
Fallen on our bed, when we draw the curtains
As I murmur   word by word
My boyfriend understands   they
Turn blood-red

(Translated by Yunte Huang)

HAI ZI
(1964–1989)

Born as Zha Haisheng to a peasant family in rural Anhui, Hai Zi is one of the most mythologized Chinese poets today. He attended Peking University from 1979 to 1983, and then taught at China University of Political Science and Law. Committing himself totally to poetry, he composed over 250 short poems and a number of long poems within the brief span of seven years. On March 26, 1989, two days after his twenty-fifth birthday, Hai Zi threw himself in front of a train in Shanhai-guan, the eastern end of the Great Wall. Although his suicide, caused probably by schizophrenia, bore no direct relation to the tragic event on Tiananmen Square two months later, the younger generation regards it as a symbol of self-sacrifice in the pursuit of spiritual salvation. A copy of Thoreau's Walden and a Bible were found in the sachet Hai Zi had carried on the day of his death.

Your Hands

the North
pulls at your hands
hands
pluck off gloves
they are two small lamps

my shoulders
are two old houses
that hold so much
they've even held the night
your hands
on top of them
illuminate them

because of this in the morning after our parting
in the light of dawn
I carry a bowl of porridge with both hands
thinking of the North
separated from me by mountains and rivers
two lamps

that I can only distantly stroke

—February 1985

Facing the Ocean, Spring Warms Flowers Open

starting from tomorrow, become a content person
feed the horses, split wood, roam the world
starting from tomorrow, I'll concern myself with grains and vegetables
I have a home, facing the ocean, spring warms flowers open

starting from tomorrow, I'll write letters to all the relatives
to tell them of my contentedness
what that content lightning flash told me
I will tell everyone

give a warm name to every river and every mountain
strangers, I send you my blessings

I hope for you a splendid future
I hope that you lovers become family
I hope that in this dusty world you become content
I only hope to face the ocean, as spring warms and flowers open

—*January 13, 1989*

Spring, Ten Hai Zis

spring, ten Hai Zis fully revive
on the brilliant landscape
mocking this savage and sorrowful Hai Zi
why your long, deep sleep?

spring, ten Hai Zis release their throaty roars
encircling you and me, dancing and singing
pulling at your black hair, riding you rushing wildly away, dust
    swirling
your pain at the cleaving spreads over the earth

in spring, only this savage and sorrowful Hai Zi
remains, the last one
child of the dark night, steeped in winter, losing his heart to death
unable to extract himself, in deep love with an empty, frigid village

where the grain is piled high, blocking the window
the six family members use half of it: mouths, eating, stomachs
half is for planting and reproduction
great winds blow from the east to the west, from north to south, with
    no thought for the dark night or the dawn
in the end what will your daybreak mean?

—*before dawn 3–4 o'clock, March 4, 1989*
(Translated by Dan Murphy)

MA YUAN

(1953–)

Hailed as the first Chinese postmodernist, Ma Yuan was born in Liaoning. A peasant and factory worker during the Cultural Revolution, he attended Liaoning University from 1978 to 1982. After graduation he was assigned to work for a radio station in Tibet, where he lived for eight years, an experience he often draws upon for his writing, as he does in "Thirteen Ways to Fold a Paper Hawk." A hardcore avant-gardist known for his use of circular narrative and embedded storytelling, Ma once declared that "the novel is dead." After a hiatus of twenty years, he resumed fiction writing in 2012 and now lives in self-imposed isolation in the tropical rain forest and monsoon jungle of Sipsongpanna, the southernmost region in Yunnan.

Thirteen Ways to Fold a Paper Hawk

1

March 3 was the Tibetan New Year. My coworkers came over in the morning to wish me Happy New Year, and got me drunk on Tibetan barley wine until I didn't know up from down, went to bed at noon, and didn't wake up until dark. When I got out of bed and splashed cold water on my face, I found a little boil on the right corner of my mouth. Just something tiny, I thought.

Half a week later this boil had swollen up incredibly, and started oozing out sickening pus mixed with blood. A scab the size of a walnut formed at the corner of my mouth, my cheek had swollen, and my face was one big mess. Traditional medicine calls the corner of your mouth "the danger triangle." From there, they say, the pus can run right through your veins straight into your brain. I had no idea if that was true. You can laugh if you like, but I cried from the pain, and not just once either. Now this wasn't just something tiny anymore.

I started going to the hospital.

In Lhasa, Tibetan New Year is a big holiday. My friends were out celebrating and here I was alone in my work unit's dormitory, where I'd crawled into bed to read a novel. It's tough for a man all alone. What could I do to while away the time, doomed as I was to a life of perpetual loneliness? But I wasn't content with being lonely. I have ways of coping with it. Reading novels is one. Or, for example . . .

At sundown I sometimes walk out onto the street and look at the shattered clay pots and bowls people leave lying all over the street. I watch the long-haired dogs chase each other playing. Sometimes I go to a sweet tea shop, sit for an hour and drink up the last fifty cents in my pocket. Or I take a walk to the south side of Medicine King Mountain to see what Buddhist worshippers have left behind. Little clay Buddhas? Prayer flags with a picture of Sakyamuni?* Stone tablets engraved with lines of scripture?

Or I could draw the curtain (my only spare bedsheet, white with blue checks—you know that pattern), shut the door, turn on the lamp on my little three-drawer desk, and spin you a story.

(Of course it's a good story . . . at least I hope so.)

It's times like this my imagination is especially active. I can call to mind things that happened and things that haven't happened. Before I write a story I always rack my brain—"What should I write? How should I put it?"—the same old problems. If my Tibetan pal Little Kel-

---

*   Sakyamuni: Siddhartha Gautama (ca. 563 B.C.–ca. 487 B.C.), the historical Buddha, founder of the Buddhist religion.

sang hadn't come by and told me what his criminal investigation squad was up to, who knows where my imagination might have galloped to?

Little Kelsang asked me if I remembered the turquoise peddler. Sure I did. Little Kelsang had just joined the police department last year—a true raw recruit. This case had him worked up. I told him to unbutton that stiff collar on his uniform, take off that visored policeman's hat, and relax a little, while I poured him a cup of tea.

Let's talk a little about the Barkhor. The Barkhor runs in a circle around the famous Jokhang Temple, with streets and alleyways criss-crossing all over the place. You can see people here from almost every country on earth. Somebody reckoned more than thirty thousand people come here every day to do business and to worship Buddha, and it must be at least double that on Sunday. The Barkhor is one big market-place. The array of goods on sale here puts to shame anything you could imagine. This is China's greatest antique and jewelry market. Millions change hands here every day. A rare peddler of indecipherable national-ity surreptitiously slips a jewel from his sleeve to show a foreign tourist. With a smile neither cringing nor haughty, he holds up his fingers in token of offer or counteroffer.*

It was here that I came across the world-famous alexandrite cat's-eye gem. From a peddler's rug on the street's second corner I bought an emerald-green turquoise, about as big as a couple of peanuts in their shells. It weighed fifty-two grams. Well, actually, I don't know anything about the quality of precious stones. I just liked its shape and color, so decided to have it. At first he wanted sixty. I offered him thirty. He laid out his rug at this same spot every day of the year. You couldn't reckon his age. Seventy was as good a guess as thirty-five. I'd been dropping over to the Barkhor for quite a while, so by now we knew each other on sight. From his face I decided he must be from South Asia. Nepal maybe. Or else India or Pakistan. He spoke Chinese clearly enough. We struck a deal at thirty-eight. That was last year, August 12—my desk calendar confirms the date.

---

*   In such bargaining one finger usually represents 1,000 yuan.

2

You remember that little street that runs off the Barkhor's southwest corner, right?

(In fact I didn't. Once I'm on the Barkhor I can't tell north from south.)

You remember how muddy it used to get there in the summer? They've been repaving it with concrete paving stones.

(I nodded. This didn't mean I remembered what it was like. It meant I was listening.)

The street has been repaired.

(I still couldn't work out what Little Kelsang was driving at.)

They widened it too, so they had to cut into the courtyards on both sides. The City Works Commission tore down the walls of the courtyard houses and then rebuilt them. In one courtyard, where nobody lived but an old lady, they dug up a man's body, not decomposed yet. Right, it was the turquoise peddler. You've noticed there's a different peddler on that street corner now, a Khampa woman selling sheepskins.

(I didn't want to tell you I'd really noticed. . . . I didn't want to interrupt your story.)

The old woman had caved-in cheeks, not a tooth in her head. She said she had no idea what had happened and didn't know the dead man. She had no children, no regular occupation, but kept body and soul together by selling used clothing on the street. She used snuff, no other unusual habits. The neighborhood committee told us that she'd moved to the Barkhor after the 1957 Lhasa uprising, a little over twenty years ago. They had no precise information about what she did before that. On the Barkhor people are always moving in and out. It is all so confusing that even old neighbors know little about each other. When we started to question her, she just stuck to her story. After we threatened her, she spilled everything.

3

The story of this old lady reminded me of another old lady who lived all by herself near the Barkhor. A guy I work with is one of her customers.

She runs an unlicensed wine shop. Her barley wine doesn't have that sour taste—if you know what I mean. So her business is good. Now, I can't drink Tibetan barley wine. They brew it with unboiled water and it gives me diarrhea. When I drop in at my friend Big Kelsang's house he always wants me to follow the Tibetan custom and drink off three cups of the stuff, so the last time I went over there I got out a copy of the doctor's diagnosis, and told Big Kelsang that I had inflammation of the stomach lining, but he swore the barley wine he bought was made with boiled water, and I wouldn't get diarrhea from it. So I couldn't refuse. That was how I learned about this old lady.

When Big Kelsang went out to her shop again to buy wine, I went along. I wanted to find out how she made her wine. I was curious to know why she brewed her wine with boiled water when everybody else used unboiled water.

She was plump, with thick, fleshy hands—a gentle, agreeable person. In my mind's eye I'd pictured this unlicensed wine shop owner as a shriveled old woman, cautious and reserved, with a thousand secrets lurking in the wrinkles of her face. But she wasn't like that. She was nothing like any character in my stories. At the time, I was a little disappointed. But anyway let's go back to Little Kelsang's story.

4

She said the dead man was her lover. He'd left her all his things to look after. She'd sold them all. She said he had a nine-eyed alexandrite cat's-eye. (A top-quality gem with just *five* eyes will bring in better than a thousand yuan.) He kept it on a cord around his neck, never took it off. She'd asked for it more than once, she said, but he always refused. All he'd given her was a few ordinary turquoises. So she got him drunk on liquor, and with the help of two itinerant Khampa peddlers, she strangled him with a cord, buried him, and then, after all, she said, she didn't get the jewel. The two guys grabbed it and took off. How could she stop them? Cheating an old woman! Her father was Muslim, she said. She'd been a jewel-trader herself.

Three times we asked for a description of the two Khampa men. Each time she gave a different description. We asked her their names and where they came from. She said people in business don't ask people questions like that. You don't ask where goods come from, or where they're going. But she said by the sound of their accents they were from the Tibetan district of Sichuan Province. Well, whether you believe her is up to you. She'd been here in Lhasa twenty years, and nobody knew anything about her. There she sat, not a tooth in her head, her mouth all puckered—her face the portrait of a lifetime of hardship. Not a word of truth in all she said, I reckon.

(And then?)

We went over her statement. We figured she might have made up the two Khampa accomplices to throw us off the trail. Think about it—thousands of Khampa traders up and down the Barkhor, how could we track them down with no description? And on top of that, she said they'd left the Barkhor, left Lhasa! Still, we're going to dispatch a couple of men to search in the Tibetan district of Sichuan.

5

Little Kelsang was one of the two men they dispatched. He said he was setting off in three or four days. I asked him to let me know what happened when he got back. He laughed, and asked if I wanted to turn it into yet another story. I didn't say yes, I didn't say no. The material was pretty flimsy, but who knows how the case might develop? I'm waiting for the outcome.

Suddenly I thought of something else. I asked Little Kelsang if the old lady believed in Buddha. He said there were some copper Buddha statues in her house, even some ceremonial items, but who could tell if they were for prayer or for sale.

That's about all Little Kelsang's story.

I'm sure you'd forgive me for not finishing this story. I'm all worn out. I fold my quilt into a pillow, lean back, light a cigarette, and close my eyes. I'm wondering why all old women involved in secrets and intrigues are thin and shriveled, and why, when I heard about the murder, the old lady selling barley wine came into my mind. What's even more interesting is that my image of the old lady who sells illegal wine should fit in so perfectly with the murderous old woman.

6

A knock on the door.

"Ma Yuan! Ma Yuan!"

It was Xinjian.

"Sitting at home all alone? God, what's the matter with you?"

"A boil. Must be a punishment for something I did."

"Dead-on. Have you eaten?"

"There's hardtack, and some cans."

"Listen, come on over and stay at my place a few days."

Xinjian's a painter. He's designing the interior of the new museum, and arranging the art exhibition there too. So I moved into his apartment with him, right there in the museum.

His place is roomy enough. As I walked in, my eyes lit on some paper hawks on his design desk. He came to Lhasa the year before last, the same as me. He studied fine art, and he brought along photos of all his murals, his sculpture, his canvases. I've seen them.

A couple of bachelors get together, things go better. His place is cleaner than mine, and the reason is a girl who comes over every once in a while, a beautiful girl with a laugh to show flashing white teeth. Her name's Nima. She's nineteen. She likes to do her laundry in the Lhasa River.

Xinjian likes to go over to the river too. He paints from life, and he's always looking for scenes to inspire his art. The Lhasa River in summer is just so enticing, at last he couldn't resist. He leaped in, and cut his foot on a piece of broken glass. The wound was deep. He grabbed his foot, howling like a devil, and Nima came running from the bank where she was washing clothes.

You can imagine what happened next. She got a bicycle and took him to the hospital, then came to the hospital to visit him, then came again, then . . .

She discovered he was a painter, and that after he shaved his beard he wasn't so old. (In fact he's only twenty-nine.) She found out the work studio where he lived was in the worst mess you could imagine. She became his student. She's been interested in art ever since she was a child. Now they talk about art together for hours on end. He's sculpted a bust for her too, abstract style. Anyone can see that they have too many romantic illusions about the future. I'm more practical, even if I'm boarding here with Xinjian for the time being. As soon as she came in, I went out. I might as well take a little break, go stroll around the Barkhor.

The Buddha may well be an idol for all eternity, I thought to myself, as I hung around outside the front gate of the Jokhang Temple. I just couldn't understand all these people prostrating themselves before the Buddha, but somehow I felt a deep respect for them. What I could see as I stood there watching them was their passion and concentration. In the dark expanse of the central hall I ran into her unexpectedly. In profile she still looked plump and kindly. She wouldn't remember me, but I watched her as she intently stuck four ten-yuan bills onto a Buddha shrine made of yak butter: I recalled that after I drank her wine at Big Kelsang's house, I didn't get diarrhea.

Spring is the season for flying paper hawks. Or maybe where you come from you call them kites.

Now, maybe Lhasa's paper hawks aren't unique, but a kite's backdrop is the sky, and there's no sky anywhere like the sky over Lhasa. On this whole planet it's the bluest sky to fly your kite in, yes, or just to watch other people fly their kites in—it's a pleasure. Just now there were three beautiful paper hawks flying in Lhasa's sky, diving and climbing together with three real hawks off in the distance. The way the kites tugged at the string almost seemed to pull the people who flew them into the sky. Well, Nima had probably left by now, so I thought I might as well go back.

By the time I returned to Xinjian's place, Nima had left. But there were two visitors. Zhuang Xiaoxiao was Xinjian's classmate at the fine art institute he attended. I already knew him.

"Let me introduce Liu Yu, from China News Agency. Liu, this is Ma Yuan from the radio station."

We nodded to each other. Liu Yu told me a friend in Beijing asked him to bring me a book, and when I had time I should go to his place to get it. The Beijing friend is a writer. In the book he gave me was a letter in which he said Liu Yu was a writer too.

Zhuang Xiaoxiao was talking about a problem he had at the exhibit of one of his best portraits. Some fine art official of the party said it distorted the image of the Tibetan people. Zhuang seethed with resentment. The model for the portrait came from the Nagchu pasturelands, and—it turned out to be Nima's granny. Nima got to know Zhuang Xiaoxiao through Xinjian. When she spotted the portrait at Xiaoxiao's studio, she stared dumbstruck. The wrinkles in the old woman's face were like the frost-scars in the bark of an old elm: the weariness of a lifetime. The portrait was called *The Years*.

Nima asked Zhuang Xiaoxiao how he got to know her granny. Xiaoxiao told her when he'd been painting up in the grasslands, he'd lived in her granny's house. The old woman had milked her yak every day to make him yak butter tea, and as she churned the butter she told him legends of the grasslands. When he mentioned that he'd like to paint her portrait, the old woman agreed. At first she kept chatting and laughing, but as Xiaoxiao became absorbed in his work, they stopped talking. The old woman was patient, but obviously she was anxious about the sheep and yaks out in the fields. She sat there, but her thoughts were elsewhere. When Xiaoxiao saw the latent exhaustion take shape in her face, he seized it.

Nima told Zhuang Xiaoxiao her father had often offered to bring her granny to come and live with them in Lhasa, but the old woman had always refused, saying she had to stay and take care of the animals. Granny was over seventy. She'd told Nima that she wouldn't live much longer, and didn't want to die anywhere else, she wanted to stay in the grasslands. She was used to the sheep, the yaks, the brown hawks.

Zhuang Xiaoxiao was planning to enter this portrait in the National Fine Art Exhibition in Shenyang this October. What about Xinjian? Nima took part in the discussion of ideas for Xinjian's sketch.

7

Liu Yu came to Xinjian's for a chat. I brought the subject of fiction into their conversation. Liu Yu wasn't much interested in discussing fiction. He was just making a few technical remarks about Zhuang Xiaoxiao's painting *The Years*, said he didn't like the picture's technique. All he really wanted to talk about was young Beijing painters. Beijing people love to go on about Beijing, just the same as Shanghai people all long to return to Shanghai. Liu Yu started asking Xinjian about his latest sketch. He wanted to know why Xinjian chose the Madonna as his subject. Xinjian told him that from ancient times right up to the present painters all over the world have been painting the Madonna, so there was no reason why he shouldn't want to paint one too. The Madonna was a Christian subject, and the Madonna was also Mother, or rather mother's love. Even if he, Xinjian, was a twentieth century Chinese, Raphael's Madonna evoked the same feeling of awe for the sacred in him.

Xinjian's sketch showed a woman with a child in her arms, eyes lowered, with two more children crouched against her feet, one on its hands and knees. It was obvious this was a Tibetan mother and her three children. The background was much less concrete: in the vague distance rose a snowcapped mountain, the Potala Palace, the Great Wall, and flocks of sheep. He'd painted the flocks of sheep stretching into the sky so at first I couldn't tell if they were sheep or clouds.

The conversation came around to the art committee's censorship. Well, Zhuang Xiaoxiao had strong feelings about this. Some of his best paintings hadn't made it because of censorship, but now, he said, he'd smartened up. He was going to find a Tibetan collaborator, and put the collaborator's name in front of his own. That way he'd be better off both in terms of censorship and in getting awards. The fine art committee has to encourage minority artists—it's government policy—so any way you looked at it the chance of getting his work before the public was better. Zhuang Xiaoxiao talked this way because he has confidence in his work. He trusted his feelings, and he trusted his wholehearted labor.

Now I thought of something else. The model for Xinjian's Madonna was Nima. Did Xinjian plan to use Zhuang Xiaoxiao's strategy? Maybe. A writer friend of mine, Hu Daguang, does the same. Her mother is Tibetan. Her father is Chinese, Mongolian, and Manchu, all mixed together. Hu Daguang uses a Tibetan pen name, Phuntsok. She grew up in China, has Chinese habits, and speaks Chinese in her daily life. She can't speak a word of Tibetan, but now she's a young Tibetan writer.

Well, I've been chattering away, now back to the story.

Liu Yu and his crew came to Tibet to shoot a news film and I heard they were planning to stay a few months. I asked Liu Yu if he'd found any material for a story since he'd arrived. He said he was collecting material for a short story about an old woman who lived near the Potala Palace.

8

They'd killed off the dogs in Lhasa couple of years ago, so I hear. In Lhasa there are just too many dogs. And in the past there had been even more dogs. They say Lhasa's dogs are a precious species that fetches a good price in London.

This old woman is dead now. She used to live at the foot of the Potala Palace, not far from your radio station. I hear she died a good few years ago, but still I feel an urge to go and see the place where she lived.

She was a devout Buddhist, never married. Every day since she was young she walked three times around the Potala Palace spinning her prayer wheel. The Potala's outer wall must be at least two thousand meters in circumference. Every day she walked around it three times. People who came regularly to Lhasa to spin their prayer wheels all knew her. She made a living selling clay Buddhas.

Every day she sat in the sun on the same flight of steps down on the Barkhor with a few copper molds, meticulously forming all different

kinds of Buddha statues out of fine yellow clay that she brought in from
the countryside. There were thousand-hand, thousand-eyed Happy
Buddhas, there were figures of Tsongkhapa* sitting erect, but most of
all there were Sakyamuni Buddhas with the rays of illumination around
their heads.

Herdsmen on pilgrimage from the countryside always used to
squat down, pick out a couple of clay buddhas, and leave a couple of
yuan in her cardboard money-box. Then there were foreign tourists buying souvenirs of Lhasa to take back home. They were her
customers too. They'd ask her how much, but she wouldn't answer,
so monkey see, monkey do, they'd imitate the pilgrims and leave a
foreign exchange certificate.† At times like this she didn't even look
up, her attention fixed on the new Sakyamuni she was turning out
of her mold.

Usually she didn't take shelter even when it rained, but just stared
blankly at the peddlers as they hurriedly gathered up their wares into
their ground cloths, stared at the people bumping and crowding in their
rush to find shelter from the rain, stared at the rain washing away the
fine yellow clay she'd brought in from the countryside, at the muddy
yellow clay flowing from beneath her feet off to lower ground.

She must have made a fair sum. She gave it all to the Buddhas. She
went at regular intervals to worship at Jokhang Temple, at Ramoche
Temple, at Drepung Temple, at Sera Temple, at the Potala. The money
she donated included every denomination of Chinese currency, besides
foreign currency exchange certificates, overseas currency remittance
certificates, even worthless old Tibetan money that went out of circulation years ago. Every time, she just poured out all she had. You could

---

*   Tsongkhapa (1357–1419) was a monk posthumously regarded as founder
of the Geluk (System of Virtue) sect, the dominant sect of Tibetan Buddhism. The Dalai Lama is its leader.
†   Special certificates in Chinese currency denominations that foreigners
received in exchange for foreign currency. The practice was discontinued
in 1994.

fairly say her heart and soul belonged to the Buddhas. She hadn't a single new piece of clothing.

This isn't the story I'm going to tell.

9

That story didn't sound true. But I believe it's true. I hadn't been in Lhasa two weeks before I'd already heard it from two people. It has made me ponder many questions.

As I was saying a minute ago, Lhasa was full of dogs a few years ago. That was before you came to Tibet. Dogs came and went wherever they pleased, in and out of shops, restaurants, all the public places. You could have called it a plague of dogs. Now Tibetans love dogs, they keep dogs as pets, they couldn't kill dogs, but back then there were just too many dogs. There were cases of rabies and other contagious diseases that were suspected of being spread by dogs. Besides, the population of Lhasa is only about a hundred fifty thousand. Such a large proportion of dogs to people caused shortages in the food supply. Packs of dogs got into fierce battles with one other. They disrupted the environment of the entire city.

So the Lhasa city government called on the populace to kill off dogs. The officials set up part-time dog-killing squads, and issued a directive forbidding staff and workers of state enterprises to keep dogs.

Most people couldn't bring themselves to kill the dogs. They just chased the family dog out of the house. All these family dogs simply swelled the numbers of the dog packs in the streets. In a short time there were many more dogs on the streets than ever before. A few young men went out with rifles and small-caliber guns and hunted them down.

This old woman started to keep dogs. She took dogs that had been terrified by all the gunfire back to her home, fed them, let them laze around basking in the sun where no one would come to frighten them.

Dogs must have a language of their own. These dogs told their friends about their good fortune. More and more dogs came to her shelter. A newcomer would slink into her yard with a group of the old tenants, watching her every move with its usual wary vigilance. If by chance she had a wooden stick in her hand, the newcomer turned and ran with its tail between its legs. In a dog's eyes, there's no great difference between a stick and a gun, especially in such times as those.

And so her little courtyard became dog-paradise. Every morning she went out the same as always to walk three times around the Potala, she molded the same clay Buddhas on the Barkhor, but she went less often to the temples to pray, and now if someone who took one of her little Buddhas didn't leave enough money, she no longer kept the same blank expression, but gave the customer a melancholy look, shook her head, and waited for them to take out more.

One of the dogs, a short-legged one with long golden fur, had a puppy again, a golden yellow puppy. When the old woman walked around the Potala spinning her prayer wheel, she carried the puppy at her bosom, with the mama dog trotting along behind to the rhythm of the spinning prayer wheel. People who knew her could see she was getting thin. Her cheeks grew sunken, her eyes hollow, her cheekbones and the bridge of her nose stood out sharply. She started to buy fresh milk every morning.

The kids who sold milk knew she never haggled about the price. They started watering down bottles of whole milk that usually sell for forty cents and sold them to her for fifty. She'd never drunk milk all her life; her neighbors said all the milk went to her puppies. Every day she'd buy four or five bottles of milk, sometimes even more. By now she had four puppies.

Her alley was narrow, just wide enough for two people to pass each other. Her little courtyard was at the very end. With a couple of dozen dogs stealing in and out, the half-lit alley assumed a mysterious air. At dusk the dogs left her courtyard one after another and came single file down her alley. If you closed in on that scene from above with a high-power zoom lens, the effect could be quite something.

(I laughed. Liu Yu was having a relapse of his professional mania. But in all fairness, Liu Yu's photography isn't bad at all. I like to hear him go on about the technical details.)

Of course this aroused resentment among the neighbors. With so many dogs living all together, there was plenty of biting and snapping, yelping and growling. The neighbors got no peace and quiet. When they complained, she didn't say much, just smiled, embarrassed. I think it must have been a bitter smile. After that she spent even more time with the dogs to get to know them better so that they would obey her, no more snapping and biting, snarling and barking, no more disturbing the neighbors. They were certainly tamer and more docile than before, but now she had even less time to spend on the Barkhor.

The old woman's favorite was the golden yellow puppy, the only puppy born right there in her yard. She treated it as if it had been her own child. When it got a little bigger she let it down from her bosom, tied a little cord around its neck, and the little puppy followed her along just like its mother used to do, trotting in step to the rhythm of the spinning prayer wheel. At night it crept up into her bed on the sly, snuggled up to the old woman's bosom, and fell peacefully asleep.

Now the old woman often appeared at the grain market. Lhasa is a city with a high cost of living and since Tibet can't produce enough grain to feed itself, the free market grain prices are high. She was a registered resident so she had grain ration coupons, but it takes a lot of grain to feed two dozen hungry dogs. What could she do? People could see that she was getting thinner and thinner, weaker and weaker. Sometimes she went out pushing a little cart, came back with it stuffed with flour sacks, leaning on the cart as she pushed it forward, the cart barely holding her up.

She didn't drink yak butter tea anymore, didn't even eat *tsampa*,* since barley is more expensive than wheat. But now, to everybody's surprise, she started drinking barley wine. I don't remember if I told you she didn't drink or take snuff. Now every noon she went into a canvas tent by the side of the street, contentedly drank off two cups, looked down with bleary, half-closed eyes at the little yellow dog at her feet, and muttered something intimate that only the two of them

* *Tsampa* is ground roast barley, the Tibetan staple.

understood. She'd just about fallen apart, but still every day she went to the Potala to spin her prayer wheel, went to the Barkhor to mold clay Buddhas, every day . . . look, Xinjian's fallen asleep. We've stayed too long. I'll tell you the rest of this when we get a chance.

10

In those days we often went to a big island in the middle of the Lhasa River. By "we" I mean Xinjian, Luo Hao, and myself. (Luo Hao's only nineteen, a professional photographer.) It was Xinjian's idea to go to the river to wash our clothes. I'm sure he wanted to relive sweet memories of his first meeting there with Nima. It was on that island that he told me their story.

I happened to mention Liu Yu's story, and told Xinjian that he'd fallen asleep before it was over. To my surprise Xinjian gave another yawn, and said he'd heard the same story from Luo Hao a long time ago. He said Luo Hao had lived in Lhasa since he was a kid, so naturally he knew a lot of these Lhasa legends.

On this particular occasion we'd brought a big load of dirty laundry, including everybody's bedclothes. Besides that, we brought lots to eat, canned food and more besides. Luo Hao brought along the white rooster his little brother had been raising, which he'd cooked into chili-sauce chicken. There was beer too. There's nothing more luxurious in Tibet than chili-sauce chicken with beer.

Our nearest neighbors were two Tibetan girls, washing clothes down the bank. Since Luo and I had no expectations of a romantic encounter, at first each group just minded their own business.

The Lhasa River is so clear you can see the bottom. First you spread your clothes out on the current, lay some stone pebbles on them to weigh them down in the water, let them soak for a while, then drag one up, lay it out on the pebble beach, sprinkle it evenly with soap powder, and rub it on with your hands, or you can tread it in with your feet if you'd rather. Then do a second one. Then a third one.

The girls started it by laughing—a brazen, unscrupulous laugh. They were laughing at us. It must have been the clumsy way we men wash our clothes. We thought about it and started laughing ourselves.

We were standing knee-deep in the current rinsing out the soap. The water was piercing cold. The waves leaped and sparkled on the stones of the riverbank. We stretched out our clothes and the swift current rinsed them quickly clean with a pleasant swish. The most interesting thing was that our checkered quilts and bedsheets spread out on the current in a decorative effect, trembling with an uncanny rhythm that seemed to remind me of something. Luo Hao had an inspiration—he went off a little way, set up his tripod, pushed the timed-release shutter, then came dashing toward us fast as he could, kicking up spray, and just made it in time to hold up a quilt like the rest of us as the shutter clicked. A souvenir photograph: three he-men washing their bedclothes in the Lhasa River with the Potala Palace in the background.

Luo Hao's second inspiration came from the girls unbinding their heavy braids to wash their hair. They were sisters—that was obvious—with thick black hair. As the younger one turned her face, her thick black hair still in the water, to say something to her sister, Luo Hao caught the unique scene on film. That was the photo he sent to the Japanese exhibition "Water and Life."

The sisters weren't one bit shy. Xinjian and I called in Chinese asking them to pose for some shots from various angles. They were plainly delighted, spoke good Chinese too. They left us their names and addresses and asked us to drop by and give them copies of the photos. They were husky and healthy-looking. I still remember their straightforward talk and their hearty laughs.

As I looked at them, I don't know why but I couldn't help recalling Liu Yu's story about the dogs who found a home with the old woman. For some reason I couldn't fathom, that story kept running through my head. The two girls brought over some barley wine and invited us to drink with them. We were afraid of getting diarrhea but nobody wanted to say so out loud. We politely turned down their offer and invited them to try what we'd brought. The cold chili chicken clearly delighted them, and after we finished the beer we had a big pot of their warm yak-butter tea.

It was the younger sister who discovered Xinjian's paper hawk hanging on a bush. She squealed with surprise and bubbled over in expressions of admiration. She asked Xinjian's permission, then with an expert hand she let the kite fly.

She said there were two paper hawks at home, her father had folded them, her father folded such beautiful paper hawks. Come spring lots of neighbors came looking for her father to fold them a paper hawk. He could fold two completely different kinds. Just then I recalled that when her older sister had given us their address a moment before, she said it was just below the Potala. I thought I'd ask them about the old woman who sheltered dogs. They were natives of Lhasa, lived here all their lives, and they came from the same neighborhood, so maybe they knew more about her.

Too bad, they didn't. But it turned out Luo Hao knew something. He said the old woman hadn't only kept dogs at the end of her life, she'd done that for years, and indeed had kept twenty or more. She didn't really make clay Buddhas. She had no relatives. She was long dead and gone, so the two girls from her neighborhood wouldn't have even heard of her. Luo Hao said the old woman often saved up her own grain for the dogs until she grew incredibly emaciated. The Lhasa people back then all knew about her. Some gave her grain out of pity, but she wouldn't eat any of it herself. They say the government even gave her an extra share of grain, but she refused to eat that too, giving it all to the dogs. She was stubborn, wouldn't listen to anyone. Some say she starved, others say she died of some disease. Anyhow, she lived alone, never had anything to do with the neighbors. They found her dead, and since she was so thin, the rumor naturally spread that she starved. Nobody knew for sure. Living together with so many dogs that roved all over, maybe she picked up some contagious disease and died.

The younger sister's mind was absorbed in flying the kite, but as the older sister turned away I happened to notice her wipe a tear from her face. I gave Luo Hao a poke and he broke off the story.

Xinjian finally gave the paper hawk to that playful girl.

But what was the matter with big sister? Could it be . . .

11

Before he left Lhasa, Liu Yu finished his version of the story for me. This time there was no interruption, and I listened to the end. I know maybe Luo Hao's version of the story is more down-to-earth, more authentic. But Liu Yu's version brings out the meaning better. Liu Yu wants to write a story, so his material is more elastic. Luo Hao's version is too restrictive on the imagination. Liu Yu doesn't just want to tell it superficially. I guess he's most concerned with the story's Buddhist elements and their deeper impact. This version gives the tale room to soar. I realized how keenly I hope for a chance to read Liu Yu's story, to discover what this tale had sparked off in another writer's imagination. That spark is what fascinates us.

Three days after Liu Yu left Lhasa I looked up the two sisters. I found their little alley, narrow and deep. Just the luck! Little sister wasn't there. I asked big sister why. She answered, "She's gone to fly her kite."

(Translated by Herbert J. Batt)

CHE QIANZI
(1963–)

*Born Gu Pan in Suzhou, a city noted for its exquisite gardens and aes-
thetic traditions, Che Qianzi is a renaissance man who is adept at
poetry, essay, painting, and calligraphy. Steeped in Chinese classics,
he represents the avant-garde, experimental spirit of contemporary
Chinese poetry. Seriously playful and profoundly witty, he once won a
sonnet contest by writing the same line fourteen times. In 1992 he graduated from Nanjing University, where he had formed a poetry group
called the "Original." A prolific essayist and noted painter, he now lives
in Beijing.*

The Night in the End

█hand

should█

eye█

left█

belly
█

nails

hea█

█d

left hand

left eye

revolver

█m

c█st

ch █

Sign: Inspired by a Letter*

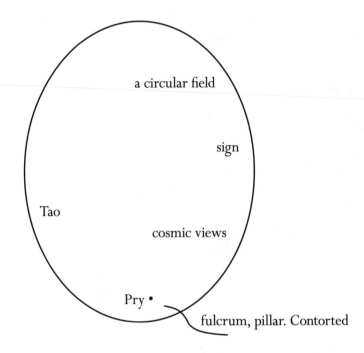

a circular field

sign

Tao

cosmic views

Pry •

fulcrum, pillar. Contorted

concave, red labyrinth, sea anemone
and the second page. No, but

---

* The Chinese word for "letter" in the title is *zimu*, literally meaning "mother of words." Hence, the title may be translated as "Sign: Inspired by Mother of Words."

A Chinese Character Comic Strip

> Eat: Titanium Oxide, Yellow No. 5, Vitamin C
> > and raisins
> > and
> > a comic strip:

1. 国 *country*   (Jade King lies on a big bed. A flea frolics on his waist.)

2. 口 *mouth*   (The king squishes the flea and gets out of the big bed. Now, it's all empty.)

3. 囚 *prisoner*   (We climb onto the big bed and become the expected unfilial sons.)

> All these are Chinese charactered on the comic strip.

An Antique Style Door Screen

1	7	it	all	I	4	1
2	2	looks	of	stand	2	2
3	3	like	a	in	3	3
4	4	rain	sudden	front	4	4
5	5	it	a	of	5	5
6	6	looks	gust	a	6	6
7	7	like	of	door	7	7
8	8	rain	spring	screen	8	8
2	8	it	wind	looking	5	2
2	2	looks	lifts	at	2	2
3	3	like	up	a	3	3
4	4	rain	my	big	4	4
5	5	it	facial	crowd	5	5
6	6	looks	skin	of	6	6
7	7	like	and	first	7	7
8	8	rain	you	graders	8	8
3	9	it	like	doing	6	3
2	2	looks	a	their	2	2
3	3	like	target	military	3	3
4	4	rain	made	drills	4	4
5	5	it	of	in	5	5
6	6	looks	empty	the	6	6
7	7	like	egg	school	7	7
8	8	rain	shell	yard	8	8

a long line of ants another long line of ants another long line

(Translated by Yunte Huang)

YU JIAN
(1954–)

Born in Kunming, Yunnan, Yu Jian worked as a riveter for ten years before entering Yunnan University in 1980. He and fellow young poets founded an unofficial journal Them *in 1984, proclaiming that "poetry stops with language," a view that foregrounds the oral, colloquial in writing. Positioning himself as a southern regional author in opposition to the cultural center dominated by the northern capital, Yu caused a stir in 1994 with the publication of his long poem "File 0." Praised by some critics as a milestone in contemporary Chinese poetry and maligned by others as a jumble of gibberish, the poem, with its accidental rhyming and ironic spacing, is a postmodern epic of the battle of discourses, a Kafkaesque fable of how private lives are recorded and examined by the state machine—the filing system.*

File 0

The File Room

in an architectural construction on the fifth floor   behind locks and more locks   in a secret room   his dossier
is held in a document folder   it is evidence of a person   two floors separating it from the person himself
he works on the second floor   the folder   is 50 meters away along a corridor   and 30 steps up on another floor
a room unlike others   with reinforced concrete on 6 sides   3 doors   no windows
1 fluorescent light   4 red fire extinguishers   200 square meters   over a thousand locks
padlocks   secret locks   drawer locks   the biggest one is an "Everstrong"   hanging outside
up the stairs   turn left   up the stairs   turn right   then turn left   then right again   unlock   unlock
by means of a combination   finally penetrate the inner sanctum   filing cabinet upon filing cabinet   this one next to that one
that one on top of this one   this one underneath that one   that one in front of this one   this one behind that one
8 aisles 64 rows   between them holding more than a ton of printing paper   black ink   paper clips and glue
his 30 years   one folder in 1,800 drawers   in the firm grasp   of a key
it is not a very thick folder   this person is young   only 50-some pages   40,000-some characters
and then   a dozen official seals   seven or eight photographs   some fingerprints   net weight 1,000 grams
in various hands   invariably arranged from left to right   first lines indented by two spaces   new line for each paragraph
from one radical to another radical   all of them words-that-name to do with him   definitions and modifiers
one third of his life   his times   places   events   patterns of who he sees and what he does

492

piled up together without words-that-move   reliably staying in the dark   will not move   will not be exposed
will not get damp   will not catch fire   there are no mice here   there are no germs here   there are no microbes of any kind here
copied out neatly   clearly   cleanly   well-trusted
on these grounds people view him as a comrade   issue him IDs   a salary   acknowledge his sex
on these grounds   he comes to work at eight every day   uses various kinds of paper   ink and correction fluid
outlines   drafts   lays out   corrects   proofreads   making everything follow standard grammar
from writing to writing   the movement of a hand   a fountain pen from left to right   from one radical
to another radical   from words-that-move to words-that-name   from plain words to metaphors   from—to—
a process by which ink is gradually used up   the movements of a good person   someone calls out "0"
his flesh and bone carrying him   like 0 he turns around and answers   someone else asks him to pass some paper
his building remains motionless   his position remains motionless   the light remains motionless
the locks remain motionless   the big steel cabinets remain motionless   his document folder remains motionless

Chapter One   History of Birth

his origin has nothing to do with writing   he came from a 28-year-old woman's labor pains
a time-honored hospital   third floor   host to inflammations   medications   doctors and a morgue
the paint is touched up every year   large quantities of gauze   of cotton wool of glass and alcohol are consumed
bricks in the walls show through   the grain has worn off the floorboards   things that come from human bodies
have replaced the varnish   no longer shiny   a little springy   nothing to do with human nature

the chrome on the scalpels has come off   the doctor is 48   the nurses are all virgins

howl   struggle   infuse   inject   pass   groan   daub

twist   grip   rip   cut   split   run   loosen   drip   trickle   flow

these words-that-move   are all on-site   words-that-move make up the site   words-that-move steeped in pools of blood

"the head's coming out"   the doctor's practiced enunciation   testimony: hands covered with blood

long white coats covered with blood   sheets covered with blood   floor covered with blood   metal covered with blood

testimony: "Obstetrics & Gynecology"   "No Spitting"   "One Child Is Best"   "Men's"

materials for investigation: influenza to the right   sore throats straight ahead

X-rays on the third floor for the inpatient department go out the door and walk west for 100 meters   surgery in 305

for injections queue on first floor   to pay bills queue at the left window   to collect medicine queue at the right window

a day crammed with all sorts of pain   a day of taut nerves   a day of incisions and sutures

a day of first visits and relapses   a day of rot and recovery   a day of deaths and births

everywhere are words of cures and words of illnesses   words of those fighting to live and words of those ready to die   everywhere are

actions to do with treating diseases and actions to do with having diseases   actions to do with final farewells and actions to do

with delivering babies

all this ancient stuff   will stick   to that first-born   that first-ever   that first-time

that new tongue   those new vocal cords   that new brain-box   those new testicles

these living things that come from countless words-that-move   are named in a notional word 0

Chapter Two   *History of Growing Up*

and his listening has begun   and his looking has begun   and his moving has begun

grown-ups give him hearing   grown-ups give him seeing   grown-ups give him movement

for mom say "mother"   for dad say "father"   for granny say "grandmother"

that dark   that turbid   that obscure   that tangled lump of flesh and blood

becomes limpid   becomes clear   understands   fills character-square upon character-square   page upon page of paper

turns into words-that-name   function words   syllables   past tense   word groups   passive voice

affixes   turns into meaning   significance   defined meaning   basic meaning   extended meaning   ambiguous meaning

turns into interrogative sentences   declarative sentences   compound and complex sentences   linguistic rhetoric semantic markers

a parasite living off words   from now on unable not to hear words   not to see words   not to meet words

some words make him public   some words give him cover   following words from simple to complex   from

shallow to profound   from childish to mature   from halting to fluent   this little person   becomes literate at six

is weaned at one   goes to nursery at two   goes to kindergarten at four

first grade to sixth   certified by   Teacher Zhang   seventh grade eighth grade ninth grade   certified by

Teacher Wang   tenth grade eleventh grade   certified by   Teacher Li   eventually he graduates from university

a thesis   thematically clear   properly composed   coherently structured   metrically neat

elegant parallelism   effective allusions   rare genius   unusual flourish   speak the mind bare the heart

appraisal: respects teachers   cares for classmates   opposes individualism   never comes late

observes the rules   delights in labor   never leaves early   is no foulmouth   bothers no women tells no lies   fights the Four Pests   is hygienic   does not take a needle or thread from the masses   is active and involved

is civilized   has a very good character   has a very good appearance   trims his fingernails   greets uncle   says hello to auntie

gives grandpa a hand   offers grandma his arm   puts his hands behind his back when class starts   actively seeks to make progress

pays attention during lectures   is conscientious in note-taking   is lively and vigorous   is modest and prudent works hard and

never complains

deficiencies: does not like physical education   sometimes whispers in class   does not regularly brush his teeth

note: report to teacher   he picked up a penny on the street   did not give it to Uncle People's Policeman

comment: this student's thinking is fine   but he is no talker   who knows what is on his mind

it is hoped that his parents   will examine his diary   report to us as necessary   to coordinate the upbringing

self-criticism: on 2 November 1968   did a bad thing

I drew a tank on a wall on a clean white wall on a public wall on everybody's wall on a collective

wall was drawn a great big tank by me I perpetrated the crime of liberalism must make a determined effort to mend my ways

history of medical allergies: symptoms reported by the doctor   the mother or the head of the family

"Darling" 4 to 6 tablets   3 times daily   after use of medication red spots appear on the face

"Good Boy"   1 tablet   3 times daily   symptoms as above   red spots less serious

"Little Dear"   (external use   apply locally)   after application of the ointment the patient suffers from drowsiness

"Here Comes the Big Bad Wolf Mummy Doesn't Want You Anymore"   (stimulant)   after taking this the patient suffers from vertigo

trace element composition: (also called For Your Health)   cherish   care for   flowers   grass

buds   seedlings   small   tender   honey-sweet   golden   (each tablet contains 25 mg)

innocent   pure   childish   naughty   (each tablet contains 25 mg) pulling   leading   cuddling   carrying   kindly watching   gently stroking

pat lightly   rock   urge   instruct   teach with skill and patience   hammer home   graft

mold   correct   rectify   purge   cultivate   show solicitude   injure accidentally   (50 mg each)

top brand sleeping pills: tomorrow or when you grow up   (take for the rest of your life)

filling: milk   language and literature   fruit candy   history   chocolate   fried rice with egg

three luminaries sun moon stars   four-syllable verse airs odes hymns   calcium tablets   voluntary labor   cod-liver oil

fruit fizz   briefing sessions   storytelling sessions   conferences 5,000 years   half a century   in the last decade

three years in succession   left center right   early this century   mid-century   recently   red-cooked   ice-cold   yellow-braised

fried   roasted   pickled   stewed   simmered   MSG   ground pepper   The Soy Sauce King   's achievements

's disgrace   's glory   's continuation   up to standard   's necessity   's victory   's greatness   's confidence

transcript: excellent   Grade A   good on all fronts   95   first-rate   top of his class

product appraisal certificate: over 1.70 m   net weight 63 kilograms   waist 32 inches

has hair   has dimples   has a beard   has testicles   has eyeballs   has biceps

has three bedrooms and a lounge room   has loudspeakers   has a salary   has hobbies   has poise   has a tender heart

can show loving care   can dance   can sing   can write   can talk   can sleep

his ears are ears   his nose is a nose   his legs are legs   his hands are hands   his anus is an anus

hearing in both ears 1.50 m   liver all clear   no abnormalities in heart lungs diaphragm   (doctor's signature)

Chapter Three   History of Romantic Love (Youth)

on that day suspended in sunlight   when the world's temperature was just right for all living things

an April noon   a temperature for unrest   a temperature for incest   a

temperature for flowerings and erections   when everything alive wanted to move   to move and seduce

all those bodies   all those joints   all those hands   all those legs   everywhere

all of them actions that cannot be named   movements that defy language   no battle-cries   no

clamor   no manifestos   no slogans   a mediocre day   unrecorded in the annals of history

it was just the details of those movements   the components of those actions   it was only to do with the flesh

to do with the skin   to do with the limbs   to do with the stem   to do with the root   to do with the round

to do with the long   to do with the springy   to do with the soft   to do with the hard

to do with juice   to do with rubbing   to do with interflow   to do with free breathing

to do with openings   to do with attacks   to do with leaps   spurts   sprints

(recollection)   on that day   they   male classmates   all of them 13 years old   surged in

to the toilet at school   on the walls was drawn all that was forbidden   a great many movements   the movement of masturbation

the movement of rape   the movement of syphilis   the movement of heroin   bad movements such as these

masturbate as the first word-that-moves   the male's admission ticket   hands all sticky   quickly over and done with

the temperature was just right   having tasted this small pleasure   the Adams   could not find the words to forgive themselves

the words they wanted did not exist outside   outside was the word-that-names Alma Mater   the word-that-names classroom

outside were words-that-name like garden   pond   blackboard   sports field   reading room   books totally irrelevant to the thing at hand   the boys felt desperately suffocated   all they could do was make ambiguous gestures

make up some code-words to murmur   tease each other   discuss the experience   walk out of the communal toilet

go to class   listen to the teacher   take notes   recite from memory   take tests   answer questions   take exams   revise

decree: delete all of the above 23 lines   must not be photocopied   circulated   published

Chapter Three   Text (Romantic Love)

at the legal age   of eighteen one may talk about marriage   talk that leads to romantic love   to collecting the relevant paperwork

romance and love   personal matters   this is a process of talking   a process in which a group of people shrinks to a few people

shrinks to three people   shrinks to two people   a process in which the back of the tongue touches the hard palate

a process in which the soft palate is lowered   air flows through the nasal cavity   lower lip and upper teeth

draw close to one another   a process in which the lips protrude   the lips assume a circular shape

a process of clustered vs scattered sounds   rough vs smooth   voiced vs unvoiced   obstructed vs unobstructed

sudden vs continuing   tense vs lax   falling vs rising intonation   tongue tip vs rounded lips

of course one has to wash one's hair   wash one's face   change one's shirt   rinse one's mouth   change one's socks   shine

one's shoes   sprinkle perfume

of course it's the best this   the best that   the best the other

of course it's getting there at seven   of course it's the main gate to the park   of course it's gazing from afar slow in coming

of course it's the moon fading at dawn where willows line the riverbank   of course it's two paper coasters   under two bottles of

soda pop

of course face to face lack words want words stop oneself smile behind one's hand want to say it hold it back saying how cool and
lovely the autumn is

of course be of one heart and mind be kindred spirits   of course deeply deeply   madly madly   endlessly endlessly
of course it's finding out what's going on   guess   "really   no kidding"   of course it's being a pretty pout   it's intimacy
of course it's brimming   overflowing   streaming   of course it's tear-filled eyes asking the flowers but the flowers won't speak
of course it's truly truly   terribly terribly   of course laden with grief   sorrow   despair
of course it's turning anger into joy   smiling through one's tears   of course it's hesitation   indecision   exploration
of course it's not finding out what's going on   it's conjecture   a puzzling smile   of course it's a small handkerchief
a swarm of mosquitoes   a caterpillar   a dandelion   a white rose
of course the very very very best   engraved on one's bones and heart   unforgettable   once in a lifetime
oh eternally the moonlight   oh eternally the narrow path   oh eternally the wind is rising   oh eternally at dusk
oh eternally 11 o'clock   oh eternally the park gates are closing   oh eternally streetlights   oh eternally long streets
oh eternally reluctant to part   oh eternally look back   oh eternally your silhouette from behind   oh eternally your eyes
it's time   please hurry up   it's time   please hurry up   see you later   Belle
see you later   Lu   till next time   Mei   till next time   Hua   see you again   Guizhen   till next time   Lan
summary: flowing cursive script   intransitive words-that-move   words-that-describe   words-that-name   modal adverbial
modifiers

description   simile   metaphor   allegory   myth   personification   irony   black humor
confessionalists   synesthesia   neoclassicism   colloquial poetry   initial rhyme   internal rhyme   end rhyme
contradictory rhetoric   functional ambiguity   palace poetics   music of Heaven   symbols   modulations

effective allusions striking a chord by referring to something close at hand if the enemy charges we retreat if the enemy retreats we harass for each inch of good there is a foot of evil

position statement: (large meeting   small meeting   neighborhood committee   the person who registers   comrades   relatives

friends   the person on duty at the door   the person in charge   the person who signs   the person who stamps)

safely   fine   while we're at it   needless to say   fantastic   don't worry   perfect match

agree   nod   approve   raise hands   applaud   sign

all right   not bad   OK then   fantastic   no problem   unanimously approved

Chapter Four   Daily Life

1 PLACE OF RESIDENCE

the address where he sleeps is no. 6 Shangyi Street   public land for building consistently used for the construction of housing   formerly with hoes   carts   saws   nails   tiles

now with mixers   pile drivers   jackhammers   blowtorches   trucks   cement

marble   reinforced steel   pour   ram   pile   lay   rivet   seal

steel windows   steel doors   steel locks   earthquake-proof up to magnitude 10   fireproof   floodproof

A-B-C-room 503   is the code in his residence booklet   A represents

the district where he lives   B represents his block   C represents his entrance
5 indicates his level   03 finally is his room

2 SLEEP SITUATION

his bed is 1.30 m from the floor   closest to the ceiling   the right height for sleeping
away from noise   dry and airy   eminently fit for storing   accumulating   shelving   stacking
at 10 p.m.   he draws the curtains   locks the door   turns the light off   this is formal sleep
at noon   he sleeps on the couch   without taking his clothes off   just his shoes   covered with a blanket
a good time to sleep   is in spring   when he sleeps much   sleeps well   sleeps and does not want to wake up
a bad time to sleep   is from June to September   hot   stuffy   when a single sleep comes in several parts
many cat naps   to get the job done   in autumn he sleeps longest   undisturbed by mosquitoes or flies
no need to scratch or catch   he sleeps with peace of mind   sleeps lots   in winter he goes to bed at 9   with an electric blanket

3 GETTING UP

puts on shorts   puts on a singlet   puts on pants   puts on slippers   goes to the toilet   squeezes out the toothpaste
fills his mouth with water
spits out the water   washes his face   looks in the mirror   rubs on moisturizer   combs his hair   changes into shoes
eats breakfast   two oil fritters and a bowl of soya-bean milk   a glass of milk and a roll   in turns

502

puts on a woolen sweater   puts on a coat   takes his briefcase   looks in the mirror once again   locks the door
checks with his hand if the door is fast   goes down the stairs   looks at the sky   looks at his watch   pushes his
bicycle   goes out the main gate

4 WORK SITUATION

goes in   nods   his mouth opens   his face moves   his hands move   his feet move
his head moves   his eyeballs and eyelids move   stands   sits   his face does not move   walks four steps
walks 10 meters   gives   takes   opens   holds   skims   taps   pushes   pulls   collects
counts up   squats down   comes out   closes up   drinks   closes up   chews   spits   measures   brushes   copies   bends
at longitude 35° east   latitude 20° north   radius 200 meters   altitude 500 meters   air temperature
22°   southeasterly wind force 3   time: from 8 to 12   from 2 to 6

5 THOUGHT REPORT

(based on inferences made by a comrade with a good grasp of the details   there are doubts   expose and sort out)
he wants to yell reactionary slogans   he wants to break the law and violate discipline   he wants to go into a frenzy   he wants
to degenerate
he wants to rape   he wants to go naked   he wants to kill a bunch of people   he wants to rob banks
he wants to be a big millionaire   a big landlord   a big capitalist   wants to be king   president

he wants to lead a life of debauchery   of dissolution and excess   to be a local despot   to act like a tyrant   to ride
roughshod over the people

he wants to capitulate   he wants to be a traitor   he wants to surrender to the enemy   he wants to recant   he wants to
turn against his own side

he wants to rebel   to engage in frantic activism

he wants to agitate   to revolt   to bring down an entire class

6 A GROUP OF WORDS-THAT-MOVE HIDDEN IN GLOOMY THOUGHT

smash   arouse   penetrate   punish   frame   accuse the innocent   hit the helpless

"do"   "work"   "fix"   shout oneself hoarse   demolish   expose

overthrow   execute   make the boot come down hard   storm!   charge!

comments and instructions: this person should be subjected to internal control   careful observation of movements

reports in duplicate   top secret

for internal reference   file with care   not for outside circulation   "it's enough that you know   don't tell him"

7 LEISURE ACTIVITIES

always thinking about the landscape outside the city (beyond Xiama Village)

hammers out one flawless sentence after another   the wheat 10 km around his native place   has been lucky enough to be
mentioned by him

(see *In the Rain*)   on occasion   stylishly corrects   *Poems by Zhimo*   (Zhimo   modern poet

studied in England   graduated from Cambridge   publications include *Sayonara*   translated into Japanese

English   French   Italian   Serbian   16 African languages)

often   strolls along a nineteenth-century street   (Shangyi Street   part of Wuhua District

altogether containing 2 public toilets   3 Sichuan hot-pot restaurants   1 post office

1 hairdresser   6 garbage cans   3 alleyways   14 front gates   3 slogan banners

2 billboards   10 posters advertising medical cures   missing persons notices   shops to let)

every week   washes his clothes once   sees 2 movies   buys 7 local papers   (the evening paper *Reader's Digest Weekly*)

does 80 sit-ups   spends 6 hours browsing in shops   (in three sessions   2 hours each time)

every day   eats snacks   20 grams of cake   20 grams of sunflower seeds   3 packets of chewing gum   1 packet of peanuts

3 grams of fruit candy   takes 1 look at the calendar   8 glances at his watch   sits down 9 times   squats for 20 minutes

lies down 11 times   sits down for 4 hours   his hands behind his back   his hands behind his head   his hands in

his trouser pockets   his hands on his mug   his hands dangling   his hands unclenched   his feet on tiptoe his feet touching

the floor

his feet arched   his feet in slippers   his feet in a basin   his feet on a cloth   his feet bare

every night   takes off the cloth cover   presses ON   watches commercials   watches the news   watches the weather forecast

watches the world of animals   watches song   and watches dance   watches 30 episodes of a soap opera   watches

watches commercials   watches foreigners   watches commercials   watches the country's natural beauty   watches

commercials   watches

sports   flowers   clothes   water   watches commercials   watches a preview of tomorrow's program   watches how today's program ends

here   goodnight everybody   watches the screen become a mass of snowflakes   presses OFF

8 DIARY

day X month X year X   sunny   not in a good mood   depressed   day X month X year X
sunny   in a good mood   sat around all morning   day X month X year X   the sky was overcast again
lonely   it rained   slept some more in the afternoon   day X month X year X   slept the whole day
on this day in that month in year X caught a cold   on this day it was windy   on that day it was hot   on this day it was
cold   on that day waited for so-and-so   New Year   this day   birthday   that day   holiday
this day in that month in this year

Chapter Five   Forms

1 CV FORM   REGISTRATION FORM   MEMBERSHIP FORM   ADMISSION NOTICE   APPLICATION FORM

a photograph   black-and-white half-inch photograph bareheaded   family name given name   stroke order   pen
names   11 (omitted)

sex   *yang* in the south   *yin* in the north   year and month of birth   in the fall of the year *jiazi*   amid great winds and rains place of birth   now there is a beautiful spot   age   thirty with mere dust and soil for honor and rank

family background   if the old man was a hero the son will be as strong   make the old man a reactionary and the son will be as wrong

occupation   my Heaven-granted talent will find its use   salary   a dish of pickled vegetables   not worth rattling one's teeth

educational level   laziness in youth   spells regret in old age   this person contains

30 kilograms of muscle   5,000 cc of blood   20 kilograms of fat   10 kilograms of bones

200 grams of hair 1pair of eyeballs 2 liver lobes 2 hands 2 feet 1 nose

marital status   one could say married   one could say unmarried   believe it or not that's up to you

political features   a ridge from this angle a peak from that   far and near and high and low none remain the same   ethnicity

in the distant East there is a dragon   zodiac sign   horoscope   animal sign   palmistry   birthmarks

heredity   nicknames   facial features   accent   fingerprints   footprints   blood group

family members and social connections   father   file weight 3,000 grams   first half of his life

in need of an additional 500 grams   awaiting supplementation   mother   file weight 2,500 grams   brothers and sisters

file weight 1,000 grams each   nephews and nieces   file weight 10 grams each   paternal grandfather   grandmother

father's elder brother   maternal   great-uncle   mother's eldest brother's wife   file weight 5,000 grams   all deceased

personal history   from this year to that year   in Chapter One   from that year to another year in Chapter Two

this year and that year   in Chapter B   (500 meters from the work unit   the district hospital's department of internal medicine)

from this year to that year   in Chapter Three   from that year to another year   in Chapter Four

2 INVENTORY OF OBJECTS

1 single bed   (two planks added for width   two mottos pasted on the head

1 picture of Belmondo   1 full-length picture of a female movie star)

1 desk   (5 drawers   semi-antique)   contents: letter paper   envelopes

diary   rice coupons   meal coupons   bathing coupons   commodity coupons

employment ID   personal ID   medical history   ballpoint pen   fountain pen

weasel hair writing brush   goat hair writing brush   7 combs   27 keys

(bicycle keys   built-in lock keys   padlock keys   flex-lock keys

copper keys   aluminum keys   iron-coated keys differing numbers of each)

1 broken Seagull watch (domestic product)   2 quartz watches (broken)   1.5 bottles of Stomach Comfort

20 sachets of painkiller powder   1 bottle of flu medicine   half a bottle of librium   1 bottle of glycerine   skin ointment

scattered pills   ampules   powders   ointments   sugarcoated tablets   some of each

3 pads of lined manuscript paper   1 bottle of black ink   1 bottle of blue ink   1 bottle of red ink

7 souvenir badges from famous scenic spots

1 bookcase   (height 1.50 m   width 1.20 m   5 shelves   altogether holding 3 sets of selected works

1 set of collected works   1 complete *Sea of Words*   1 complete *Modern Chinese*   *Teach-Yourself Handbook of Chinese*

Autodidact magazine   *Handbook of Sexual Knowledge*   *Essays on Jin Ping Mei*   *All-in-One*

Erudition   *World Atlas*   *330 Poems in Chinese Parallel Verse*   *Health and Nutrition*

Two Hundred Things to Know about Photography   *The World of Will and Ideas*   *Japanese Primer*)

15 kilos of old magazines   5 kilos of old wall calendars   20 kilos of waste paper

unit price   for old magazines   0.20 *yuan* per kilo (same price for wall calendars and waste paper)

books   0.40 *yuan* per kilo

6 arts and crafts objects: a plaster bust of the Venus de Milo   a plaster statue of David   1 porcelain galloping horse

ceramics: 1 lion   1 eagle   1 American panther

1 leather trunk   (brand-new   smells of camphor balls   with a combination lock)   containing 2 brand-new Western suits

1 Goldlion tie (red)   1 piece of Milton scarlet woolen cloth   (length 4 m   width

1.50 m)   2 silk quilt covers   1 brand-new photo album   (no pictures inside)

1 wooden trunk (i.e. an old soap box)   containing   1 cotton-padded jacket (on the bottom)   2 old military uniforms

2 old Mao suits   3 old zip-up jackets   1 pair of bell-bottoms   (frayed at the hem)

2 pairs of jeans (halfway worn)   old socks (7 pairs)   shorts   singlets   towels   some of each

1 guitar (as good as new   broken strings   brand name *Hongmian*)

1 glass presse-papier (pressing on 2 postcards   3 photographs   1 soft-focus picture of himself

8-inch-size   in autumn   with fallen leaves in the foreground   the second is a group shot   all together at the park gate

he   sitting ninth from left in the front row   the third is a picture of a woman   this person's

name   age   work unit   background   politics   track record are all unclear)

1 black-and-white television set   1 army thermos   1 inner tube   1 spittoon

13 empty bottles   1 flashlight   8 pairs of slippers (5 pairs unusable)

1 sneaker (whereabouts of other shoe unknown, surviving one as good as new)

2 pairs of leather shoes (with medium heels and heel reinforcements) one pair is a reddish brown

1 bundle of letters   35 in all   (sender's addresses included   this city   name and address enclosed

a television station's audience mailbox   the organizing committee of a hygiene knowledge competition

X City X Alley no. X   room 707 no. 246a XX Street)

1 small *Hongmei* radio   1 large enamel bowl   1 chair

(the rattan broken in many places)   1 couch (length 1.80 m   the cover gone shiny two of the springs showing)

7 packets of instant noodles   half a jar of coffee (Nescafé)   1 hot plate (1,000 watt)

3 mattress covers   (all old   spotted and worn)   2 badminton shuttles   1 ping-pong bat

3 decks of cards   (one deck as good as new   the other two are incomplete   and mixed together)

7 Chinese chess pieces   (3 white 4 black)   71 coins (on the floor

and in the drawers there are 18 five-cent coins in all   30 two-cent coins   the rest are one-cent coins   and small notes)

Last Chapter   (*No Text on This Page*)

510

APPENDIX ONE   FILE PRODUCTION AND STORAGE

write   transcribe   print   compile   always use a fountain pen   permanent ink
in a clear hand   invalid if altered   forgery strictly prohibited   not to be transferred   office use only
300 characters per page   simplified script   make Arabic numerals large   classify   differentiate   file away
add category number and subcategory number   in chronological order   divided according to nature of content into
category A category B category C   add page numbers   before final binding   take out staples
paper clips   pins and other metal objects   bind with thread   ensure that the content is not obscured by stapling
the pages of each chapter to be cut uniformly   pressed flat   tightly stapled   finally delivered to the file room   sorted
counted checked found correct

signed by the person who delivers the file and the person who accepts the file   go by the numbers to find his room   his aisle
his category   his level   his row   his cabinet   his space   put it in there   lock it away
close the cabinet   insert the key   turn it 360 degrees   switch off the light   close the first door
insert the key   turn it 360 degrees   close the second door   insert the key
turn it 360 degrees   close the third door   insert the key   turn it 360 degrees
close the iron security door   insert the key   turn it 360 degrees
remove

(Translated by Maghiel van Crevel)

CHI ZIJIAN
(1964–)

*Born in Mohe, Heilongjiang—a city often called "China's North Pole"—
Chi Zijian began writing in high school and had her literary debut while
still in college. Her novella* Fairy Tales from an Arctic Village *(1986)
brought her into prominence. Like her predecessor Xiao Hong, Chi also
writes about the northeastern region of China with a rare, gripping
poetic sensibility. Under Chi's pen, the frozen northern land is turned
into a magic fairyland for dramas of love and human vulnerability. Currently the chairperson of the Heilongjiang Provincial Writers Association, Chi has the unique distinction among Chinese writers of having
won the most prestigious Lu Xun Literary Prize three times.*

Night Comes to Calabash Street

If Calabash Street can ever justly be described as humming with prosperity, it is at that fleeting moment as the bright golden sun slips into
the mountain cool.

This impression derives mainly from the reflected brilliance of the sky.
The streets of the town gain a certain dignity where two of them, ash-
gray, crisscross in a minute intersection. Passersby marvel, not just at the
new dome-roofed traffic control box, but at long-established landmarks—
Xizi's mom's noisy jellied bean curd shop, Old Yu Fa's splendid pancake

shop, and Skinny's ever more profitable shoe repair shop——these too contribute to the impression of a robust yet peaceable life outside the city.

As he stepped through the school gates, Minghua spotted his granddad, birdcage in hand, waiting for him by the gray gatepost. Grandfather and grandson smiled at each other knowingly across the sunset; neither one offered the other a greeting. The young one took the cage from the old one and raised it level with his eyes to tease the bird; the old one took the young one's book bag and slung it over his shoulder like a soldier off on a rapid march.

Together they strode off toward Calabash Street.

The gray street was engulfed by the setting sun. They stepped into the boundless brilliance and were transformed into celestial beings. The thrush in its cage set up a spellbinding warbling just then, as if it was dreaming it had flown back to the forest. Trills of birdsong blended with the footsteps, the peddlers' cries, and the fragrance of frying pancakes, all wafting gently up from Calabash Street.

The street lay before them in all its glory. It wouldn't be going too far to compare it to a bride in her wedding finery. The sign in front of Xizi's mom's jellied bean curd shop was as smart as the coil of her hair. The shop was certain to be full already, a clutch of men and women under the awning outside stippling the benches with all the colors of the spectrum. There was always laughter in Xizi's mom's voice, you could hear it a mile away.

The muscles in the old one's face relaxed all at once, the way dried wood-ear fungus does when you pour boiling water over it. Though he was a man of seventy-odd and frosty white at the temples, when he got to Calabash Street, he'd go all red in the face with excitement, like a child. The little one smiled, showing teeth gilded by the setting sun, as if someone had stuck a wild chrysanthemum in his mouth.

"Kept late again?" the old one grumbled.

"We had these endless practice tests today. The teachers took turns bombarding us in every subject," the little one said with unaffected humor.

"Battle readiness," the old one responded, as though that were an end to it.

They had reached the door of the jellied bean curd shop. White snow floated in all the bowls, glittering like coral. Small spoons, the six *fen* apiece kind, dug into the fragrant, tender stuff, making it quiver, making everyone's mouth water.

A nod, a smile, but no words: that was their protocol for greeting friends. Everyone's appetite was as clear as the skies, and immediately they were raring to eat.

Xizi's mom spied them through an opening in the door curtain and her voice immediately came spilling through the chinks in the woven bamboo:

"Xizi, seat the customers!"

"Ai . . ." That voice, crisp as a chisel cutting through a block of ice, could belong to none other than ten-year-old Xizi. He was small-boned and spindly, but his body was crowned with a magnificent head, as if a weak plant had by some miracle produced a gigantic fruit. The effect he had on people was half pleasing and half frightening. That head was as big as the setting sun—and as round.

Minghua was into the shop before his granddad. Xizi, wiping off tables in the kitchen, cocked his head to smile at Minghua. The soy sauce bottle on the table boasted a number of flies disporting themselves like ladies of the night. Their tryst with the bottle interrupted by Xizi's movements, they flickered off one after another to the windowsill.

"Xizi—bowls!" Xizi's mom's voice seemed fused with piping hot beads of sweat.

"Ai . . . I'm coming—" Xizi threw down his cloth, put two round stools into position, and, dusting off his hands, went off to fetch the bowls.

"Why so slow?"

"I wiped off the tables and put the stools around first."

"You should get the bowls first and then do the stools; that's the right way."

"If I do the stools last, people have to stand around too long."

"You can never be wrong, can you?" Xizi's mom laughed.

They always got good service in Xizi's mom's jellied bean curd shop.

If the place was full, they were invited into the inner sanctum, where they could eat in peace.

"Have a couple of bowls, Minghua. Jellied bean curd is good for the brain and you wear yours out!" Xizi's mom stood behind them brimming with cheer.

Minghua turned and gave her a smile, which made Xizi convulse with laughter, his huge head swaying on his slender neck as he rocked to and fro.

"Just look at these two kids, would you?" The old one swallowed down a mouthful of jellied bean curd and beads of sweat bubbled out on the tip of his nose.

"I give up!" In a single swoop, Xizi's mom took the white-flowered blue apron from her waist and slipped it over Xizi's head. "What is that stupid laughter of yours all day long about?"

"Minghua's gone to school so long it's made him stupid." He'd seen Minghua grip the spoon as though it was a pen.

"You're a big dope yourself and don't know it."

Xizi had already yanked the apron from his head and thrown it onto the pastry board. The setting sun swelled like a tide against the windowpane. Inside the shop tranquillity reigned.

"Go buy me a pancake," the old one ordered Minghua. There was still an edge to his appetite. When Xizi's mom heard that a pancake was wanted, she seemed to see Old Yu Fa's shriveled-walnut face glow among thousands of pancakes, round yellow orbs like huge suns scorching her heart. She blinked; there was a barely discernible tightening at the corners of her mouth. In a strongly nasal voice she put in: "Xizi will go."

"No, let me." Minghua's figure was already stirring the curtain and there was a crisp rustle of bamboo.

Old Yu Fa's pancake shop sprang up in response to Xizi's mom's jellied bean curd shop. Generally, people who eat jellied bean curd want some steamed buns or pastries to go with it. Xizi's mom's wasn't a large shop and they were short of hands, she couldn't handle these as well, so Old Yu Fa's pancake shop wafted onto Calabash Street like a rosy cloud drifting over from the horizon.

Actually, Old Yu Fa wasn't old, not more than fifty, twelve years older than Xizi's mom. He had been a carter in a production team for most of his life, had never married, and had a bit of money put by.

The fact that he was without a wife was partly due to his looks and personality. He was only 1.53 meters tall, stocky, with short legs, a paunch, and a thick waist. His arms were in fact quite beefy, and because his head resembled a big iron ball stuck in the mire, he seemed to have no neck. At first glance, he looked like an oaf. But appearances can be misleading; he was one clever fellow. To give his pancake shop a boost, he bought a dark red donkey and several granite millstones. His busiest time of day was dusk and his face became as lively as a bridegroom's then.

Standing there under the awning in the open air, in a sunset fine as this, with lots of people gathered around—now, that was sheer bliss, rare in this mortal world, and Old Yu Fa the presiding genius of the moment. Anyone hearing his tone of voice and watching the way he moved as he fried the pancakes would envy him his lot in life.

"The usual, Minghua . . . nice and brown?"

"Mmm!"

"You're sure to pass all your exams with flying colors. Seen the big bright sun in your dreams?"

"No, but I have seen stars."

"Ah—stars!" shouted Old Yu Fa as he turned the pancake with the spatula. "Stars mean official position. You've got a bright future ahead of you."

Bursts of hearty laughter came from the bystanders. The pancake was rolled and ready: a long cylinder of hot and fragrant crispy-soft dough, like a rice-colored napkin tucked under Minghua's chin. He began taking big bites of it.

As a result of his recent exertions, Old Yu Fa's face grew even redder and shinier. Seeing that he was about to serve the other customers, Minghua said quickly, "Fry another, not too brown this time."

"One for Granddad?" Old Yu Fa's eyes sparkled and the ladle rattled against the pan.

"Yup, for Granddad."

"Having jellied bean curd at Xizi's mom's again, is he? Of all the luck!"

As he spoke, Old Yu Fa splashed a ladleful of batter into the pan, evened it out with the wooden spatula, and then gave it a few good turns, making the pan wheeze clouds of white steam.

"What d'ya need all that flour for? Pancakes got to be thin or they ain't any good," a very old woman said as she licked the remains of one from her palm.

"Missus, you're not familiar with the size of our county magistrate's belly!"

"Hahaha . . ."

Minghua took his granddad's pancake and, rubbing the enchanting dusk from his eyes, ambled off in the direction of the jellied bean curd shop. Just then, from the empty square around the traffic control box at the head of Calabash Street, came the golden tones of a gong.

Skinny's trained monkey was about to perform again.

Men women young old gathered around in a circle; some were eating, others just stood there. The monkey was really very clever. He wore a cunning black Chaplinesque waistcoat and an absurd pair of bright green velvet trousers. After a day spent mending shoes, Skinny would squeeze into his jeans, near-white from washing, and tuck a flowered shirt into them. He made a sight for sore eyes as he put the monkey through its paces.

When the monkey had enough of banging on the gong, he handed it over to Skinny and picked up a square of rosy red cloth, which he slipped over his head as he minced coyly about playing the bride. Following laughter from the satisfied crowd, a silvery shower of coins pelted the monkey, sliding suggestively down his rump to sigh contentedly onto the black and white pavement.

All the glory of Minghua's granddad's life was congealed in that fifteen meters of street.

"Another bowl?"

"No, I've had enough."

"You shouldn't drink too much in the evening. You're getting on in years, and if you got something stuck in your throat, you might choke to death."

"Nothing to worry about. I'm off."

"Just like that?" Xizi's mom's voice suddenly darkened like the skies at dusk. "Minghua and Xizi are watching Skinny's monkey."

The dusk had been shattered, and the golden light fringing the horizon died swiftly away. The interior of the small shop grew unusually warm and quiet. More and more people poured into Calabash Street to watch the monkey, until finally the traffic cop had to disperse the dense crowd.

"Minghua, don't take the school entrance exam. Just look at Jin San. A couple of years studying only got him back to standing on the street and he doesn't even make as much as Skinny does with his shoe repair shop and performing monkey."

"Xizi! Thinking about money at your age. . . ."

"But my mom says so."

"Your mom is old-fashioned—narrow-minded. How many times has my granddad told you—you should go to school; you're ten years old and here you are still waiting tables in the shop. Is that what you want to do with your life?"

"Well, I don't know," said Xizi, somewhat at a loss.

"Keep on like this and you'll never find a wife."

"My mom says as long as you have money you don't have to worry."

"Then you're sure to get an idiot for a wife."

Xizi heard him out and started to giggle. He giggled like a little girl, his pinkie in the corner of his mouth, like a star towing a crescent moon.

The monkey began to make his bows to the crowd and numerous coins again shot out at the animal's hindquarters. The coins tinted the gray street bright and sparkling, like sunlight after a storm makes the bubbles in the hollows of the pavement glisten.

Skinny guffawed. He had teeth the color of tea, a color that made you think of filth and unpleasantness. There was a weak, dirty look to the gummy matter borne out of the corners of his eyes when they watered.

Seeing Skinny laugh, looking like a crook-necked willow tree, Xizi laughed too, laughed until he cried. Minghua pinched the boy's ear between his fingers and scolded him for "laughing like an idiot."

OLD YU FA had shut up his pancake shop, blocking out the dusk by closing the shutters. Alone in the room, he stripped and began to wash himself with a towel dipped in tepid water, attacking his ears, neck, armpits with gusto. The neighbors were always complaining about his grubbiness. They said he had a strong smell about him. Never mind what the neighbors said, tonight he was going to have a thorough wash and then put on a spanking clean jacket and go see *The White Snake* with Xizi's mom. That morning he had given the tickets to Xizi to take over with the instruction:

"If your mom isn't going, bring the tickets back."

The sun had been gone for some time now and so far Xizi hadn't come back with the tickets. It looked as if his mom had accepted.

Xizi's dad had died of lung cancer. Someone's getting cancer had the same effect on the folks of Calabash Street as a flash of lightning splitting the heavens: it terrified them; its dying brilliance made them gasp. It was with the same sort of emotion that Old Yu Fa had regarded Xizi's dad's death. He watched as Xizi's dad, like a full moon on the wane, grew thinner day by day. Later he witnessed the man's pallid face after he gave up the ghost in the emergency room and the worrisome, merciless oxygen tube sprouting from his nostrils. When he pulled the oxygen tube from the dead man's nose, Xizi's mom wailed and threw herself at Old Yu Fa, tearing at his face and neck. She swore at him for being wicked and cruel and ordered—begged—him to reinsert the tube. That was his first encounter with the violent yet docile female temperament. Unfortunately, taking place as it did in the emergency room, the experience made no soul-stirring impression on him. But the memory of that moment always aroused him.

People said the look in Xizi's mom's eyes was too intense, too brilliant, her man couldn't withstand her sexual appetites, she ate him alive. Though Old Yu Fa had no experience of women, his powers of imagination concerning sexual encounters were as prodigious as anyone else's. From then on, whenever he beheld Xizi's mom's vivacious face and sultry eyes, he couldn't resist further glances at the quivering breasts lurking under her blouse and her ample rounded buttocks, as a way of corroborating the opinion of others as well as his own imagination.

These complicated emotions filled him now as he took a sponge bath. As he schussed the black balls of dirt from his chest to the floor, he began to whistle softly, a song learned in his days as a carter:

> A cart, a whip, a lone shadow, and a jug of wine,
> I can bear the wind and the snow in my face,
> Just let the sound of my hooves
> Carry to the mountain fastness, calling out—Sweetheart
> Bolt the door fast when night comes.

A hot breeze crept into the room through a chink in the shutters like a soft fuzzy caterpillar. The odor of pancakes was as strong as ever. The cloying, sweet smell raised visions of autumn wheat fields in his mind's eye, their grand vista of golden yellow spreading all the way to the horizon, right up to the setting sun. In the midst of the fields stood a yellow wattle hut; inside, Xizi's mom went contentedly about her work. As he came in from the fields he could see from far off a wisp of cooking smoke floating tenderly into the sky, and at the same time, catch a whiff of what he'd been longing for.

Someone was knocking on the shutters.

"Pancakes!" came a shrill insistent voice.

"Here!" Old Yu Fa responded immediately, as if he were a pancake himself.

"I'm so hungry my stomach is shriveling up!" The tone was aggressive, rising to a note of dissatisfaction and doubt: "What are you up to anyway, shutting up so early?"

"I haven't done anything to be ashamed of!" Old Yu Fa, terrified that his innermost secrets might be found out, rushed to defend himself.

He wrung out the towel, gave himself a once-over, and threw on his clothes. Then, taking two steps to his usual three, he unbolted the door.

"Performance over, is it?"

"Yep."

"And the monkey?"

"Xizi's keeping an eye on it."

"A good take, a washbasin full of coins, was it?"

"Enough for pancakes." Skinny licked at the sweat that was running down to the corner of his mouth.

"Enough to get your brother a wife, then." Old Yu Fa laughed.

"Enough my eye! The price has gone up again. This morning she wanted seven thousand."

"Geez. She's no fairy princess either. . . ."

"Women are nothing but trouble." The way Skinny shook his head implied he'd been cheated innumerable times by innumerable women.

Old Yu Fa gave Skinny the leftover pancakes that had been wrapped up in cheesecloth and asked if he wanted some cucumbers. They'd only just been salted down and weren't too salty yet, very cool and refreshing. "Mmm." Skinny's chicken-claw hand was into the plate of cucumbers on its own.

Skinny had an older brother who was paralyzed, thirty-five years old, and unmarried. As Skinny's dad lay dying, he'd been pointing at the paralytic and his eyes had refused to close. Skinny's mother too was so broken up her hair turned white. Now Skinny had taken up shoe repair, a modest enough sort of trade, but it had brought brighter days to his impoverished family. To see the paralytic married was the one dream of his mother's remaining days.

"At the start, Yinhua asked for two thousand, after a year it went up to five, now she wants seven. Seems like she doesn't want to marry my brother."

"Well, if Yinhua marries your brother, she'll be like a widow with a living husband, won't she?"

"It's only his legs that are out of commission."

"Haha, it's still no good—a paralytic—think about it . . . you'd have
to . . ."

"Yinhua's no prize either!"

"Because she got pregnant once? It's not as if it was her fault, she just
picked the wrong guy and then he dumped her." Old Yu Fa didn't feel
like arguing with Skinny anymore. All he could think of was sitting
in the theater with Xizi's mom to watch the opera as soon as possible;
nothing could top that.

"If you've got what it takes, get Xizi's mom out from under the county
magistrate's thumb."

"What would I want to do that for?"

"Cooking, cleaning, having kids."

"She's too good at burying men alive."

"Isn't that just talk?" With one foot out the door, Skinny turned and
said, "As for having what it takes, you're no match for His Lordship."

"He can lick my boots!" Old Yu Fa flew into a sudden rage, cursing
furiously. But the moment the words were out, he clapped a hand over
his mouth, thinking fearfully to himself: "Lucky no outsider heard; you
can't badmouth somebody that important and get away with it."

Old Yu Fa knew the magistrate only too well. That whitish paved
road led to the residence of the former county magistrate, Geng Ming.
Old Yu Fa had taken his cart to the quarry to dig out the best gravel
for it. Just after it was finished, Minghua's granddad, county chief pro-
curator at the time, just back from a meeting, found out about it. Subsequently, Old Yu Fa had seen with his own eyes how David took on
Goliath. In the end, Geng Ming had been relieved of his post and transferred out of the county. The paved road had been a symbol of Geng
Ming's power; now it had also become a witness to the chief procura-
tor's strict enforcement of the law.

Now Old Yu Fa ran this hole-in-the-wall pancake shop. How would
someone with as little ingenuity as himself fare against the magistrate?
He was nothing but the old nag that pulled the cart, while that other
was the driver. It was fate. Old Yu Fa sighed. Even his enthusiasm for the
opera had waned, and he stood there blankly.

||||||||||||||||

Skinny went back to his shoe repair shop and had just taken up his work when Xizi ran in sputtering and shouting:

"The monkey's eaten some bananas!"

"Whose?"

"The state's. I was picking the money up off the ground, not paying him any mind and he jumped up onto the state vegetable stall, ate the bananas, and left a whole pile of peels behind!"

"Where were the stall-keepers?"

"At the department store buying leather shoes at the sale."

"Serves them right." Skinny sniggered.

"You'll have to pay."

"Like hell." Skinny didn't care.

"Really, you will, they've caught the monkey."

"Shit." Skinny cursed, closed up shop, and said:

"Where's Minghua's grandaddy?"

"Talking to my mom."

"Ask him to come out and act as judge."

As he thought, Skinny walked toward Xizi's mom's jellied bean curd shop.

Daylight had gone, the last rays of the setting sun receding from the earth like an outgoing wave. . . . People didn't feel its warm lingering breath—an altogether different feeling, cool and refreshing, swept over them.

As they were walking along, Old Yu Fa came up to them and took Xizi to one side. Skinny observed them, one young, one old, jabbering together for some time. Finally, Old Yu Fa drew a ticket out of Xizi's pocket, tore it into pieces in the breeze, and with a mixture of exasperation and relief patted Xizi on the head. Then, humming to himself, he drifted away.

"Old fool," Skinny whispered.

"Hehe. Some fun." Xizi giggled.

"What're you laughing at?"

"I'm laughing at myself because I have such a terrible bad memory."
And Xizi scratched his cheek, just like the monkey.

THINGS WERE PICKING UP on Calabash Street again. There were
few vehicles left on the street, but the old folks gathered to chew
the fat shone like the silvery snowflakes of midwinter scattered over
the ground. They held mugs of tea, stools, even grandkids. Perspiration
from the hot dinners they'd eaten filmed their foreheads. The curiously
shaped clouds in the sky had thinned out, dispersing until finally you
couldn't make out the shapes, or even tell the clouds from the sky. . . .

Just then a boy who'd been out searching for wild duck eggs suddenly
ran up from the river to report:

"Yinhua's thrown herself into the river!"

Even Calabash Street, that drunken Arhat, reeled with shock at
the news.

(Translated by Janice Wickeri)

YU HUA
(1960–)

Born in Zhejiang, Yu Hua never went to college but had his literary training from reading books in mutilated form—in the age of censorship young Chinese readers often secretly circulated books with covers torn to conceal the titles and the authors. He worked as a small-town dentist for five years, and then shifted from looking at cavities in people's mouths to cavities in a nation on the verge of an economic boom. His short story "On the Road at Eighteen" (1986) made him famous, followed by the novel To Live *(1993), which was adapted for the screen by Zhang Yimou to international acclaim. Author of six novels and many stories and essays, Yu was awarded Italy's Premio Grinzane Cavour (1998), France's Chevalier de l'Ordre des Arts et des Lettres (2004), and other honors.*

On the Road at Eighteen

The asphalt road rolls up and down like it's pasted on top of ocean waves. Walking down this little highway in the mountains, I'm like a boat. This year, I turned eighteen. The few brownish whiskers that have sprouted on my chin flutter in the breeze. They've only just taken up residence on my chin, so I really treasure them. I've spent the whole day walking down the road, and I've already seen lots of mountains and lots of clouds. Every one of the mountains and every one of the clouds made me think of people I know. I shouted out each of their nicknames as I walked by. So even though I've walked all day, I'm not tired, not at all. I walked through the morning, now it's the tail end of the afternoon, and it won't be long until I see the tip of dusk. But I haven't found an inn.

I've encountered quite a few people along the road, but none of them has known where the road goes or whether there's an inn there. They all tell me: "Keep walking. You'll see when you get there." I think what everyone said was just terrific. I really am just seeing when I get there. But I haven't found an inn. I feel like I should be worried about that.

I think it's weird that I've walked all day and only seen one car. That was around noon, when I'd just begun to think about hitchhiking. But all I was doing was thinking about hitchhiking. I hadn't started to worry about finding an inn—I was only thinking about how amazing it would be to get a lift from someone. I stood by the side of the road waving at the car, trying my best to look casual. But the driver hardly even looked at me. The car or the driver. They hardly even looked at me. All they fucking did was drive right by. So I ran, chasing the car as fast as I could, just for fun, because I still hadn't started to worry about finding an inn. I ran until the car had disappeared, and then I laughed at myself, but I discovered that laughing too hard made it difficult to breathe, so I stopped. After that I kept walking, happy and excited, except that I started to regret that I hadn't picked up a rock before I started waving at the car.

Now I really want a lift, because dusk is about to fall and I can't get that inn out of my goddamned head. But there haven't been any cars all afternoon. If a car came now, I think I could make it stop. I'd lie down in the middle of the road, and I'm willing to bet that any car would come to a screeching halt before it got to my head. But I don't even hear the rumble of an engine, let alone see a car. Now I'm just going to have to keep walking and see when I get there. Not bad at all: keep walking and see when you get there.

The road rolls up and down from hill to valley, and the hills tempt me every time, because before I charge up to the top, I think I'll see an inn on the other side. But each time I charge up the slope, all I see is another hill in the distance, with a depressing trough in between. And still I charge up each hill as if my life depended on it. And now I'm charging up another one, but this time I see it. Not an inn, but a truck. The truck is pointed toward me, stalled in the middle of the highway in a gully between two hills. I can see the driver's ass pointing skyward and, behind it, all the colors of the approaching sunset. I can't see the driver's head because it's stuffed under the hood. The truck's hood slants up into the air like an upside-down lip. The back of the truck is piled full of big wicker baskets. I'm thinking that they definitely must be packed with some kind of fruit. Of course, bananas would be best of all. There are probably some in the cab too, so when I hop in, I can eat a few. And I don't really care if the truck's going in the opposite direction as me. I need to find an inn, and if there's no inn, I need a truck. And the truck's right here in front of me.

Elated, I run down to the truck and say, "Hi!"

The driver doesn't seem to have heard me. He's still fiddling with something under the hood.

"Want a smoke?"

Only now does he pull his head out from under the hood, stretch out a black, grimy hand, and take the cigarette between his fingers. I rush to give him a light, and he sucks several mouthfuls of smoke into his mouth before stuffing his head back under the hood.

I'm satisfied. Since he accepted the smoke, that means he has to give me a lift. So I wander around to the back of the truck to investigate what's in the wicker baskets. But they're covered, and I can't see, so I sniff. I smell the fragrance of apples. And I think: Apples aren't too bad either.

In just a little bit, he's done repairing the truck, and he jumps down from the hood. I rush over and say, "Hey, I need a ride." What I don't expect is that he gives me a hard shove with those grimy hands and barks, "Go away!"

I'm so angry I'm speechless, but he just swings on over to the driver's side, opens the door, slides into the cab, and starts the engine. I know that if I blow this opportunity, I'll never get another one. I know I should not just give up. So I run over to the other side, open the door, and hop in. I'm ready to fight if necessary. I turn to him and yell: "Then give me back my cigarette!" The truck's already started to move by now.

He turns to look at me with a big, friendly smile and asks, "Where you headed?"

I'm bewildered by this turnaround. I say, "Doesn't matter. Wherever."

He asks me very nicely, "Want an apple?" He's still glancing over at me.

"That goes without saying."

"Go get one from the back."

How am I supposed to climb out of the cab to the back of the truck when he's driving so fast? So I say, "Forget it."

He says, "Go get one." He's still looking at me.

I say, "Stop staring at me. There's no road on my face."

With this, he twists his eyes back onto the highway.

The truck's driving back in the direction I just came from; I'm sitting comfortably in the cab, looking out the window and chatting with the driver. By now we're already the best of friends. I've found out that he's a private entrepreneur. It's his own truck. The apples are his too. I hear change jingling in his pockets. I ask him, "Where are you going?"

He says, "I just keep driving and see when I get there."

It sounds just like what everyone else said. That's so nice. I feel closer to him. I want everything I see outside the window to be just as close, just as familiar, and soon all those hills and clouds start to bring more friends to mind, so I shout out their nicknames as we drive by.

Now I'm not crying out for an inn anymore. What with the truck, the driver, the seat in the cab, I'm completely at peace. I don't know where the truck's going, and neither does he. Anyway, it doesn't matter, because all we have to do is keep driving, and we'll see when we get there.

But the truck broke down. By that time, we were as close as friends can be. My arm was draped over his shoulder and his over mine. He was telling me about his love life, and right when he'd got to the part about how it felt the first time he held a woman's body in his arms, the truck broke down. The truck was climbing up a hill when it broke down. All of a sudden the squeal of the engine went quiet like a pig right after it's been slaughtered. So he jumped out of the truck, climbed onto the hood, opened up that upside-down lip, and stuffed his head back under it. I couldn't see his ass. But I could hear the sound of him fiddling with the engine.

After a while, he pulled his head out from under the hood and slammed it shut. His hands were even blacker than before. He wiped them on his pants, wiped again, jumped down, and walked back to the cab.

"Is it fixed?" I asked.

"It's shot. There's no way to fix it."

I thought that over and finally asked, "Now what do we do?"

"Wait and see," he said, nonchalantly.

I was sitting in the cab wondering what to do. Then I started to think about finding an inn again. The sun was just falling behind the mountains, and the hazy dusk clouds looked like billows of steam. The notion of an inn stole back into my head and began to swell until my mind was stuffed full of it. By then, I didn't even have a mind. An inn was growing where my mind used to be.

At that point, the driver started doing the official morning calisthenics that they always play on the radio, right there in the middle of the highway. He went from the first exercise to the last without missing a beat. When he was finished, he started to jog circles around the truck. Maybe he had been sitting too long in the driver's seat and needed some exercise. Watching him moving from my vantage point inside the truck, I couldn't sit still either, so I opened the door and jumped out. But I didn't do calisthenics or jog in place. I was thinking about an inn and an inn and an inn.

Just then, I noticed five people rolling down the hill on bicycles. Each bike had a carrying pole fastened to the back with two big baskets on either end. I thought they were probably local peasants on their way back from selling vegetables at market. I was delighted to see people riding by, so I welcomed them with a big, "Hi!" They rode up beside me and dismounted. Excited, I greeted them and asked, "Is there an inn around here?"

Instead of responding they asked me, "What's in the truck?"

I said, "Apples."

All five of them pushed their bikes over to the side of the truck. Two of them climbed onto the back, picked up about ten baskets full of apples, and passed them upside down to the ones below, who proceeded to tear open the plastic covering the top of the wicker and pour the apples into their own baskets. I was dumbstruck. When I finally realized exactly what was going on, I made for them and asked, "Just what do you think you're doing?"

None of them paid the slightest bit of attention to me. They continued to pour the apples. I tried to grab hold of someone's arm and screamed, "They're stealing all the apples!" A fist came crashing into my nose, and I landed several feet away. I staggered up, rubbed my nose. It felt soft and sticky, like it wasn't stuck to my face anymore but only dangling from it. Blood was flowing like tears from a broken heart. When I looked up to see which of them had hit me, they were already astride their bikes, riding away.

The driver was taking a walk, lips curling out as he sucked in deep draughts of air. He had probably lost his breath running. He didn't seem to be at all aware of what had just happened. I yelled toward him, "They stole your apples!" But he kept on walking without paying any attention to what I had yelled. I really wanted to run over and punch him so hard that his nose would be left dangling too. I ran over and screamed into his ear, "They stole your apples." Only then did he turn to look at me, and I realized that his face was getting happier and happier the longer he looked at my nose.

At that point, yet another group of bicycles descended down the slope. Each bike had two big baskets fastened to the back. There were even a few children among the riders. They swarmed by me and surrounded the truck. A lot of people climbed onto the back, and the wicker baskets flew faster than I could count them. Apples poured out of broken baskets like blood out of my nose. They stuffed apples into their own baskets as if they were possessed. In just a few seconds, all the apples in the truck had been lowered to the ground. Then a few motorized tractor carts chugged down the hill and stopped next to the truck. A few big men dismounted and started to stuff apples into the carts. One by one, the empty wicker baskets were tossed to the side. The ground was covered with rolling apples, and the peasants scrabbled on their hands and knees like ants to pick them all up.

It was at that point that I rushed into their midst, risking life and limb, and cursed them: "Thieves!" I started swinging. My attack was met with countless fists and feet. It seemed like every part of my body got hit at the same time. I climbed back up off the ground. A few children began to hurl apples at me. The apples broke apart on my head, but my head didn't break. Just as I was about to rush the kids, a foot came crashing into my waist. I wanted to cry, but when I opened my mouth, nothing came out. There was nothing to do but fall to the ground and watch them steal the apples. I started to look around for the driver. He was standing a good distance away, looking right at me, and laughing as hard as he could. Just so I knew that I looked even better now than I had with a bloody nose.

I didn't even have the strength for anger. All I could do was gaze out at everything that was making me so angry. And what made me the angriest of all was the driver.

Another wave of bicycles and tractors rolled down the hill and threw themselves into the disaster area. There were fewer and fewer apples rolling on the ground. A few people left. A few more arrived. The ones who had arrived too late for apples began to busy themselves with the truck. I saw them remove the window glass, strip the tires, pry away the planks that covered the truck bed. Without its tires, the truck obviously felt really low, because it sank to the ground. A few children began to gather the wicker baskets that had been tossed to the side a moment before. As the road got cleaner and cleaner, there were fewer and fewer people. But all I could do was watch, because I didn't even have the strength for anger. I sat on the ground without moving, letting my eyes wander back and forth between the driver and the thieves.

Now there's nothing left but a single tractor parked beside the sunken truck. Someone's looking around to see if there's anything left to take. He looks for a while and then hops on his tractor and starts the engine.

The truck driver hops onto the back of the tractor and looks back toward me, laughing. He's holding my red backpack in his hand. He's stealing my backpack. My clothes and my money are in the backpack. And food and books. But he's stealing my backpack.

I'm watching the tractor climb back up the slope. It disappears over the crest. I can still hear the rumble of its engine, but soon I can't even hear that. All of a sudden, everything's quiet, and the sky starts to get really dark. I'm still sitting on the ground. I'm hungry, and I'm cold, but there's nothing left.

I sit there for a long time before I slowly stand up. It isn't easy because my whole body aches like crazy every time I move, but still I stand up and limp over to the truck. The truck looks miserable, battered. I know I've been battered too.

The sky's black now. There's nothing here. Just a battered truck and battered me. I'm looking at the truck, immeasurably sad, and the truck's looking at me, immeasurably sad. I reach out to stroke it. It's cold all over. The wind starts to blow, a strong wind, and the sound of the wind rustling the trees in the mountains is like ocean waves. The sound terrifies me so much that my body gets as cold as the truck's.

I open the door and hop in. I'm comforted by the fact that they didn't pry away the seat. I lie down in the cab. I smell leaking gas and think of the smell of the blood that leaked out of me. The wind's getting stronger and stronger, but I feel a little warmer lying on the seat. I think that even though the truck's been battered, its heart is still intact, still warm. I know that my heart's warm too. I was looking for an inn, and I never thought I'd find you here.

I lie inside the heart of the truck, remembering that clear warm afternoon. The sunlight was so pretty. I remember that I was outside enjoying myself in the sunshine for a long time, and when I got home

I saw my dad through the window packing things into a red backpack. I leaned against the window frame and asked, "Dad, are you going on a trip?"

He turned and very gently said, "No, I'm letting you go on a trip."

"Letting me go on a trip?"

"That's right. You're eighteen now, and it's time you saw a little of the outside world."

Later I slipped that pretty red backpack onto my back. Dad patted my head from behind, just like you would pat a horse's rump. Then I gladly made for the door and excitedly galloped out of the house, as happy as a horse.

(Translated by Andrew F. Jones)

SU TONG
(1963–)

Born in Suzhou, Su Tong graduated from Beijing Normal University in 1984 and became an editor. A prolific author of nine novels and hundreds of short stories, he is best known for Wives and Concubines, *a collection of four novellas published in 1990, later adapted for the screen by the director Zhang Yimou under the title* Raise the Red Lantern, *which was nominated for an Oscar for Best Foreign Film. He won the Man Asian Literary Prize in 2009 for the novel* The Boat to Redemption. *Reminiscent of William Faulkner and Gabriel García Márquez, Su often writes about pain, torture, and desire in the south, where tradition crumbles like a house of cards and humanity struggles to keep its sanity, as depicted in the excerpt that follows.*

Raise the Red Lantern (excerpt)

When Fourth Mistress, Lotus, was carried into the Chen family garden, she was nineteen; she was carried into the garden through the back gate on the west side at dusk, by four rustic sedan bearers. The servants were washing some old yarn by the side of the well when they saw the sedan chair slip quietly in through the moon gate and a young college girl, dressed in a white blouse and black skirt, step down from it. The servants thought it was the eldest daughter returning from her studies in Beiping; when they rushed forward to welcome her, they realized their mistake: it was a female student, her face covered with dust and looking unbearably exhausted. That year Lotus's hair was cut short, level with her ears, and tied up with a sky-blue silk scarf. Her face was quite round; she wore no makeup; and she looked a little pale. Lotus climbed out of the sedan chair, stood on the grass, and looked blankly all around; a rattan suitcase was placed horizontally beneath her black skirt. In the autumn sunlight, Lotus's slender figure appeared tenuous and delicate; she looked as dull and lifeless as a paper doll. She raised her hand and wiped the sweat off her face; the servants noticed that she wiped the sweat not with a handkerchief but with her sleeve; this minor detail made a deep impression on them.

Lotus walked over to the edge of the well and spoke to Swallow, who was washing yarn. "Let me wash my face. I haven't washed my face in three days."

Swallow drew a pail of water for her and watched her plunge her face into the water; Lotus's arched-over body shook uncontrollably like a waist drum played by some unseen hands. Swallow asked, "Do you want some soap?" Lotus did not speak, and Swallow asked again, "The water's too cold, isn't it?" Lotus still did not speak. Swallow made a face in the direction of the other maidservants standing around the well, covered her mouth, and laughed. The maidservants thought this newly arrived guest was one of the Chen family's poor relations. They could tell the status of nearly all the Chen family's guests. Just then Lotus suddenly turned her head back toward them. Her expression was much more wide-awake after washing her face; her eyebrows were very fine and very black, and they gradually knit together. Lotus gave Swallow a sidelong glance and said, "Don't just stand there laughing like a fool; wipe the water off my face!"

Swallow kept on laughing. "Who do you think you are, acting so fierce?"

Lotus pushed Swallow away violently, picked up her rattan suitcase, and walked away from the well; she walked a few paces, turned to face them, and said, "Who am I? You'll all find out, sooner or later."

‖‖‖‖‖‖‖‖‖‖‖‖

THE FOLLOWING DAY everyone in the Chen household learned that Old Master Chen Zuoqian had taken Lotus as his Fourth Mistress. Lotus would live in the south wing off the back garden, right beside Third Mistress Coral's room. Chen Zuoqian gave Swallow, who had been living in the servants' quarters, to Fourth Mistress as her private bondmaid.

When Swallow went to see Lotus, she was afraid; she lowered her head as she called out, "Fourth Mistress." Lotus had already forgotten Swallow's rudeness, or perhaps she just did not remember who Swallow was. Lotus changed into a pink silk cheongsam and put on a pair of embroidered slippers; the color had returned overnight to her face, and she looked much more amiable. She pulled Swallow over in front of her, examined her carefully for a minute, and said to Chen Zuoqian, "At least she doesn't look too dreadful." Then she spoke to Swallow. "Squat down; let me look at your hair."

Swallow squatted down and felt Lotus's hands picking through her hair, carefully searching for something; then she heard Lotus say, "You don't have lice, do you? I'm terribly afraid of lice."

Swallow bit her lip and did not speak; she felt Lotus's hands, like the ice-cold blade of a knife, cutting into her hair, hurting her slightly. Lotus said, "What's in your hair? Smells terrible; take some perfumed soap and hurry over and wash your hair."

Swallow stood up; she stood there motionless, with her hands hanging down. Chen Zuoqian glared at her. "Didn't you hear what Fourth Mistress said?"

Swallow said, "I just washed my hair yesterday."

Chen Zuoqian yelled at her, "Don't argue about it; if she tells you to go wash, you go wash. Careful I don't beat you."

Swallow poured out a pan of water and washed her hair under the crabapple trees. She felt she'd been horribly wronged; hatred and anger pressed on her heart like an iron weight. The afternoon sun shone down on the two crabapple trees; a clothesline was strung between them, and

Fourth Mistress's white blouse and black skirt were waving in the breeze. Swallow looked all around; the back garden was completely quiet, and no one was there. She walked over to the clothesline, spat right on Lotus's white blouse, then turned and spat again on her black skirt.

CHEN ZUOQIAN WAS exactly fifty years old that year. When Chen Zuoqian took Lotus as his concubine at the age of fifty, the affair was carried out in a half-secretive manner. Right up until the day before Lotus came through the gate, the First Mistress, his first wife, Joy, still didn't know a thing about it. When Chen Zuoqian took Lotus to meet her, Joy was in the Buddhist chapel counting out her rosary and chanting the sutras. Chen Zuoqian said, "This is my First Mistress."

Just as Lotus was about to step forward and greet her, the string broke on Joy's Buddhist rosary, sending the beads rolling all over the floor; Joy pushed away her amboyna chair and knelt down on the floor to pick up the beads, mumbling all the while, "It's a sin, it's a sin." Lotus went over to help her pick up the beads and was pushed lightly away by Joy, who just repeated, "It's a sin, it's a sin," and never once raised her head to look at Lotus. As Lotus watched Joy's fat body crouching down on the damp floor to pick up the Buddhist beads, she covered her mouth and laughed silently. She looked at Chen Zuoqian, who said, "All right, we're going."

Lotus stepped over the raised threshold of the Buddhist chapel, took Chen Zuoqian's arm, and asked, "Is she really a Buddhist? Why's she chanting the sutras at home?"

Chen Zuoqian said, "A Buddhist! Ha! She's just too lazy, hasn't anything to do, so she plays at being a Buddhist, that's all."

Lotus was enthusiastically welcomed into the rooms of Second Mistress, Cloud. Cloud had her maid bring out watermelon, sunflower, and pumpkin seeds, and several kinds of candied fruits for Lotus. The first thing Cloud said after they sat down concerned the melon seeds. "There aren't any good melon seeds around here; I have someone buy all the melon seeds I eat in Suzhou."

Lotus spent some time cracking melon seeds at Cloud's, cracking and eating until she was quite bored; she didn't like snacks like that, but she could hardly show it. Lotus stole a sidelong glance at Chen Zuoqian, hinting she wanted to leave, but he seemed to be intent on staying a little longer at Cloud's and acted as though he didn't see Lotus's expression. Lotus inferred from this that Chen Zuoqian was particularly fond of Cloud; then her gaze couldn't help lingering on Cloud's face and figure. Cloud's facial features had a kind of warmth and delicate grace, even though she couldn't hide the tiny wrinkles and the somewhat noticeable slackness of her skin; in her movements she had even more the appearance of a cultured young woman from a good family. Lotus thought a woman like Cloud could easily attract men, and women would not dislike her either. She very quickly addressed Cloud as Elder Sister.

Of the Chen household's three earlier wives, Coral's room was closest to Lotus's, but Coral was the last one Lotus met. Lotus had heard of Coral's extraordinary physical beauty, and she wanted very much to meet her; but Chen Zuoqian refused to take her there. He said, "It's so close, you go on over yourself."

Lotus said, "I've gone over there; the maid said she was sick, blocked the door, and wouldn't let me in."

Chen Zuoqian snorted through his nose. "Huh, whenever she's unhappy she says she's sick." He went on, "She wants to be more important than I am."

"Are you going to let her?"

Chen Zuoqian waved his hand and said, "Don't be ridiculous! Women can never be more important than men."

Lotus walked by the north wing and noticed that Coral's windows were hung with curtains of pink lace drawnwork; a sweet scent of flowers emanated from inside. Lotus stopped in front of the windows for a moment; suddenly unable to control her desire to peek in, she held her breath and gently pulled open the curtains. The shock she received then nearly frightened her to death: Coral was also watching her from behind the curtain. Their eyes met straight on for only a matter of seconds, then Lotus ran away in dismay.

When night came, Chen Zuoqian came to Lotus's room to spend the night. Lotus helped him take his clothes off and handed him some nightclothes, but Chen Zuoqian said, "I don't wear anything. I like to sleep naked."

Lotus just looked the other way and said, "Suit yourself, but it's better to wear something, otherwise you'll catch a chill."

Chen Zuoqian started to laugh. "You're not afraid I'll catch a chill, you're afraid of seeing me naked."

Lotus said, "I am not afraid." But as she turned away, her cheeks were already crimson. This was the first time she had a clear look at Chen Zuoqian's body. Chen Zuoqian had a body like a red-crowned Manchurian crane, bony and skinny, and his penis was as taut as a well-drawn bow. Lotus felt a little out of breath, and she asked, "Why're you so skinny?"

Chen Zuoqian climbed onto the bed, crawled under the quilt, and answered, "They've worn me out."

When Lotus rolled over on her side to put out the lamp, Chen Zuoqian held her back. "Don't put it out. I want to see you. Put out the lamp and you can't see anything."

Lotus touched his cheek and said, "Suit yourself. I don't know anything about it anyway, so I'll follow you."

Lotus seemed to fall from a high place into a dark valley where pain and dizziness were accompanied by a feeling of lightness. The strangest thing was that Coral's face continually intruded into her consciousness; that most beautiful face was also hidden in the darkness. Lotus said, "She's really strange."

"Who?"

"Third Mistress. She was behind the curtain watching me."

Chen Zuoqian's hand moved from Lotus's breast to her mouth. "Don't talk. Don't talk now."

Just at that moment someone knocked lightly on the bedroom door. The two of them were startled; Chen Zuoqian looked at Lotus and shook his head, then put out the lamp. In a little while the knocking started again. Chen Zuoqian jumped up and shouted angrily, "Who's that knocking?"

A timid girlish voice came from outside the door. "Third Mistress is sick; she's calling for the Master."

Chen Zuoqian said, "She's lying, lying again. Go back and tell her I've already gone to bed."

The girl outside the door said, "Third Mistress is very sick; she says you have to come. She says she's about to die."

Chen Zuoqian sat on the bed and thought for a minute, mumbling to himself, "What's she up to this time?" Lotus watched his uneasiness, then pushed him. "You better go. It would be terrible if she really died."

Chen Zuoqian did not return that night. Lotus listened carefully to hear what transpired in the north wing, but nothing at all seemed to be happening. Only a robin in the pomegranate tree called out a few times, leaving a clear and mournful sound lingering in the distance. Lotus drifted between disappointment and sorrow, and could not sleep. Very early the next morning, when she got up to put on her makeup, she saw that her face had undergone some sort of profound transformation; the rims of her eyes were dark black. Lotus already knew what Coral was up to, but the next day, when she saw Chen Zuoqian emerge from her north wing room, she went up to him anyway and inquired about Coral's illness. "Did you call a doctor for Third Mistress?"

Chen Zuoqian shook his head in embarrassment. He looked completely exhausted and was too enervated to speak; he merely took hold of Lotus's hand and gave it a long, soft squeeze.

THE REASON LOTUS was married to Chen Zuoqian after already spending one year in college was very simple: her father's tea factory went broke, and he could not afford her tuition. The third day after Lotus had quit school and returned home, she heard members of her family shouting wildly in the kitchen; she ran in and saw her father propped against the side of the sink; the sink was full of fresh bubbling blood. Her father had slashed his wrists open and gone effortlessly down to the Yellow Springs of the Dead. Lotus remembered the feeling of despair she had at that time. When she held up her father's icy cold corpse, she felt even colder all over than his body did.

When this misfortune occurred, she couldn't even cry. No one else used that sink for many days after, but Lotus still washed her hair in it. She did not feel the nameless fear and trembling that most young women would. She was very practical. As soon as her father died, she had to be responsible for herself. Lotus stood beside that sink washing and combing her hair out over and over again; it was her way of calmly planning for her future. Thus when her stepmother came right to the point and asked her to choose between going to work and getting married, she answered dryly, "I'll get married, of course."

Her stepmother asked further, "You want to marry into an ordinary family or a rich family?"

Lotus answered, "A rich family, naturally; do you have to ask?"

Her stepmother said, "It's not the same. If you go to a rich family, you'll be small."

"What does it mean: 'be small'?" Lotus asked.

Her stepmother thought for a moment and said, "It means to be a concubine; your status will be a little lower."

Lotus laughed coldly. "What is status? Is status something people like me can be concerned about? No matter what, I've been given to you to sell; if you have any consideration for my father's affections, then sell me to a good master."

The first time Chen Zuoqian went to call on her, Lotus barred the door and refused to see him; "Meet me at the Restaurant Occidental," she said from inside the door. Chen Zuoqian thought to himself that since she was a college student she would naturally be different from most vulgar young women. He reserved a table for two at the Restaurant Occidental and waited for Lotus to show up. It was raining that day, and as Chen Zuoqian waited and looked through the window at the street made misty by the rain, his emotions were unusually warm and sweet—feelings he had never experienced before in his first three marriages. Lotus came walking slowly along, carrying a delicate little flower-patterned silk umbrella. Chen Zuoqian smiled happily. Lotus was just as pure and pretty as he had imagined, and just as young. Chen Zuoqian remembered that Lotus sat down opposite him and pulled a big handful of little candles out of her purse. She whispered to Chen Zuoqian, "Order me a cake, all right?"

Chen Zuoqian had the waiter bring them a cake; then he watched Lotus stick the candles one by one into the cake until she had put in a total of nineteen candles; she put the remaining candles back into her bag. Chen Zuoqian said, "What's all this; is this your birthday?"

Lotus only smiled. She lit the candles and watched them burn with nineteen bright little flames. In the light of the candles Lotus's expression grew exquisitely beautiful; she said, "Look how lovely the flames are."

"They are lovely," Chen Zuoqian agreed.

After she finished talking, Lotus took a long deep breath and blew out all of the candles at once. Chen Zuoqian heard her say, "Let's celebrate my birthday early; nineteen years have gone by."

Chen Zuoqian felt that there was something to think about in what Lotus said. Much later he still often recalled that scene of Lotus blowing out those candles; it made him feel that Lotus possessed a kind of elusive yet beguiling power. As a man with an abundance of sexual experience, Chen Zuoqian was even more obsessed with Lotus's skill and passion in bed. He seemed to envision many kinds of ecstasy the first time he met her, and later on they all came to be confirmed in practice. It is difficult to judge whether Lotus was like that by nature or was reshaping her own disposition in order to please him, but Chen Zuoqian was very satisfied; the way he doted on Lotus was noticed by everyone high and low in the Chen household.

IN THE CORNER of the back garden wall there was a wisteria vine; from summer to fall the wisteria flowers weighed heavily on the branches. From her window, day after day, Lotus saw only those fluffy clumps of purple flowers delicately swaying in the autumn breeze. She noticed there was a well beneath the wisteria vine and there was also a stone table and stone benches. It was a very quiet, comfortable place, but no one was ever there, and the path leading up to it was overgrown with weeds. Butterflies flew by and cicadas sang on the wisteria leaves; Lotus remembered that last year at that time she was sitting under the wisteria at school studying—it all seemed like suddenly waking from a dream. Lotus walked slowly over to the vine, carefully pulling up her skirt so as not to let the weeds and the insects rub against it; slowly she pulled back a few branches of wisteria, and saw that the stone tables and benches were covered with a thick layer of dust. The walls of the well were covered with moss. Lotus bent over and looked down into the well; the water was a bluish black color, and there were some ancient dry leaves floating on the surface. Lotus saw the broken reflection of her face in the water and heard the sound of her breathing being sucked down into the well and amplified, weak yet oppressively deep and low. A gust of wind rushed up; Lotus's skirt billowed out like a bird taking flight, and at that instant she felt a coldness as hard as stone rubbing slowly up against her body. She started back, walking very quickly now, and when she reached the hallway of the south-side wing, she heaved a long sigh. Just as she looked back at the wisteria vine, two or three clumps of flowers suddenly dropped off; they tumbled down quite abruptly, and Lotus felt it was awfully strange.

Cloud was sitting in her room waiting for Lotus. She immediately noticed that Lotus looked very troubled; she stood up and patted her on the shoulder: "What's wrong with you?"

Lotus answered, "What's wrong with me? I was walking around outside."

Cloud said, "Your complexion looks awful."

Lotus laughed and said that she had just got her period. Cloud laughed too and said, "I wondered why in the world you came over to see me again." She opened a parcel and took out a roll of silk: "Real Suzhou silk; it's for you to make a dress with."

Lotus pushed back Cloud's hands. "No, no, no—how could I accept gifts from you? I should be giving you gifts."

"Shush," said Cloud. "What do you mean by that? When I saw how very likable you are, I immediately thought about this piece of silk; if it were that woman next door, I wouldn't give it to her if she tried to pay me; that's just the way I am."

Lotus took the silk, put it in her lap, and ran her hands over it. Then she said, "Third Mistress is a little strange. But she's very good looking."

"Good looking? If you scraped Coral's face, a pound of makeup would come off."

Lotus laughed again and changed the subject. "I was just walking around by the wisteria vine. I really like that place."

"You went to the Well of Death?" Cloud shrieked. "Don't go there, that place is bad luck."

"Why do you call it the Well of Death?" Lotus asked in alarm.

Cloud answered, "No wonder you looked so bad when you came in here. Three people have died in that well."

Lotus stood up, leaned against the window frame, and looked over at the wisteria vine. "What sort of people died in the well?"

Cloud said, "They were all family members from earlier generations, all women."

Lotus still wanted to ask more, but Cloud could not tell any more; she only knew that much. She said everybody high and low in the Chen family avoids the subject; everybody's lips are sealed tight as a jar. Lotus stood there puzzled for a moment, then said, "Things like that, I guess it's just as well not to know about them anyway."

THE YOUNG MASTERS and young ladies of the Chen family all lived in the central compound. Lotus once saw the two sisters Yirong and Yiyun digging for worms in the muddy ditch; from their radiantly cheerful faces, so natural and innocent, Lotus could tell at a glance that they were Cloud's children. She stood to one side, quietly observing them. The two sisters noticed Lotus, but went on stuffing the worms into a little bamboo container as if no one were there. Lotus asked, "What are you digging worms for?"

Yirong answered, "To go fishing," but Yiyun stared rudely at Lotus and said, "None of your business."

Lotus felt unpleasantly awkward; walking on a few steps, she heard the two girls whisper, "She's a concubine too, just like Mom." Lotus was suddenly stunned; she looked back and stared angrily at them. Yirong giggled out loud, but Yiyun stared back at her with unyielding contempt and whispered something else. Lotus thought, "It's terrible for them to be so young and already saying such nasty things. Heaven knows what sort of education Cloud is giving those girls."

The next time Lotus ran into Cloud, she could not help telling her what Yirong had said. Cloud said, "That child just can't hold her tongue. When I get home, I'll pinch her lips good." After Cloud apologized, she went on. "Actually those two girls of mine are still pretty easy to handle. You've never seen the Little Master from next door. He's just like a dog, biting and spitting on anyone he runs into. Hasn't he ever bitten you?"

Lotus shook her head. She recalled the little boy next door, Feilan, standing on the porch eating a piece of bread and peering over at her, his oily hair combed back and shiny, with a pair of little leather shoes on his feet. Sometimes Lotus could catch a glimpse of something like Chen Zuoqian's expression on Feilan's face. Probably she was more disposed to accept Feilan because she hoped to give Chen Zuoqian another son. "A boy is better than a girl," thought Lotus. "Who cares if he bites people or not?"

After a long time only Joy's son and daughter remained unseen by Lotus. From this it was easy to discern their high status in the Chen household. Lotus regularly heard discussions concerning the son Feipu and the daughter Yihui. Feipu was always out collecting rents and carrying on real estate transactions, while Yihui was studying at a women's college in Beiping. Lotus casually asked her maid Swallow about Feipu, and she said, "Our Eldest Young Master is very resourceful."

Lotus asked, "How is he resourceful?"

Swallow answered, "Well, anyway, he is resourceful; the whole Chen household depends on him now."

Lotus further asked Swallow, "What's the Eldest Young Mistress like?"

Swallow replied, "Our Eldest Young Mistress is pretty and demure; she's going to marry a rich man someday."

Lotus laughed to herself. The tone of Swallow's praise for those two implied a criticism of her, and Lotus found it quite irritating. Taking out her anger on the Persian cat curled up at her feet, she kicked it away and cursed, "Stop licking your ass over here, you little tramp!"

Lotus became increasingly annoyed with Swallow; mostly because, whenever she had nothing to do, she would run over to Coral's room. But also because every time Lotus gave her a chemise and underpants to be washed, her face would take on a sullen expression. Sometimes Lotus would scold her. "Who are you trying to impress, frowning like that? If you don't like being with me, you can go back to the servants' quarters, or even go next door, it's all right."

Swallow would defend herself. "I'm not. I wouldn't dare frown; I was born with this face."

Lotus would grab a hairbrush and throw it at her, and Swallow would shut up. Lotus guessed that Swallow slandered her quite a bit throughout the rest of the house. But she could not treat her too harshly because she had once seen Chen Zuoqian come into her room and take the opportunity to fondle Swallow's breasts. Although it was a fleeting and altogether natural thing, Lotus had to control herself somewhat; if it were not for her master's fondling, Swallow would not dare act so insolently toward her. Lotus reflected, "Even a common servant girl also understands how to rely on a little fondling to build up her courage. A woman is just that sort of creature."

ON THE EIGHTH DAY of the ninth lunar month, one day before the Double Ninth Festival, the Eldest Young Master, Feipu, returned home.

Lotus was in the central courtyard admiring the chrysanthemums when she saw Joy and the servants crowding around a group of men; one in the middle, dressed in white, was very young and, viewed from behind and far away, looked quite tall. Lotus guessed that he must be Feipu. She watched as the servants carried a whole cartload of luggage to the back courtyard, running around and around like colorful carousel animals. Gradually everyone went inside, but Lotus was still embarrassed to go in.

She picked some chrysanthemums and walked slowly toward the back garden; on the way she spied Cloud and Coral coming her way with their children in tow. Cloud grabbed her arm and said, "Eldest Young Master has come home, aren't you going to go meet him?"

Lotus answered, "*I* go to meet *him*? He should come to meet me, shouldn't he?"

Cloud said, "That's right, he should be the one to come to meet you first."

Standing to one side, Coral impatiently pushed Feilan on the back of the head. "Hurry up, hurry up."

It was at the dinner table that Lotus actually met Feipu. That evening Chen Zuoqian had the cooks prepare a banquet to welcome Feipu back home. The table was covered with sumptuous and exquisitely prepared delicacies; Lotus looked at the food and could not help thinking that the welcoming banquet on the day she first entered the Chen household was not nearly as grand as this one. She felt a little hurt, but her attention very quickly shifted to Feipu himself. Feipu was sitting next to Joy; Joy said something to him, and then he leaned over toward Lotus, smiled, and nodded his head. Lotus smiled and nodded back at him. Her first impression of Feipu was that he was unexpectedly young and handsome; her second impression was that he was very thoughtful. Lotus always liked to evaluate people's character on meeting them.

The next day was the Double Ninth Festival. The gardeners brought all of the chrysanthemum pots in the garden together in one place and arranged them in various colors to form the characters for "good fortune, prosperity, longevity, and happiness." Lotus got up very early and walked all around, by herself, looking at the chrysanthemums. There was a chilly morning breeze, and she was wearing only a sleeveless woolen sweater; she just folded her arms across her chest, held her shoulders, and walked around, looking at the flowers. A long way off she saw Feipu coming out of the central courtyard and walking her way. Lotus was hesitating, trying to decide whether or not to greet him first, when Feipu called out, "Good morning, Lotus."

Lotus was rather startled at his direct use of her given name; she nodded and said, "According to our generational difference, you shouldn't call me by my name."

Feipu stood on the other side of the flower beds, smiled as he buttoned up his shirt collar, and said, "I should call you Fourth Mistress, but you must be a few years younger than I am. How old are you?"

Lotus turned to look at the flowers in an obvious display of displeasure. Feipu said, "You like chrysanthemums too? I thought I'd be the first one to enjoy the scene this early in the morning; didn't think you'd be up even earlier."

Lotus replied, "I've liked chrysanthemums ever since I was little; I certainly didn't just start liking them today."

Feipu asked, "What's your favorite kind?"

Lotus answered, "I like them all, but I just hate crab claws."

"Why's that?" asked Feipu.

"Crab claws bloom too impudently."

Feipu laughed again and said, "That's interesting; I just happen to like crab claws best."

Lotus glanced over at Feipu a moment. "I figured you would."

Feipu asked further, "Why is that?"

Lotus took a few steps forward and said, "Flowers are not flowers and people are not people; flowers are people and people are flowers; don't you understand such a simple principle?" Lotus suddenly raised her head and caught sight of a strange gleam drifting by briefly, like a leaf, on the surface of Feipu's moist eyes; she saw it and she understood it.

Feipu stood with his hands on his hips on the other side of the chrysanthemums and said suddenly, "I'll take all the crab claws away, then."

Lotus said nothing. She watched Feipu take all the crab claws away and put some black chrysanthemums in their place. After a short interval, Lotus spoke again. "The flowers are all fine, but the characters are no good; they're too vulgar."

Feipu wiped the mud off his hands and winked at Lotus. "Nothing can be done about that. Good fortune, prosperity, longevity, and happiness is what the Old Master told them to arrange. It's the same every year, a custom passed down from our ancestors."

Whenever Lotus thought of the time she spent enjoying the chrysanthemums on the Double Ninth Festival, she felt happy inside. It seemed as though from that day on she and Feipu had some sort of secret understanding between them. Sometimes, when she thought of how Feipu had moved the crab claws away, she would laugh out loud. Only Lotus herself knew that she really didn't particularly dislike crab claw chrysanthemums.

"WHO DO YOU like best?" Lotus regularly asked Chen Zuoqian while he shared her pillow, "Of the four of us, who do you like best?"

Chen Zuoqian said, "Why, you, of course."

"What about Joy?"

"She turned into an old hen long ago."

"And Cloud?"

"Cloud's still tolerable, but she's a little flabby."

"What about Coral, then?" Lotus could never control her curiosity about Coral. "Where does Coral come from?"

Chen Zuoqian said, "I don't know where she comes from; she doesn't even know herself."

Lotus said, "You mean Coral is an orphan?"

Chen Zuoqian answered, "She was an actress. She sang the female lead in a traveling Peking opera troupe. I was an amateur performer myself. Sometimes I'd go backstage and invite her out for dinner; one thing led to another, and she just came along with me."

Lotus stroked Chen Zuoqian's face and said, "All the women want to go along with you."

Chen Zuoqian said, "You're half right there; all women want to go along with a rich man."

Lotus began to laugh. "You're only half right too; you should've said, 'When a rich man gets rich he wants women, wants them so much he can never get enough.'"

Lotus had never heard Coral sing Peking opera, but that morning she was awakened from her dreams by a few crisp, clear, long, drawn-out

words sung in opera style. She poked Chen Zuoqian lying next to her
and asked if that was Coral singing. Chen Zuoqian responded groggily,
"That bitch, when she's happy, she sings, and when she's unhappy, she
cries." Lotus opened the window and saw that a layer of snow-white
autumn frost had fallen during the night. A woman dressed all in black
was singing and dancing under the wisteria vine. It *was* Coral after all.

Lotus draped a cloak over her shoulders and stood in the doorway
watching Coral from afar. Coral was already totally absorbed in her
song; Lotus felt that she sang in a delicately plaintive manner, and her
own emotions were aroused. After a long time Coral stopped abruptly.
She seemed to have noticed that Lotus's eyes were brimming with
tears. Coral threw her long flowing sleeves back over her shoulders and
walked toward the compound. Some crystalline specks of brightness
danced on her face and clothing in the morning light; her round, tightly
coiled chignon was moist with dew, and thus her entire appearance was
damp and laden with sorrow, like a blade of grass in the wind.

"Are you crying? You're living a very happy life, aren't you? Why are
you crying?" Coral asked dryly as she stood facing Lotus.

Lotus took out a handkerchief and wiped the corners of her eyes, then
said, "I don't know what happened. What was that you were singing?"

"It's called *The Hanged Woman*," Coral answered. "Did you like it?"

"I don't know a thing about Peking opera; it's just that you sang so
movingly that I felt sad too, just listening." As Lotus spoke, she noticed
Coral's face take on an amiable expression for the first time.

Coral lowered her head, looked at her opera costume, and said, "It's
only acting; it's not worth feeling sad about. If you act very well, you
can fool other people, but if you act badly, you only fool yourself."

In Lotus's room Chen Zuoqian started to cough, and Lotus looked
at Coral with obvious embarrassment. Coral said, "Aren't you going to
help him get dressed?"

Lotus shook her head and said, "He can dress himself. He's not
a child."

Coral looked resentful. She laughed and said, "Why does he always want me to help him on with his shoes and clothes? Looks like people are divided into the worthy and the unworthy."

Just then Chen Zuoqian shouted from inside the room, "Coral! Come in and sing something for me!"

Coral immediately raised her willow-thin eyebrows; she laughed coldly, ran to the window, and yelled inside, "This old lady doesn't care to!"

Lotus had experienced Coral's temper. When she talked about it in an indirect manner with Chen Zuoqian, he said, "It's all my fault for spoiling her years ago. When she feels defiant, she curses my ancestors for eight generations. That little bitch of a whore, sooner or later I'll really have to punish her."

Lotus said, "You shouldn't be too cruel to her; she's really quite pitiful; she has no other family, and she's afraid you don't care about her, so she's developed a bad temper."

After that Lotus and Coral had some lukewarm contact. Coral was crazy about mah-jongg. She regularly called a group together at her place to play; they played from right after dinner until very late into the night. From the other side of the wall, Lotus could hear the clicking sound of the tiles noisily shuffled all night, and it kept her awake. She complained to Chen Zuoqian, and he said, "I guess you'll just have to stand it; when she plays mah-jongg, she's a little more normal. Anyway, when she loses all of her money, I won't give her any more. Let her play. Let her play until she drops."

On one occasion Coral sent her maid over to invite Lotus to play mah-jongg, but Lotus sent her back with these words: "Invite me to play mah-jongg? It's a wonder you could even think of it." After her maid returned, Coral herself came over. She said, "There are only three of us—we need one more; do me a favor."

Lotus replied, "But I don't know how; won't I just lose my money?"

Coral took Lotus by the arm. "Let's go. If you lose, we won't take your money. Better yet, if you win, you can keep it, and if you lose, I'll pay for you."

Lotus said, "You don't have to go that far; it's just that I don't like to play."

She saw Coral's smile turn into a frown as she was speaking. Coral said, "Huh, what have you got here that's so great? You act like you're sitting on a big pot of gold and won't move an inch; it's only a dried-up old man, that's all."

Lotus was so irritated that her temper began to flare up; just as she'd decided to tell her off and the curses were already boiling up onto her tongue, she swallowed them back again, bit her lip, and thought for a few seconds. Then she said, "All right, then, I'll go with you."

The other two players were already seated at the table waiting; one was the steward, Chen Zuowen, but she didn't know the other one. Coral introduced him as a doctor. The man wore gold-rimmed glasses; his complexion was quite swarthy, but his lips were moist, crimson, and softly expressive in a feminine manner. Lotus had seen him going in and out of Coral's room before and, for some unknown reason, could not believe he was a doctor.

Lotus was quite absentminded as she sat at the mah-jongg table; she really could not play very well and listened, bewildered, as they shouted out, "My game," and "Just the tile I needed." All she did was shell out money, and gradually she began to feel bad about it. Finally she said, "My head aches, I need a little rest."

Coral said, "Once you sit down, you have to play eight rounds—that's the rule. You're probably feeling bad about your losses." Chen Zuowen chimed in, "It doesn't matter, to lose a little money wards off many calamities." Coral retorted, "Just consider that tonight you're doing Cloud a favor; she's been terribly bored lately. Loan the old man to her for one night and let her give you back the money you lose."

The two men at the table began to laugh. Lotus laughed and said, "Coral, you really know how to amuse people." But in her heart she felt like she'd just swallowed a hornet.

Lotus coldly observed the flirtatious glances passing between Coral and the doctor; she felt that nothing could escape her intuitive under-standing. A tile fell off the table while they were being shuffled, and when Lotus bent down to pick it up she discovered that their four legs were wrapped in a tight embrace; they separated quite quickly and naturally, but Lotus definitely saw what they were doing.

Her expression did not change, but she did not look directly at Coral and the doctor's faces any longer. At that moment her emotions were very complicated; she was a little apprehensive, a little nervous, and also a little exultant at finding them out. "Coral," she thought to herself, "you're living too freely, too brazenly."

IN THE AUTUMN there were many times when the sky outside her window was dark and damp as a fine rain fell unceasingly onto the garden, splashing off the aspen and pomegranate leaves with a sound like shattering jade. At times like those Lotus would sit by the window, wearily staring at a handkerchief hanging on the clothesline being drenched by the rain; her feelings at the time were turbulent and complex, and some of her thoughts were so personal she could not reveal them to anyone.

She simply could not understand why every time it was dark and rainy her sexual desires were heightened. Chen Zuoqian was incapable of noticing how the weather affected her physiology; he could only feel embarrassed at his inability to keep up with her. He'd say, "Age is unforgiving, and I can't stand using aphrodisiacs like three-whip spirit ointment." He caressed Lotus's warm, pink flesh until countless little frissons of desire pulsated just under her skin. His hands gradually grew wild in their movements, and his tongue also began to caress her body. Lotus lay sideways on the sofa; with her eyes closed and her face flushed, she listened to the pearls of rain crashing onto the window, and spoke in a low moan, "It's all because of the cold rain."

Chen Zuoqian did not hear her clearly. "What did you say? Gold chain?"

"Yes," Lotus lied, "gold chain; I want a beautiful gold chain necklace."

Chen Zuoqian said, "There's nothing you want that I won't give you, but whatever you do, don't tell the others."

Lotus rolled over and sat up quickly. "The others? Who the hell are they? I don't give a damn about them."

Chen Zuoqian said, "Yes, of course, none of them can compare with you." He saw Lotus's expression change rapidly; she pushed him away, quickly slipped on her underclothes, and walked over to the window. Chen Zuoqian asked what was wrong. Lotus turned her head back and said with slightly veiled resentment, "I don't feel like it now. Why did you have to start talking about them?"

Chen Zuoqian stood sullenly beside Lotus and watched the rain falling outside the window. At times like those the entire world was unbearably damp. The garden was completely empty; the leaves on the trees were green and cold; in the far corner the wisteria vine swaying in the wind took on the appearance of a person. Lotus remembered the well and some of the stories she'd heard about it. She said, "This garden is a little spooky."

"What do you mean, 'spooky'?" Chen Zuoqian asked.

Lotus just pursed her lips and faced the wisteria vine. "You know, it's that well."

Chen Zuoqian said, "A couple of people died in that well, that's all; jumped in and committed suicide."

Lotus asked, "Who was it who died?"

Chen Zuoqian answered, "You don't know them, anyway; a couple of family members from earlier generations."

Lotus said, "I suppose they were concubines."

Chen Zuoqian's expression immediately grew severe. "Who told you that?"

Lotus laughed and said, "No one told me. I saw for myself. I walked over to the side of that well and immediately saw two women floating on the bottom; one of them looked like me, and the other one also looked like me."

Chen Zuoqian said, "Don't talk nonsense, and don't go there anymore."

Lotus clapped her hands and said, "That's no good; I still haven't asked those two ghosts why they threw themselves into the well."

"Why would you have to ask?" said Chen Zuoqian. "It could only be because of some filthy affair."

Lotus was silent for a long time and then suddenly burst out, "No wonder there are so many wells in this garden. They were dug for people to throw themselves into to commit suicide."

Chen Zuoqian put his arm around Lotus. "You're talking crazier all the time. Don't go on imagining things like that." As he spoke, he took hold of Lotus's hand and made her rub him down there. "He's ready again now, come on; if I die in your bed, I'll be perfectly happy."

In the garden the autumn rain was bleak and dreary, and for that reason their lovemaking had an aura of death about it. Everything that came before Lotus's eyes was black; only a few daisies on her dressing table emitted a faint red glow. When she heard a noise outside the door, she grabbed a perfume bottle close at hand and threw it in that direction. Chen Zuoqian said, "What's the matter now?"

Lotus answered, "She's spying on us."

"Who's spying?"

"Swallow."

Chen Zuoqian laughed. "What's there to see? And besides, she can't see us anyway."

Lotus replied in a severe tone, "Don't defend her; I can smell that slut's foul odor from miles away."

AT DUSK A crowd of people were sitting around in a circle in the garden listening to Feipu play a bamboo flute. Dressed in a silk shirt and silk pants, Feipu looked even more elegant and charming. He sat in the middle holding the flute while his listeners, for the most part his business companions, sat around in a circle. That crowd of people had become the center of attraction for everyone in the Chen household. The servants whispered back and forth as they stood on the porches observing them from afar. The rest of the people inside the rooms could hear the sound of Feipu's wooden flute through the windows, like the faint sound of gently flowing water; no one could ignore that sound.

Lotus was frequently very moved by the sound of Feipu's flute, sometimes so much that tears rolled down her cheeks. She wanted very much to sit down with that crowd of men and be much closer to Feipu. When

Feipu took up his flute, he reminded her of a young man at college who used to sit alone in an empty room playing a zither; she could not remember that young man's face very clearly and did not have any hidden, secret affection for him. But she was easily transported by that sort of exquisitely beautiful scene; her emotions flowed forth like ripples on an autumn stream. She hesitated quite a while, then moved a rattan chair out onto the porch, sat down, and quietly listened to Feipu's playing. It was not long before the sound of the flute grew still and was replaced by the voices of the men talking. Lotus immediately felt it most uninteresting, and she thought to herself, "Talking is such a bore; it's nothing more than you lying to me and me cheating you; as soon as people start talking, they put on a hypocritical display of affection."

She stood up and went back into her room, where she suddenly remembered she also had a long flute, an heirloom left by her father, in her rattan suitcase. She opened the suitcase; it had not been in the sun for a long time and was already a little musty; all those abandoned and unworn schoolgirl dresses and skirts were neatly arranged in it as though all the days of her past were sealed there in dust, radiating tiny sparks from disappointed dreams. Lotus took out all the clothes, but did not see the flute. She clearly remembered putting the flute into her suitcase when she left home. How could it be missing?

"Swallow, Swallow, come here," she called toward the porch.

Swallow came in and said, "Fourth Mistress, why aren't you listening to the Young Master play the flute?"

Lotus asked, "Have you touched my suitcase?"

Swallow replied, "A long while ago you asked me to straighten up your suitcase, and I folded all your clothes, didn't I?"

Lotus asked further, "Did you see a wooden flute?"

"Flute?" said Swallow. "I didn't see one. Only a man can play a flute!"

Lotus stared straight into Swallow's eyes, laughed coldly, and said, "Then you must have stolen my flute, didn't you?"

Swallow replied, "Fourth Mistress, you shouldn't just insult people any old way; why would I steal your flute?"

"Naturally you'd have your own mischievous plans," said Lotus, "running around with a head full of clever schemes all day and still pretending to be little miss innocent."

Swallow said, "Fourth Mistress, you shouldn't wrongly accuse people like that. Go and ask Old Master, Young Master, First Mistress, Second Mistress, and Third Mistress, when did I ever steal so much as a single copper from my masters?"

Lotus paid no more attention to Swallow's words; she stared contemptuously into Swallow's face, then ran into her little bedroom, stepped on her cheap wooden trunk, and ordered, "You talk so tough; open up and let me see!"

Swallow pulled at Lotus's leg and pleaded with her, "Fourth Mistress, don't step on my trunk; I really didn't take your flute!"

Looking at Swallow's frightened expression, Lotus was even more sure of herself; she picked up an ax from the corner of the room and said, "I'll hack it open and see; if it's not there, I'll buy you a new trunk tomorrow." She bit her lips, swung the ax down, and Swallow's trunk split right open as clothing, copper coins, and various sorts of trinkets spilled out all over the floor.

Lotus shook out all the clothes, but the flute was not there. Then, suddenly, she caught hold of a bulging little white cloth package; when she opened it up, there was a small cloth figurine. The figurine had three fine needles stuck into its chest. At first she thought it was pretty funny, but she soon realized that the little doll-like figure looked an awfully lot like herself; on close inspection she saw that it had one word faintly written on it in black ink: "Lotus." She felt a sudden sharp pain in her chest, just as though she really was being pierced by three fine needles. Her face immediately went white. Swallow leaned back against the wall and stared at her in alarm. Lotus suddenly let out a shrill scream, jumped up, grabbed Swallow by the hair, and bashed her head repeatedly against the wall. She swallowed back her tears and shouted, "You trying to curse me to death? You trying to curse me to death?"

Swallow did not have the strength to struggle free; she just stood there limp and immobile, sobbing without end. Lotus grew tired, and while she was catching her breath she suddenly remembered that Swallow was illiterate. Who was it, then, who wrote her name on the cloth doll? This question distressed her even more. She squatted down and started wiping away Swallow's tears, then spoke in a gentle tone of voice. "Don't cry. It's all over now; just don't do it anymore. I won't hold it against you, but you've got to tell me who wrote my name for you."

Swallow was still sobbing as she shook her head. "I won't tell. I can't tell."

Lotus said, "You don't have to be afraid; I won't make a big fuss about it. All you have to do is tell me, and I definitely won't get you in trouble." Swallow still shook her head. Then Lotus began to prompt her. "Was it Joy?" Swallow shook her head. "Then it must have been Coral, right?" Swallow still shook her head. Lotus swallowed back a breath of cold air, and her voice was shaking slightly. "Then it was Cloud?" Swallow stopped shaking her head; she looked both despondent and ridiculous. Lotus stood up, looked up into the sky, and said, "You can know a person's face, but not her heart; I guessed it long ago."

CHEN ZUOQIAN SAW Lotus sitting woodenly on the sofa with red and swollen eyes, twisting a bunch of wilted daisies lying limply in her hand. He said, "You've been crying?"

Lotus answered, "No. You treat me so well, why would I cry?"

Chen Zuoqian thought a moment and said, "If you're feeling bored, we could walk around the garden, or we could go out for a midnight snack too."

Lotus twisted the daisies again, tossed them out the window, and asked flatly, "What did you do with my wooden flute?"

Chen Zuoqian hesitated a moment and answered, "I was afraid you'd think of someone else, so I put it away."

The trace of a cold smile formed in the corners of Lotus's mouth. "All my heart is right here; who else would I be thinking about?"

Chen Zuoqian replied quite seriously, "Well, then, tell me, who gave you that flute?"

"It's not a love token, it's an heirloom; my father left it to me."

"I was too suspicious," Chen Zuoqian said with a slight air of embarrassment. "I thought some young student gave it to you."

Lotus held out her hands and said, "Hurry up and bring it here; it's mine, and I want to keep it here."

Chen Zuoqian grew even more embarrassed. He walked back and forth, rubbing his hands together. "This is terrible," he said. "I already had one of my servants burn it." He did not hear Lotus say another word as the room gradually grew dark. When he turned on the light, he saw that Lotus's face was white as snow and tears were flowing silently down her cheeks.

That night was a very unusual one for the two of them. Lotus curled herself up like a lamb and stayed far away from Chen Zuoqian's body; Chen Zuoqian reached over and caressed her, but did not receive any response. He turned the lights off a while, then turned them on again and looked at Lotus's face; it was as indifferent and unfeeling as a piece of paper. "You're going too far," he said. "I've almost got down on my knees and begged for forgiveness."

Lotus was silent a moment, then said, "I don't feel good." Chen Zuoqian said, "I hate it when people frown at me." Lotus turned over and said, "Why don't you go to Cloud's, she always smiles at you." Chen Zuoqian jumped out of bed and pulled on his clothes. "I will go, then; thank God I still have three other wives!"

(Translated by Michael S. Duke)

ZHANG ZAO
(1962–2010)

Born in Hunan, Zhang Zao was a prominent poet who came of age after the Misty School. Trained in foreign languages and literature, he graduated from Hunan Normal University with a bachelor's degree. In 1986 he went to study in Germany and received a Ph.D. in literature from Tübingen University. For years he was the poetry editor for the journal Today. In 2010 he died of lung cancer in Tübingen, Germany, the hometown of his favorite poet, Friedrich Hölderlin, whose work was introduced to China during the "culture fever" in the 1980s.

A Starry Moment

My first real agony
When whiteness blurs transparency
Beads of sweat commit suicide
And you are naked as the walls

Our first, how pure it is
And pretty like math

A fever seizes me
Light and skin hanging upside down

You, a dismembered body of flowing water
Choke me in the night
And scorch me in arrays of clarity
My purple friend, the Emperor, weeps for me

Even the moon, as a blessing, opens the white door
At ten o'clock the desk lamp stops its walk
Scraps of paper behave like bewildered caresses
You ask me to forget the abysmal alleys nearby
Where year upon year the elderly fill up the windows

Even a cup of shining stars
Even the childlike dawn to the left,
That obscures the hanging constellations, is too weak
To support the torrents of yesterday's wind
Oh, how white with purity I am now, like

The air before you were born
You once blossomed like a real pomegranate

Into the Mirror

As long as there are regrets
plum blossoms fall.
To see her swim for the far shore
or climb a pine ladder,
there is beauty in dangerous acts.
Better yet, to watch her return on horseback
cheeks flush with shame,
bowing her head, as if answering the Emperor.
A mirror always waits for her
And bids her to sit at her usual spot in the mirror,

looking out the window.
As long as there are regrets
plum blossoms fall
and cover the southern mountain.

Elegy

a letter opens, someone says
that the sky's turned cold

another letter opens
it's empty, empty
but heavier than the world

a letter opens
someone says he's singing from the heights
someone says, no, even if a potato is dead
by inertia
it can still grow small hands

another letter opens
you sleep soundly like an orange
but peeling you naked, someone says
he has touched another you inside

another letter opens
everyone is laughing
everything around is uproarious with laughter

a letter opens
clouds and whitewater run wild outdoors

a letter opens
I am chewing certain darkness

another letter opens
a bright moon high in the sky

another letter opens, crying
death is a real thing.
(Translated by Yunte Huang
and Glenn Mott)

XI CHUAN
(1963–)

Born Liu Jun in Xuzhou, Jiangsu Province, Xi Chuan graduated from Peking University with a degree in English in 1985. He worked as an editor for various magazines, including the literary journal Tendency (1988-91). In the wake of the Tiananmen crackdown and after the death of his two poet friends (Hai Zi and Luo Yihe) in 1989, Xi Chuan stopped writing for three years. He is currently a professor at China Central Academy of Fine Arts in Beijing.

On the Other Side of the River

on the other side of the river
there is a flame
a flame
having burnt May
now burning August

when the pagoda tree blooms, the freckled old professor bows to her
when orange blossoms fall, a debonair heir waves and smiles to her

yet she remains burning
on the other side of the river

like red coral dazzling underwater
like a red straw hat
blown away by wind

yesterday when I saw her
she was looking to the sky
standing still
and today she lowers her head
watching the water

if it's overcast or raining
what will she do
on the other side of the river?
——her flame won't go out

a poet sees her
a peasant sees her
a Marxist sees her
she's on the other side of the river, burning
having burnt May
now burning August

Blackout

a blackout, convincing me
I live in a developing country

a country where people read by moonlight
a country that abolished imperial exams

a blackout, letting me hear
wind chimes and a cat's crawl upstairs

a running motor dies with a thud in the distance
the battery-powered radio still sings by my side

with every blackout, time turns back quickly:
candles lit in a little eatery

the fatso devouring crow meat
finds crows crowding the limbs of a tree

and the pitch-black before me
so much like the womb of a surging sea

a mother hangs herself on a beam
to each room belongs a scent of its own

a blackout. I fish out a slipper
but mutter: "Quit hiding, matches!"

in the candlelight I see myself
a giant wordless shadow cast upon the wall

Far Away

for Akhmatova

there in a dream is a snowfield
there in the snowfield is a white birch
there a small house about to resound in prayer
there a shingle about to fall off the North Star

far away

there a crowd of people green as cabbage
there a pot of hot water drunk up by beasts
there a wooden chair sunk in recollection
there a desk lamp representing me in illumination

far away

a sheet of glass scrawled in words I can't read
a white page overgrown with soybeans and sorghum
a face forces me to drop my pen
picking it up again, I find the ink frozen

far away

December's wandering clouds rise from treetops
my soul's train in the cold stops
I see me treading a bleak road
coughing thrice at a woman's door

(Translated by Yunte Huang)

YU XINQIAO
(1968–)

Born in Fujian and raised in Zhejiang, Yu Xinqiao is one of the most popular and important poets in China today. His maternal grandfather was a wealthy overseas businessman, a factor that doomed Yu's prospects in a period when the Communist ideology pitched the working class against the "exploitive" class. A middle school dropout, Yu became a popular speaker on the subjects of poetry and Chinese culture in the years following the June 4 crackdown. In 1993 he called for a "Chinese Renaissance Movement," a proposal welcomed by many but frowned upon by the government. He was subsequently jailed for eight years on dubious charges. While many mainstream journals, in fear of censorship, shy away from his work, Yu is tremendously popular among Chinese readers. His poem "If I Have to Die," set to music, was a big hit; even real estate developers borrowed his lines for use on billboards.

If I Have to Die

What you didn't ignite
Can't be called fire
What you haven't touched
Can't be called sapphire
Ah you, you're finally here

As soon as we meet
My heart breaks into bits
The whole world crumbles
Your beauty is an unsheathed blade
What you didn't kill
Has no reason to live
What you didn't shatter
Can never be patched together
If I have to die in this life
I must die in your hand

Epitaph

In my country
Only you have not read my poetry
Only you have not loved me
When you find my grave
Please select the prettiest spring day
Walk the sunniest path
And come apologize to me
If there're raindrops
Ask them to fall another day
If the milkweed hasn't yet blossomed
Ask them to bloom instantly
In my sunlit country
In my moonlit country
In my well lit country
Only you have not read my poetry
Only you have not loved me
You're the only shadow in my bright land
You must apologize to the sky
Apologize to the clouds

Apologize to the mountains and rivers
Finally apologize to me
Finally say: If Yu Xinqiao were still alive
How great would that be

The Dead Are Mourning the Living

It's time
Lily-white and jade-green Chinese
Demolishes in silence all platforms of good-bye
A voiceless train
Slows down in Tang and Song poetry
At present I wish
This country, addicted to forgery
Can at least speed up forgery today
Let all the calamities
All the deaths
At least turn out to be fictional today
Let earthquakes happen only in heaven
Let beautiful lies cover the earth
Ah, it's time
The dead are mourning the living

Self-Introduction

I'm from the most beautiful country
Where filth and chaos are only a legend
The only trash to clean up
Are the fresh flowers littering the fields

I'm from the freest country
Where prison never exists
No wrongful conviction, or false claim
Anytime anywhere we're free to dream

Where fault finders throng in number
But even among thistles and thorns
There is no bone to pick

Listen, I don't agree you are happy
I'm from the country of truth
Except for ours, there's no other path
                    (Translated by Yunte Huang)

GAO XINGJIAN

(1940-)

The résumé of the first Chinese Nobel laureate in literature reads like a chronicle of government censorship. Born in Ganzhou, Jiangxi, to a father who was a bank clerk and a mother who was a play actress, Gao graduated from Beijing Foreign Studies University with a degree in French in 1962. A translator of Samuel Beckett and Eugène Ionesco, Gao first became known as a playwright devoted to absurdist drama— an artistic form that was frowned upon by the Communist regime, resulting in censorship of Gao's plays in the 1980s. In 1986 Gao was misdiagnosed with lung cancer, which led him to make a ten-month trek along the Yangtze. This soul-searching pilgrimage became the basis of his magnum opus, Soul Mountain (1990). In 1989 he resigned from the Communist Party and continued his unrelenting criticism of ortho- dox ideology. Thereafter, all his works were banned in China. He was awarded the Nobel Prize in Literature in 2000.

Soul Mountain (excerpts)

1

The old bus is a city reject. After shaking in it for twelve hours on the potholed highway since early morning, you* arrive in this mountain county town in the south.

In the bus station, which is littered with ice-block wrappers and sugarcane scraps, you stand with your backpack and a bag and look around for a while. People are getting off the bus or walking past, men humping sacks and women carrying babies. A crowd of youths, unhampered by sacks or baskets, have their hands free. They take sunflower seeds out of their pockets, toss them one at a time into their mouths, and spit out the shells. With a loud crack the kernels are expertly eaten. To be leisurely and carefree is endemic to the place. They are locals and life has made them like this, they have been here for many generations and you wouldn't need to go looking anywhere else for them. The earliest to leave the place traveled by river in black canopy boats and overland in hired carts, or by foot if they didn't have the money. Of course at that time there were no buses and no bus stations. Nowadays, as long as they are still able to travel, they flock back home, even from the other side of the Pacific, arriving in cars or big air-conditioned coaches. The rich, the famous, and the nothing in particular all hurry back because they are getting old. After all, who doesn't love the home of their ancestors? They don't intend to stay so they walk around looking relaxed, talking and laughing loudly, and effusing fondness and affection for the place. When friends meet they don't just give a nod or a handshake in the meaningless ritual of city people, but rather they shout the person's name or thump him on the back. Hugging is also common, but not for women. By the cement trough where the buses are washed, two young women hold

---

* The "you" in this chapter and the "I" in the next are two unnamed characters of the novel. We may read such a contrapuntal narration as one man's inner dialogue.

hands as they chat. The women here have lovely voices and you can't help taking a second look. The one with her back to you is wearing an indigo-print headscarf. This type of scarf, and how it's tied, dates back many generations but is seldom seen these days. You find yourself walking toward them. The scarf is knotted under her chin and the two ends point up. She has a beautiful face. Her features are delicate, so is her slim body. You pass close by them. They have been holding hands all this time, both have red coarse hands and strong fingers. Both are probably recent brides back seeing relatives and friends, or visiting parents. Here, the word *xifu* means one's own daughter-in-law and using it like rustic northerners to refer to any young married woman will immediately incur angry abuse. On the other hand, a married woman calls her own husband *laogong*, yet your *laogong* and my *laogong* are both used. People here speak with a unique intonation even though they are descendants of the same legendary emperor and are of the same culture and race.

You can't explain why you're here. It happened that you were on a train and this person mentioned a place called Lingshan. He was sitting opposite and your cup was next to his. As the train moved, the lids on the cups clattered against one another. If the lids kept on clattering or clattered and then stopped, that would have been the end of it. However, whenever you and he were about to separate the cups, the clattering would stop, and as soon as you and he looked away the clattering would start again. He and you reached out, but again the clattering stopped. The two of you laughed at the same instant, put the cups well apart, and started a conversation. You asked him where he was going.

"Lingshan."

"What?"

"Lingshan, *ling* meaning spirit or soul, and *shan* meaning mountain."

You'd been to lots of places, visited lots of famous mountains, but had never heard of this place.

Your friend opposite had closed his eyes and was dozing. Like anyone else, you couldn't help being curious and naturally wanted to know which famous places you'd missed on your travels. Also, you liked doing things properly and it was annoying that there was a place you've never even heard of. You asked him about the location of Lingshan.

"At the source of the You River," he said, opening his eyes.

You didn't know this You River either, but were embarrassed about asking and gave an ambiguous nod which could have meant either, "I see, thanks" or "Oh, I know the place." This satisfied your desire for superiority, but not your curiosity. After a while you asked how to get there and the route up the mountain.

"Take the train to Wuyizhen, then go upstream by boat on the You River."

"What's there? Scenery? Temples? Historic sites?" you asked, trying to be casual.

"It's all virgin wilderness."

"Ancient forests?"

"Of course, but not just ancient forests."

"What about Wild Men?" you said, joking.

He laughed without any sarcasm, and didn't seem to be making fun of himself, which intrigued you even more. You had to find out more about him.

"Are you an ecologist? A biologist? An anthropologist? An archaeologist?"

He shook his head each time, then said, "I'm more interested in living people."

"So you're doing research on folk customs? You're a sociologist? An ethnographer? An ethnologist? A journalist, perhaps? An adventurer?"

"I'm an amateur in all of these."

The two of you started laughing.

"I'm an expert amateur in all of these!"

The laughing made you and him cheerful. He lit a cigarette and couldn't stop talking as he told you about the wonders of Lingshan. Afterward, at your request, he tore up his empty cigarette box and drew a map of the route up to Lingshan.

‖‖‖‖‖‖‖‖‖‖‖‖‖

IN THE NORTH it is already late autumn but the summer heat hasn't completely subsided. Before sunset, it is still quite hot in the sun and sweat starts running down your back. You leave the station to have a look around. There's nothing nearby except for the little inn across the road. It's an old-style two-story building with a wooden shopfront. Upstairs the floorboards creak badly but worse still is the grime on the pillow and sleeping mat. If you wanted to have a wash, you'd have to wait till it was dark to strip off and pour water over yourself in the damp and narrow courtyard. This is a stopover for the village peddlers and craftsmen.

It's well before dark, so there's plenty of time to find somewhere clean. You walk down the road looking around the little town, hoping to find some indication, a billboard or a poster, or just the name "Lingshan," to tell you you're on the right track and haven't been tricked into making this long excursion. You look everywhere but don't find anything. There were no tourists like you among the other passengers who got off the bus. Of course, you're not *that* sort of tourist, it's just what you're wearing: strong sensible sports shoes and a backpack with shoulder straps, no one else is dressed like you. But this isn't one of the tourist spots frequented by newlyweds and retirees. Those places have been transformed by tourism, coaches are parked everywhere and tourist maps are on sale. Tourist hats, tourist T-shirts, tourist singlets, and tourist handkerchiefs printed with the name of the place are in all the little shops and stalls, and the name of the place is used in the trade names of all the "foreign exchange currency only" hotels for foreigners, the "locals with references only" hostels and sanatoriums, and of course the small private hotels competing for customers. You haven't come to enjoy yourself in one of those places on the sunny side of a mountain where people congregate just to look at and jostle one another and to add to the litter of melon rind, fruit peel, soft drink bottles, cans, cartons, sandwich wrappings, and cigarette butts. Sooner or later this place will also boom but you're here before they put up the gaudy pavilions and terraces, before the reporters come with their cameras, and before the celebrities come to put up plaques with their calligraphy. You can't help feeling rather pleased with yourself, and yet you're anxious. There's no sign of anything here for tourists, have you made a blunder? You're only going by the map on the cigarette box in your shirt pocket, what if the expert amateur you met on the train had only heard about the place on his travels? How do you know he wasn't just making it all up? You've never seen the place mentioned in travel accounts and it's not listed in the most up-to-date travel guides. Of course, it isn't hard to find places like Lingtai, Lingqiu, Lingyan, and even Lingshan on provincial maps and you know very well that in the histories and classics, Lingshan appears in works dating back to the ancient shamanistic work *Classic of the Mountains and Seas* and the old geographical gazetteer *Annotated Water Classic*. It was also at Lingshan that Buddha enlightened the Venerable Mahakashyapa. You're not stupid, so just use your brains, first find this place Wuyizhen on the cigarette box, for this is how you'll get to Lingshan.

You return to the bus station and go into the waiting room. The busiest place in this small town is now deserted. The ticket window and the parcel window are boarded up from the inside, so knocking is useless. There's no one to ask, so you can only go through the lists of stops above the ticket window: Zhang Village, Sandy Flat, Cement Factory, Old Hut, Golden Horse, Good Harvest, Flood Waters, Dragon Bay, Peach Blossom Hollow . . . the names keep getting better, but the place you want isn't there. This is just a small town but there are several routes and quite a few buses go through. The busiest route, with five or six buses a day, is to Cement Factory but that's definitely not a tourist route. The route with the fewest buses, one a day, is sure to go to the farthest destination and it turns out that Wuyizhen is the last stop. There's nothing special about the name, it's just like any other place name and there's nothing magical about it. Still, you seem to have found one end of a hopeless tangle and while you're not ecstatic, you're certainly relieved. You'll need to buy a ticket in the morning an hour before departure and you know from experience that with mountain buses like this, which run once a day, just to get on will be a fight. Unless you're prepared to do battle, you'll just have to queue up early.

But, right now, you've lots of time, although your backpack's a nuisance. As you amble along the road, timber trucks go by noisily sounding their horns. In the town the noise worsens as trucks, some with trailers, blast their horns and conductors hang out of windows loudly banging the sides of the buses to hasten the pedestrians off the road.

The old buildings on both sides stand flush with the road and all have wooden shopfronts. The downstairs is for business and upstairs there is washing hung out to dry—diapers, bras, underpants with patched crotches, floral-print bedspreads—like flags of all the nations, flapping in the noise and dust of the traffic. The concrete telegraph poles along the street are pasted at eye level with all sorts of posters. One for curing body odor catches your attention. This is not because you've got body odor but because of the fancy language and the words in brackets after "body odor."

> Body odor (known also as scent of the immortals) is a disgusting condition with an awful, nauseating smell. It often affects social relationships and can delay life's major event: marriage. It disadvantages young men and women at job interviews or when they try to enlist, therefore inflicting much suffering and anguish. By using a new total treatment, we can instantly eradicate the odor with a rate of up to 97.53% success. For joy in life and future happiness, we welcome you to come and rid yourself of it. . . .

After that you come to a stone bridge: no body odor here, just a cool, refreshing breeze. The bridge spanning the broad river has a bitumen surface but the carved monkeys on the worn stone posts testify to its long history. You lean on the concrete railing and survey the township alongside the bridge. On both banks, black rooftops overlapping like fish scales stretch endlessly into the distance. The valley opens out between two mountains where the upper areas of gold paddy fields are inlaid with clusters of green bamboos. The river is blue and clear as it trickles over the sandy shores, but close to the granite pylons dividing the current it becomes inky green and deep. Just past the hump of the bridge the rushing water churns loudly and white foam surfaces from whirlpools. The ten-meter-high stone embankment is stained with water levels—the new grayish yellow lines were probably left by the recent summer floods. Can this be the You River? And does it flow down from Lingshan?

The sun is about to set. The bright orange disc is infused with light but there's no glare. You gaze into the distance at the hazy layers of jagged peaks where the two sides of the valley join. This ominous black image nibbles at the lower edges of the glowing sun, which seems to be revolving. The sun turns a dark red, gentler, and projects brilliant gold reflections onto the entire bend of the river: the dark blue of the water fusing with the dazzling sunlight throbs and pulsates. As the red sphere seats itself in the valley it becomes serene, awesomely beautiful, and there are sounds. You hear them, elusive, distinctly reverberating from deep in your heart and radiating outward until the sun seems to prop itself up on its toes, stumble, then sink into the black shadows of the mountains, scattering glowing colors throughout the sky. An evening wind blows noisily by your ears and cars drive past, as usual sounding their deafening horns. You cross the bridge and see there a new dedication stone with engraved characters painted in red: "Yongning Bridge. Built in the third year of the Kaiyuan reign period of the Song Dynasty and repaired in 1962. This stone was laid in 1983." It no doubt marks the beginning of the tourist industry here.

Two food stalls stand at the end of the bridge. In the one on the left you eat a bowl of bean curd, the smooth and tasty kind with all the right ingredients. Hawkers used to sell it in the streets and lanes but it completely disappeared for quite some years and has recently been revived as family enterprises. In the stall on the right you eat two delicious sesame-coated shallot pancakes, straight off the stove and piping-hot. Then at one of the stalls, you can't remember which, you eat a bowl of sweet *yuanxiao* dumplings broiled in rice wine. They are the size of large pearls. Of course, you're not as academic about food as Mr. Ma the

Second who toured West Lake, but you do have a hefty appetite nevertheless. You savor this food of your ancestors and listen to customers chatting with the proprietors. They're mostly locals and all know one another. You try using the mellifluous local accent to be friendly, you want to be one of them. You've lived in the city for a long time and need to feel that you have a hometown. You want a hometown so that you'll be able to return to your childhood to recollect long-lost memories.

On this side of the bridge you eventually find an inn on an old cobblestone street. The wooden floors have been mopped and it's clean enough. You are given a small single room which has a plank bed covered with a bamboo mat. The cotton blanket is a suspicious gray—either it hasn't been washed properly or that's the original color. You throw aside the greasy pillow from under the bamboo mat and luckily it's hot so you can do without the bedding. What you need right now is to off-load your luggage, which has become quite heavy, wash off the dust and sweat, strip, and stretch yourself out on the bed.

There's shouting and yelling next door. They're gambling and you can hear them picking up and throwing down the cards. A timber partition separates you and, through the holes poked into the paper covering the cracks, you make out the blurred figures of some bare-chested men. You're not so tired that you can drop off to sleep just like that. You tap on the wall and instantly there's loud shouting next door. They're not shouting at you but among themselves—there are always winners and losers and it sounds as though the loser is trying to get out of paying. They're openly gambling in the inn despite the public security office notice on the wall prohibiting gambling and prostitution. You decide to see if the law works. You put on some clothes, go down the corridor, and knock on the half-closed door. Your knocking makes no difference, they keep shouting and yelling inside and nobody takes any notice. So you push open the door and go in. The four men sitting around the bed in the middle of the room all turn to look at you. But it's you and not they who gets a rude shock. The men all have bits of paper stuck on their faces, on their foreheads, lips, noses, and cheeks, and they look ugly and ridiculous. They aren't laughing and are glaring at you. You've butted in and they're clearly annoyed.

"Oh, you're playing cards," you say, putting on an apologetic look.

They go on playing. The long paper cards have red and black markings like mah-jongg and there's a Gate of Heaven and a Prison of Hell. The winner penalizes the loser by tearing off a strip of newspaper and sticking it on a designated spot. Whether this is a prank, a way of letting off steam, or a tally, is something agreed upon by the gamblers and there is no way for outsiders to know what it's all about.

You beat a retreat, go back to your room, lie down again, and see a thick mass of black specks around the light globe. Millions of mosquitoes are waiting for the light to go out so that they can come down and feast on your blood. You quickly let down the net and are enclosed in a narrow conical space, at the top of which is a bamboo hoop. It's been a long time since you've slept under a hoop like this, and you've long since passed the age of being able to stare at the hoop to lose yourself in reverie. Today, you can't know what traumas tomorrow will bring. You've learned through experience everything you need to know. What else are you looking for? When a man gets to middle age, shouldn't he look for a peaceful and stable existence, find a not-too-demanding sort of a job, stay in a mediocre position, become a husband and a father, set up a comfortable home, put money in the bank, and add to it every month so there'll be something for old age and a little left over for the next generation?

2

It is in the Qiang region halfway up Qionglai Mountain, in the border areas of the Qinghai-Tibetan highlands and the Sichuan Basin, that I witness a vestige of early human civilization—the worship of fire. Fire, the bringer of civilization, has been worshipped by the early ancestors of human beings everywhere. It is sacred. The old man is sitting in front of the fire drinking liquor from a bowl. Before each sip he puts a finger into it and flicks some on the charcoals, which splutter noisily and send out blue sparks. It is only then that I perceive that I too am real.

"That's for the God of the Cooking Stove, it's thanks to him that we can eat and drink," he says.

The dancing light of the fire shines on his thin cheeks, the high bridge of his nose, and his cheekbones. He tells me he is of the Qiang nationality and that he's from Gengda Village down the mountain. I can't ask straight out about demons and spirits, so I tell him I'm here to do some research on the folk songs of the mountain. Do traditional song masters and dancers still exist here? He says he's one of them. The men and women all used to form a circle around the fire and dance right through to daybreak, but later on it was banned.

"Why?" I know quite well but I ask. I'm being dishonest again.

"It was the Cultural Revolution. They said the songs were dirty, so we turned to singing *Sayings of Mao Zedong* songs instead."

"And what about after that?" I persist in asking. This is becoming a habit.

"No one sings those anymore. People are doing the dances again but not many of the young people can do them, I'm teaching the dances to some of them."

I ask him for a demonstration. Without any hesitation, he instantly gets to his feet and proceeds to dance and sing. His voice is low and rich, he's got a good voice. I'm sure he's Qiang even if the police in charge of the population register insist that he isn't. They think anyone claiming to be Tibetan or Qiang is trying to evade birth restrictions so they can have more children.

He sings song after song. He says he's a fun-loving person, and I believe him. When he finished up as village head, he went back to being one of the mountain people, an old mountain man who likes good fun, though unfortunately he is past the age for romance.

He also knows incantations, the kind hunters employ when they go into the mountains. They are called mountain black magic or hexes and he has no qualms about using them. He really believes they can drive wild animals into pits or get them to step into snares. They aren't used only on animals, they're also used against other human beings for revenge. A victim of mountain black magic won't be able to find his way out of the mountains. They are like the "demon walls" I heard about as a child: when a person has been traveling for some time at night in the mountains, a wall, a cliff, or a deep river appears right in front of him, so that he can't go any farther. If the spell isn't broken the person's feet don't move forward, and even if he keeps walking, he stays exactly where he started off. Only at daybreak does he discover that he has been going around in circles. That's not so bad, the worst is when a person is led into a blind alley—that means death.

He intones strings of incantations. It's not slow and relaxed like when he is singing, but just *nan-nan-na-na* to a quick beat. I can't understand it at all but I can feel the mystical pull of the words and a demonic, powerful atmosphere instantly permeates the room, the inside of which is black from smoke. The glow of the flames licking the iron pot of mutton stew makes his eyes glint. This is all starkly real.

While you search for the route to Lingshan, I wander along the Yangtze River looking for this sort of reality. I had just gone through a crisis and then, on top of that, a doctor wrongly diagnosed me with lung cancer. Death was playing a joke on me, but now that I've escaped the demon wall, I am secretly rejoicing. Life for me once again has a wonderful freshness. I should have left those contaminated surroundings long ago and returned to nature to look for this authentic life.

In those contaminated surroundings I was taught that life was the source of literature, that literature had to be faithful to life, faithful to real life. My mistake was that I had alienated myself from life and ended up turning my back on real life. Life is not the same as manifestations of life. Real life, or in other words the basic substance of life, should be the former and not the latter. I had gone against real life because I was simply stringing together life's manifestations, so of course I wasn't able to accurately portray life and in the end only succeeded in distorting reality.

I don't know whether I'm now on the right track, but in any case I've extricated myself from the bustling literary world and have also escaped from my smoke-filled room. The books piled everywhere in that room were oppressive and stifling. They expounded all sorts of truths, from historical truths to truths on how to be human. I couldn't see the point of so many truths but still got enmeshed in the net of those truths and was struggling hopelessly, like an insect caught in a spider's web. Fortunately, the doctor who gave the wrong diagnosis saved my life. He was quite frank and got me to compare the two chest X-rays taken on two separate occasions—a blurry shadow on the left lobe of the lung had spread along the second rib to the wall of the windpipe. It wouldn't help even to have the whole of the left lobe removed. The outcome was obvious. My father had died of lung cancer. He died within three months of it being discovered and it was this doctor who had correctly diagnosed it. I had faith in his medical expertise and he had faith in science. The chest X-rays taken at two different hospitals were identical, there was no possibility of a technical mistake. He also wrote an authorization for a sectional X-ray, the appointment was in two weeks' time. This was nothing to get worried about, it was just to determine the extent of the tumor. My father had this done before he died. The outcome would be the same whether or not I had the X-ray, it was nothing special. That I in fact would slip through the fingers of Death can only be put down to good luck. I believe in science but I also believe in fate.

I ONCE SAW a four-inch length of wood which had been collected in the Qiang region by an anthropologist during the 1930s. It was a carved statue of a person doing a handstand. The head had ink markings for the eyes, nose, and mouth, and the word "longevity" had been written on the body. It was called "Wuchang Upside Down" and there was something oddly mischievous about it. I ask the Qiang retired village head whether such talismans are still around. He tells me these are called "old root." This wooden idol has to accompany the newborn from birth to death. At death it accompanies the corpse from the house and after the burial it is placed in the wilderness to allow the spirit to return to nature. I ask him if he can get me one so that I can carry it on me. He laughs and says these are what hunters tuck into their shirts to ward off evil spirits, they wouldn't be of any use to someone like me.

"Is there an old hunter who knows about this sort of magic and can take me hunting with him?" I ask.

"Grandpa Stone would be the best," he says after thinking about it.

"How can I find him?" I ask right away.

"He's in Grandpa Stone's Hut."

"Where's this Grandpa Stone's Hut?"

"Go another twenty *li* on to Silver Mine Gully, then follow the creek right up to the end. There you'll find a stone hut."

"Is that the name of the place or do you mean the hut of Grandpa Stone?"

He says it's the name of the place, that there's in fact a stone hut, and that Grandpa Stone lives there.

"Can you take me to him?" I ask.

"He's dead. He lay down on his bed and died in his sleep. He was too old, he lived to well over ninety, some even say well over a hundred. In any case, nobody's sure about his age."

"Are any of his descendants still alive?"

"In my grandfather's generation and for as long as I can remember, he was always on his own."

"Without a wife?"

"He lived on his own in Silver Mine Gully. He lived high up the gully, in the solitary hut, alone. Oh, and that rifle of his is still hanging on the wall of the hut."

I ask him what he's trying to tell me.

He says Grandpa Stone was a great hunter, a hunter who was an expert in the magical arts. There are no hunters like that these days. Everyone knows that his rifle is hanging in the hut, that it never misses its target, but nobody dares to go and take it.

"Why?" I'm even more puzzled.

"The route into Silver Mine Gully is cut."

"There's no way through?"

"Not anymore. Earlier on people used to mine silver there, a firm from Chengdu hired a team of workers and they began mining. Later on, after the mine was looted, everyone just left, and the plank roads they had laid either broke up or rotted."

"When did all this happen?"

"When my grandfather was still alive, more than fifty years ago."

That would be about right, after all he's already retired and has become history, real history.

"So since then nobody's ever gone there?" I become even more intrigued.

"Hard to say, anyway it's hard to get there."

"And the hut has rotted?"

"Stone collapses, how can it rot?"

"I was talking about the ridgepole."

"Oh, quite right."

He doesn't want to take me there, nor does he want to find a hunter for me, so that's why he's leading me on like this, I think.

"Then how do you know the rifle's still hanging on the wall?" I ask, regardless.

"That's what everyone says, someone must've seen it. They all say that Grandpa Stone is incredible, his corpse hasn't rotted and wild animals don't dare to go near. He just lies there all stiff and emaciated, and his rifle is hanging there on the wall."

"Impossible," I declare. "With the high humidity up here on the mountain, the corpse would have rotted and the rifle would have turned into a pile of rust."

"I don't know. Anyway, people have been saying this for years." He refuses to give in and sticks to his story. The light of the fire dances in his eyes and I seem to detect a cunning streak in them.

"And you've never seen him?" I won't let him off.

"People who have seen him say that he seems to be asleep, that he's emaciated, and that the rifle is hanging there on the wall above his head," he says, unruffled. "He knew black magic. It's not just that people don't dare go there to steal his rifle, even animals don't dare to go near."

The hunter is already myth. To talk about a mixture of history and

legend is how folk stories are born. Reality exists only through experience, and it must be personal experience. However, once related, even
personal experience becomes a narrative. Reality can't be verified and
doesn't need to be, that can be left for the "reality-of-life" experts to
debate. What is important is life. Reality is simply that I am sitting by
the fire in this room which is black with grime and smoke and that I
see the light of the fire dancing in his eyes. Reality is myself, reality is
only the perception of this instant, and it can't be related to another
person. All that needs to be said is that outside, a mist is enclosing the
green-blue mountain in a haze and your heart is reverberating with the
rushing water of a swift-flowing stream.

17

You come to the end of the village. A middle-aged woman with an
apron tied over her long gown squats by the creek in front of her door,
gutting fish no bigger than a finger. The blade of her knife flashes in the
glow of a pine torch burning by the creek. Farther on are darkening
mountain shadows and only the peak shows some slight traces of the
setting sun. There are no more houses in sight. You turn back, perhaps
it is the pine torch which draws you there. You go up and ask if you can
stay the night.

"People often stop here for the night." The woman understands what
you want, glances at your companion, but doesn't ask any questions.
She puts down the knife, wipes her hands on her apron, and goes into
the house. She lights the oil lamp in the hall and brings it along. You
follow behind, the floorboards creaking beneath your feet. Upstairs is
the clean smell of paddy straw, freshly harvested.

"It's empty up here, I'll fetch some bedding. It gets cold in the mountains at night." The woman puts the lamp on the windowsill and goes
downstairs.

She says she won't stay downstairs, she says she's afraid. And she
won't stay in the same room as you, she says she's afraid of that too. So
you leave the lamp for her, kick the paddy straw piled on the floor, and

go to the adjoining room. You say you don't like sleeping on plank beds but like rolling about in straw. She says she will sleep with her head next to yours so you will be able to talk through the wall. The wooden partition doesn't go right to the ceiling and you can see the circle of light projected onto the rafters in her room.

"This is unique," you say.

She asks for some hot water when the woman of the house returns with the bedding.

The woman brings her a small wooden pail of hot water. Afterward you hear her latching the door.

You strip to the waist, throw a small towel over your shoulder, and go downstairs. There is no light, probably the only kerosene lamp in the house is upstairs in her room. In the kitchen, you see the woman of the house by the stove. Her expressionless face, lit by the light of the open stove, is gentler. The burning straw crackles and you can smell the aroma of cooking rice.

You take a bucket and go down to the creek. The last remnants of sunset on the mountain vanish and the haziness of dusk descends. There are spots of light in the clear rippling water—the stars are out. A few frogs are croaking.

Opposite, deep in the mountain shadows, you hear children laughing on the other side of the creek. Paddy fields are over there. You seem to see a threshing lot in the mountain shadows, and the children are probably playing hide-and-seek. In the thick dark mountain shadows, separated by paddy fields, a big girl is laughing on the threshing lot. It's her, she's in the darkness opposite: a forgotten past is relived as one of that crowd of children one day recalls his childhood. One day the squeaky voice of the boy screaming cheeky nonsense thickened, became throaty and deep, and his bare feet pattering on the stones of the threshing lot left wet footprints as he departed from childhood to enter the big wide world. You hear the patter of bare feet on black cobblestones. A child by a pond is using his grandmother's embroidery frame for a tugboat. At a shout from his grandmother he turns and runs off, the patter of his bare feet resounding on the cobblestones. Once again you see the back of her, her single long black plait, in a small lane. In the wet lanes of Wuy-izhen the winter wind is icy. She has a bucket of water on a carrying pole and is walking with quick short steps on the cobblestones as the bucket presses on her young frail shoulder, straining her body down to the waist. The water in the bucket wobbles and splashes the black cob-blestones as she comes to a halt when you call out to her. She turns to smile at you, then goes on walking with more quick short steps. She is wearing purplish red cloth shoes. In the darkness children are laughing and shouting. Their voices are loud, even if you can't make out what it is they are shouting, and there seem to be layers of echoes. It is in this instant that everything comes back to life, Yaya. . . .

In an instant your childhood memories become stark and vivid. The roar of dive-bombing planes, then black wings suddenly swoop up and fly into the distance. You are huddled in your mother's arms under a small sour date tree and the thorns on the branches have torn her cot-ton jacket, showing her plump arms. Then it's your wet nurse. She's carrying you. You like her cuddling you, she's got big floppy breasts. She sprinkles salt on rice *guoba* toasted a delicious crunchy golden brown for you. You love spending time in her kitchen. The bright red eyes in the dark belong to the pair of white rabbits you kept. One of them was mauled in the cage by a weasel and the other one disappeared. You later found it floating in the urine pot in the lavatory in the back courtyard, its fur all dirty. In the back courtyard there was a tree growing in a heap of broken tiles and bricks, the tiles had moss growing on them. You could only see as high up as the branch which came to the top of the wall, so you didn't know what it looked like after it grew over the wall. You only knew if you stood on your toes you could reach a hole in the trunk, and you used to throw stones into it. People said trees have feel-ings and tree demons are sensitive just like people and don't like being tickled. If you poked something into the hole of the trunk, the tree would shake all over laughing, just like when you tickled her under the arms and she immediately pulled away and laughed until she was out of breath. You can always remember the time she lost a tooth: "Tooth-less, toothless, her name is Yaya!" She was furious with you for calling her toothless and went off in a huff. Dirt spews up like a pall of black smoke and rains down on everyone's head, your mother scrambles to her feet, feels you, you're all right. But then you hear a long shrill wail, it's another woman: it doesn't sound human. Next you are being shaken about on endless mountain roads in a tarpaulin-covered truck, squashed between the grown-ups' legs and the luggage, rain is dripping off the end of your nose. Mother's cunt, everyone down to push the truck. The wheels are spinning in the mud, splashing everyone in the face. Mother's cunt, you say, imitating the driver, this is the first bit of swearing you've picked up, you're swearing because the mud has pulled off your shoe. Yaya . . . The shouting of the children is still coming from the threshing lot, they are laughing and yelling as they chase one another about. But your childhood no longer exists, and all that confront you are the dark shadows of the mountain. . . .

YOU COME TO her door and beg her to open it. She says stop making a fuss, leave things as they are, she feels good now. She needs peace, to be free of desire, she needs time, she needs to forget, she needs understanding not love, she needs to find someone she can pour out her heart to. She hopes you won't ruin this good relationship, she's just starting to trust you, she says she wants to keep traveling with you, to go right to Lingshan. There's plenty of time for getting together but definitely not right now. She asks you to forgive her, she doesn't want to, and she can't.

You say it's something else. You've found a faint light coming through a crack in the wall. Someone else is upstairs apart from the two of you. You ask her to come and have a look.

She says no! Stop trying to trick her, stop frightening her like this.

You say there's a light flickering in a crack in the wall. You're quite sure there's another room behind the wall. You come out of your room and stumble through the straw on the floorboards. You can touch the tiles of the sloping roof when you put up an arm, and farther on you have to bend down.

"There's a small door," you say, feeling your way in the dark.

"What do you see?" She stays in her room.

"Nothing, it's solid timber, without any joins, oh, and there's a lock."

"It's really scary," you hear her say from the other side of the door.

You go back to your room and find that by putting a big bamboo tub upside down onto a pile of straw you can stand on it and climb onto a rafter.

"Quick, what can you see?" she asks anxiously.

"An oil lamp burning in a small altar," you say. "The altar is fixed to the gable and there's a memorial tablet inside. The woman of the house must be a shaman and this is where she summons back the spirits of the dead. The spirits of living persons are possessed and they go into a trance, then the ghosts of the dead attach themselves to these persons and speak through their lips."

"Stop it!" she pleads. You hear her sliding against the wall onto the floor.

You say the woman wasn't always a shaman, when she was young she was the same as everyone else, just like any other women of her age. But when she was about twenty, when she needed to be passionately loved by a man, her husband was crushed to death.

"How did he die?" she asks quietly.

You say he went off at night with a cousin to illegally cut camphor in the forest of a neighboring village. The tree was about to fall when he somehow tripped on a root and lost his bearings. The tree was creaking loudly and he should have run away from it but instead ran toward it, right where it fell. He was pulverized before he could yell out.

"Are you listening?" you ask.

"Yes," she says.

You say the husband's cousin was frightened out of his wits and absconded, not daring to report the accident. The woman saw the hessian shoes hanging on the carrying pole of a man bringing charcoal down from the mountain, he was calling as he went for someone to identify a corpse. How could she not recognize the red string woven into the soles and heels of the hessian shoes she had made with her own hands? She collapsed and kept banging her head on the ground. She was frothing at the mouth as she rolled around, shouting: Let all the ghosts of the dead and the wronged all come back, let them all come back!

"I also want to shout," she says.

"Then shout."

"I can't."

Her voice is pitifully muffled. You earnestly call out to her but she keeps saying no from the other side of the wall. Still, she wants you to go on talking.

"What about?"

"Her, the madwoman."

You say the women of the village couldn't subdue her. It took several men sitting on her and twisting her arms before they managed to tie her up. From then on she became crazy and always predicted the calamities which would befall the village. She predicted that Ximao's mother would become a widow and it really happened.

"I want revenge too."

"On whom? That boyfriend of yours? Or on the woman who's having an affair with him? Do you want him to discard her after he's had his fun with her? Like he treated you?"

"He said he loved me, that he was only having a fling with her."

"Is she younger? Is she prettier than you?"

"She's got a face full of freckles and a big mouth!"

"Is she more sexy than you?"

"He said she was uninhibited, that she'd do anything, he wanted me to be like her!"

"How?"

"Don't be inquisitive!"

"Then you know about all that went on between the two of them?"

"Yes."

"Then did she know all that went on between the two of you?"

"Oh, stop talking about that."

"Then what shall I talk about? Shall I talk about the shaman?"

"I really want revenge!"

"Just like the shaman?"

"How did she get revenge?"

"All the women were frightened of her curses but all the men liked chatting with her. She seduced them and then discarded them. Later on she powdered her face, installed an altar, and openly invoked ghosts and spirits. Everyone was terrified of her."

"Why did she do this?"

"You have to know that at the age of six she was betrothed to an unborn child in the womb—her husband in the belly of her mother-in-law. At twelve she entered her husband's home as a bride, when her husband was still a snotty-nosed boy. Once, right on these floorboards upstairs, she was raped in the straw by her father-in-law. At the time she was just fourteen. Thereafter, she was terrified whenever there was no one else in the house but the father-in-law and her. Later on, she tried cuddling her young husband but the boy only bit her nipples. It was hard waiting years until her husband could shoulder a carrying pole, chop wood, use the plow, and eventually reach manhood and know that he loved her. Then he was crushed to death. The parents-in-law were old and were totally dependent upon her to manage the fields and the household, and they didn't dare to exercise any restraints on her as long as she didn't remarry. Both parents-in-law are now dead and the woman really believes she can communicate with the spirits. Her blessings can bring good fortune and her curses can bring disaster, so it's reasonable for her to charge people incense money. What is most amazing is that she got a ten-year-old girl to go into a trance, then got the girl's long-dead grandmother, whom the girl had never seen, to speak through the child's mouth. The people who saw this were petrified. . . ."

"Come over, I'm frightened," she pleads.

47

Walking along a road on the shady side of a mountain, no one ahead or behind me, I get caught in a downpour. At first it's light rain and feels good falling on my face, then it gets heavier and heavier and I have to run. My hair and clothes are drenched, and seeing a cave on the slope,

I hurry to it. Just inside is a big pile of chopped firewood. The ceiling is quite high and one corner of the cave goes farther inside. Light is coming from over there. A stove built of rocks with an iron pot on it stands at the top of a few roughly hewn steps and light is streaming in through a crack in the rock running at an angle above the stove.

I turn around. Behind me is a roughly-nailed-together wooden bed with the bedding rolled up. A Taoist priest is sitting there reading a book. I get a surprise but don't dare disturb him and just look at the gray-white line of rain shivering in the crack. It is raining so heavily that I don't want to venture back out.

"It's all right, you can stay awhile." It is he who speaks first as he puts down his book.

He has shoulder-length hair and is wearing a loose gray top and gray trousers. He looks to be around thirty.

"Are you one of the Taoists of this mountain?" I ask.

"Not yet. I chop firewood for the Taoist temple," he replies. On his bed, cover up, is a copy of *Fiction Monthly*.

"Are you also interested in this?" I ask.

"I read it to pass time," he says frankly. "You're all wet, dry yourself first." Saying this, he brings a basin of hot water from the pot on the stove and gives me a towel.

I thank him, then, stripping to the waist, have a wash and instantly feel much better.

"This is really a good place to shelter!" I say as I sit down on a block of wood opposite. "Do you live in this cave?"

He says he is from the village at the foot of the mountain but that he hates the whole lot of them, his older brother and his wife, the neighbors, and the village cadres.

"They all put money first and only think about profit," he says. "I no longer have anything to do with them."

"So you chop firewood for a living?"

"I renounced society almost a year ago but they haven't formally accepted me yet."

"Why?"

"The old head Taoist wants to see whether I am sincere, whether my heart is constant."

"Will he accept you then?"

"Yes."

This shows he firmly believes he is sincere of heart.

"Don't you feel bored living in this cave on your own all the time?" I go on to ask, casting a glance at the magazine.

"It's more peaceful and relaxed than in the village," he calmly replies, unaware that I'm trying to provoke him. "I also study every day," he adds.

"May I ask what you are studying?"

He pulls out a stone-block-print copy of *Daily Lessons for Taoists* from under his bedding.

"I was reading some fiction because on rainy days like this I can't work," he explains when he sees me looking at the magazine on his bed.

"Do these stories affect your study?" I am curious to find out.

"Ha, they're all about common occurrences between men and women," he replies with a dismissive laugh. He says he went to senior high school and studied some literature and when there's nothing to do he reads a bit. "In fact human life just amounts to this."

I can't go on to ask him whether he ever had a wife and I can't question him about the private concerns of one who has renounced the world. The pelting rain is monotonous but soothing.

I shouldn't disturb him any further. I sit with him for a long time in meditation, sitting in forgetfulness in the sound of the rain.

I don't notice the rain has stopped. But when I do, I get up, thank him, and bid him farewell.

He says, "No need to thank me, it is fate."

This is on Qingcheng Mountain.

AFTERWARD, AT THE old stone pagoda on the island in the middle of the Ou River, I encounter a monk with a shaven head wearing a crimson cassock. He presses his palms together then kneels and prostrates himself in front of the pagoda. Sightseers crowd around to watch. He unhurriedly completes his worship, removes his cassock, puts it into a black artificial leather case, picks up his umbrella, which has a curved handle and doubles as a walking stick, then turns and leaves. I follow him, then, some distance from the crowd of sightseers who were watching him pray, I go up and ask, "Venerable Master, can I invite you to drink tea with me? I would like to ask your advice about some Buddhist teachings."

He thinks about it, then agrees.

He has a gaunt face, is alert, and looks to be around fifty. His trouser legs are tied at the calves and he walks briskly so that I have to half run to keep up.

"The Venerable Master seems to be leaving for a distant journey," I say.

"I'm going to Jiangxi first to visit a few old monks, then I have to go to a number of other places."

"I too am a lone traveler. However, I am not like the Venerable Master, who is steadfastly sincere and has a sacred goal in his heart." I have to find something to talk about.

"The true traveler is without goal, it is the absence of goals which creates the ultimate traveler."

"Venerable Master, are you from this locality? Is this journey to bid farewell to your native village? Don't you intend coming back?"

"For one who has renounced society all within the four seas is home, for him what is called native village does not exist."

This leaves me speechless. I invite him into a tea stall in the park and choose a quiet corner to sit down. I ask his Buddhist name, tell him my name, and then hesitate.

It is he who speaks first. "Just ask what you wish to know, there is nothing one who has renounced society cannot talk about."

I then blurt out, "If you don't mind, I wish to ask, Venerable Master, why you renounced society."

He smiles, blows at the tea leaves floating in his cup, and takes a sip. Then, looking at me, he says, "It seems that you are not on an ordinary trip, are you on a special mission?"

"I'm not carrying out any sort of investigation but when I saw the Venerable Master's serene person, I was filled with admiration. I don't have a specific goal but I still can't abandon it."

"Abandon what?" A smile lingers on his face.

"Abandon the human world." After I say this, he and I both laugh.

"The human world can be abandoned just by saying it." His response is straightforward.

"That's indeed so," I say nodding, "but I would like to know how the Venerable Master was able to abandon it."

Without holding anything back, he then tells me about his experience.

He says that when he was sixteen, and still at junior high school, he ran away from home to join the revolution and fought for a year as a guerrilla in the mountains. At seventeen he went with the army into the city and was put in charge of a bank. He could have become a party leader but he had his mind set on studying medicine. After graduating he was allocated work as a cadre in the city health bureau although he really wanted to continue to work as a doctor. One day he offended the branch party secretary of the hospital and was expelled from the party, branded a rightist element and sent to work in the fields in the country. It was only when the village built a commune hospital that he got to work as a doctor for several years. During this time he married a village girl and three children in succession were born. However for some reason he wanted to convert to Catholicism and when he heard that a Vatican cardinal had arrived in Guangzhou, he traveled there to ask the cardinal about the faith. He ended up not seeing the cardinal and instead came under suspicion for illicit dealings with foreigners. For this crime he was expelled from the commune hospital and he had no option but to spend his time studying traditional medicine on his own and mixing with vagrants in order to eat. One day he came to a sudden realization—the Pope was far away in the West and inaccessible, so he might as well rely on Buddha. From that time he renounced society and became a monk. When he finishes telling this he gives a loud laugh.

"Do you still think of your family?" I ask.

"They can all feed themselves."

"Don't you have some lingering fondness for them?"

"Those who have renounced society have neither fondness nor hatred."

"Then do they hate you?"

He says he never felt inclined to ask about them, but some years after he entered the monastery, his eldest son came to tell him he had been exonerated from the charge of being a rightist element and having illicit dealings with foreigners. If he returned he would be treated as a senior cadre and veteran revolutionary, reinstated in his former position, and also receive a large sum of unpaid salary due to him. He said he didn't want any of the money and they could divide it up. The fact that his wife and children had not been unjustly treated could be considered recompense for his devotion to the Buddhist faith and thereafter they should not come again. After that he started wandering and they had no means of knowing his whereabouts.

"Do you now seek alms along the way to support yourself?"

He says people are mean-spirited nowadays. Seeking alms is worse than begging, if you seek alms you don't get anything. He mainly supports himself by practicing as an itinerant doctor. When practicing he wears ordinary clothes, he doesn't want to damage the image of the Buddhist order.

"Does Buddhism allow this flexibility?" I ask.

"Buddha is in your heart." His face is serene and I believe he has achieved liberation from the worries of the inner heart. He is setting out on a distant journey and he is very happy.

I ask him how he finds lodgings on the way. He says wherever there are temples and monasteries he only needs to show his monk's certificate to be accorded hospitality. However, the situation at present is bad everywhere. There are not many monks and all of them have to work in order to feed and clothe themselves: generally long stays aren't possible because no one is providing support. Only the big temples and monasteries get any government subsidies but these are only minuscule amounts and, naturally, he doesn't want to add to people's burdens. He says he's a traveler and has already been to many famous mountains. He thinks he is in good health and that he can still walk a ten-thousand-*li* journey.

"Would it be possible for me to see your monk's certificate?" It seems that this is more useful than the credentials I have.

"It's not a secret document, the Buddhist order doesn't have secrets and is open to all."

He takes from a breast pocket a big piece of folded silk paper with an ink-print Buddha sitting with legs folded on the lotus throne in the top section. It is stamped with a large vermilion square seal. His Buddhist name at initiation, academic achievements, and rank are all written on it. He has reached the rank of abbot and is permitted to lecture on the sutras and to deal with Buddhist matters.

"Maybe one day I'll follow in your footsteps." I don't know whether I am joking or not.

"In that case we are linked in destiny." He, however, is quite earnest. Saying this, he gets up, presses his palms together, and bids me farewell.

He walks very quickly and I follow him for a while but in an instant he vanishes among the thronging sightseers. I am clearly aware that I am still rooted in the mundane world.

LATER, WHILE READING an inscription in the Abandon Profit Pagoda, built in the Sui Dynasty, which stands in front of the Guoqing Monastery at the foot of Tiantai Mountain, I suddenly overhear a conversation.

"You'd best return with me," says a man's voice from the other side of the brick wall.

"No, you should leave now." It is also a man's voice, but it is louder.

"It's not for my sake, think of your mother."

"Just tell her I'm doing very well."

"Your mother asked me to come, she's ill."

"What illness is it?"

"She keeps saying she has pains in the chest."

The son makes no response.

"Your mother got me to bring you a pair of shoes."

"I've got shoes."

"They're the sports shoes you wanted, they're for basketball."

"They're very expensive, why did you buy them?"

"Try them on."

"I don't play basketball now, I don't have any use for them. You'd best take them back, nobody wears them here."

In the early morning, birds in the forest are singing cheerfully. In the midst of the twittering of many sparrows, a single thrush warbles but it is concealed by the dense leaves of the nearby ginkgo tree so I can't see which branch it's on. Then a few magpies arrive and make a raucous clamor. It is silent for a long time by the brick pagoda and thinking they have gone I go around and see a youth looking up at the singing birds, his gleaming black shaven head does not yet have the initiation burns made with incense sticks. He is wearing a short monk's jacket, and the ruddy complexion of his handsome face is unlike the dark yellowish complexions of monks who have been vegetarian for a long time. His young father, a peasant, is holding the new white-soled basketball shoes with red-and-blue striped uppers he has taken out of their box. He is breathing heavily. I surmise the father is putting pressure on his son to get married and I wonder if the youth will take his vows.

(Translated by Mabel Lee)

CUI JIAN
(1961–)

Cui Jian, the godfather of Chinese rock and roll, was born to ethnic Korean parents in Beijing in 1961. His father was a professional trumpet player and his mother was a dancer in a Korean minority troupe. At the age of twenty, Cui secured a position as a classical trumpet player in Beijing Philharmonic Orchestra. Inspired by Western rock music (Simon & Garfunkel, the Beatles, the Rolling Stones, Bob Dylan, etc.) which had found its way into China's cultural underground, Cui formed a band called Seven-Ply Board in 1984. Two years later, his sensational performance at a concert in Beijing propelled him to national stardom, and the song "Nothing to My Name" became the biggest hit in Chinese history. His first album, Rock 'n' Roll on the New Long March, *was released in 1987. In the post-Tiananmen years, Cui has remained the most popular and politically contentious musician in China, a powerful spokesperson for the powerless silent majority.*

Nothing to My Name

I keep asking endlessly
When will you go with me?
But you always laugh at me.
I've nothing to my name.

I'll give you all my dreams,
Give you my freedom too.
But you always laugh at me.
I've nothing to my name.

Oh-o-o-o-oh! When will you go with me?
Oh-o-o-o-oh! When will you go with me?

The ground beneath my feet is moving.
The water by my side is flowing.
But you always laugh at me.
I've nothing to my name.
Why do you always laugh?
Why do I always chase you?
Do I in your eyes forever
Have nothing to my name?

Oh-o-o-o-oh! When will you go with me?
Oh-o-o-o-oh! When will you go with me?

I tell you I've waited too long.
I tell you my last wish.
I want to take your hands in mine
Then you'll go with me.
This time your hands are trembling.
This time your tears are flowing.
Perhaps you're saying you love me
Tho' I've nothing to my name.

Oh-o-o-o-oh! Then you'll go with me.
Oh-o-o-o-oh! Then you'll go with me.

(Translated by Yunte Huang)

Permissions